I0709770

icons by oscar

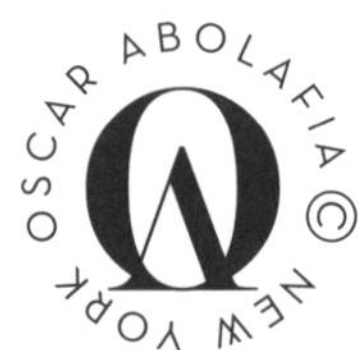

TERRA

icons

by oscar

the works of photographer
Oscar Abolafia

"We couldn't have done this without each other!"

Oscar Abolafia & Yoke Abolafia-van Berge Henegouwen

Frank. Sammie. Paul. Andy. Twiggy. Jack. Elizabeth. Elvis. Jim. Marlene. John. Priscilla. Yoko. Ginger. Janis. Mick. Fred. Salvador. Cher. Audrey. Not many are so iconic that a first name is enough to tell us who they are. They were captured by a photographer who goes by the name of Oscar Abolafia.

You can call him Oscar.

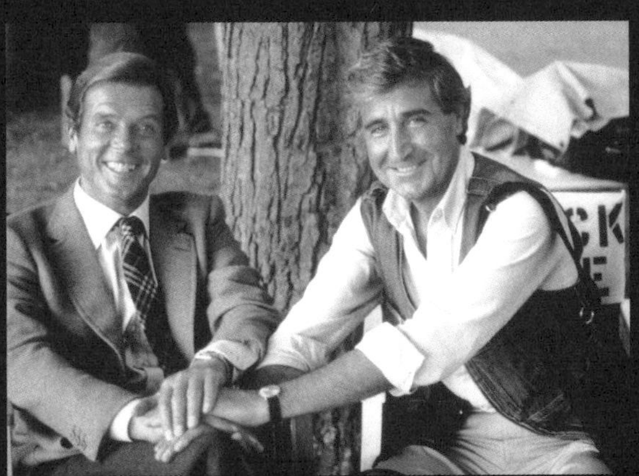

Opening up.

Oscar Abolafia (born in 1935) is an American photographer known for his outstanding photojournalism of the celebrities that made the 1960s and 70's truly extraordinary. Abolafia's work made the pages of world-famous magazines such as People Magazine, Vanity Fair and Harper's Bazaar.

Over a span of 50 years of work in the field of photography, he was able to build personal and intimate relationships with the most enduring stars of our age, such as the Kennedys, Liz Taylor, Elvis Presley and Frank Sinatra, to name but a few.

Icons by Oscar has opened up, for the first time ever, Oscar Abolafia's treasure trove of more than 300,000 intimate and iconic photographs. A carefully curated conversation with the iconic figures from our past starts now. *Icons by Oscar* is just the beginning.

Jacqueline Kennedy Onassis
1974, New York City

On her way to see Rudolf Nurevey
dance at City Center.

———

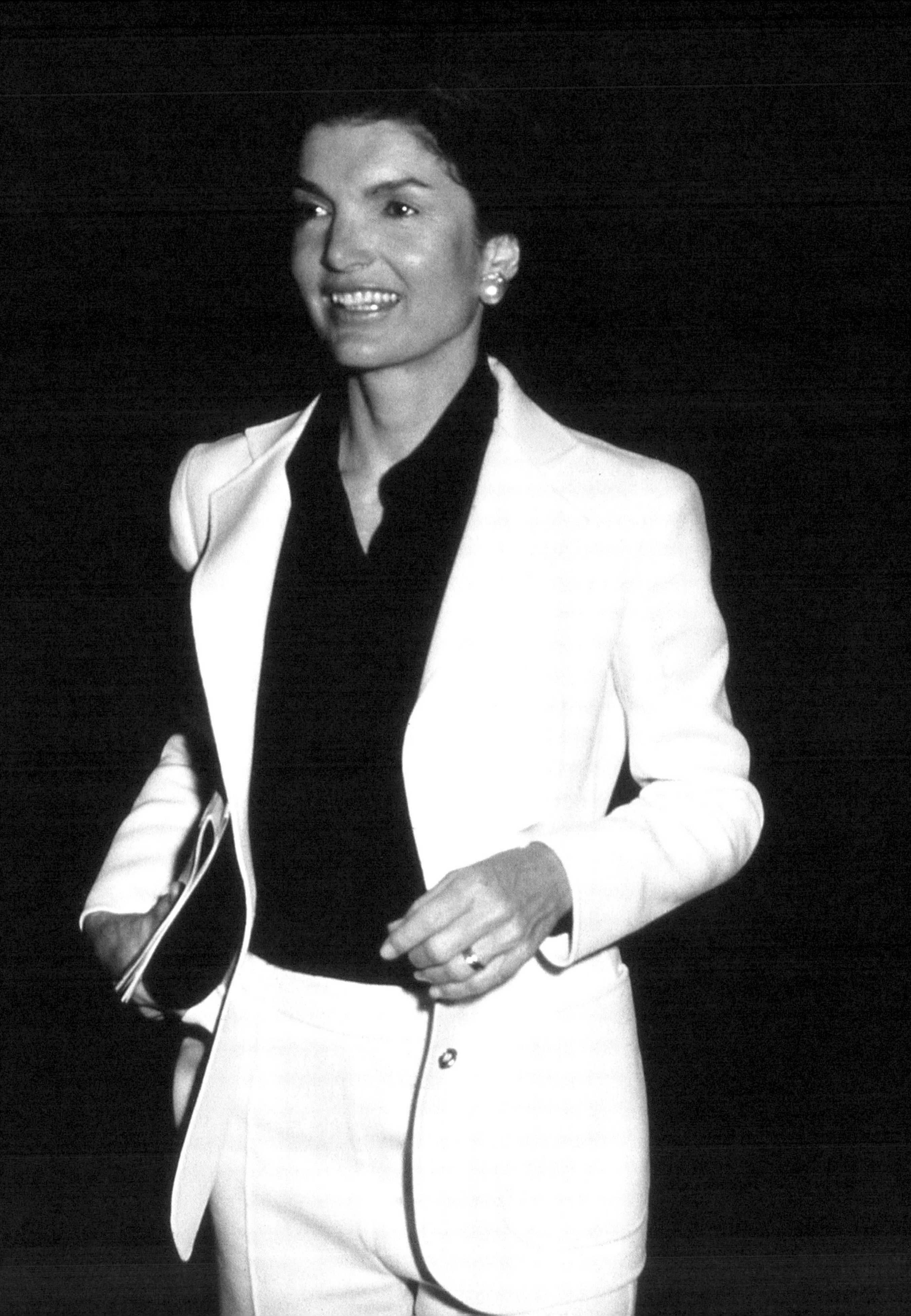

Priscilla Presley
1983, Dallas

On her first day of shooting
the TV series *Dallas*.

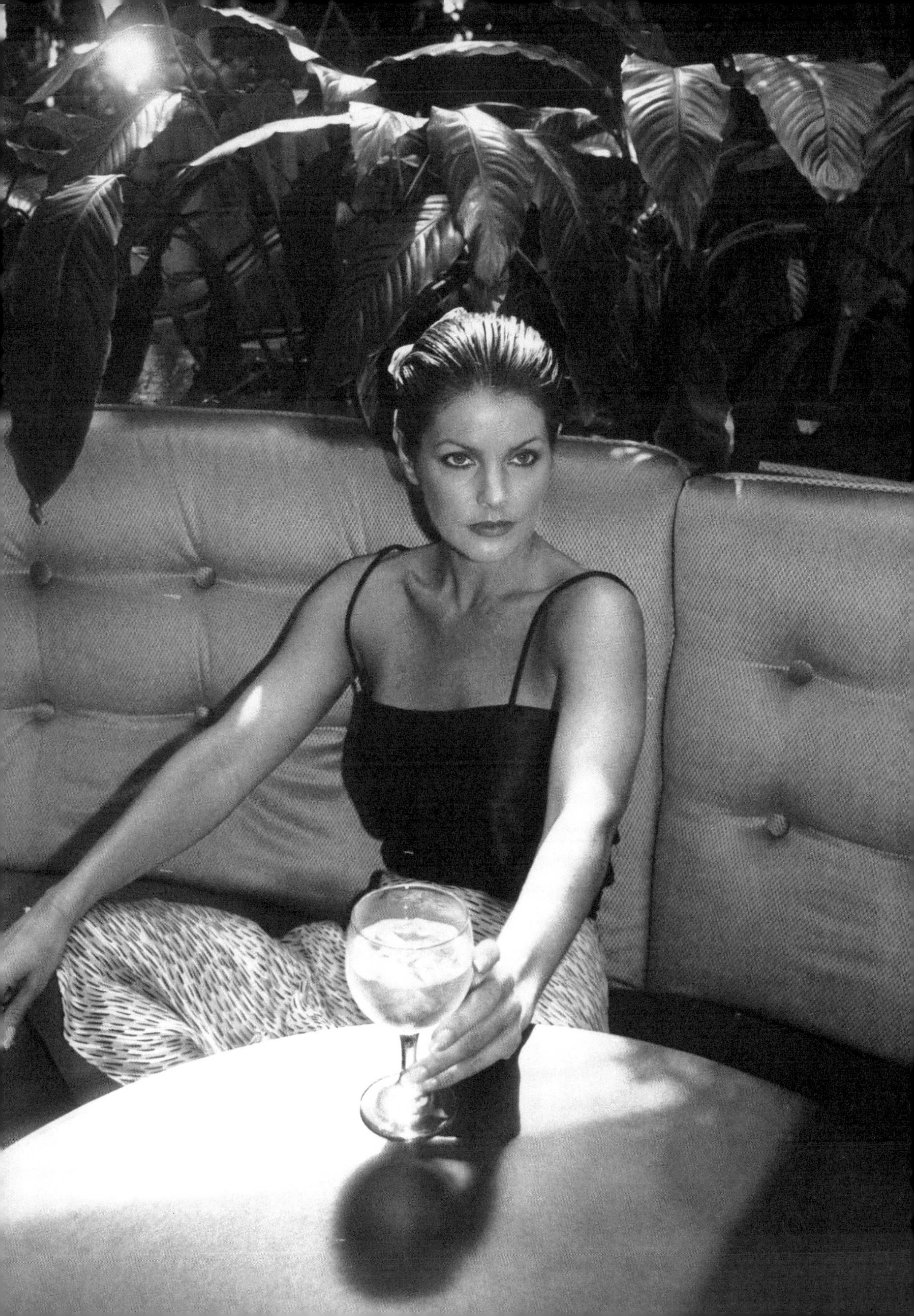

Robert De Niro and Liza Minnelli
1977, New York City

At the premiere of their movie
New York-New York.
———

Following double page

Liza Minnelli and Bianca Jagger
1972, New York City

Opening night party for the movie *Cabaret*,
starring Liza Minnelli.
———

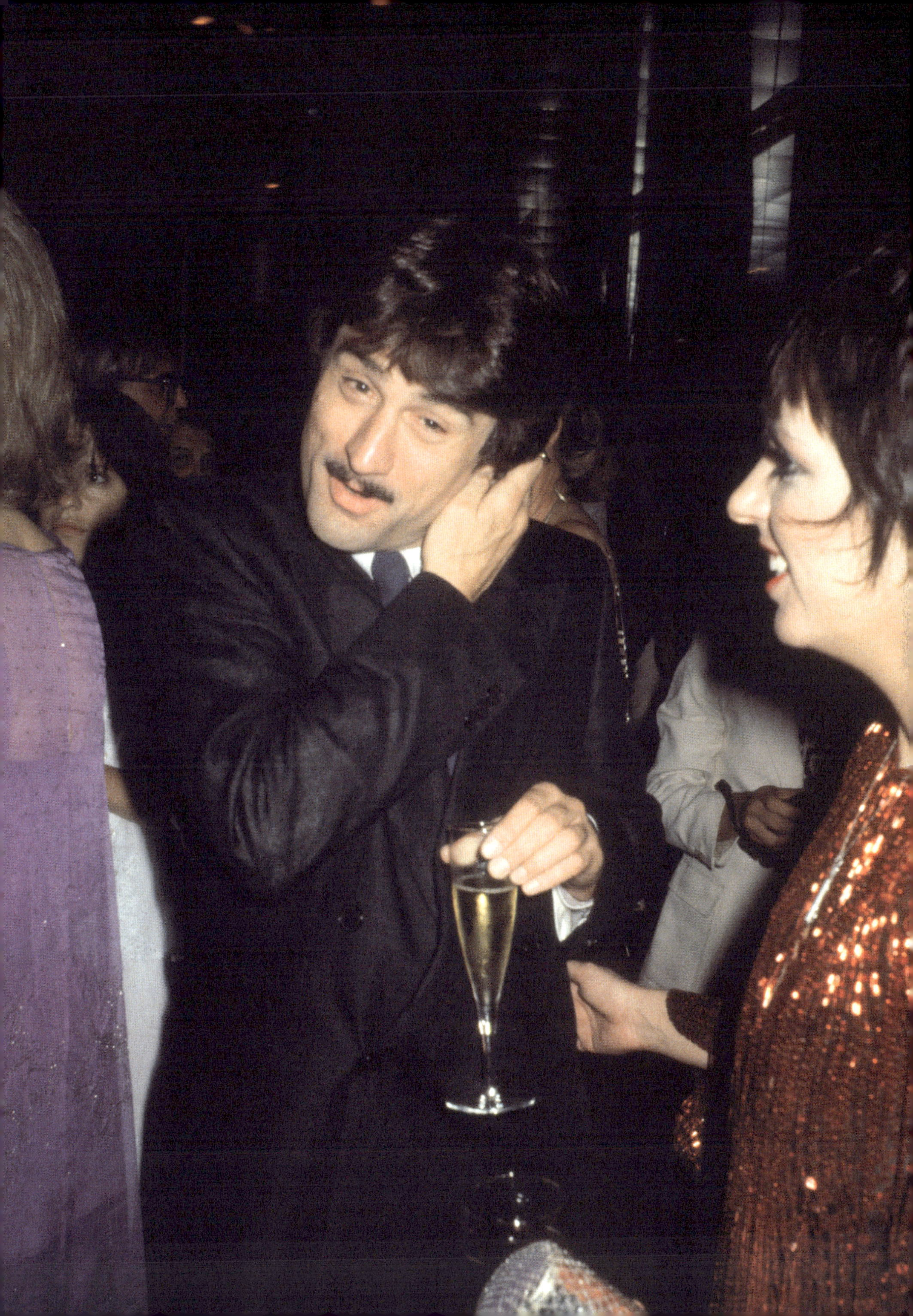

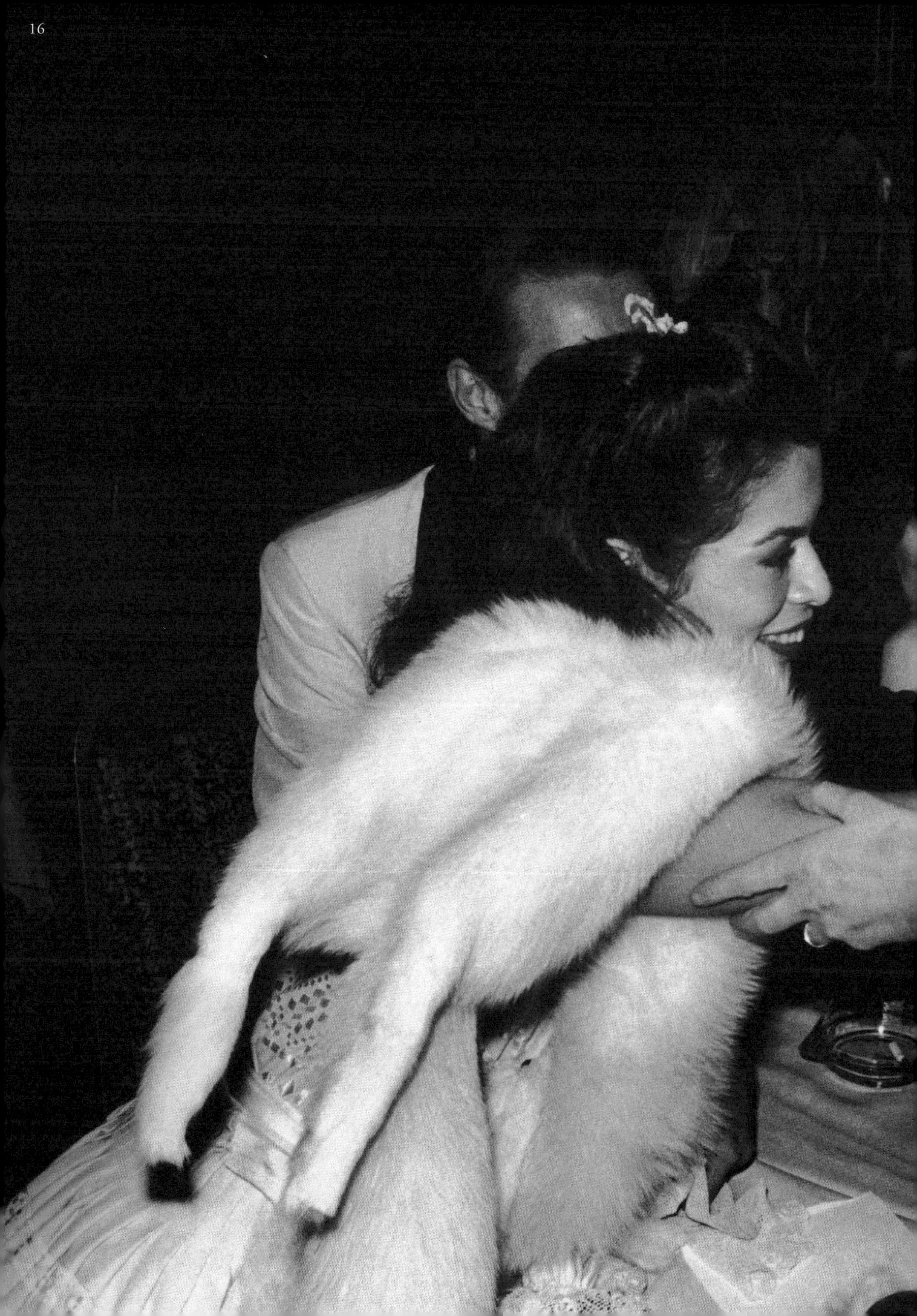

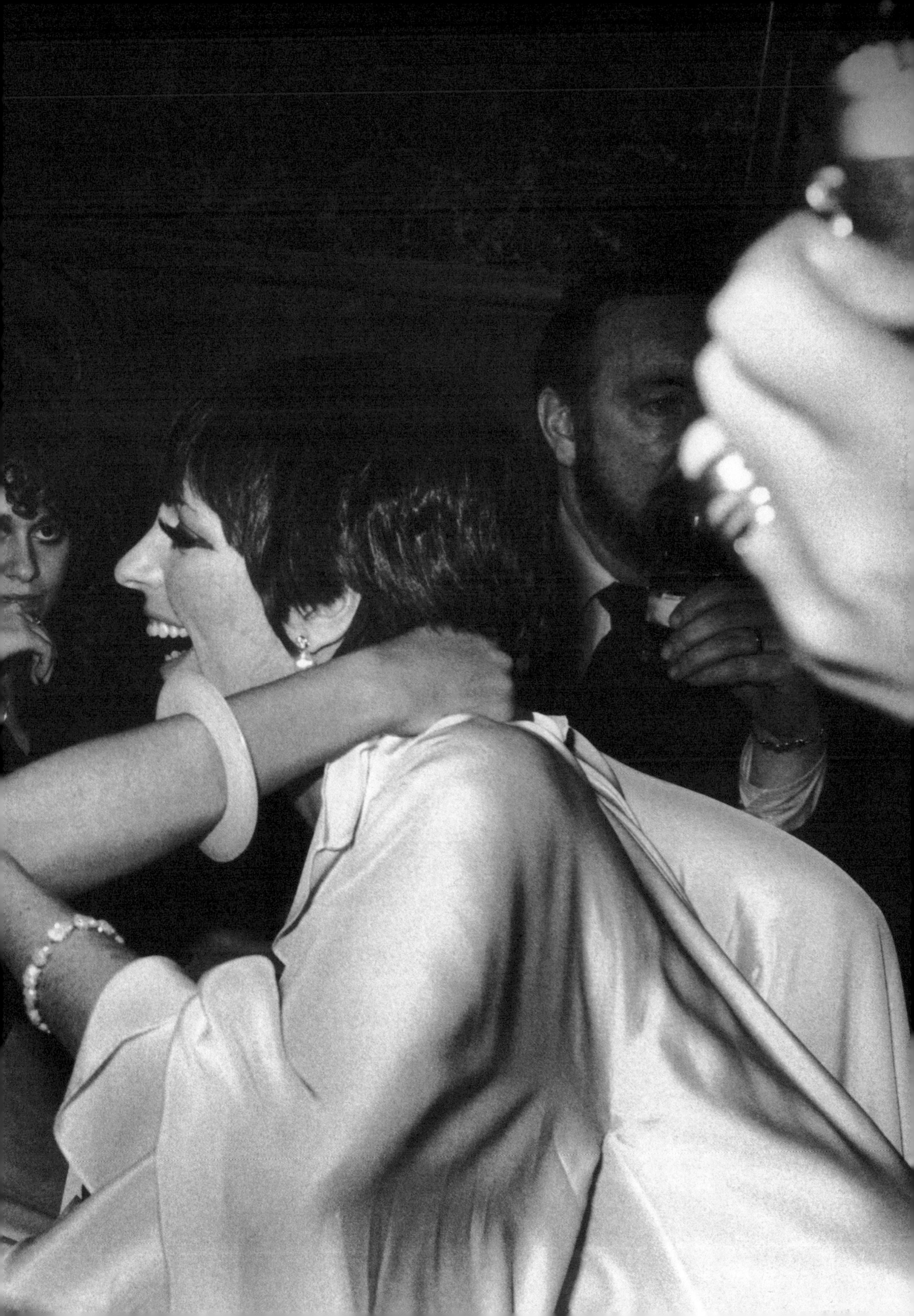

Grace Jones
1981, New York City

At a nightclub.

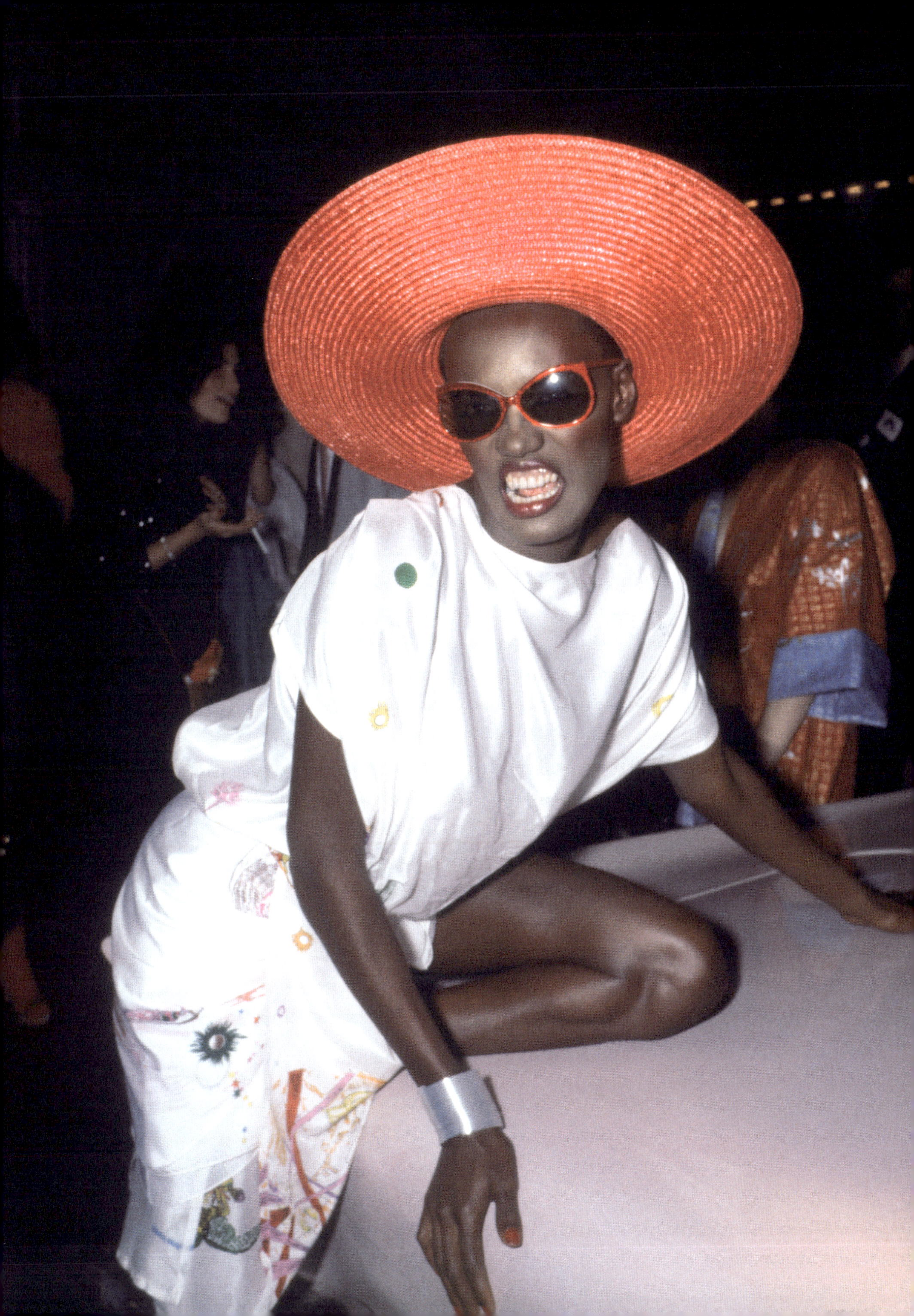

Roger Moore
1973, Jamaica

On location for the James Bond
movie, *Live and Let Die*.

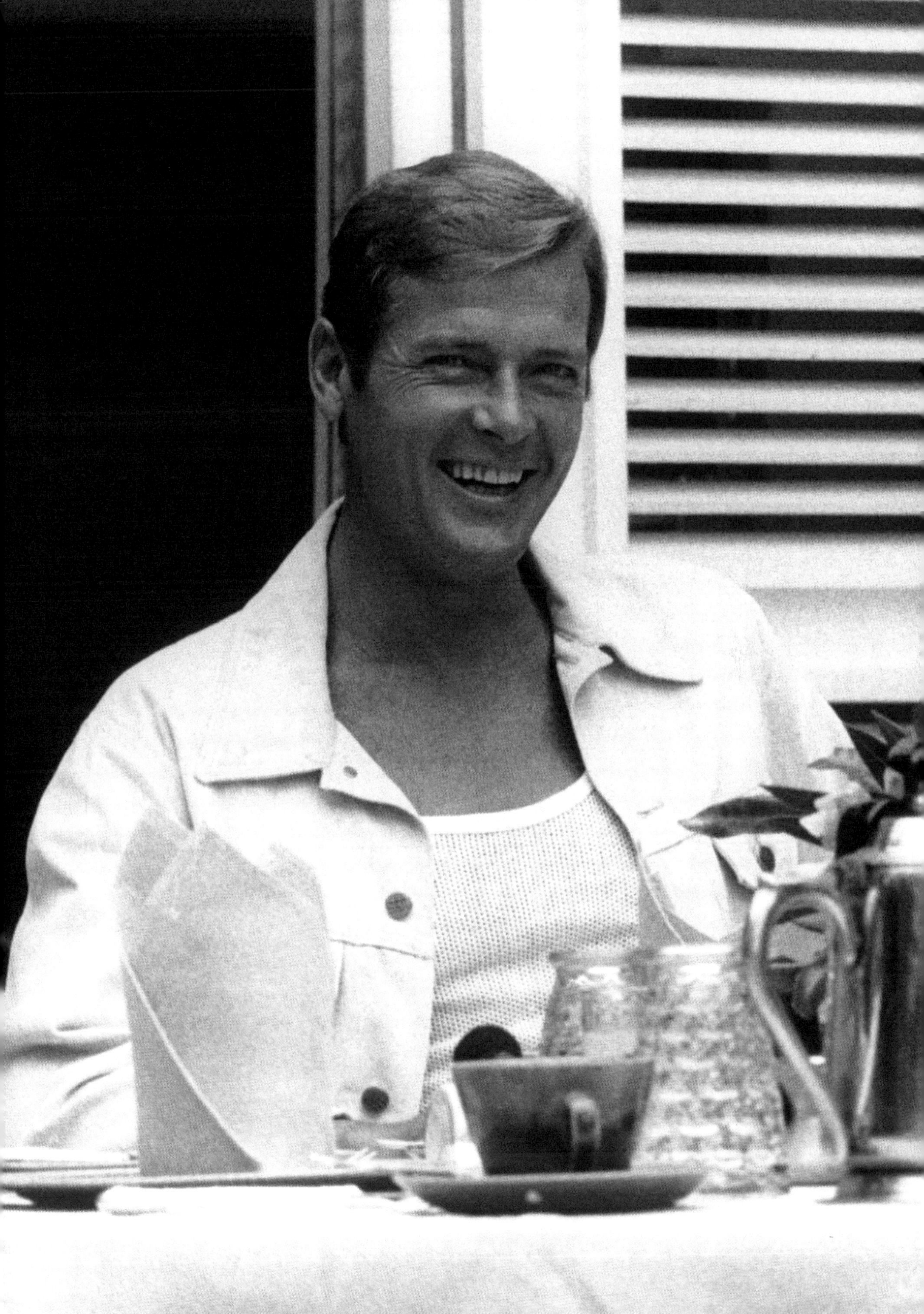

Barbra Streisand
1975, New York City

At the press conference for the movie
Funny Lady, with James Caan.

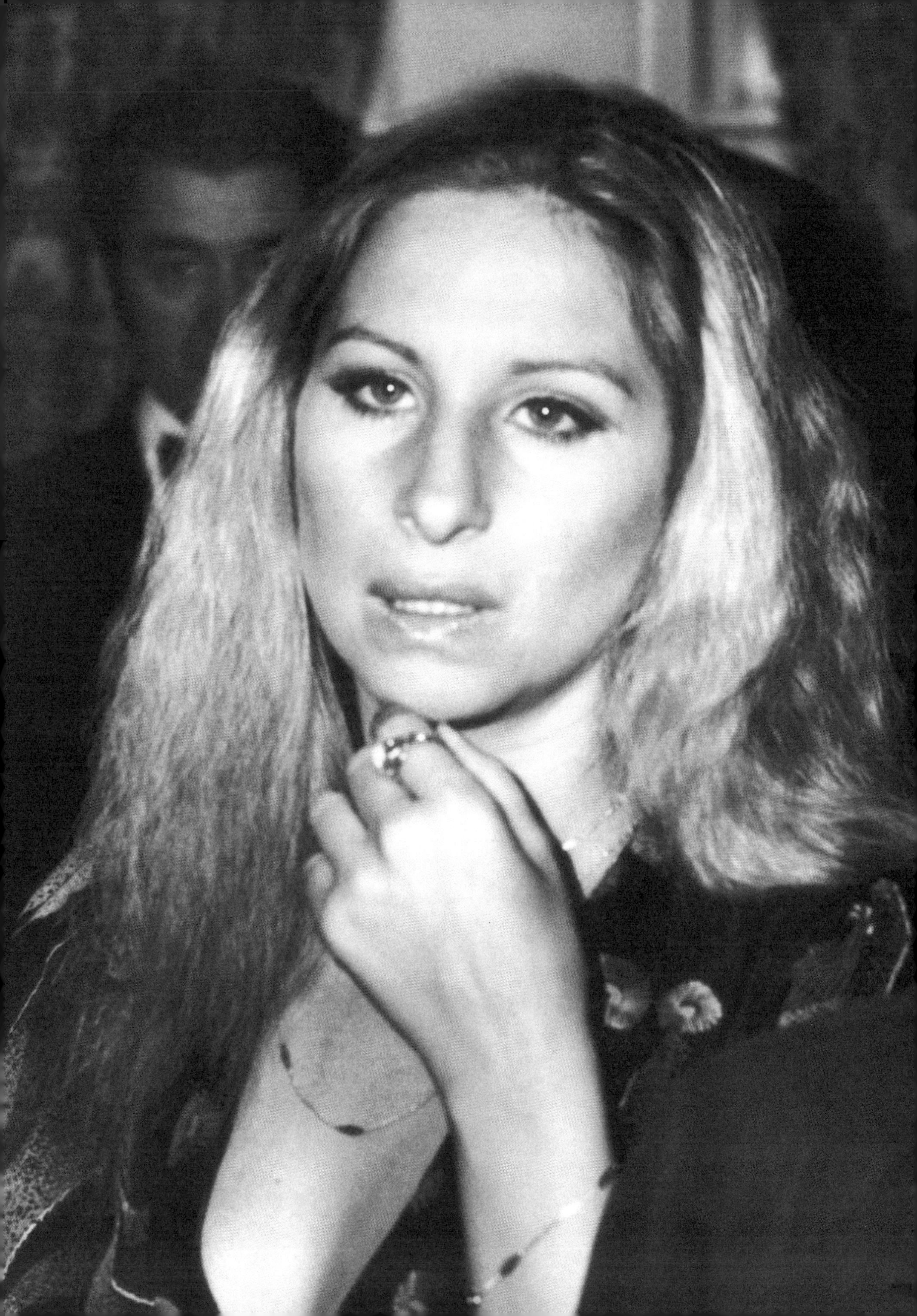

Neil Diamond
1969, New York City

In a recording studio rehearsing
Sweet Caroline.
___

Following double page

Roman Polanski
1976, New York City

In a car before fleeing the country
under suspicion of rape.
___

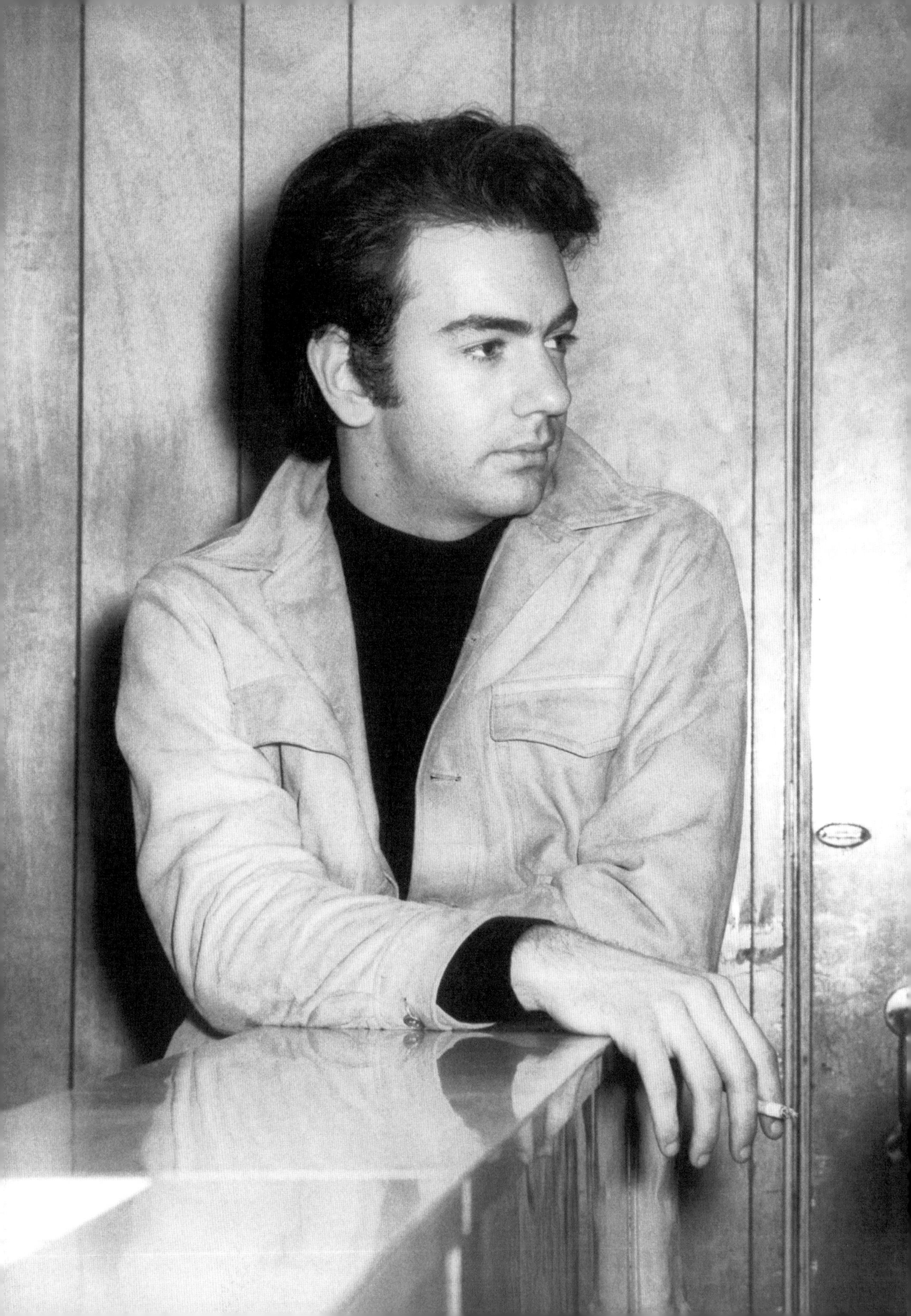

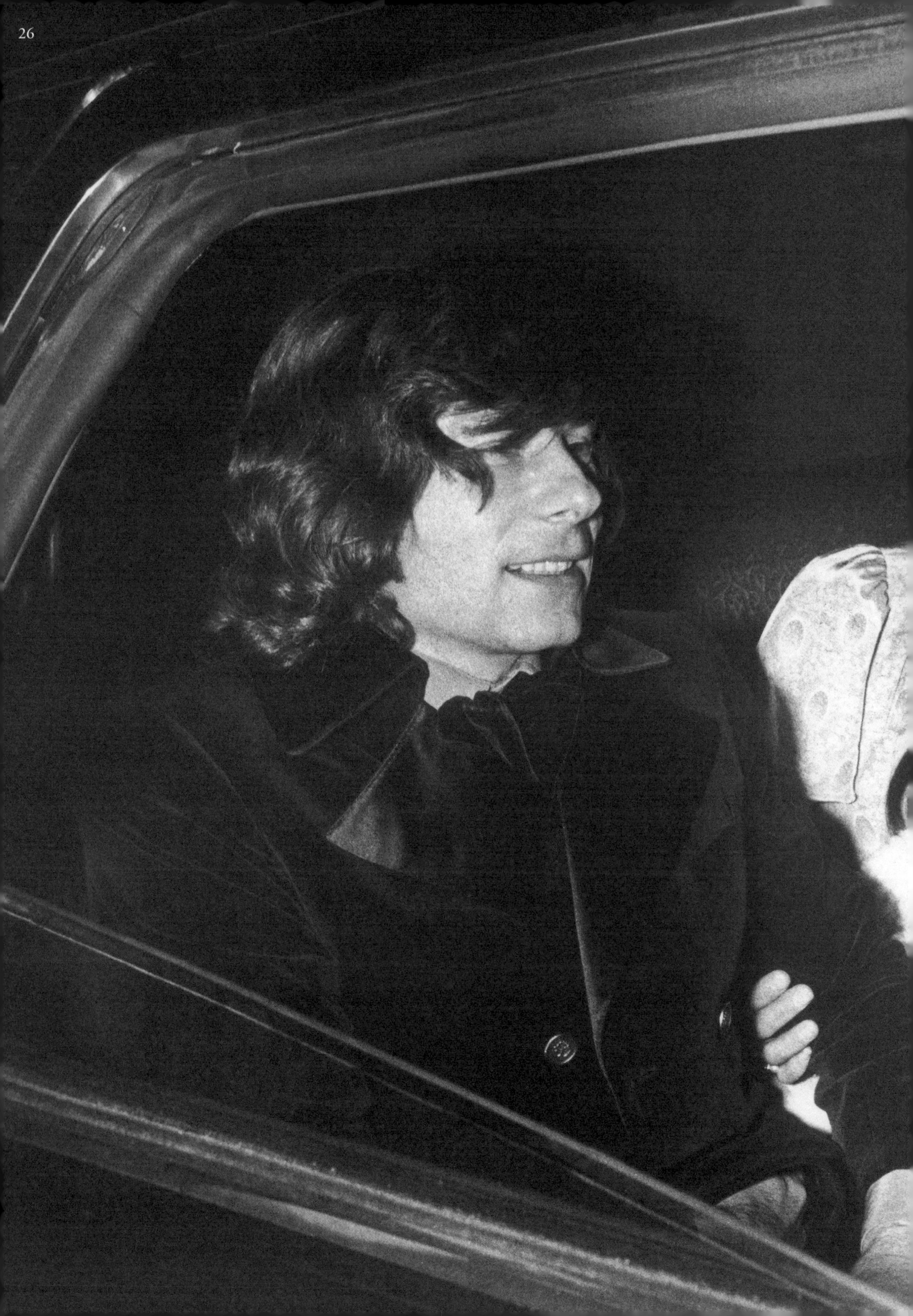

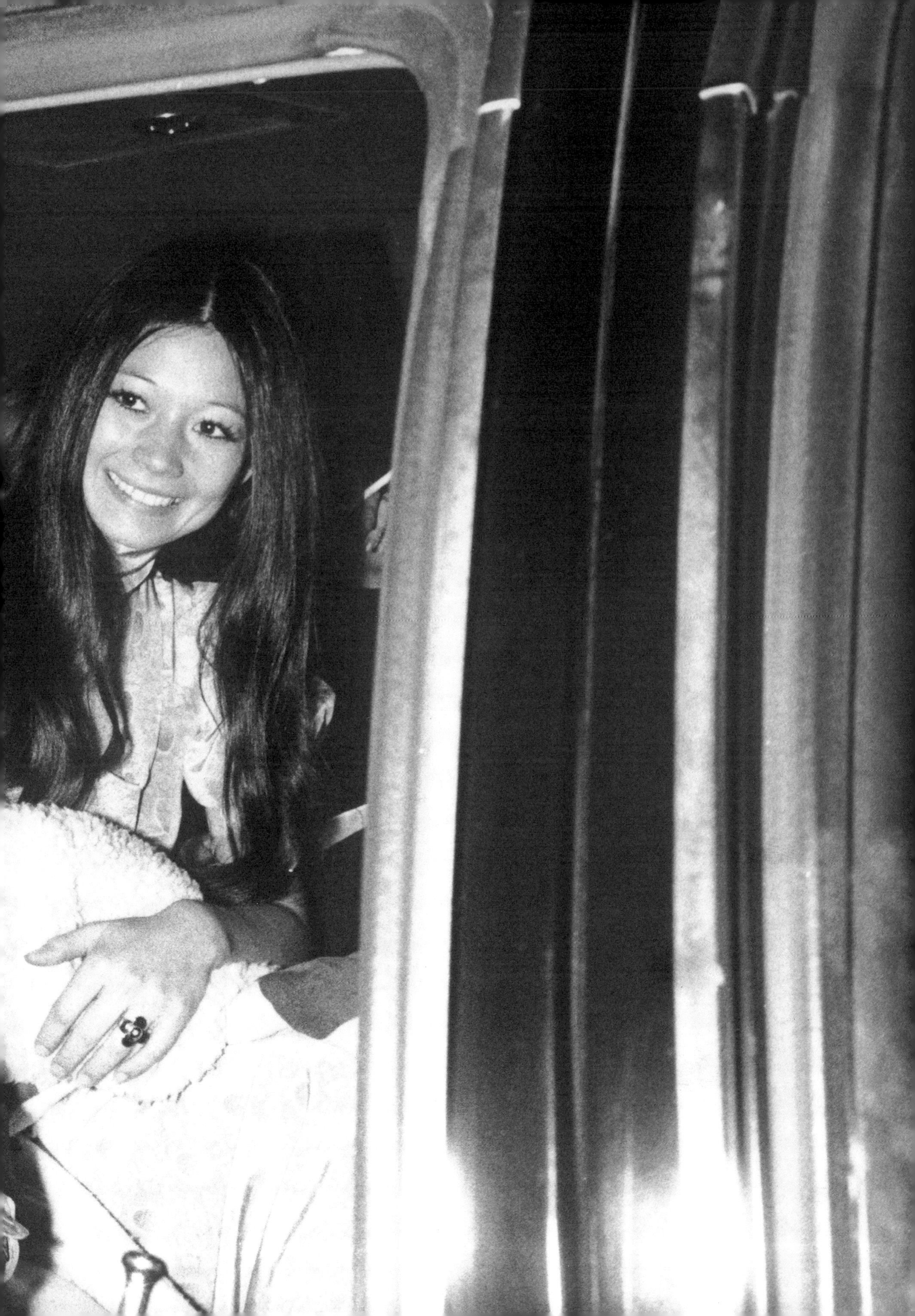

Twiggy
1967, New York City

In the dressing room of the
Tonight Show with Johnny Carson.
———

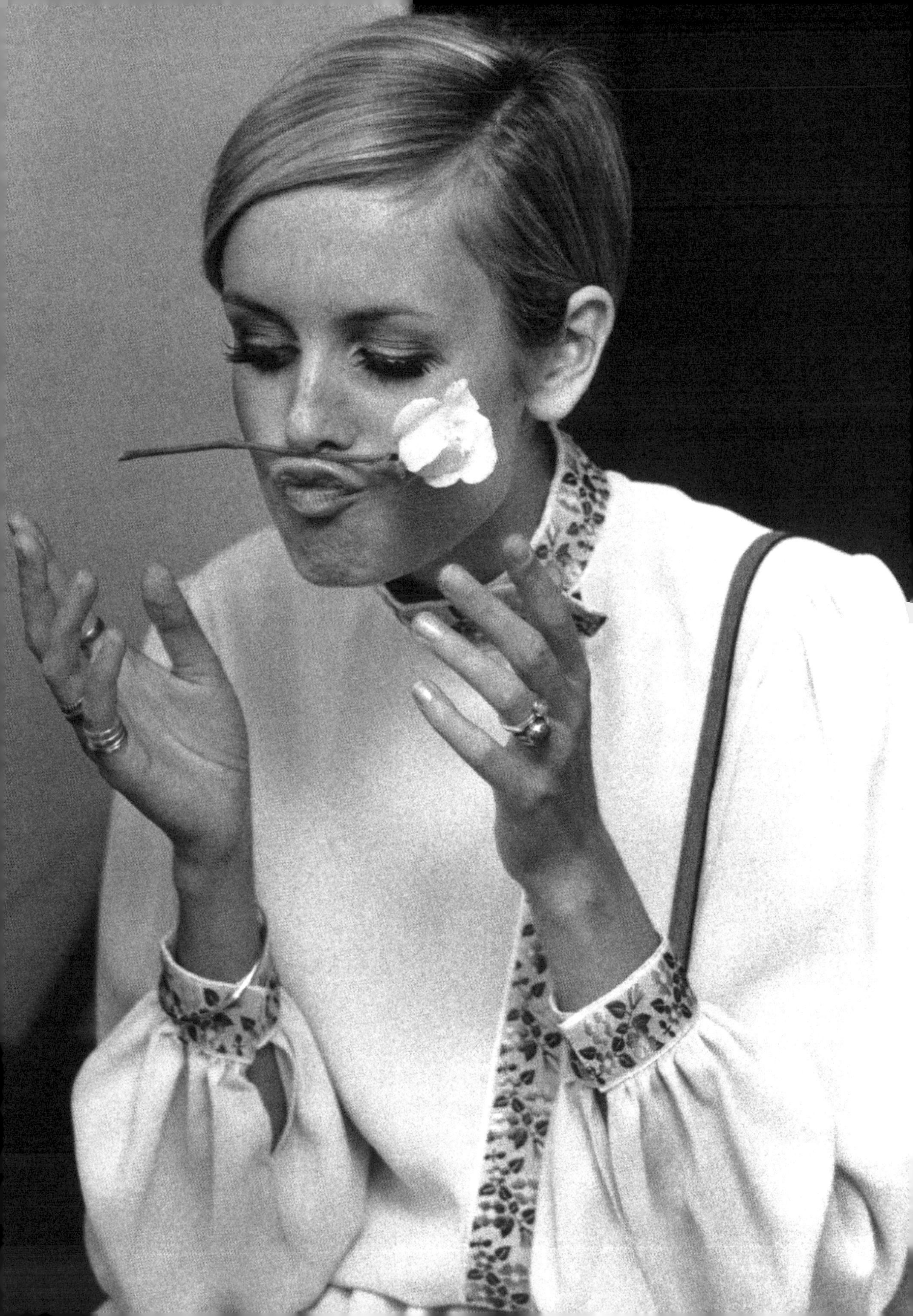

Donald Sutherland
1982, New York City

At *The Night of 100 Stars* at the Hilton Hotel.
———

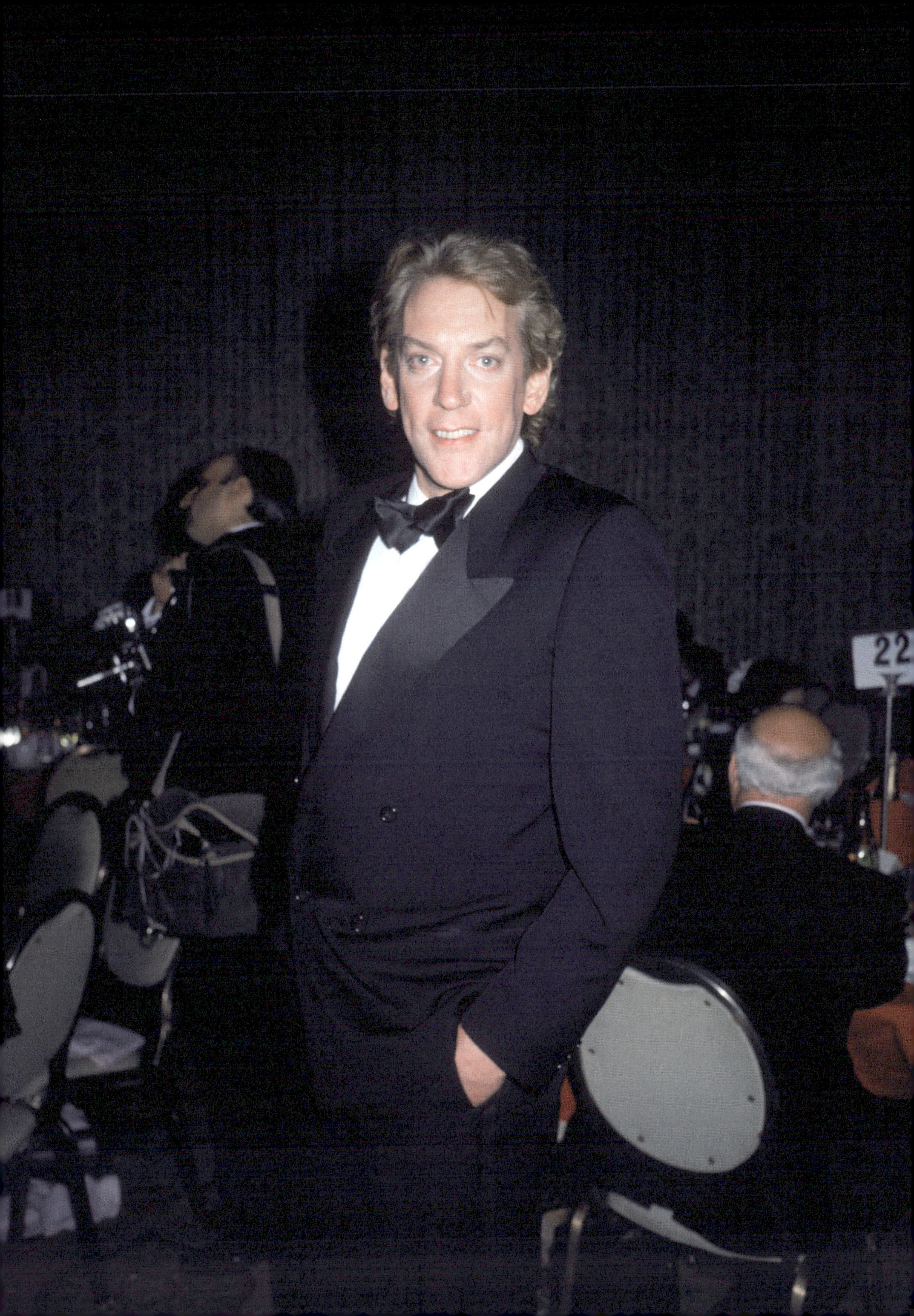

Cher
1971, New York City

Outside the St. Regis Hotel.

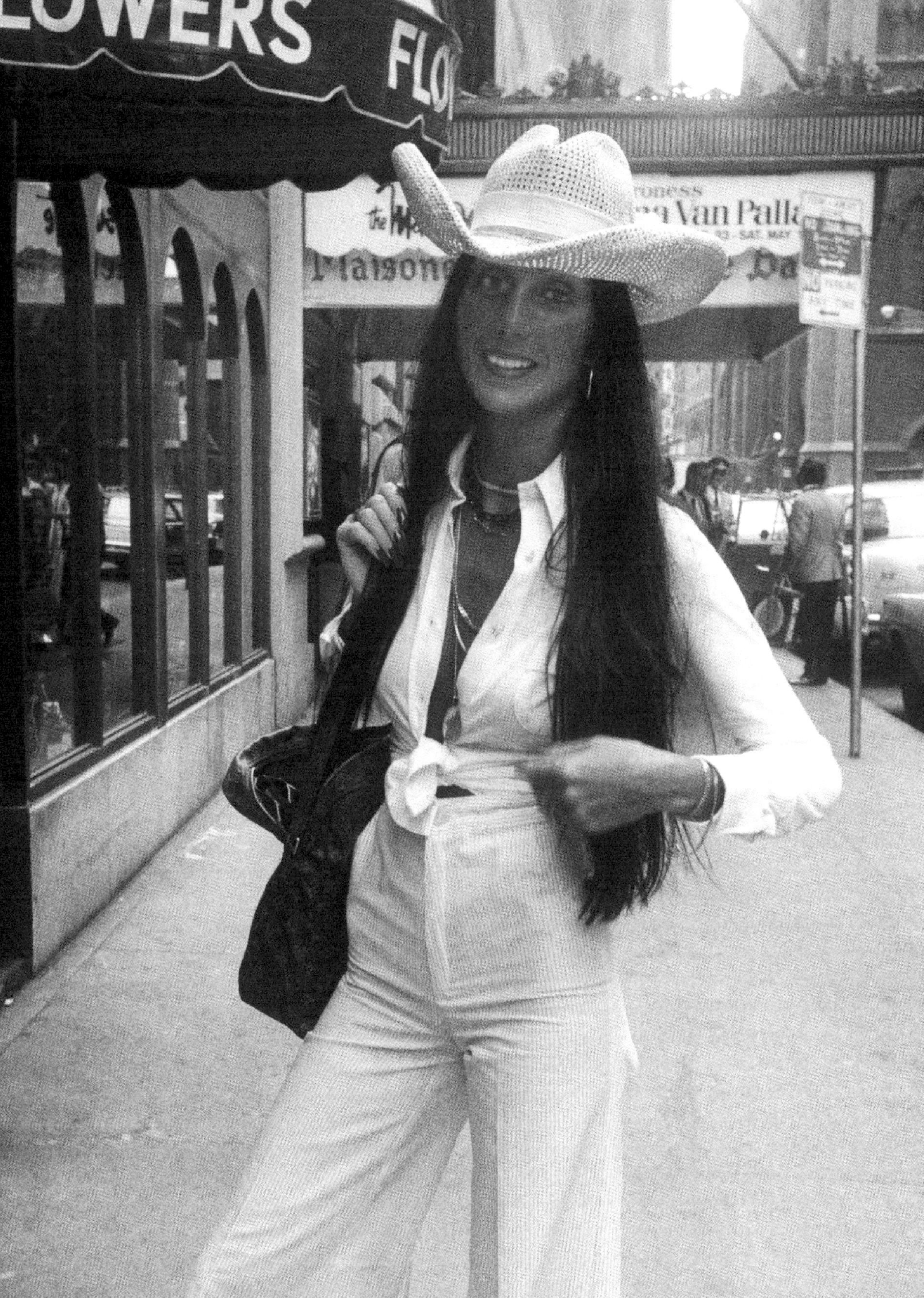

FLOWERS
FLO
Van Pall
SAT. MAY

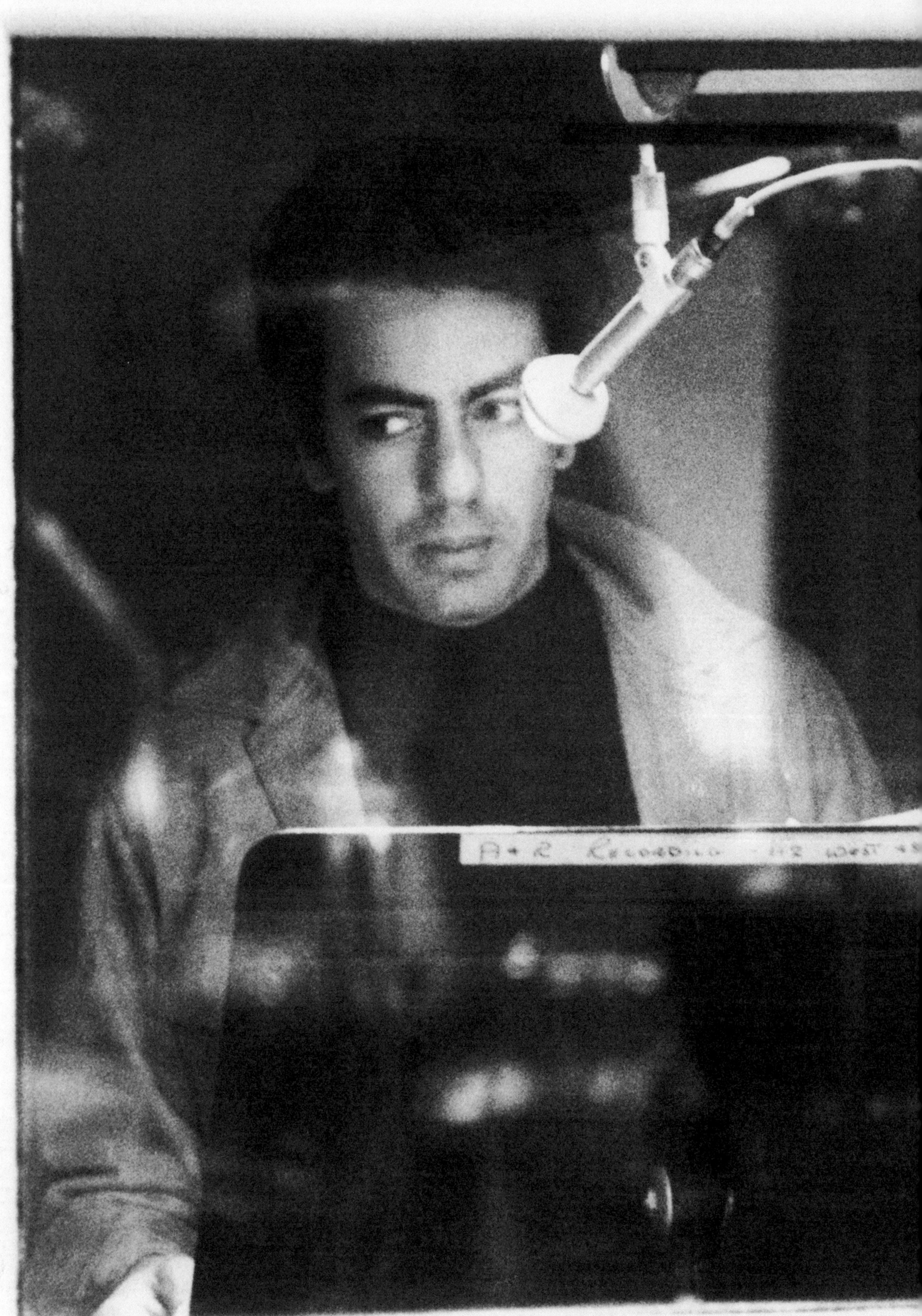
A & R Recording - 112 West 48

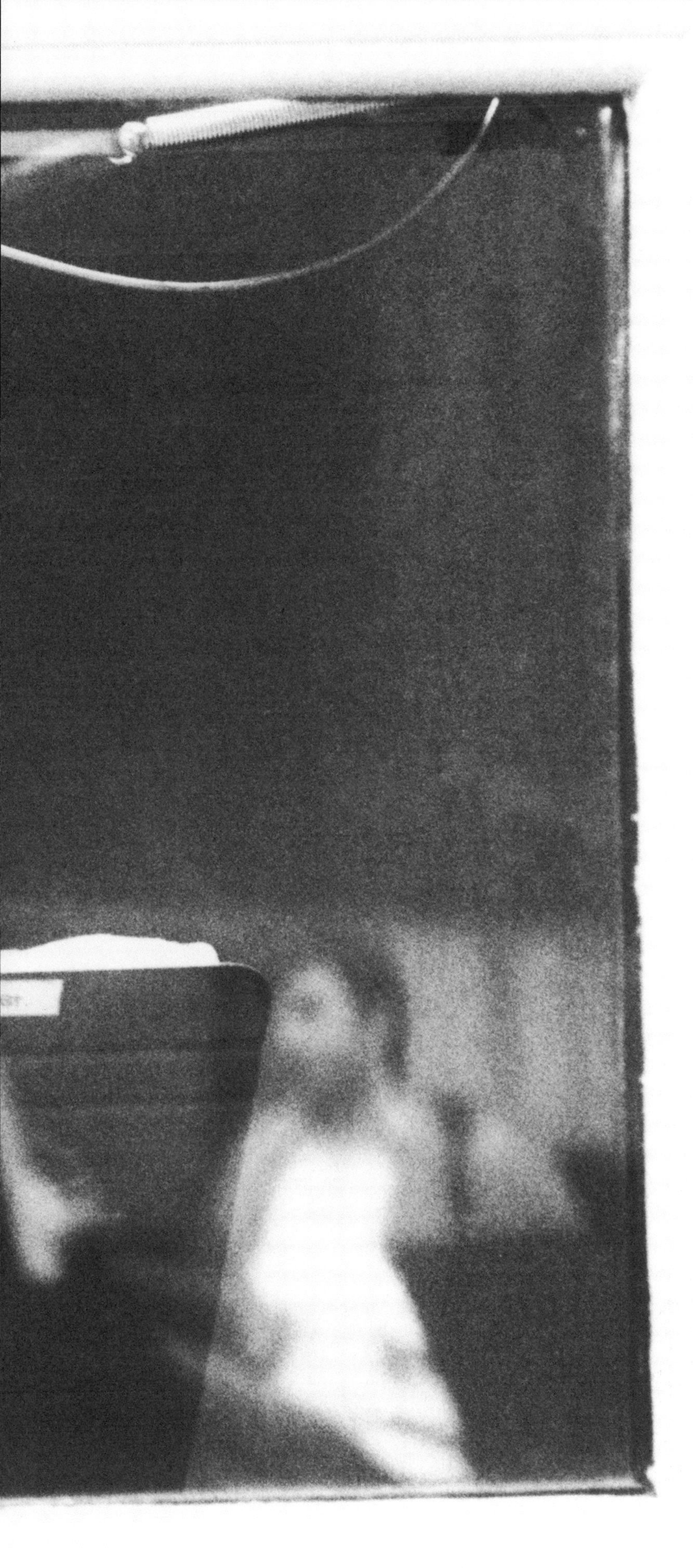

Neil Diamond
1969, New York City

In the recording studio singing
Sweet Caroline.

Siegfried and Roy
1991, Las Vegas

Showing their new tiger cubs at the
Mirage Resort and Casino Hotel.

———

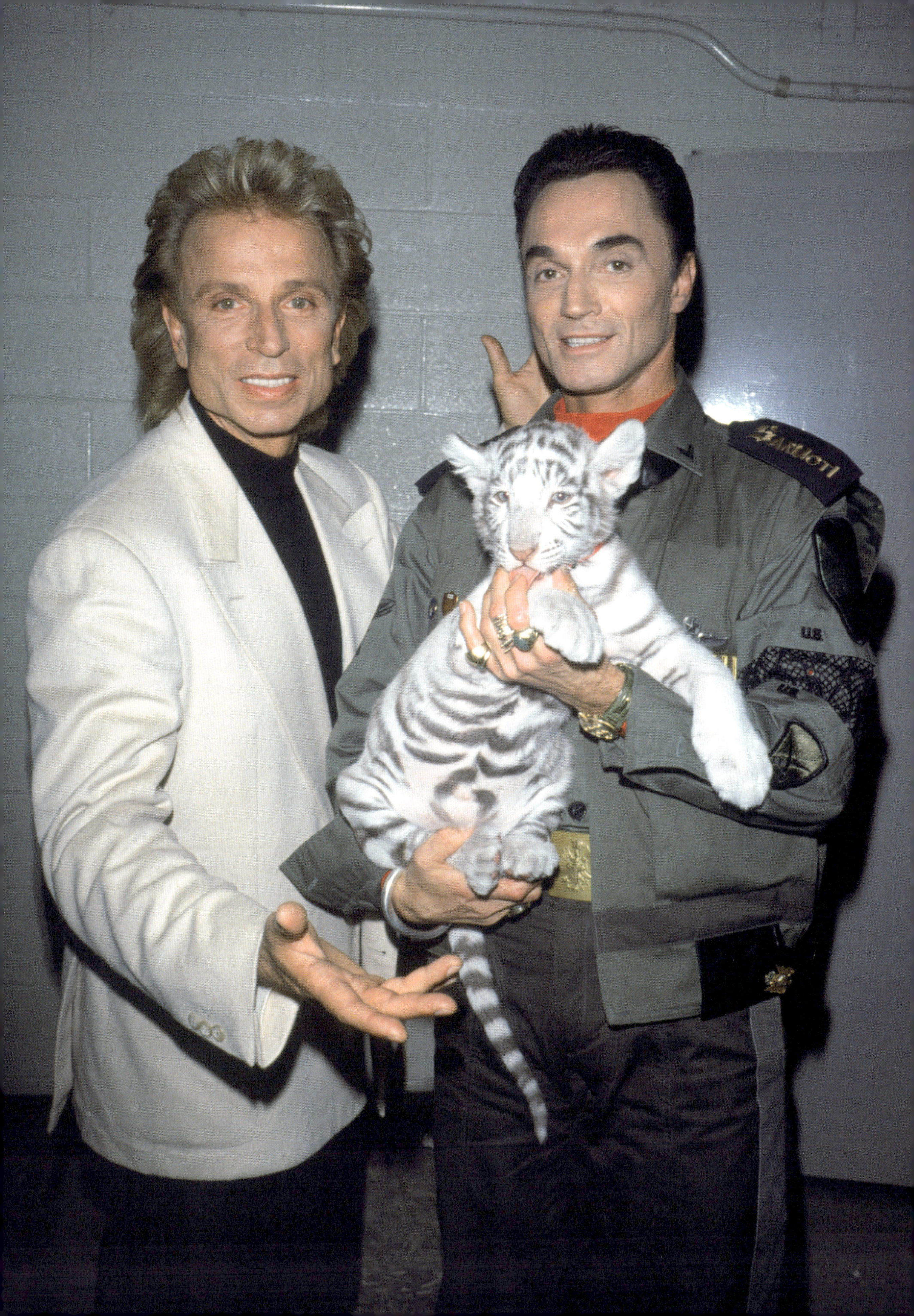

Diana Ross
1982, New York City

Skating in the New York City streets.

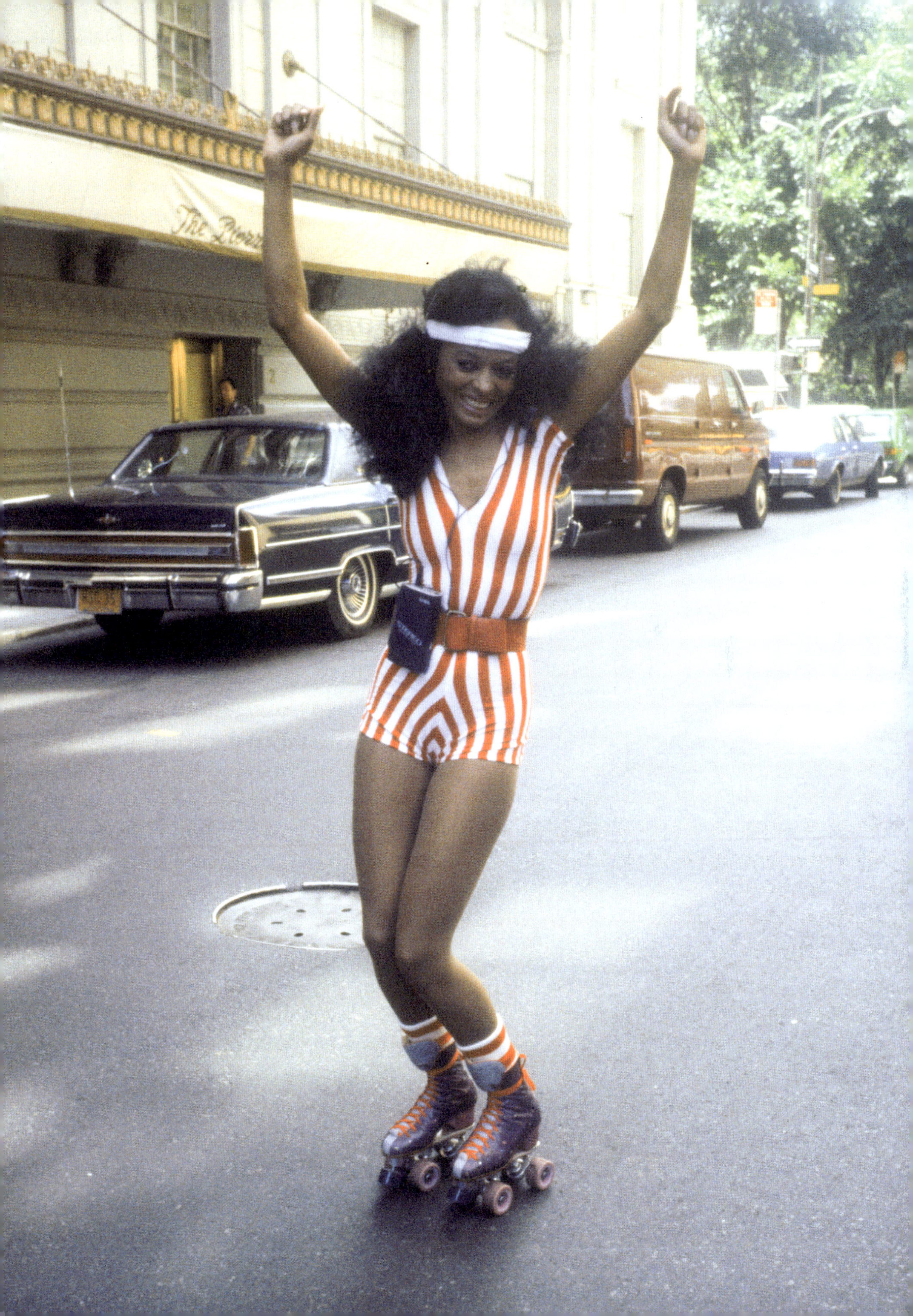

Luciano Pavarotti
1980, New York City

Playing a champagne bottle for the
New Year's celebration at Lincoln Center.

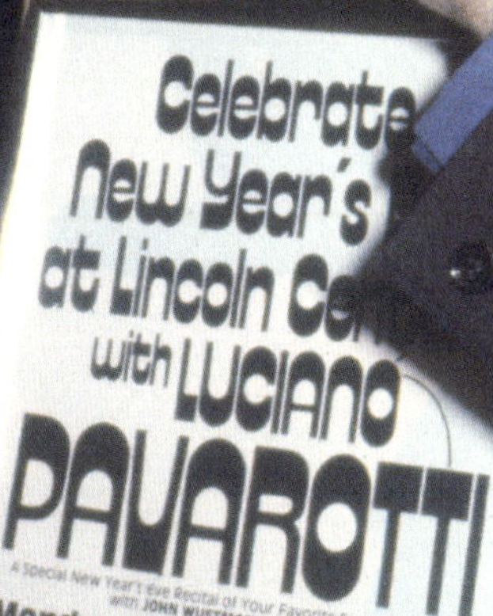
Celebrate
New Year's
at Lincoln Center
with LUCIANO
PAVAROTTI
A Special New Year's Eve Recital of Your Favorite Songs and Arias,
with JOHN WUSTMAN at the piano.
Monday, December 31 at 8pm
Avery Fisher Hall
SOLD OUT!
Including
stage seats

A Finger Splint for Elizabeth Taylor.

I had just returned from the South, flying in a private plane chartered by People Magazine, following the Senatorial campaign of John Warner and his wife Elizabeth Taylor. The magazine is reserving the cover and quite a few inside pages for this feature and the pressure is on. It has been quite an experience not simply trying to keep up with them, but taking pictures at the same time. We have had breakfasts together, done meet and greets, and all the while Elizabeth has been a great sport, donning aprons and hats to get the attention John Warner needs for his campaign, despite a painful fracture on her finger, which is in a splint.

A while later at the *New York Film Critics Circle Awards* at Sardi's, Elizabeth is happy to see me, but I notice she is not wearing her splint, and thinking it healed (since it was a nasty fracture) I ask her about it. To my surprise she informs me that it is still very painful, but she has lost the splint and has not been able to replace it. I offer to help, and tell her I'll be in touch with her later in the evening at the Waldorf Astoria Towers, where she is staying.

But getting a splint proves to be more difficult than I had imagined, and after some bargaining and pleading on the phone to anyone who would listen, and out of desperation saying it is for Elizabeth Taylor, I finally find a sympathetic emergency room doctor at Roosevelt Hospital. He tells me to come over, shows me how to apply it, and asks me again if it is really for Elizabeth Taylor. I confirm, and I'm on my way to the Towers.

But if I thought getting a splint was challenging, getting through to Elizabeth is even more of a headache! Her public relations agent John Springer is clearly annoyed, not only at the late hour but upon hearing it's me! I explain again and again why I'm calling and finally tell him to go to Elizabeth and ask. He does, and when he gets back on the phone he is even more annoyed, not only because I was right, but because he has to tell me to come up.

I spend about 15 minutes taking care of Elizabeth 's finger. She is appreciative and thanks me, even though she is not always happy with the way I photograph her. Too human, she says!
We laugh and I leave.....
———

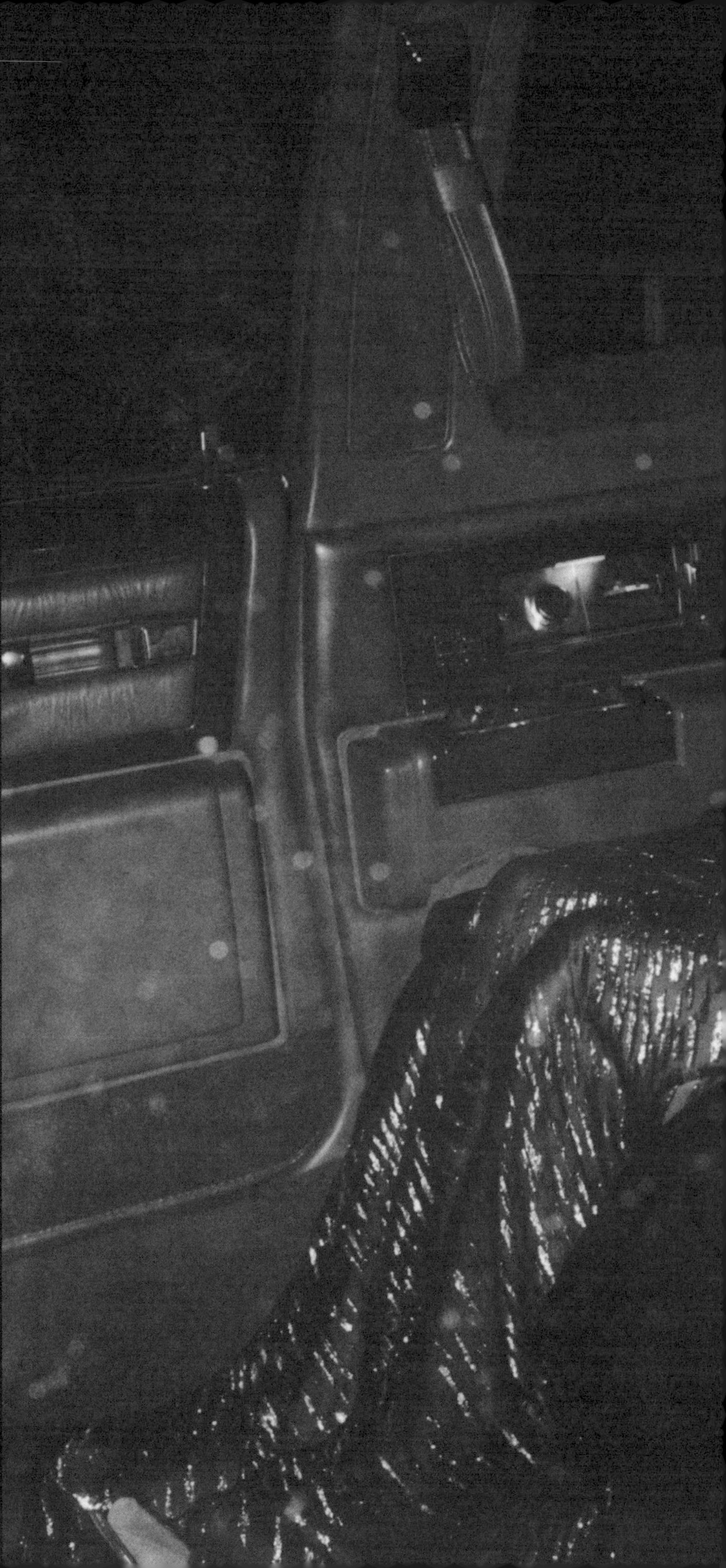

**Elizabeth Taylor and
John Warner**
1977, New York City

On the campaign trail for
his Senatorial race.

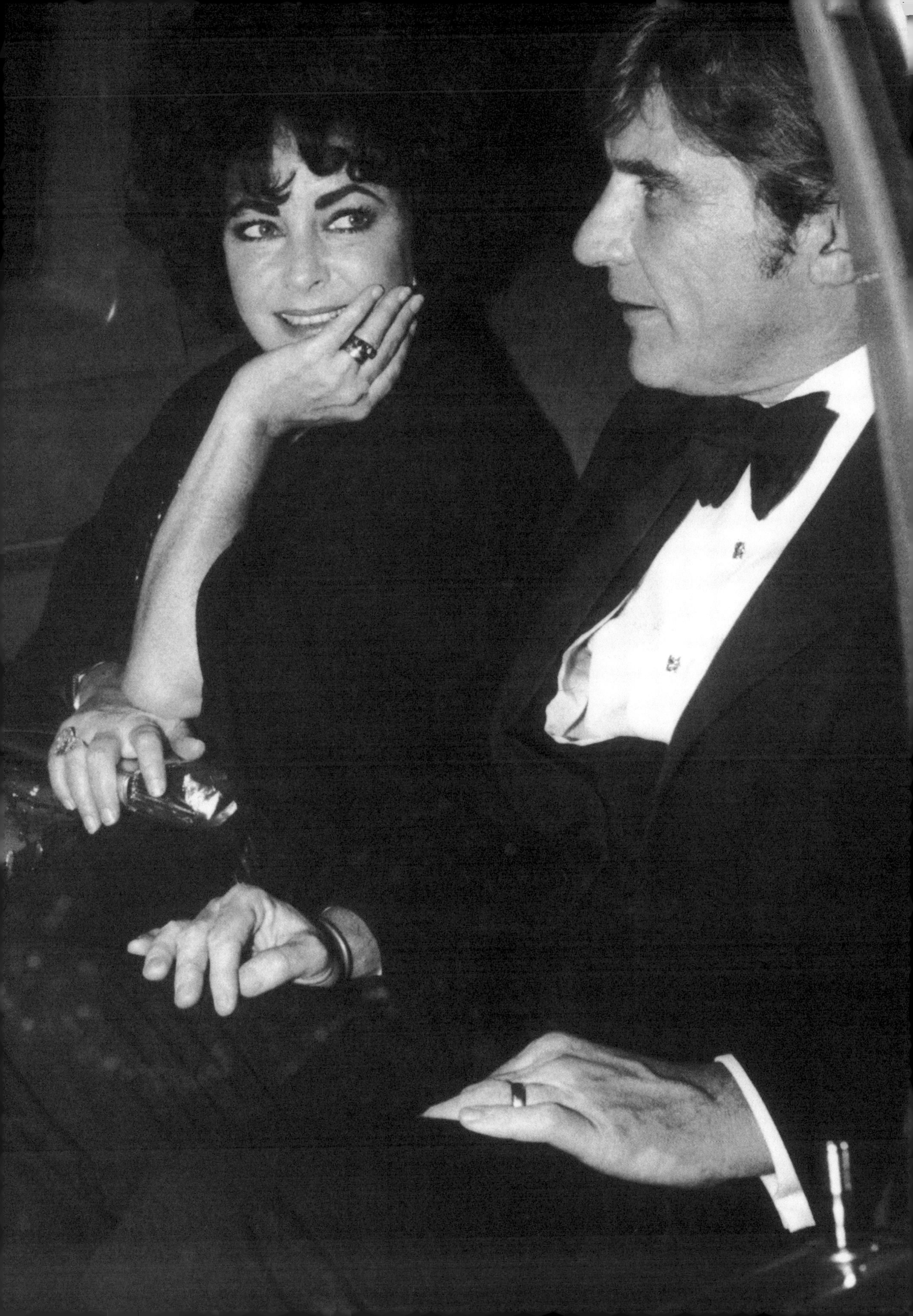

Elizabeth Taylor
1967, New York City

At a press conference at the Plaza Hotel, New York City,
promoting her movie *The Taming of the Shrew*.
———

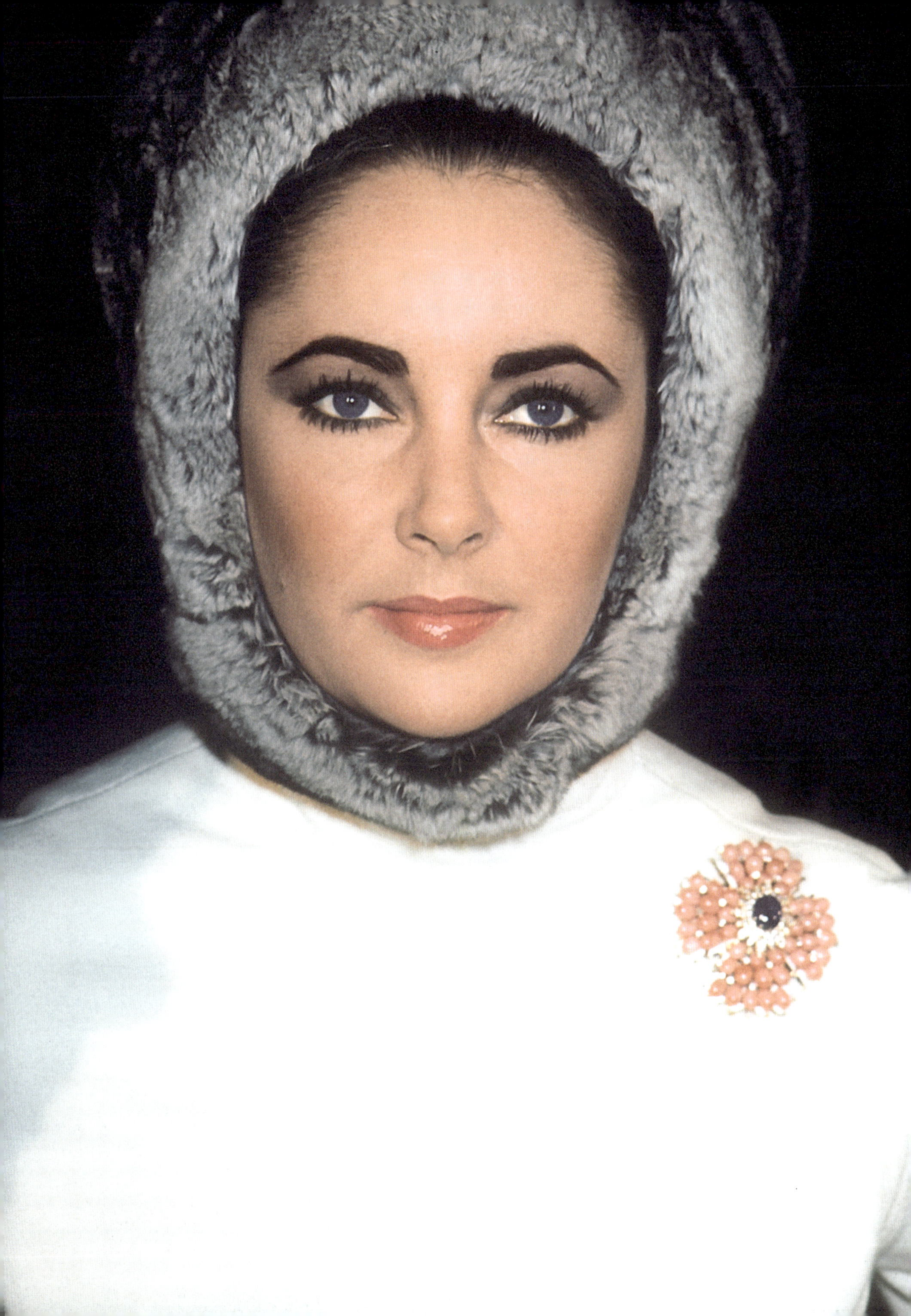

Drew Barrymore
1985, New York City

At the Hard Rock Cafe.

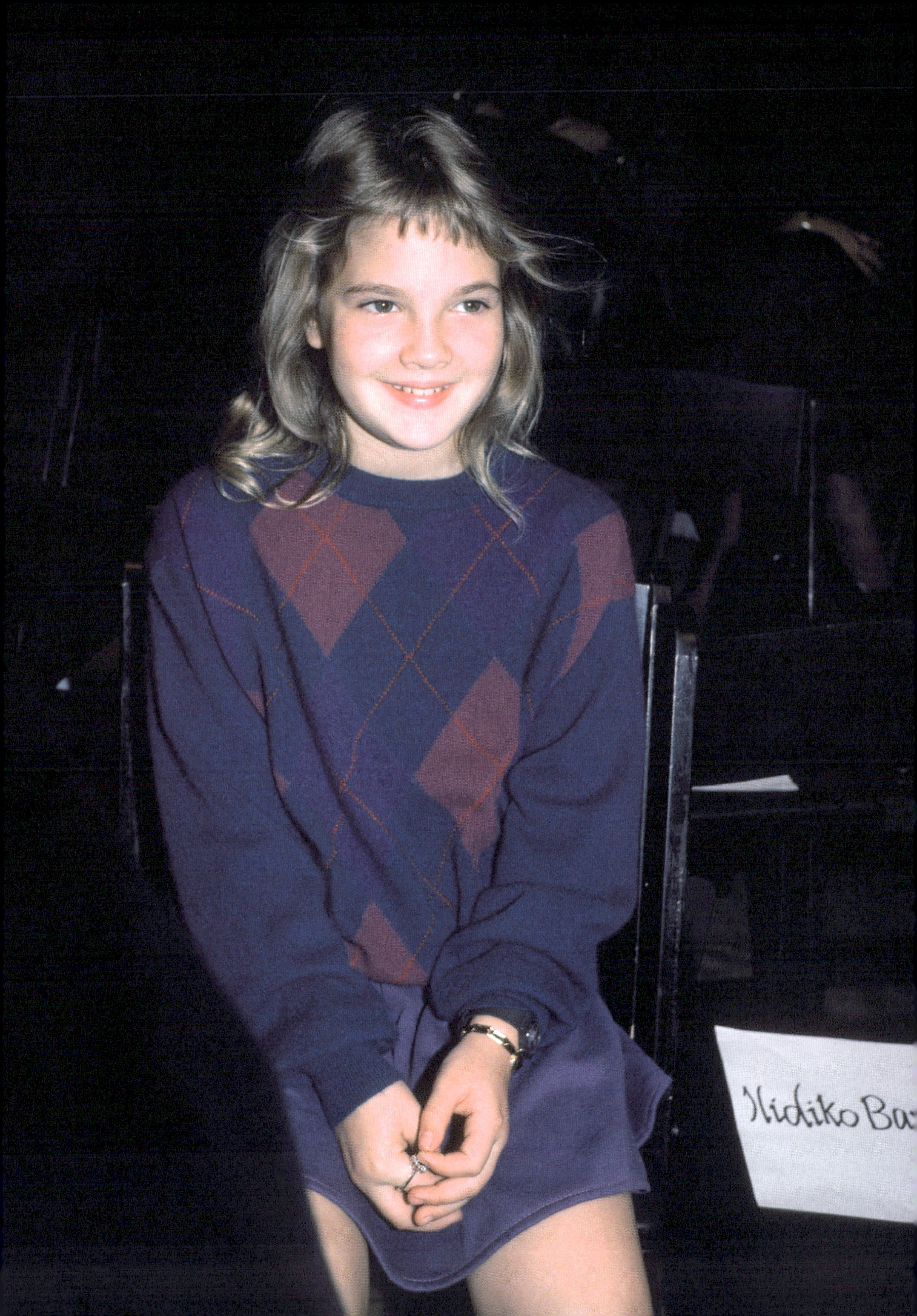
Ilidiko Ba

Elton John
1974, New York City

——

Following double page

David Bowie
1981, New York City

At the premiere of the restored version
of *Napoleon* at Radio City Music
Hall, New York City.

——

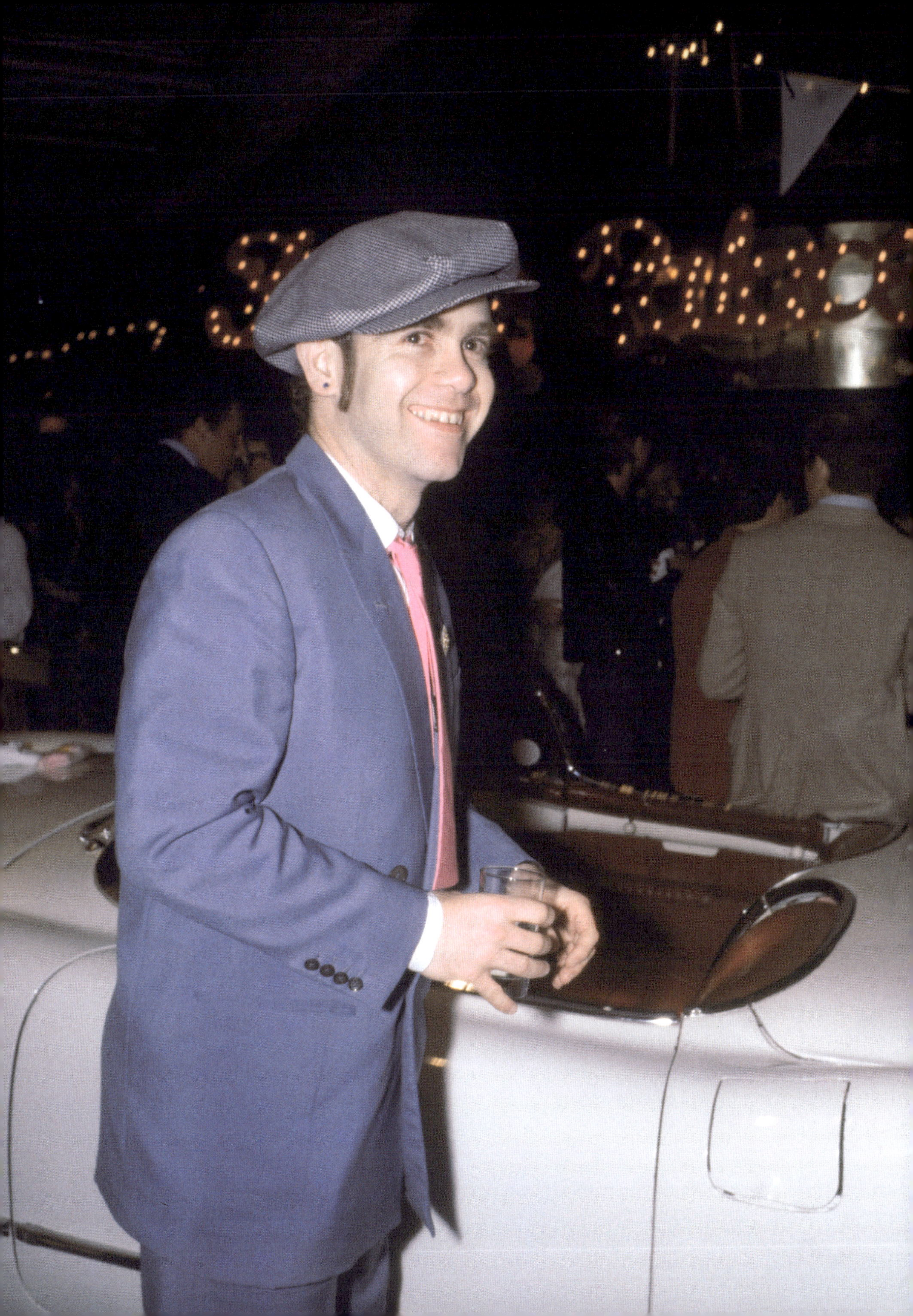

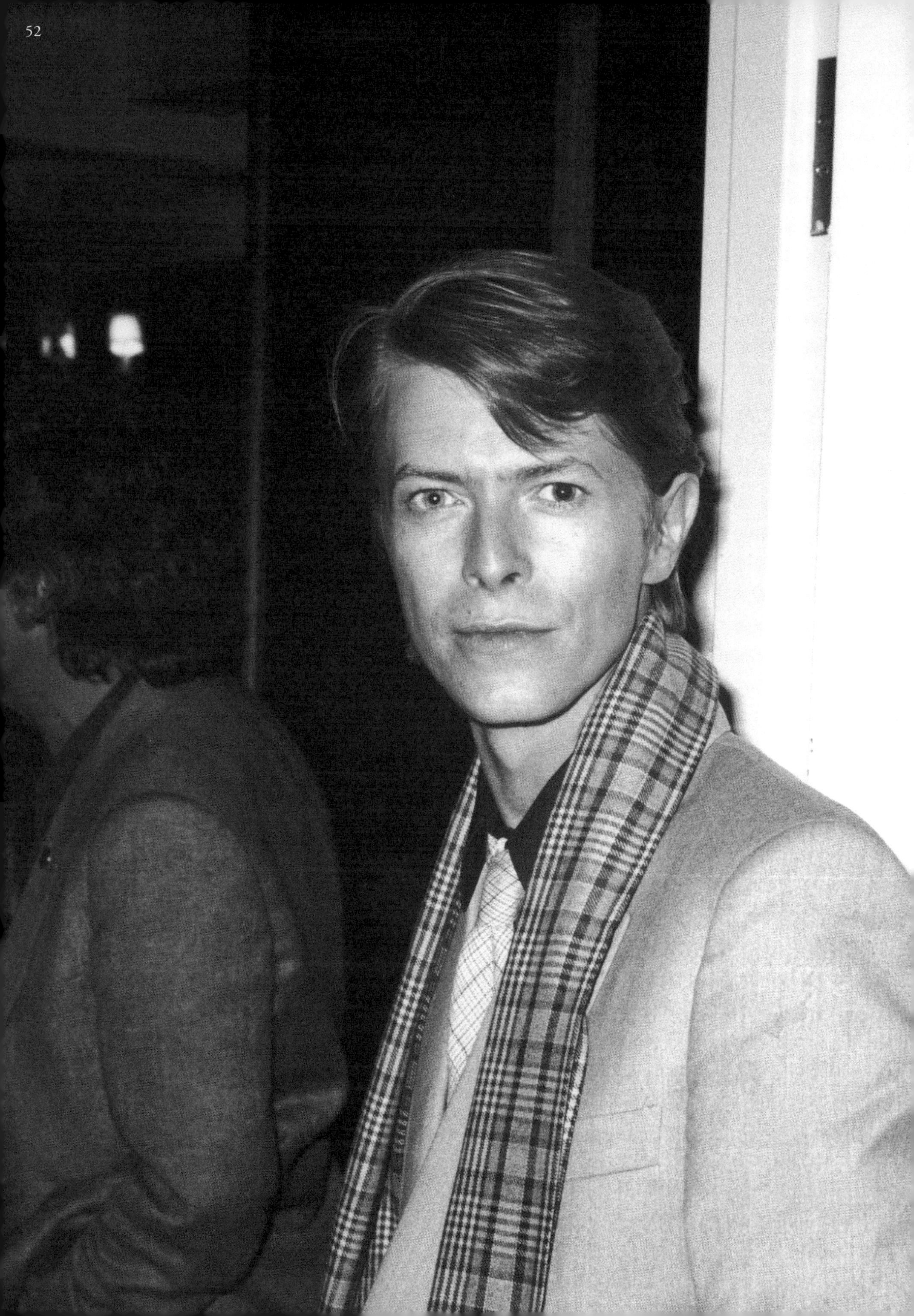

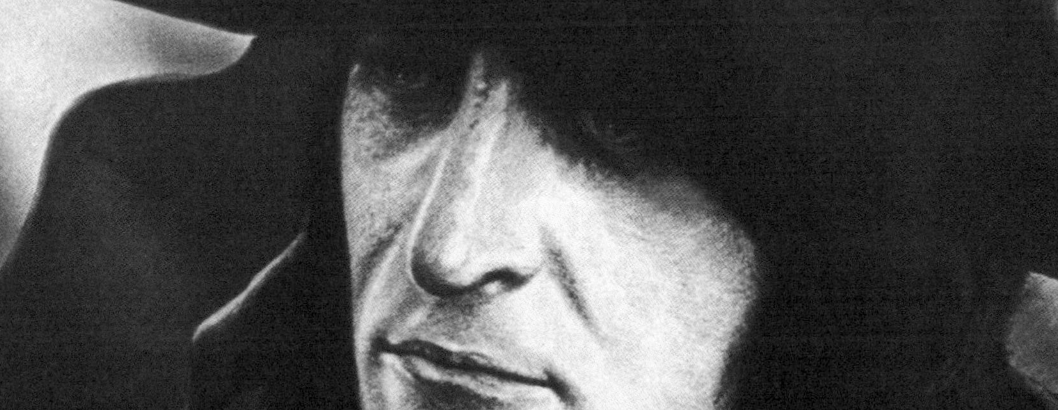

FRANCIS FORD COPPOLA
PRESENTS
NAPOLEO
ABEL GANCE'S 1927 MASTER

Rutger Hauer
1982, New York City

At the *New York Film Critics Circle Awards,*
at Sardi's.
———

Following double page

**James Gardner, Julie Belafonte,
Harry Belafonte and Lena Horne**
1970, New York City

At a charity event at the Pierre Hotel.
———

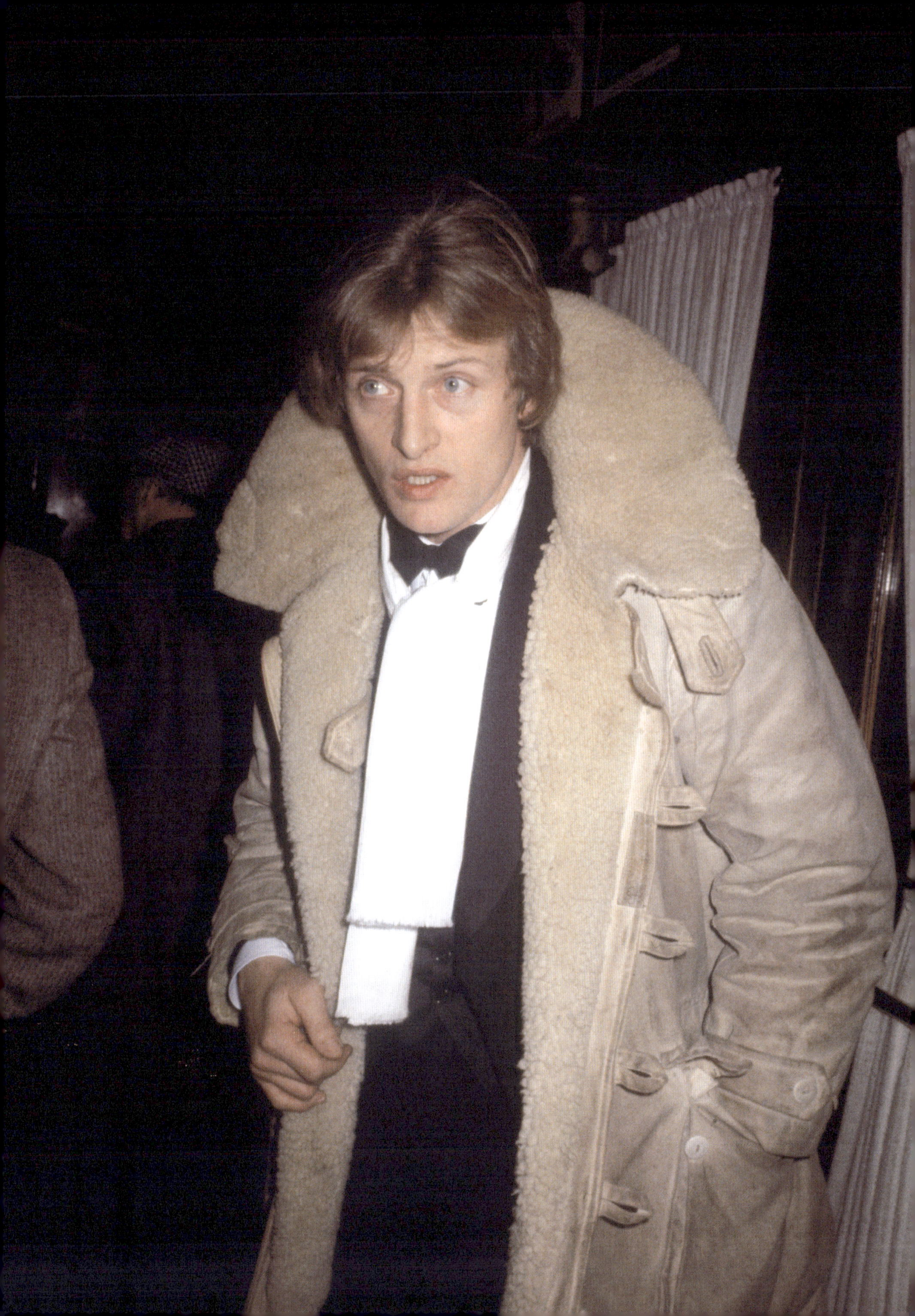

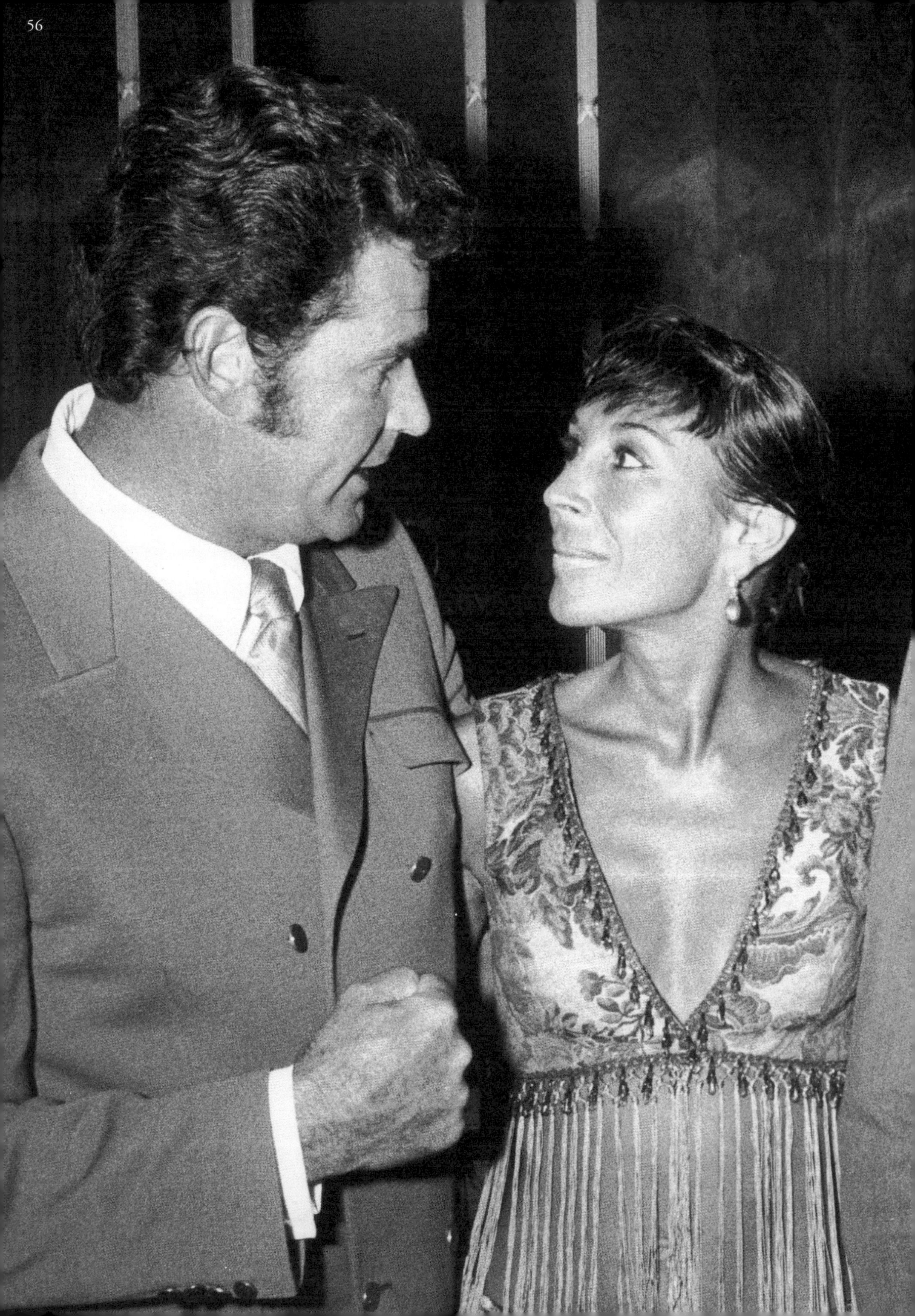

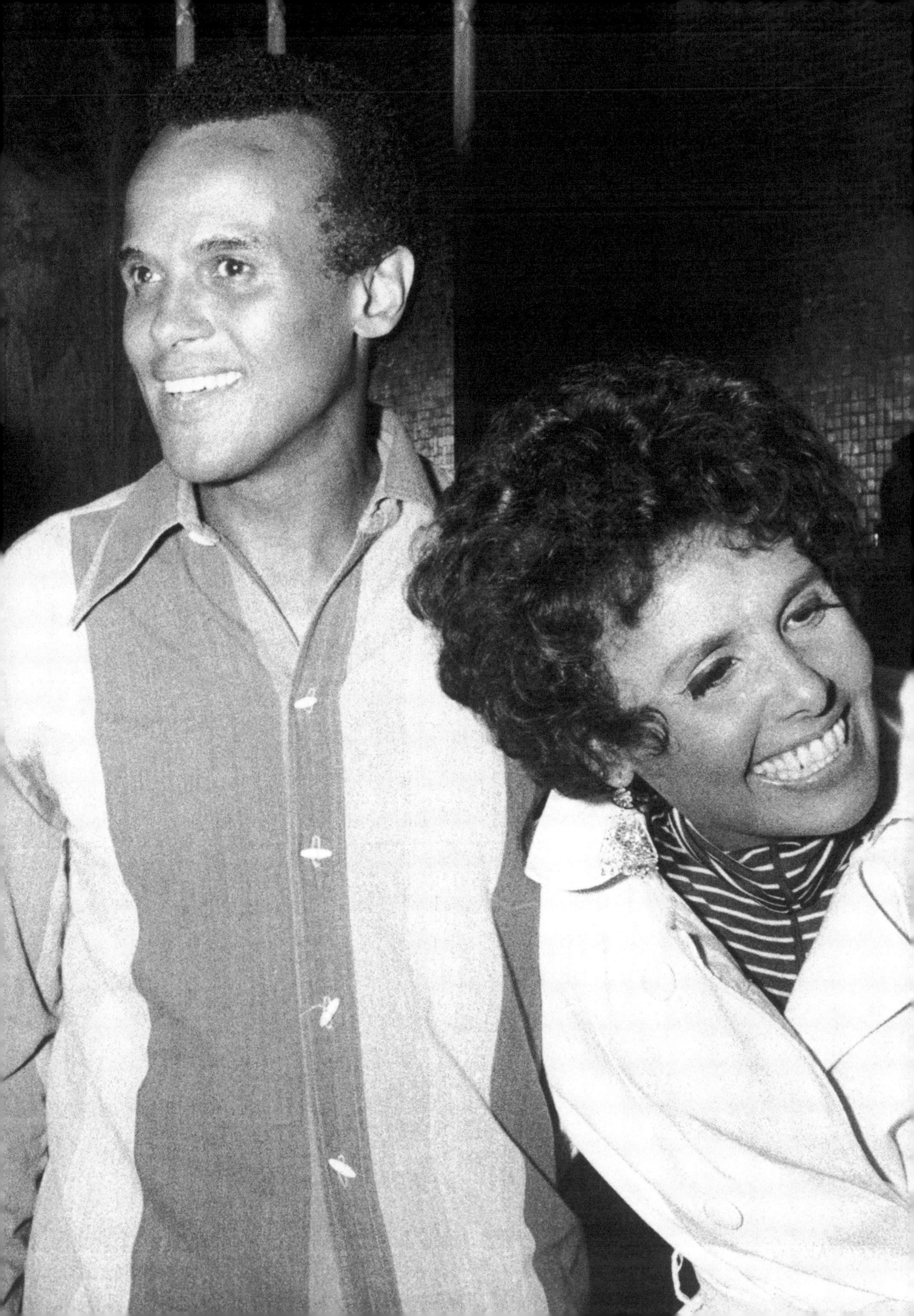

**Muhammad Ali and
Harry Belafonte**
1970, New York City

At a charity event at the Pierre Hotel.
——

Following double page

Sly Stone and Kathy Silva
1974, New York City

Sly getting married to Kathy Silva during
a sold out performance at Madison Square
Garden. They had a party at the Waldorf-Astoria
Starlight Roof.
——

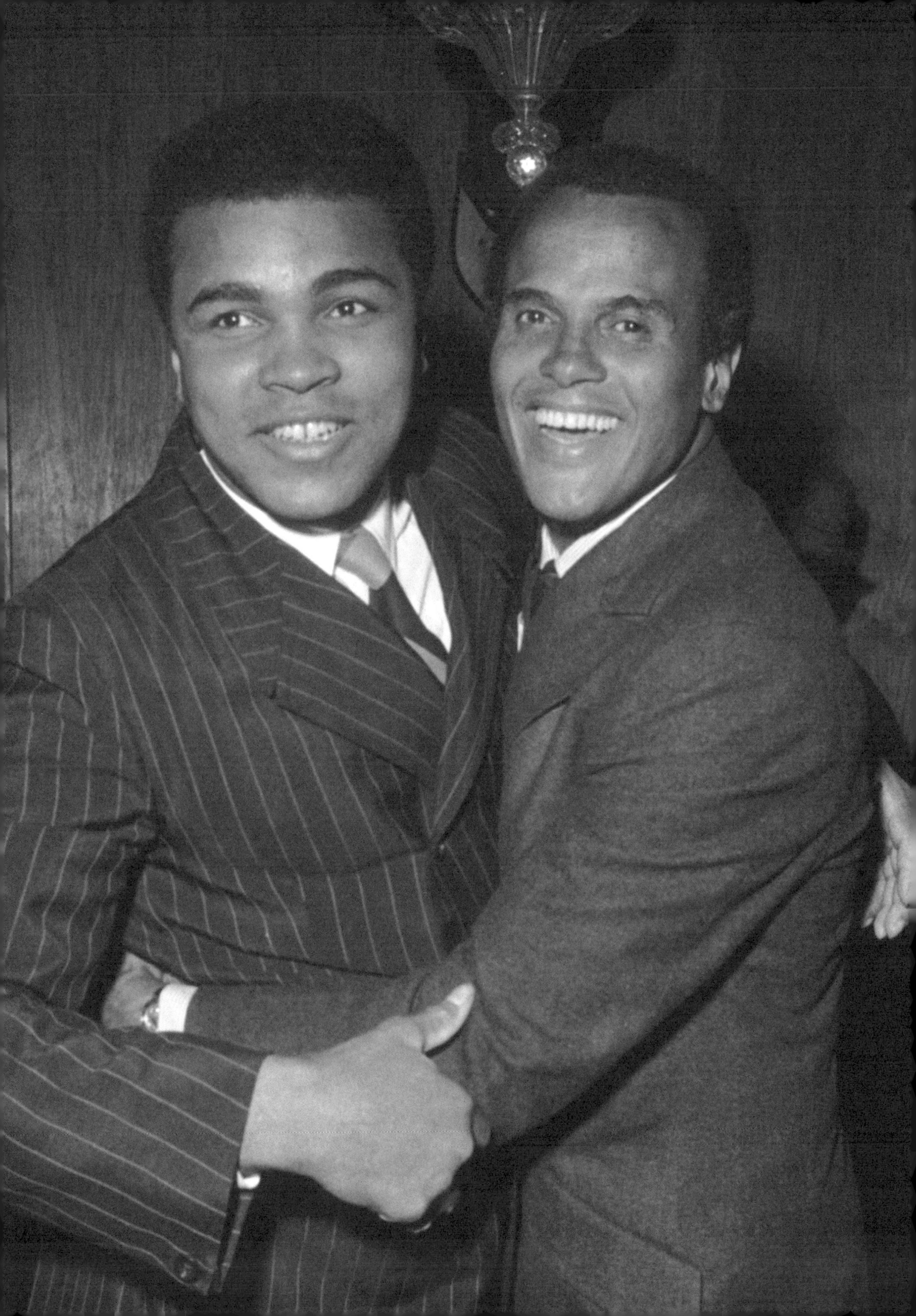

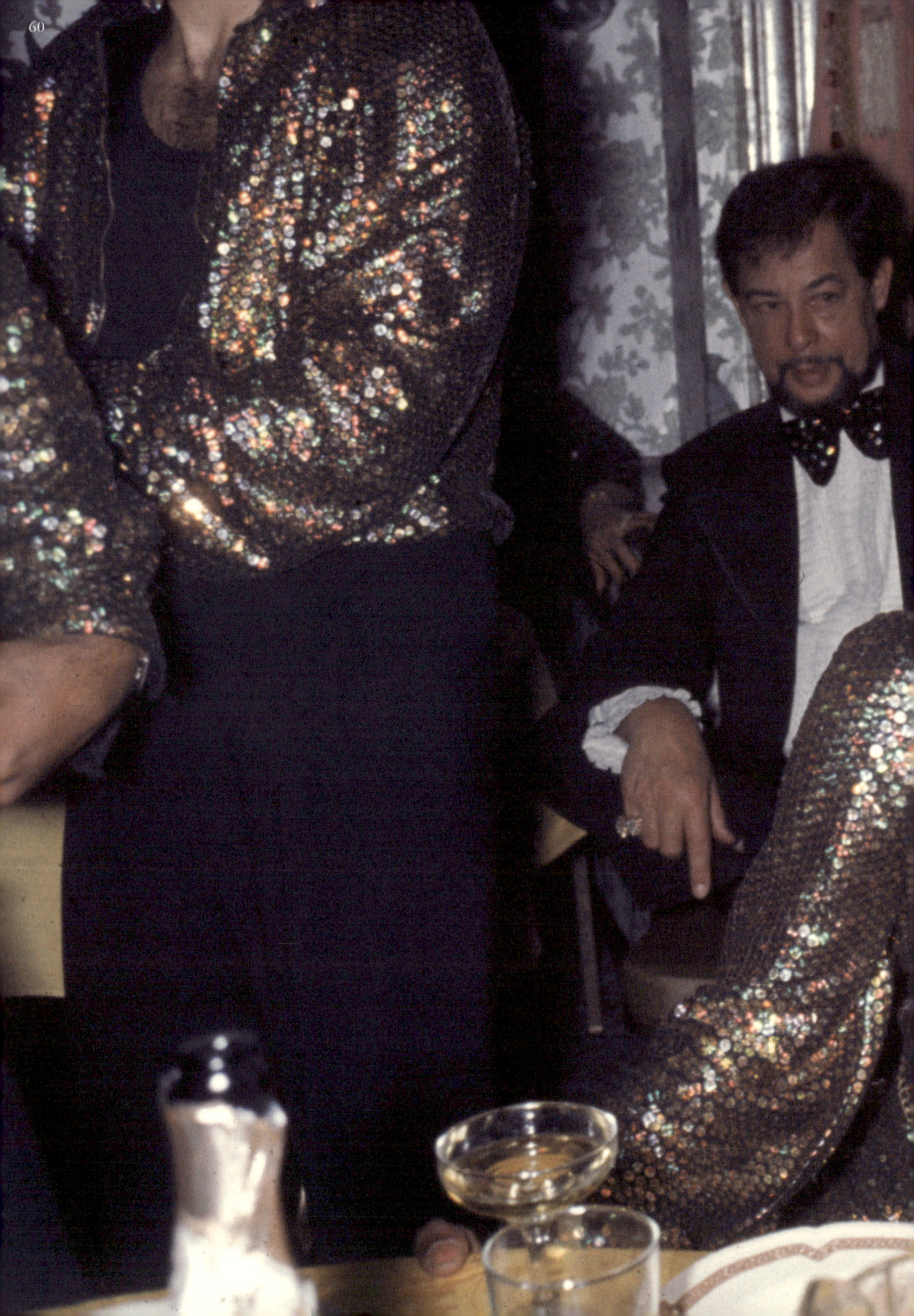

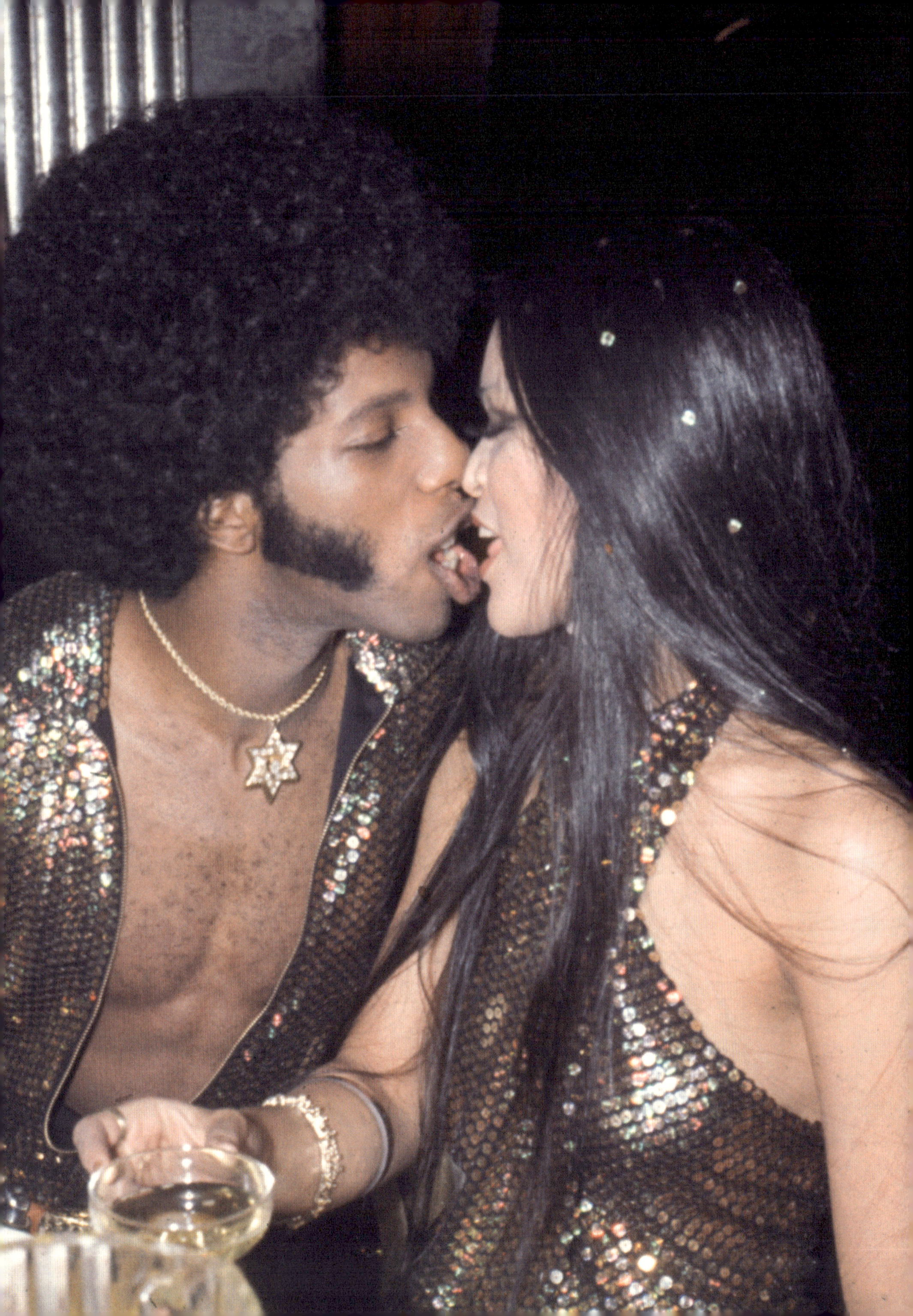

Danny DeVito
1978, New York City

In an Off Broadway play.

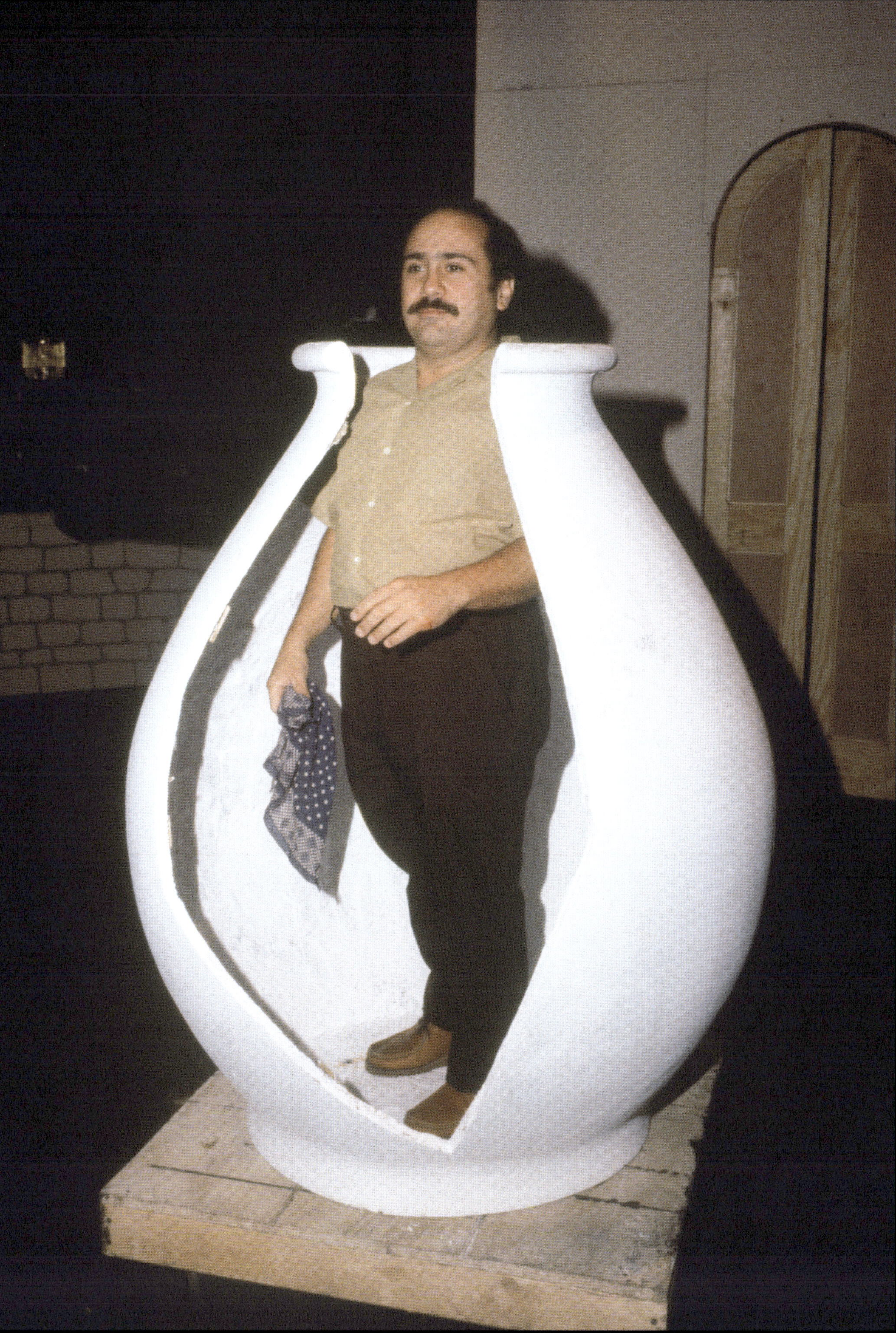

Andy Warhol and Bianca Jagger
1978, New York City

Arriving at Studio 54.
——

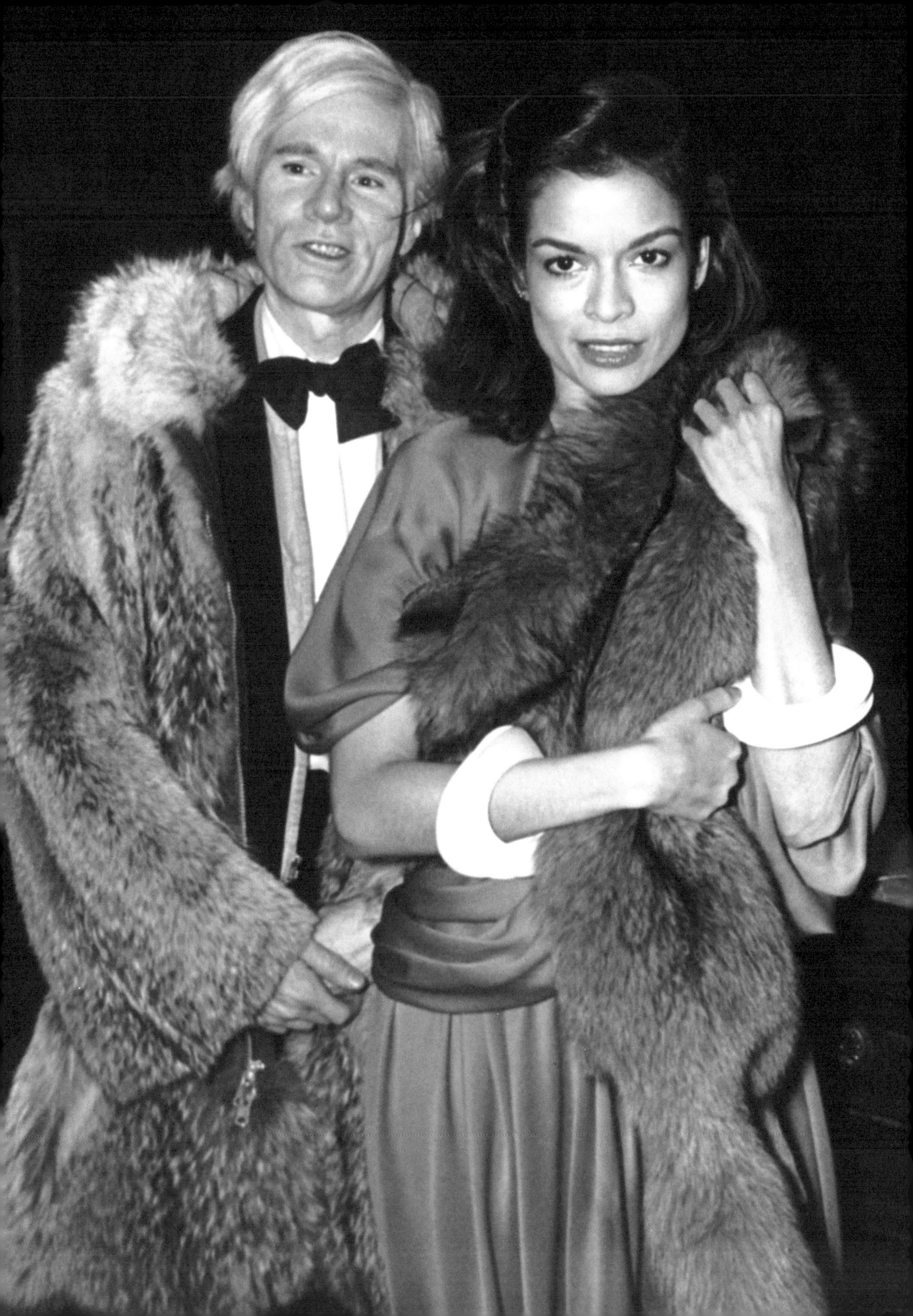

Ted Kennedy
1969, New York City

At the Hilton Hotel.

———

Following double page

John Lennon and Yoko Ono
1975, New York City

At the Astor Theatre for the *Grammy Awards*.

———

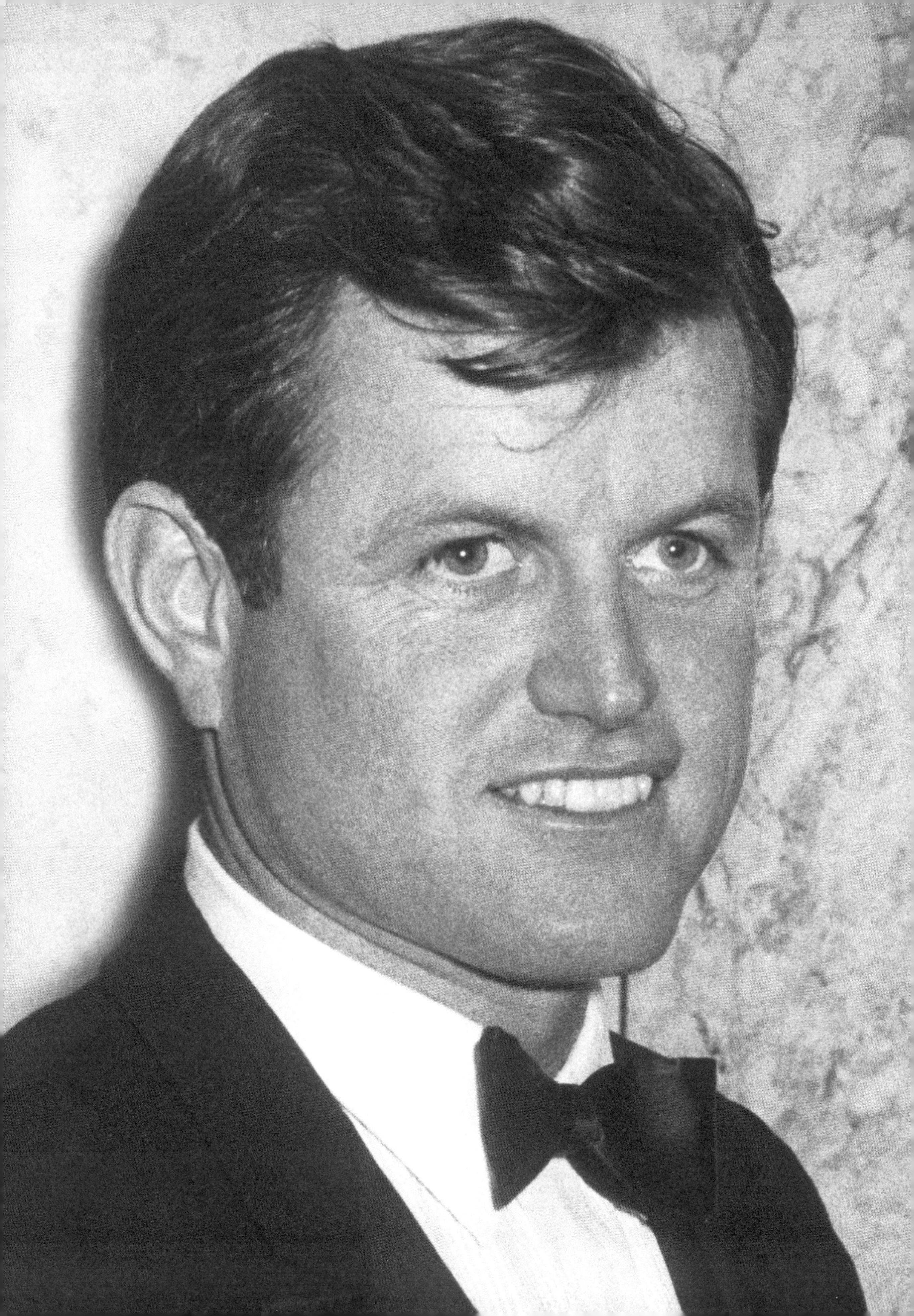

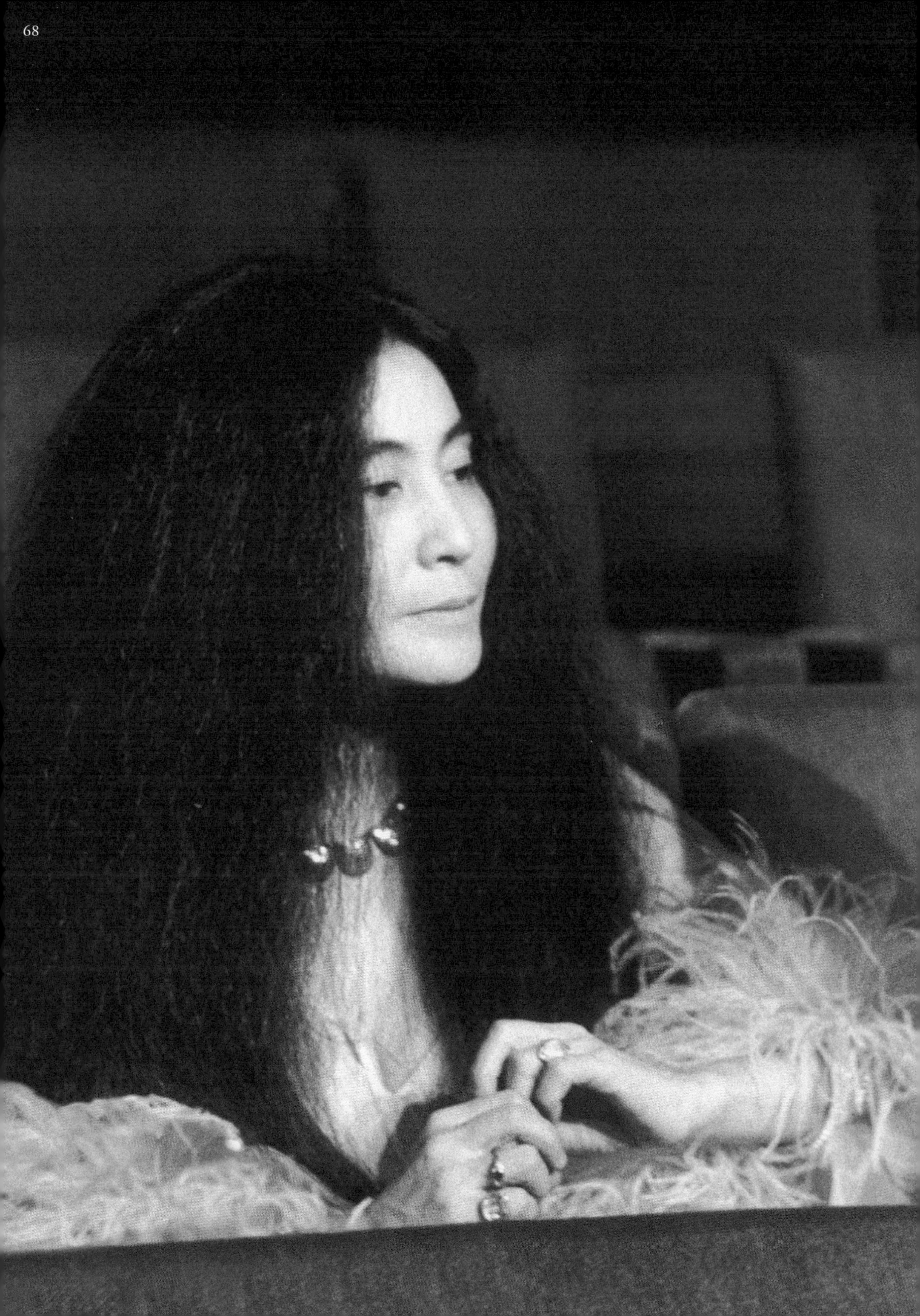

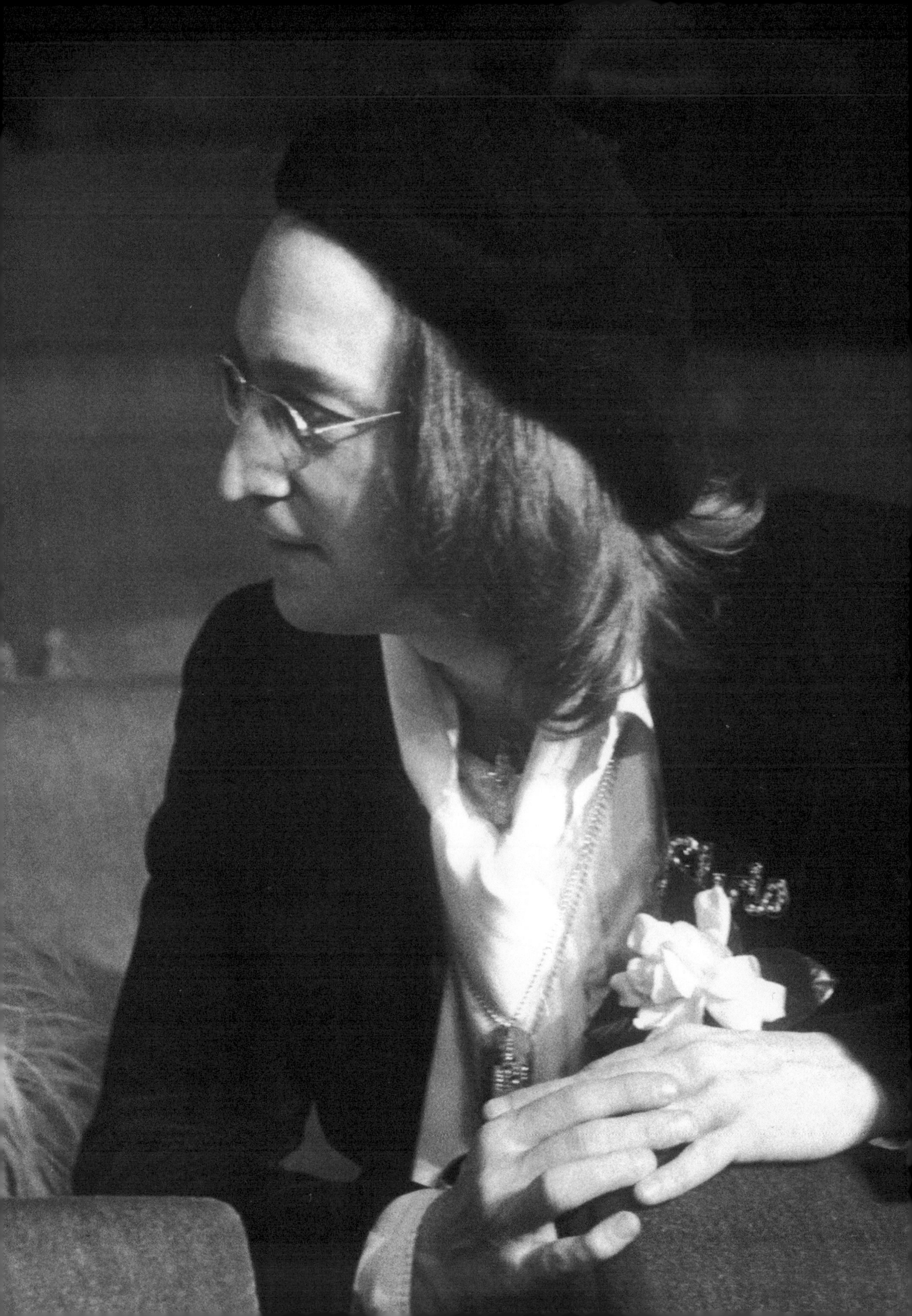

Charles Aznavour
1967, New York City

Rehearsing before his Carnegie Hall concert.
———

Following double page

Barbra Streisand
1969, New York City

In a car after the *New York Film Critics Circle Awards,*
at Sardi's.
———

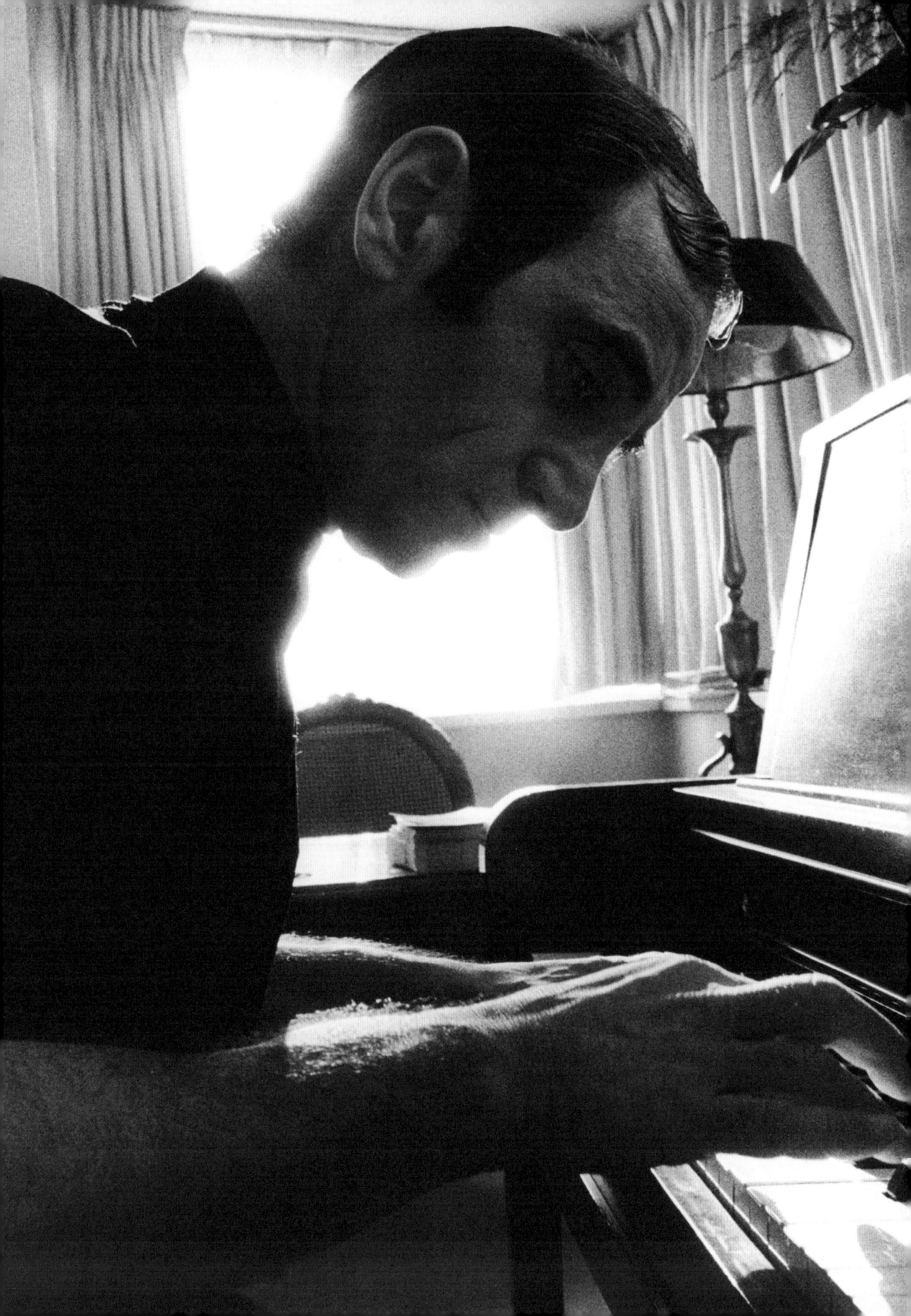

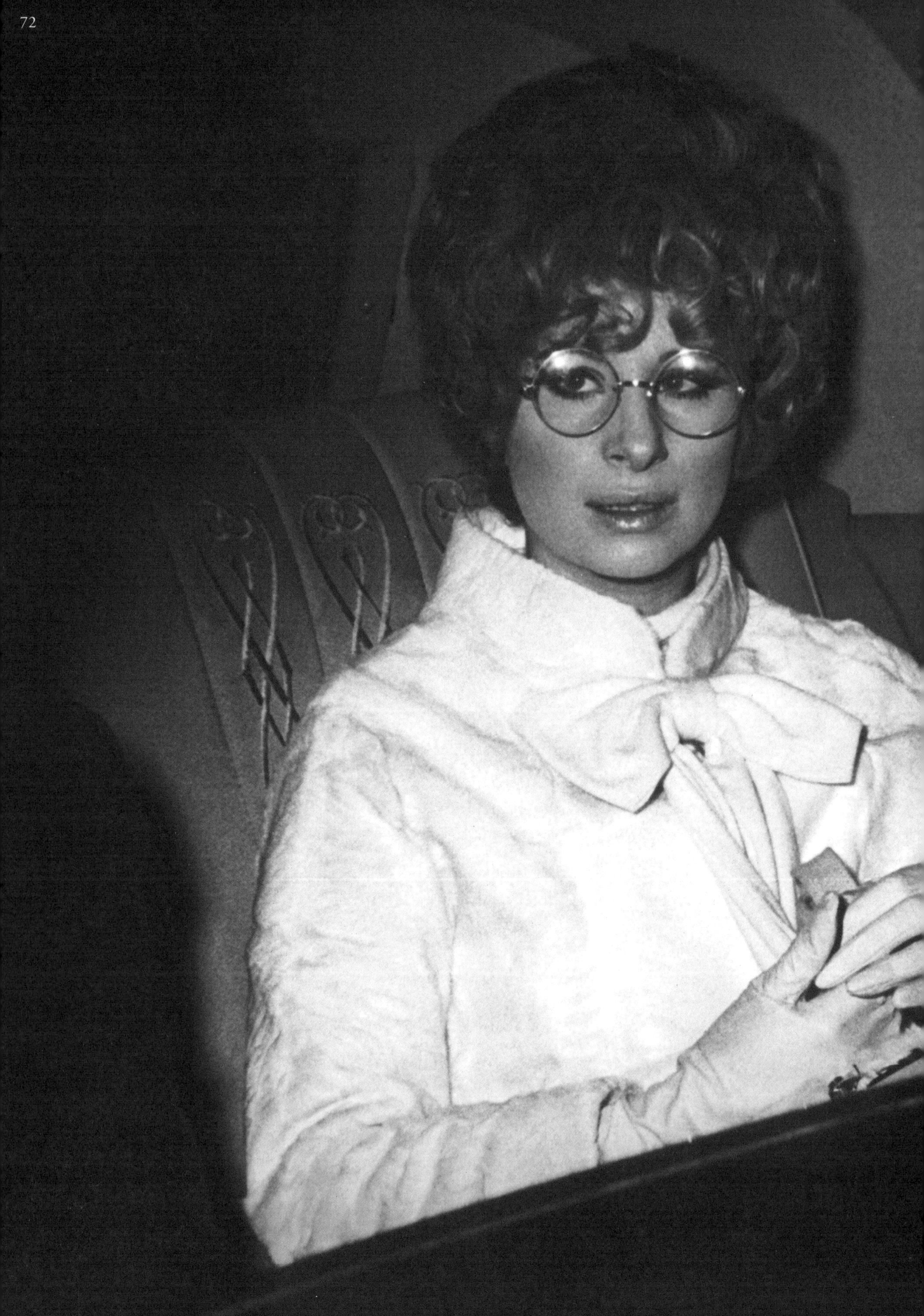

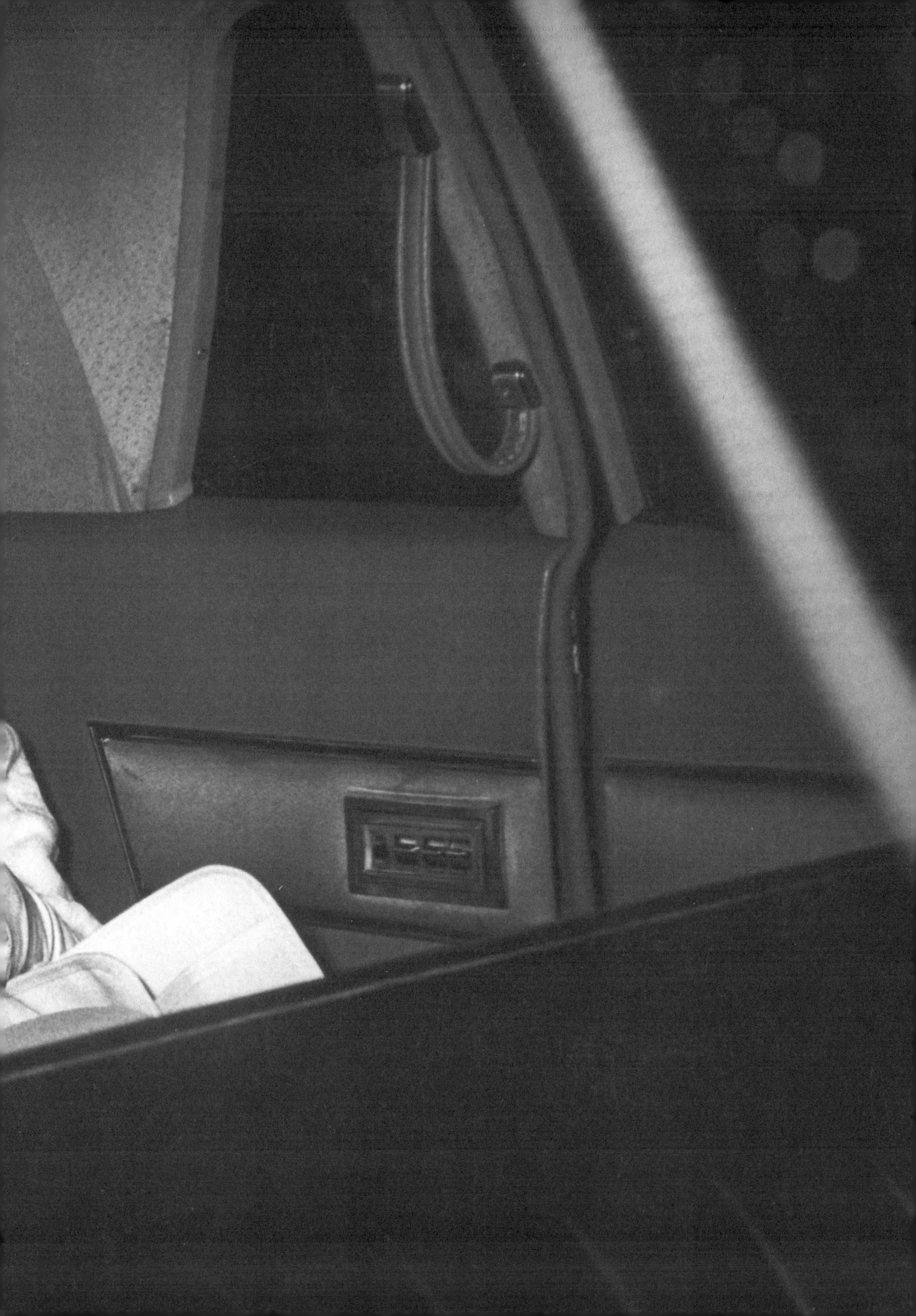

Dolly Parton
1980, Nashville

At the Grand Ole Opry
for the *CMA Awards*.

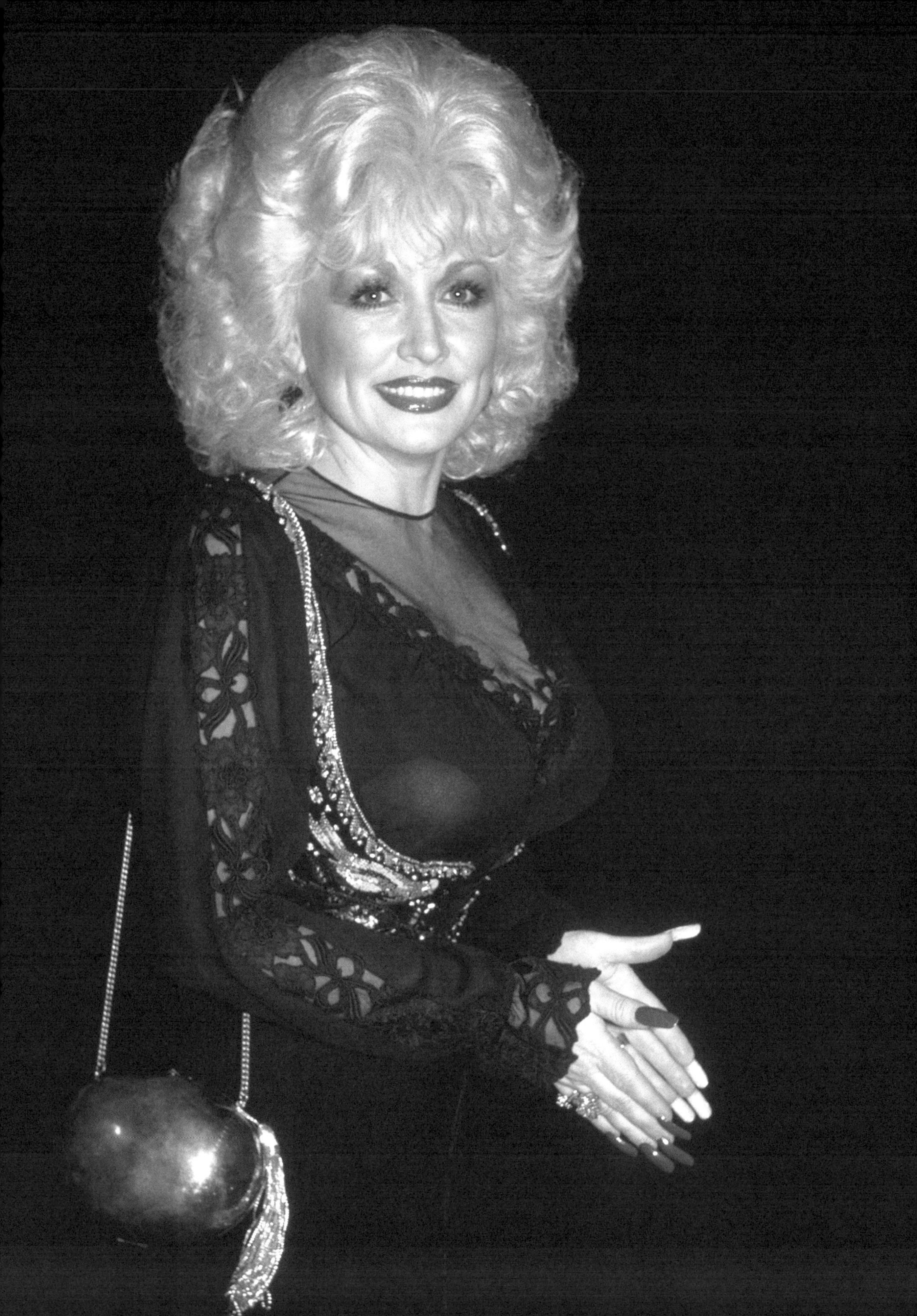

Mick Jagger and John Phillips
1977, New York City

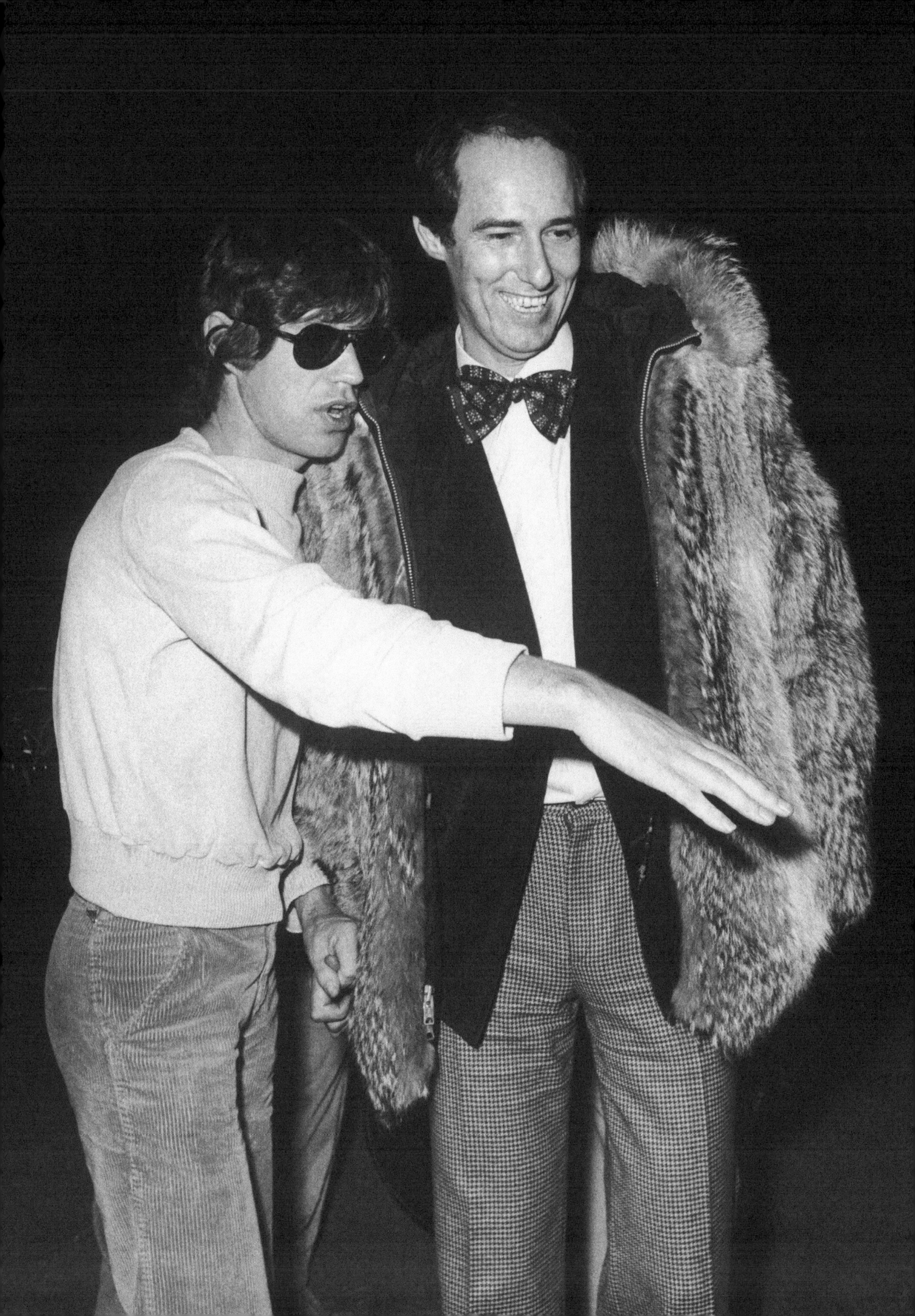

Mae West
1970, New York City

At the movie premiere of her last
movie *Myra Breckinridge*.
———

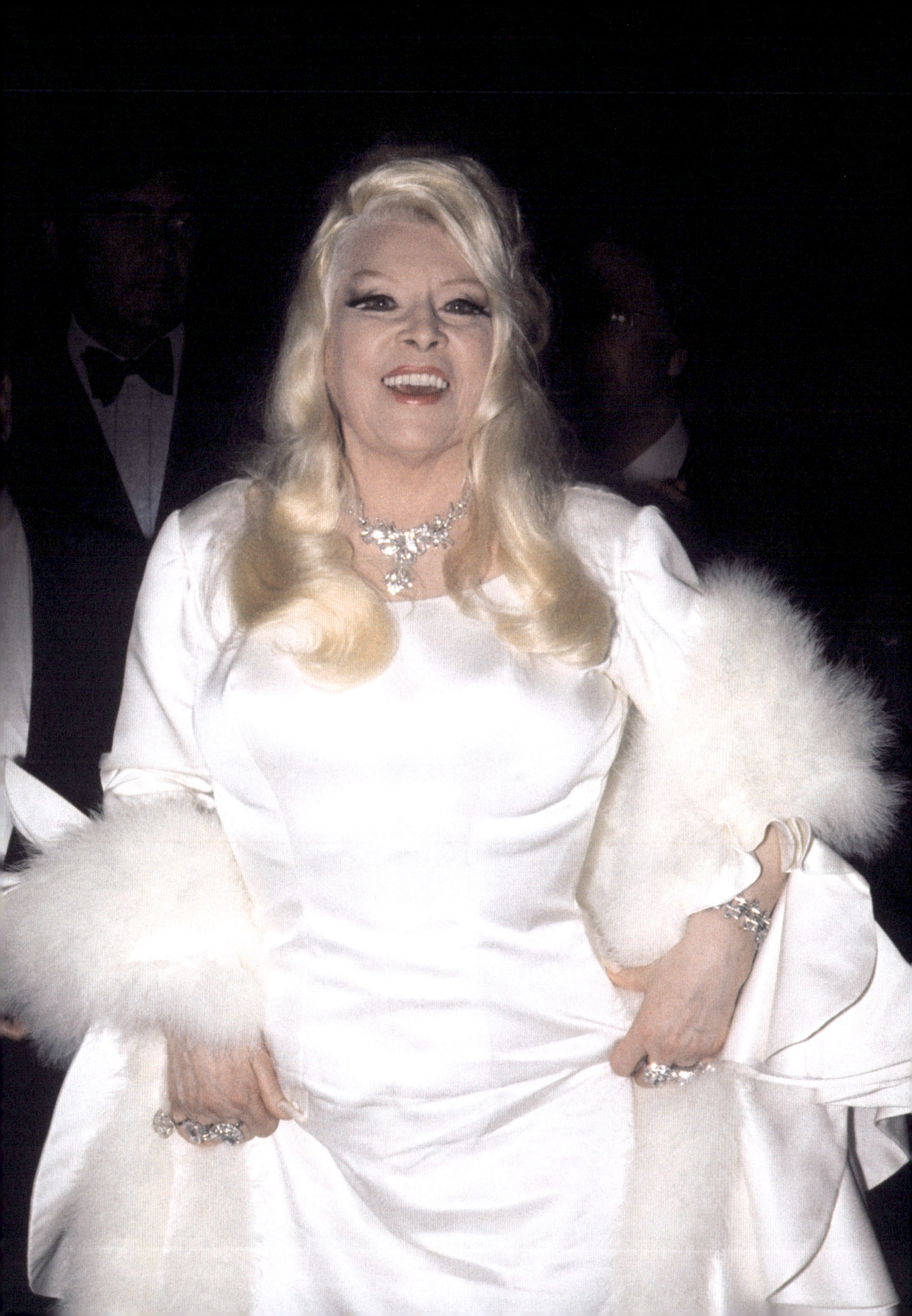

Anthony Quinn
1968, New York City

Premiere of his movie *Shoes of the Fisherman* at the MoMA.

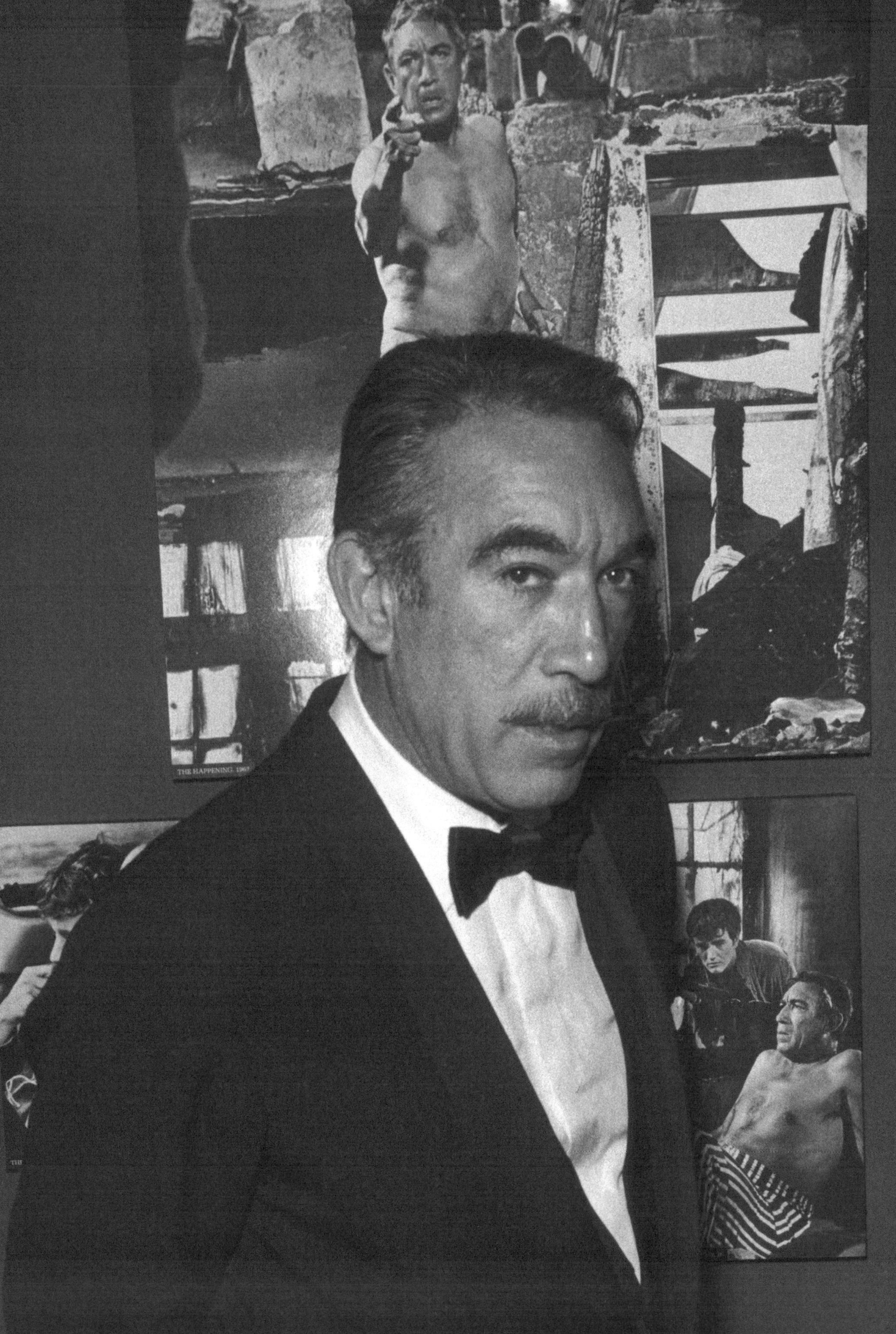
THE HAPPENING. 1967

Sylvester Stallone
1978, New York City

Filming *Paradise Alley* in Hell's Kitchen.

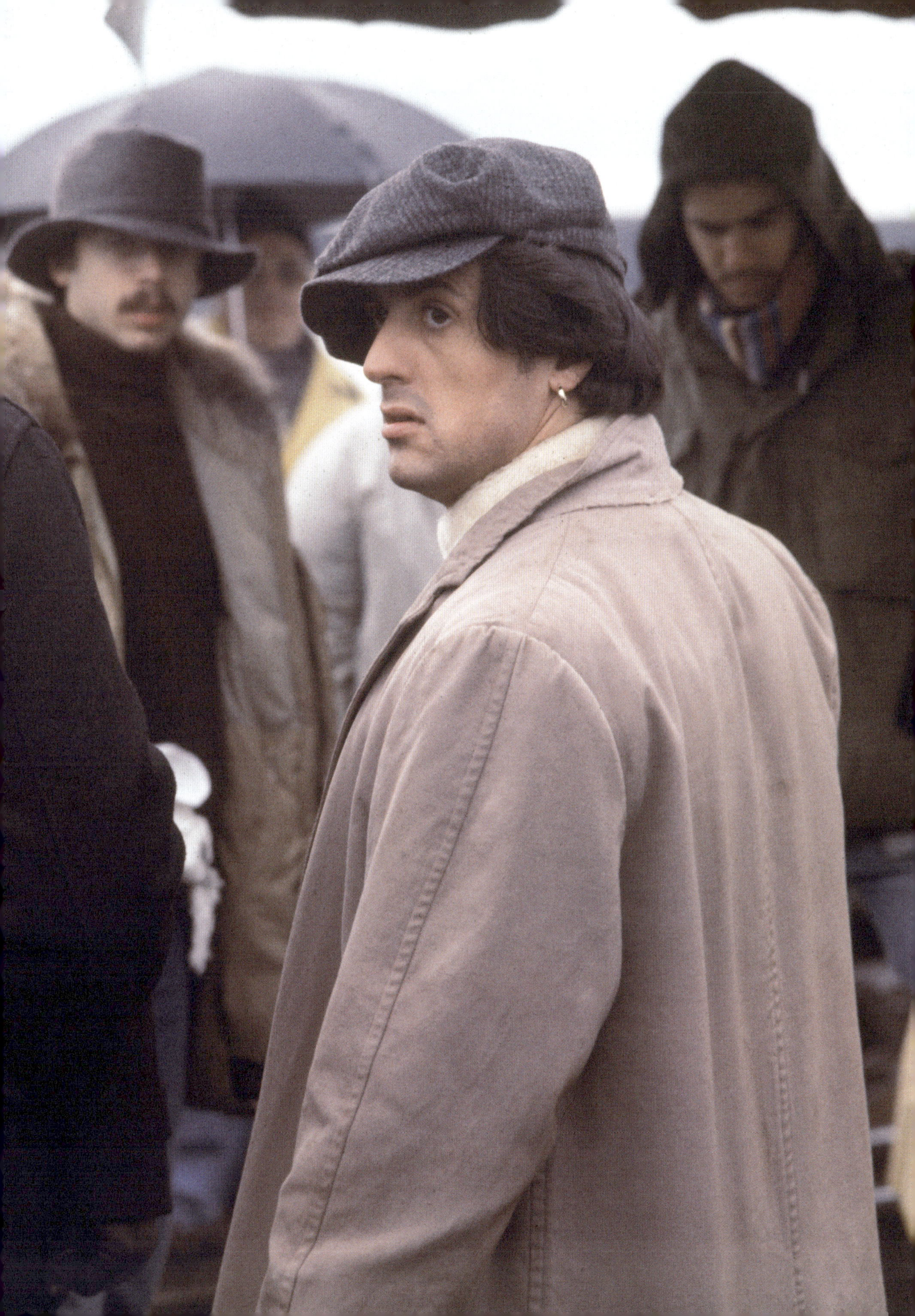

Michael Jackson
1984, New York City

At a press conference for the
Pepsi Cola commercial.

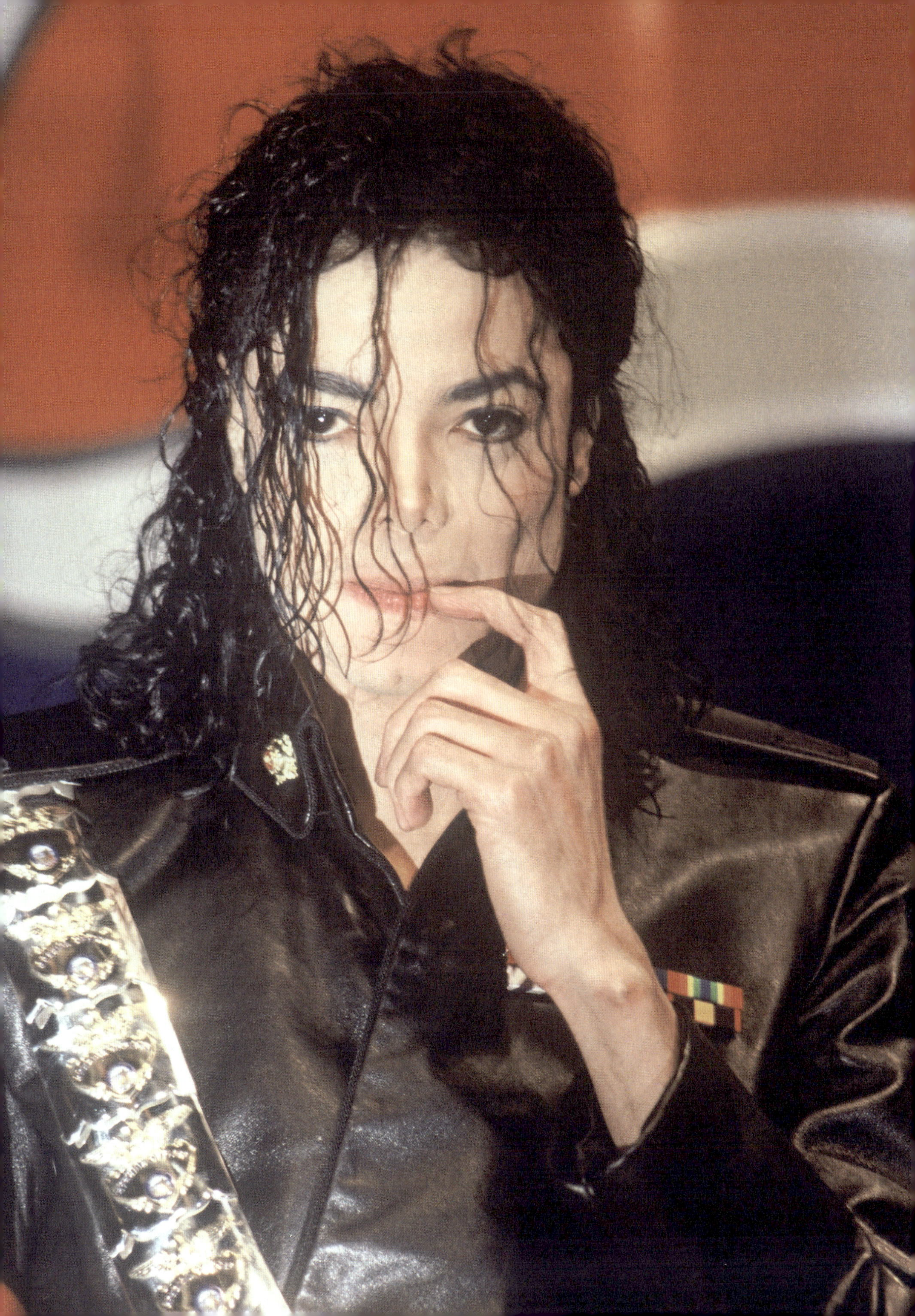

Dalí Knows.

I had met Dalí on several occasions, but never one on one. I really want to do a private shoot with him so I go to the St. Regis Hotel on 5th Avenue, where I know he stays during his New York visits. In fact, he likes this hotel so much, he even painted a mural behind the bar. This was at the height of his fame and career and I know if I can get something that is the real "Dalí" I will be able to place it.

Dalí meets me in the lobby and we discuss the possibility-not an easy feat as he speaks with a very heavy accent. It becomes almost comical. But we agree on one thing. He loves publicity, so he wants this shoot to happen! Dalí asks me to wait ten minutes and for us to meet again in one of the smaller conference rooms on the 2nd floor.

I walk into a totally dark room and when I ask where he is he says, "you are here with Dalí!" I turn on the light and find him sitting at the end of a large conference table, his walking stick laid out in front of him. Interesting, but this is not really what I'm looking for.

While sitting there, he has noticed a large hedge of artificial bushes. Excited, he gets up, saying "Dalí Knows! Dalí Knows!" I keep my camera focused on him while he moves around, and take pictures without really looking at what he is up to, but when I look at my contact sheets later, I say to myself, "Dalí knew! Dalí knew!" Staring me in the face is Salvador Dalí personified on a cross! Genius.

———

At the St. Regis Hotel.

Salvador Dali
1967, New York City

At the St. Regis Hotel.
——

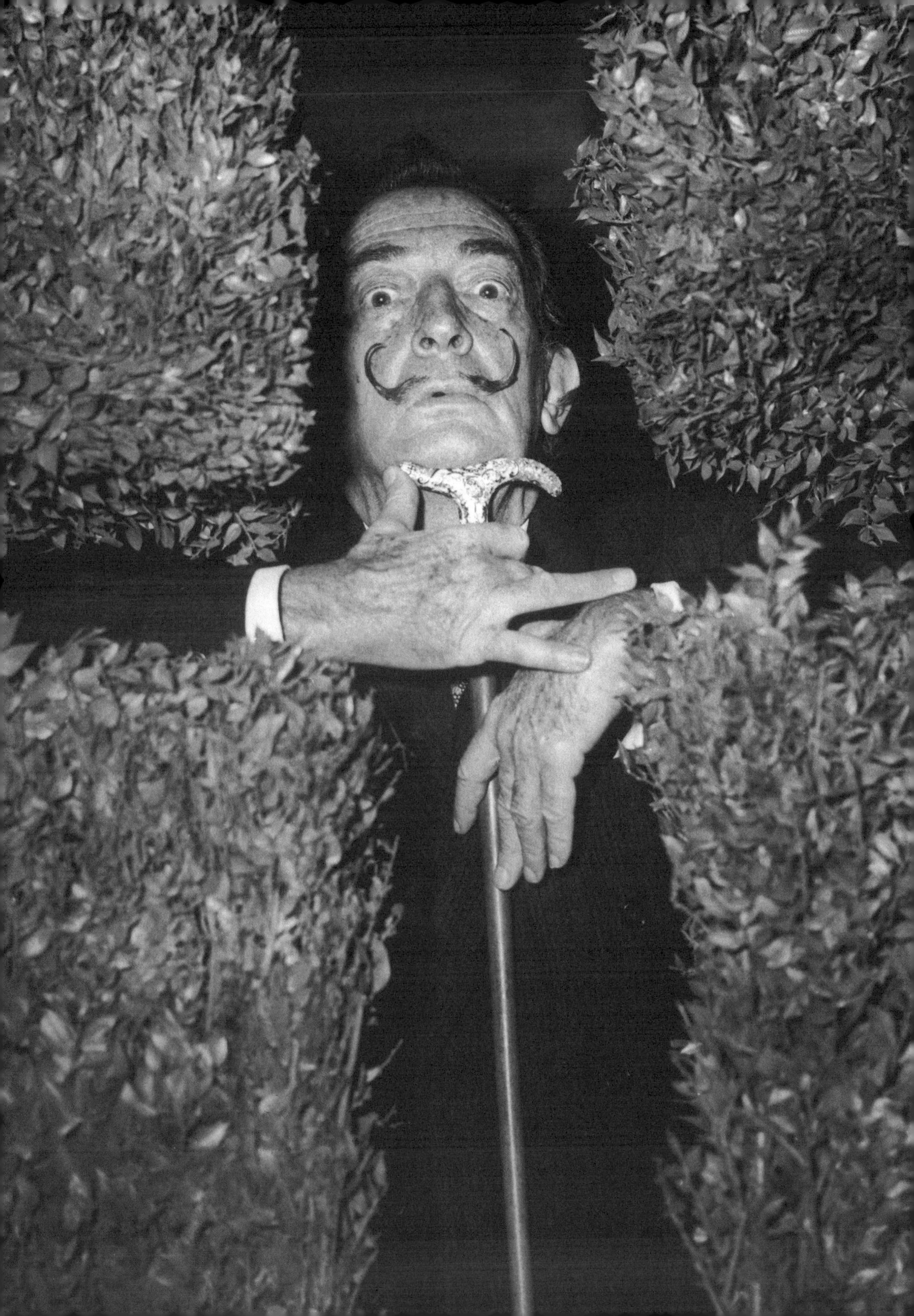

At the Guggenheim Museum where
some of his paintings were on exhibit.

Salvador Dali
1969, New York City

At the Guggenheim Museum where
some of his paintings were on exhibit.

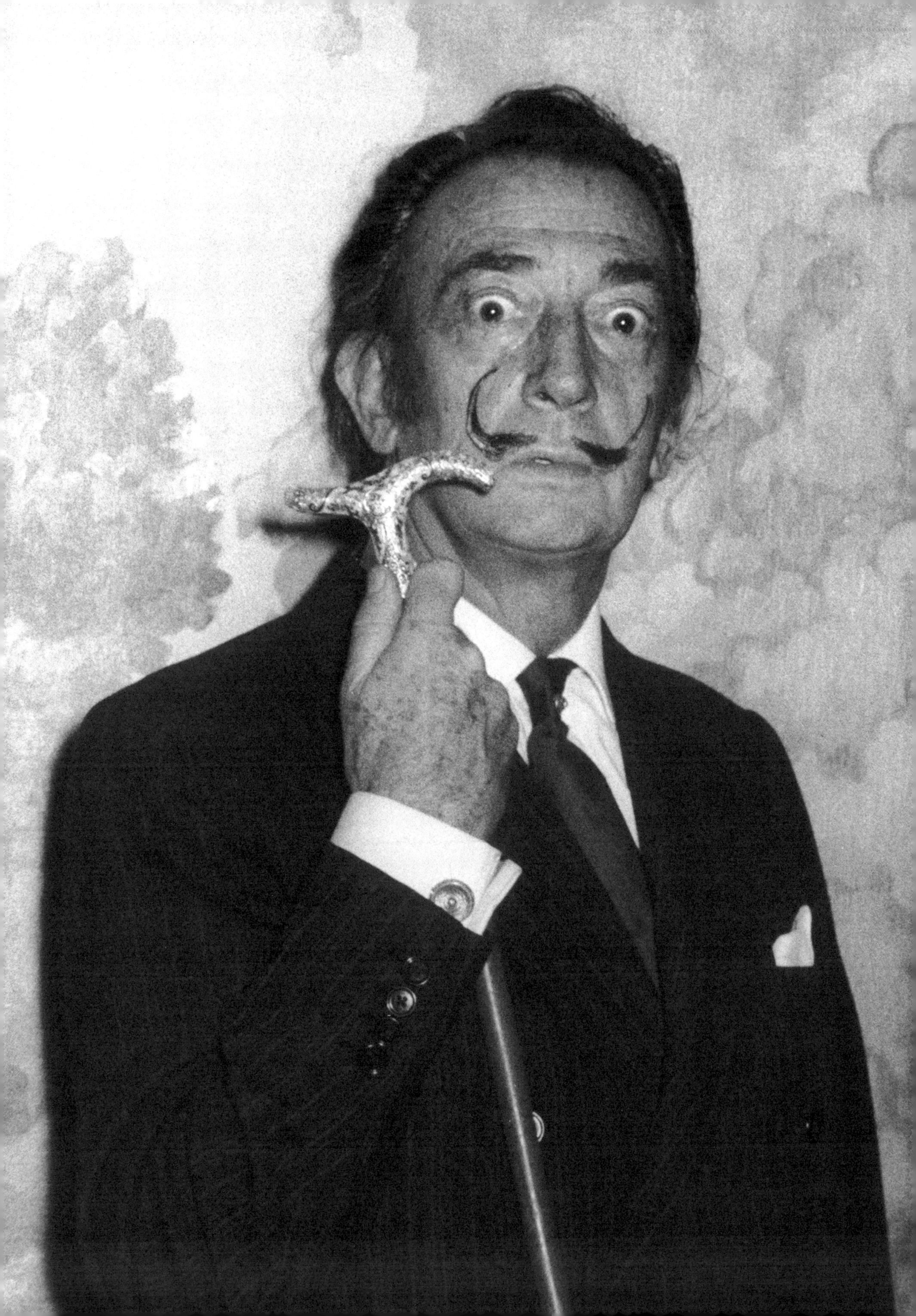

Liza Minnelli and Desi Arnaz Jr.
1973, New York City

At the Waldorf Astoria Hotel.

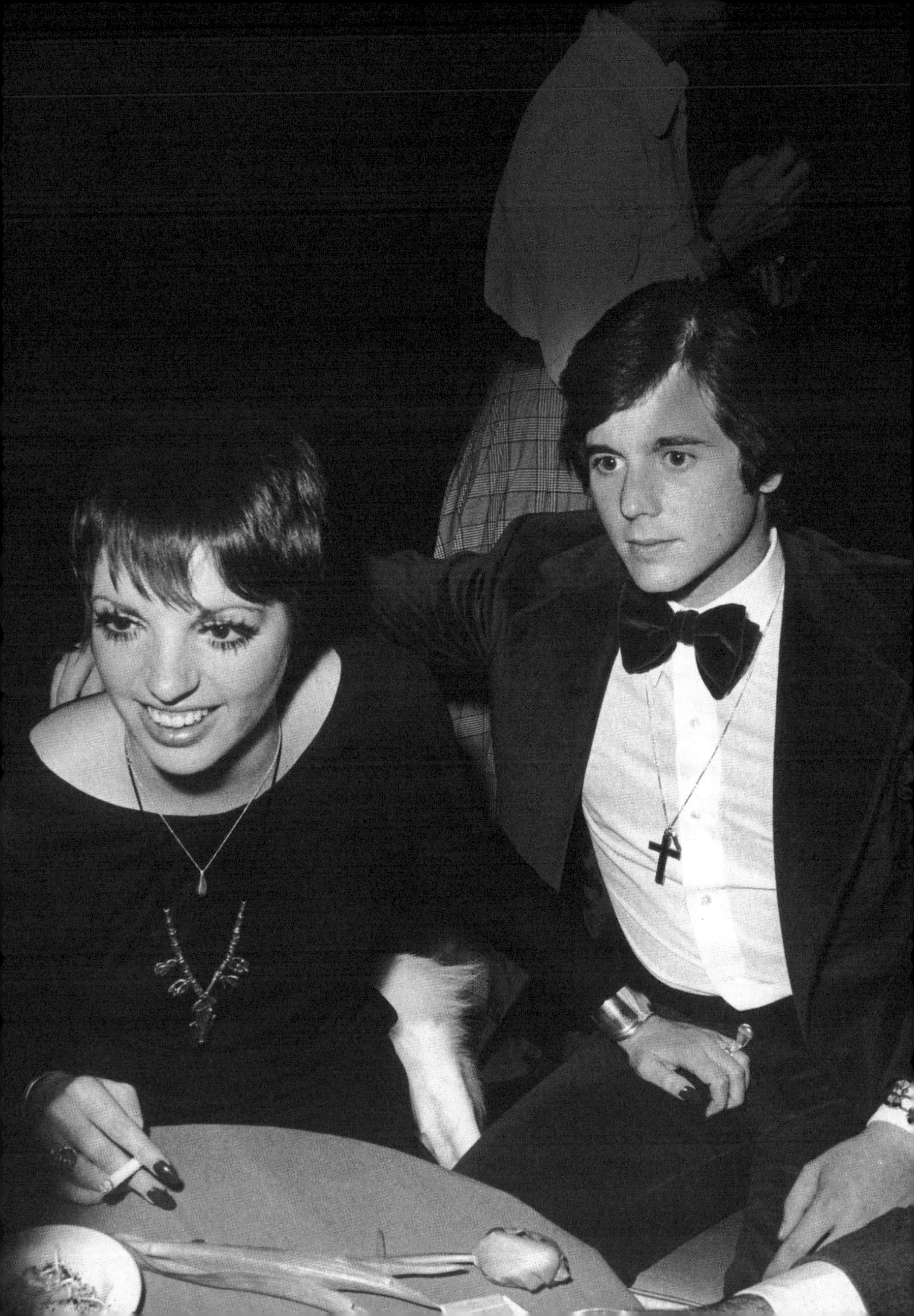

Elton John with his wife Renate Blauel
1984, Monaco

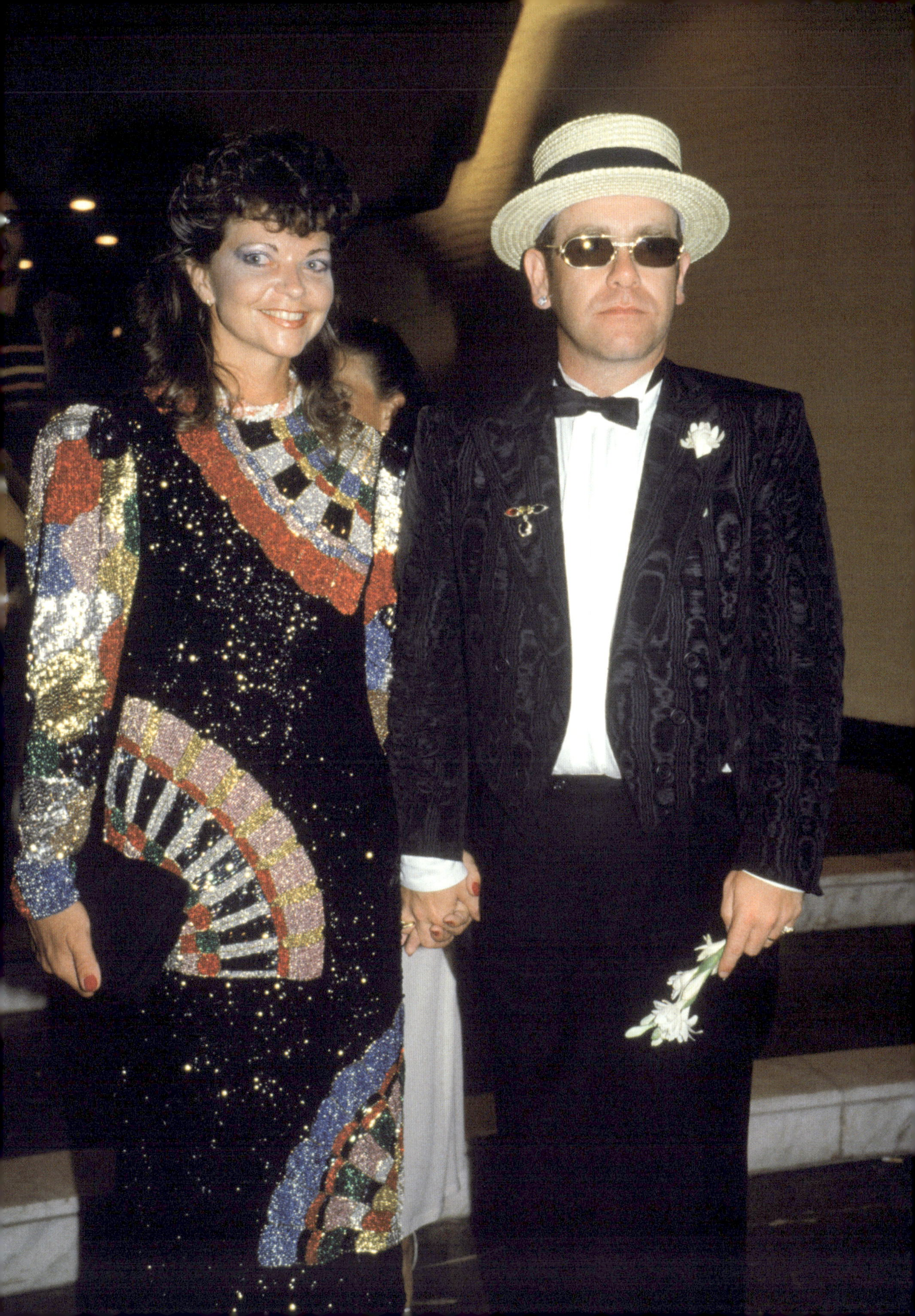

Dustin Hoffman and his wife Anne Byrne
1969, New York City

At the wrap party for *Midnight Cowboy*.

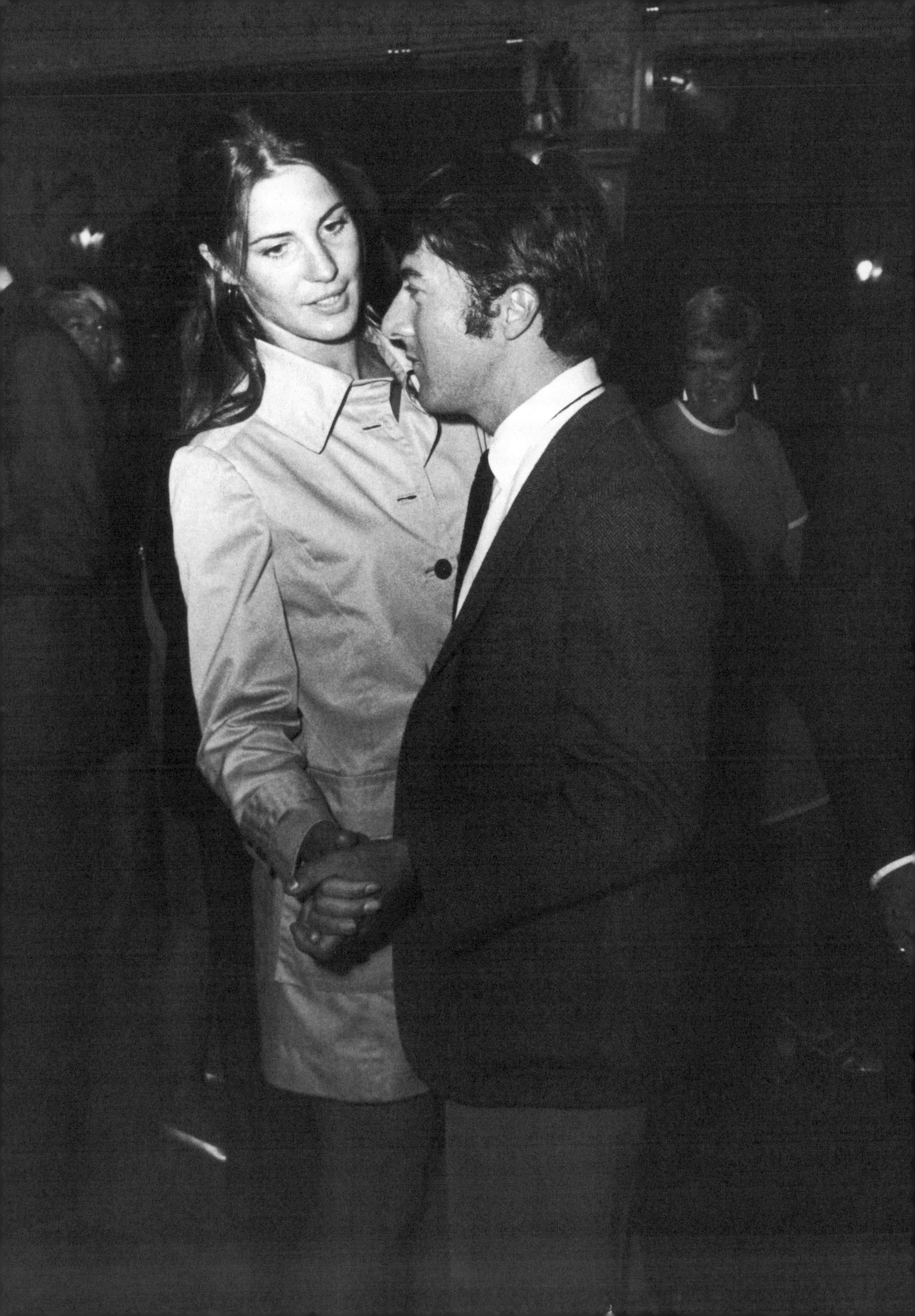

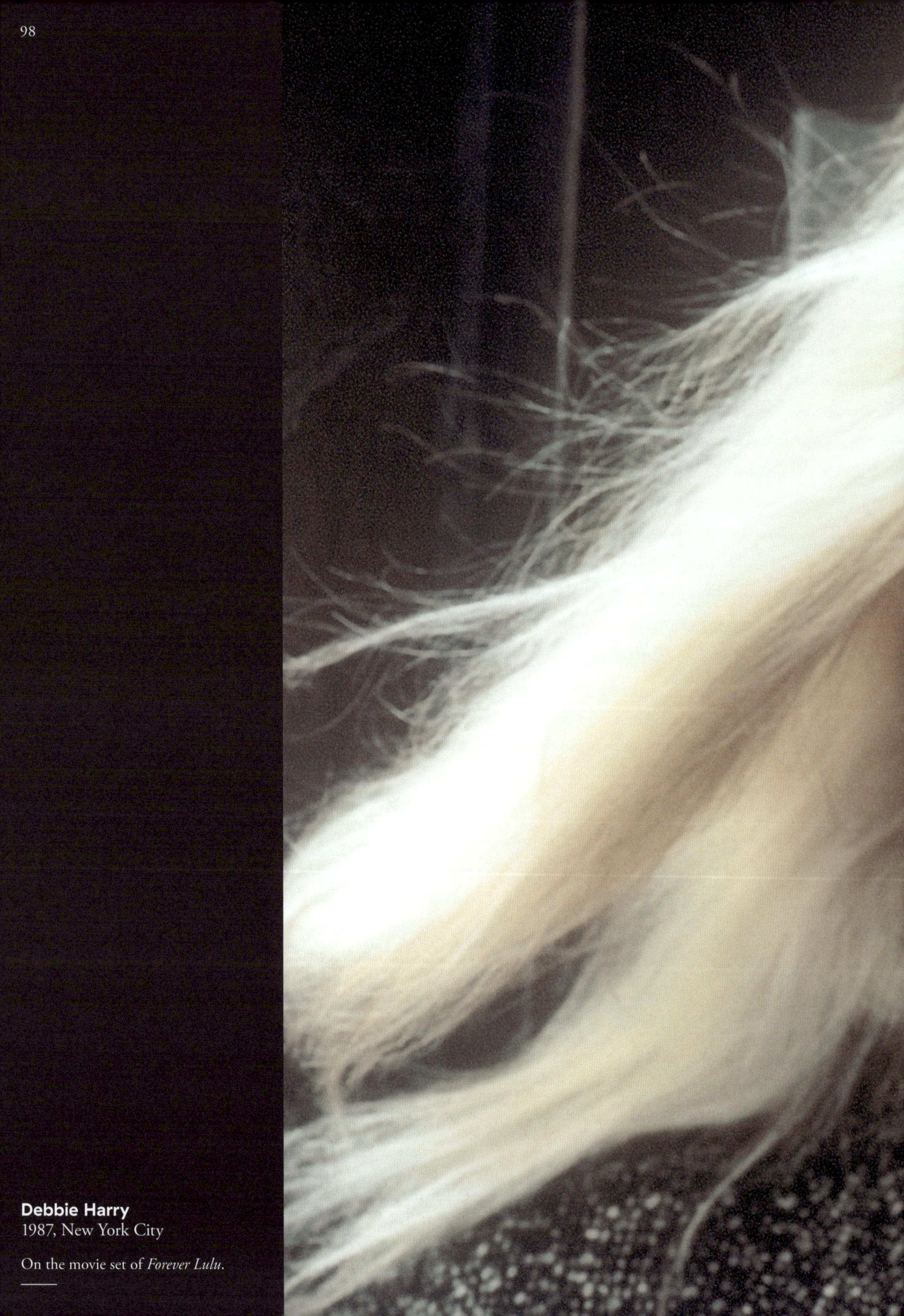

Debbie Harry
1987, New York City

On the movie set of *Forever Lulu*.

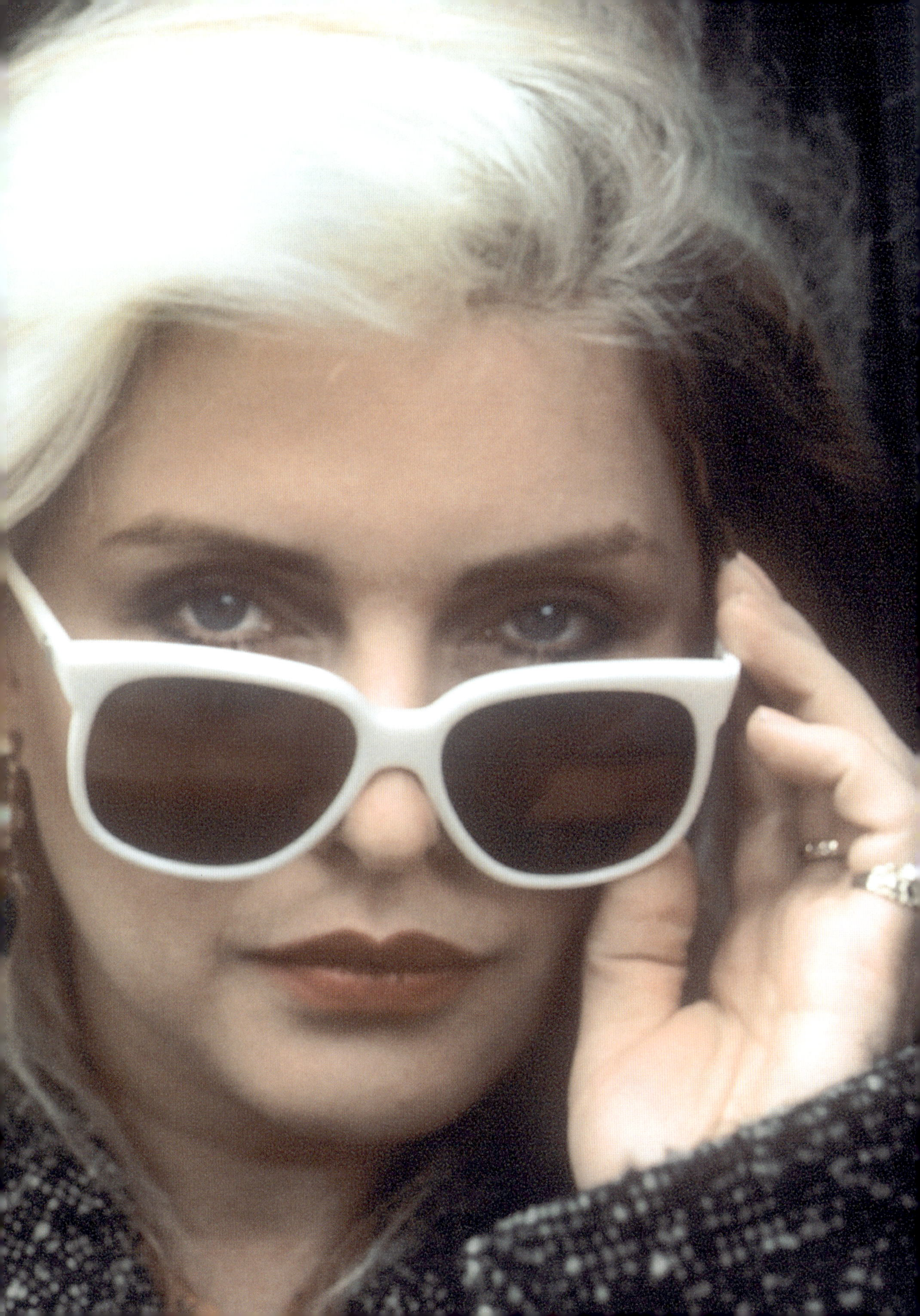

Rod Stewart
1979, New York City

Backstage, before his concert at
Madison Square Garden.

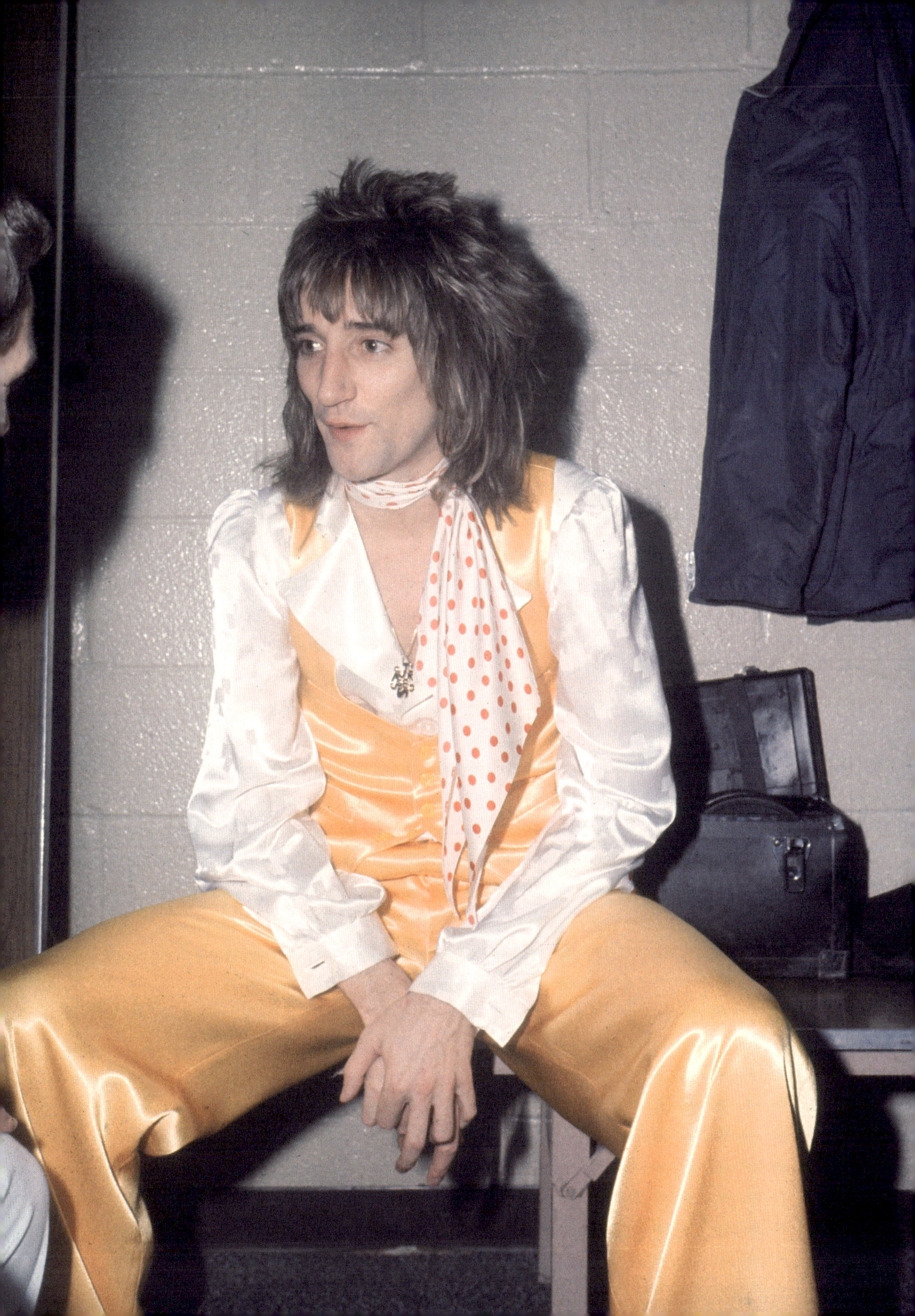

Marlon Brando
1968, New York City

At the *New York Film Critics Circle Awards,*
at Sardi's.

—

Following double page

Fred Astaire and Adele Astaire
1972, New York City

At the American Theater Hall of
Fame's induction of Fred Astaire.

—

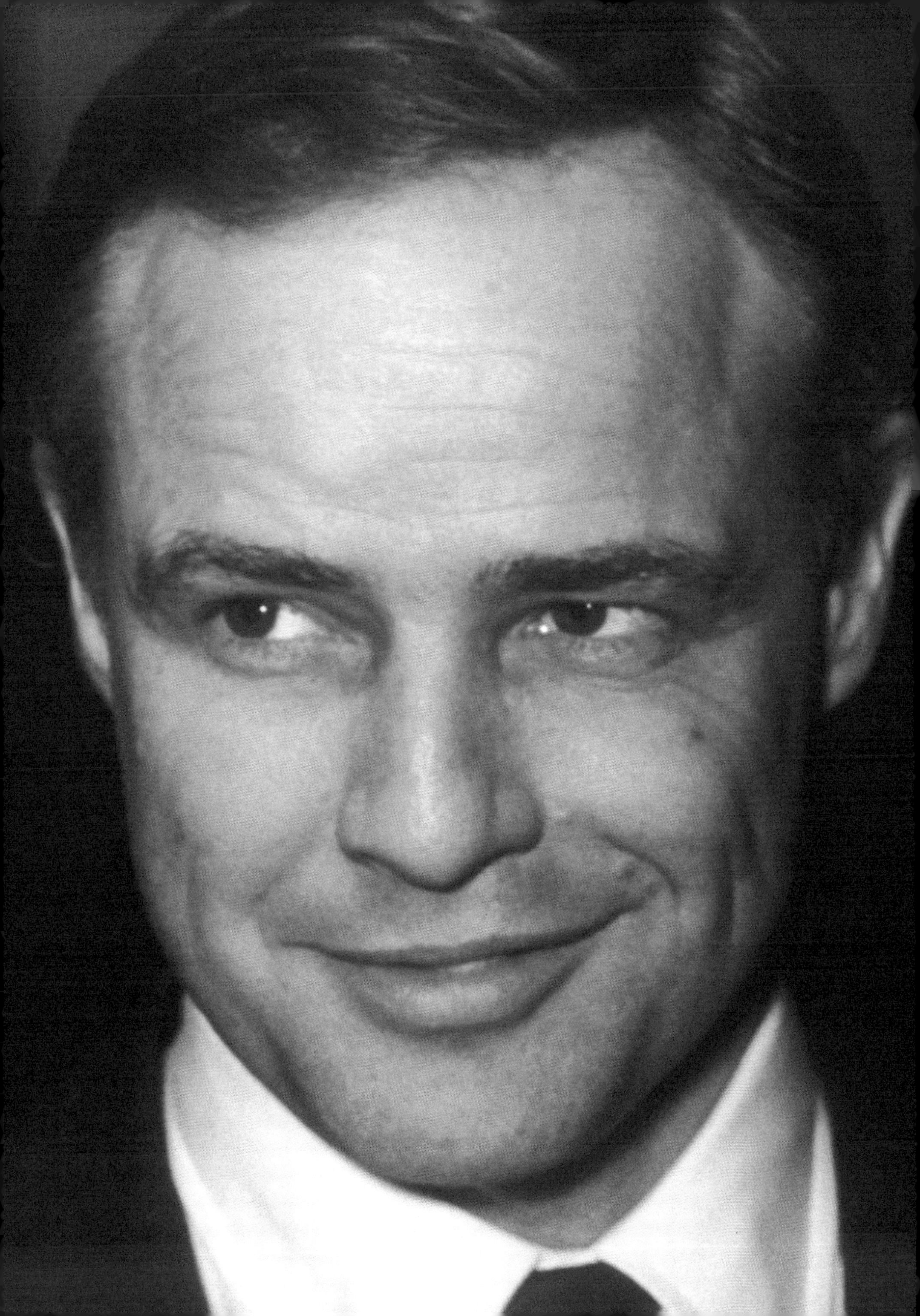

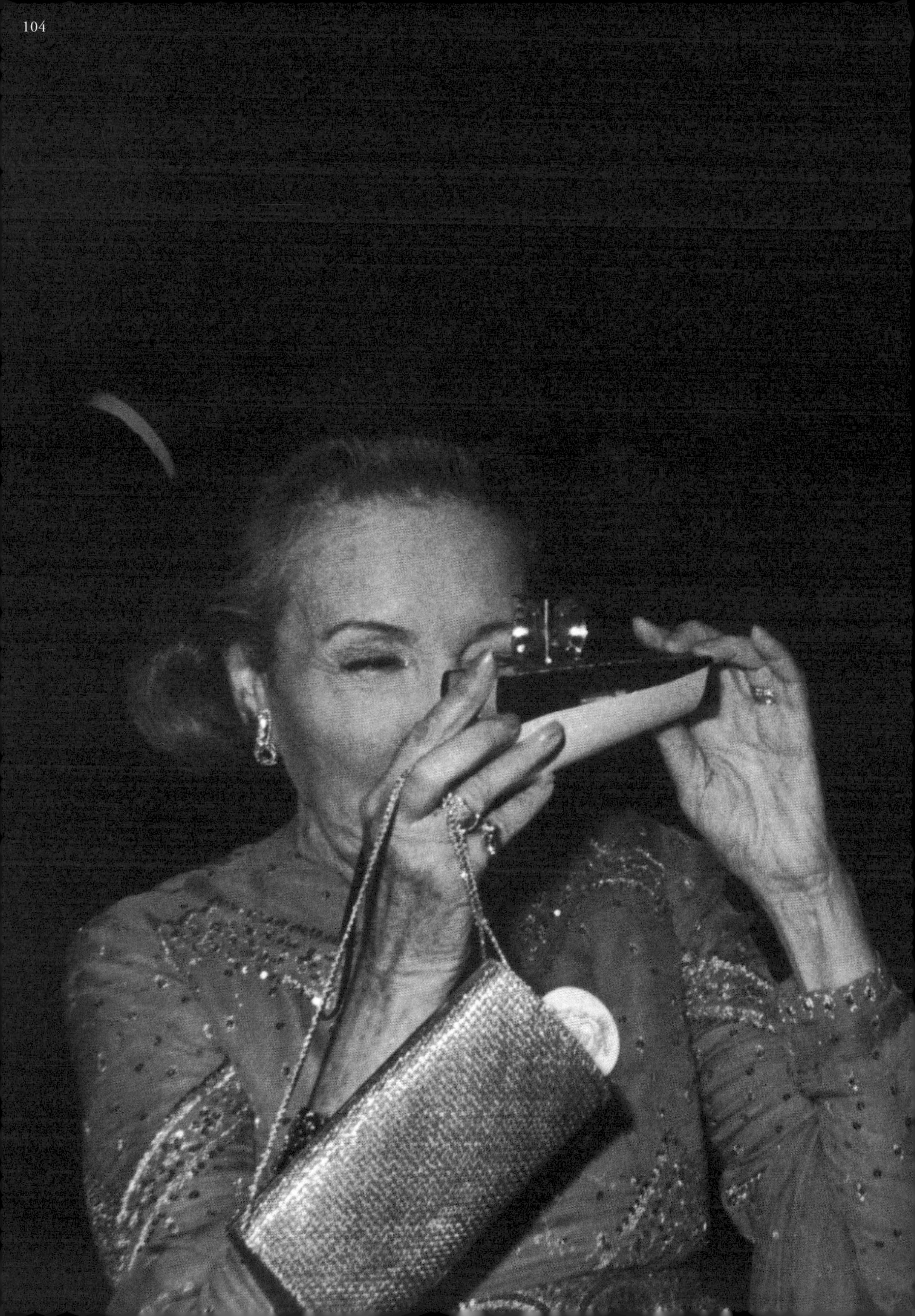

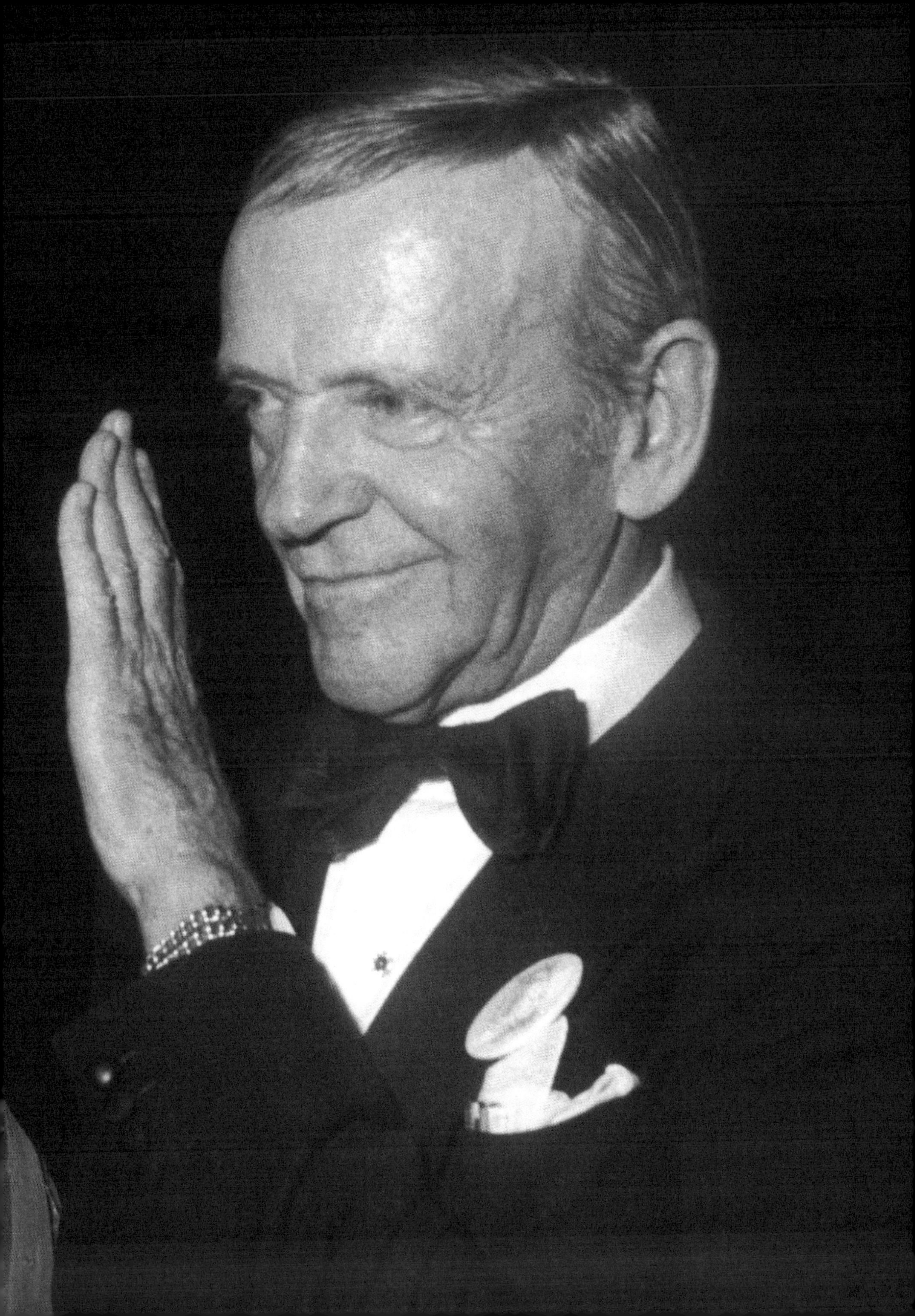

Gene Hackman
1971, New York City

At the *New York Film Critics Circle Awards,* at Sardi's,
winning a award for *The French Connection.*

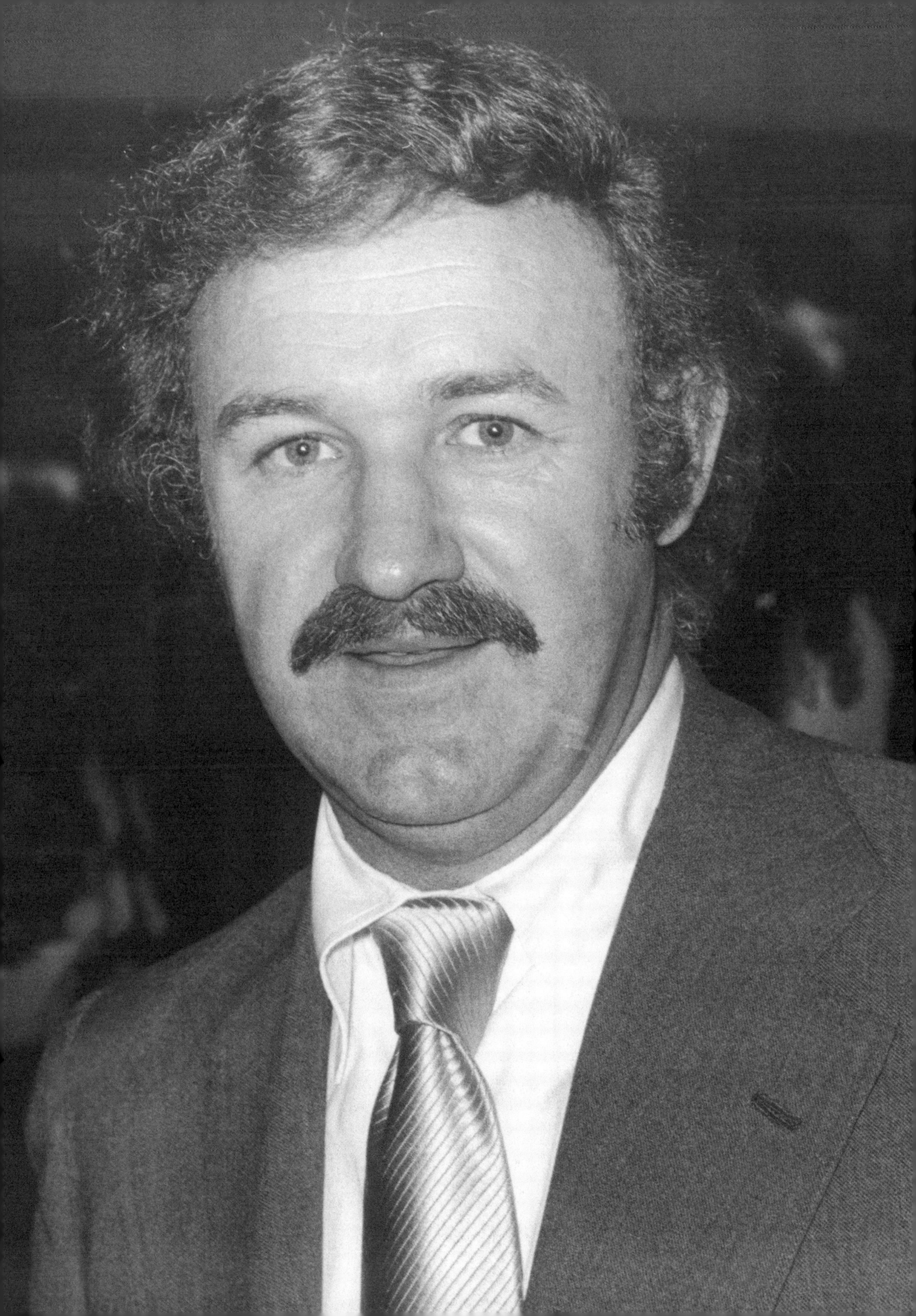

John Lennon
1975, New York City

At the New York Film Festival
at Lincoln Center.

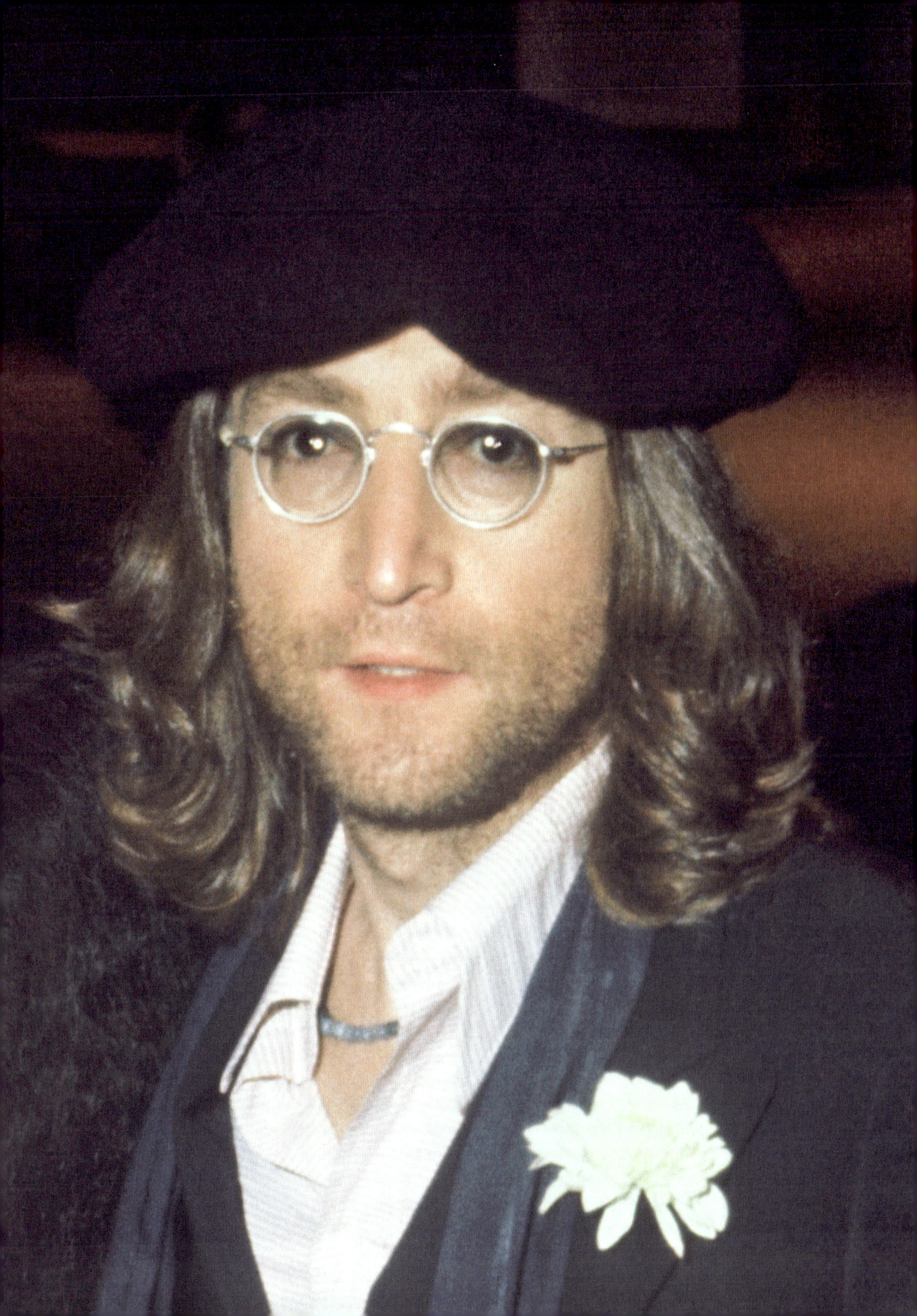

Donald Sutherland and Jane Fonda
1971, New York City

On the movie set of *Klute*.

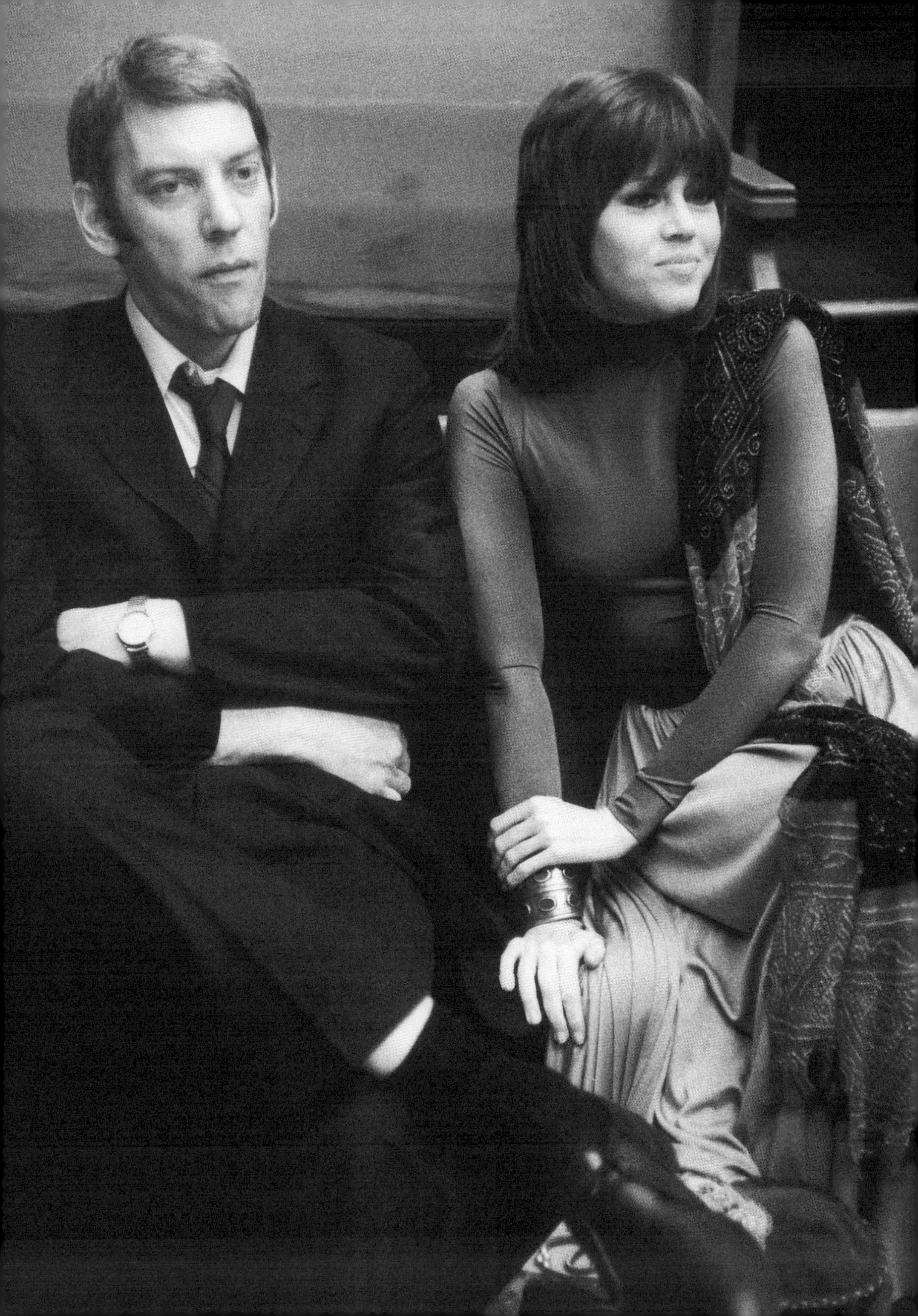

Grace Kelly
1977, New York City

At a Red Cross charity event
at the Pierre Hotel.

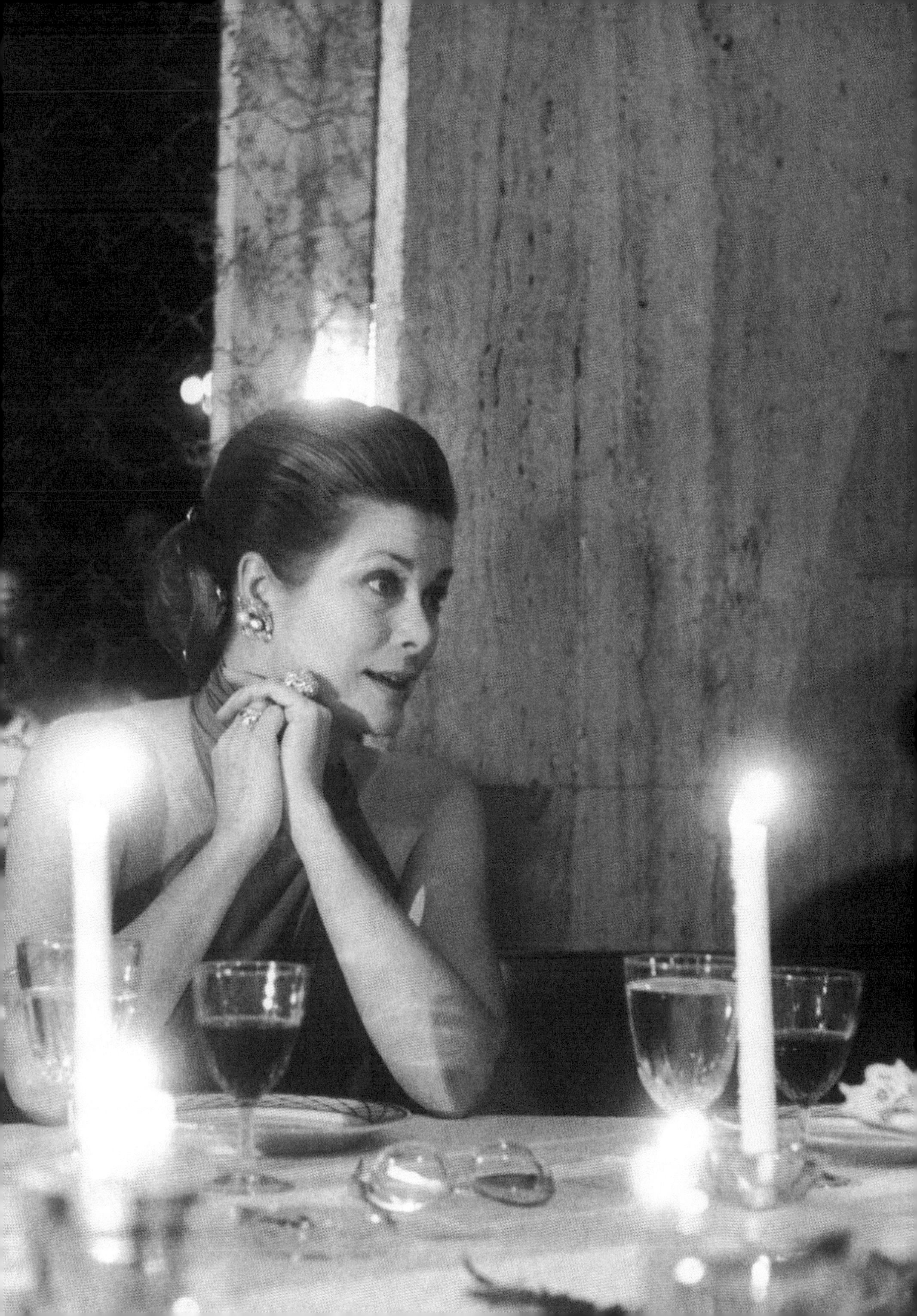

Andy Warhol and Monique van Vooren
1974, New York City

At Lincoln Center for a Rudolph
Nureyev ballet performance.
——

Following double page

Elvis Presley
1975, Long Island

Concert at the Nassau Coliseum.
——

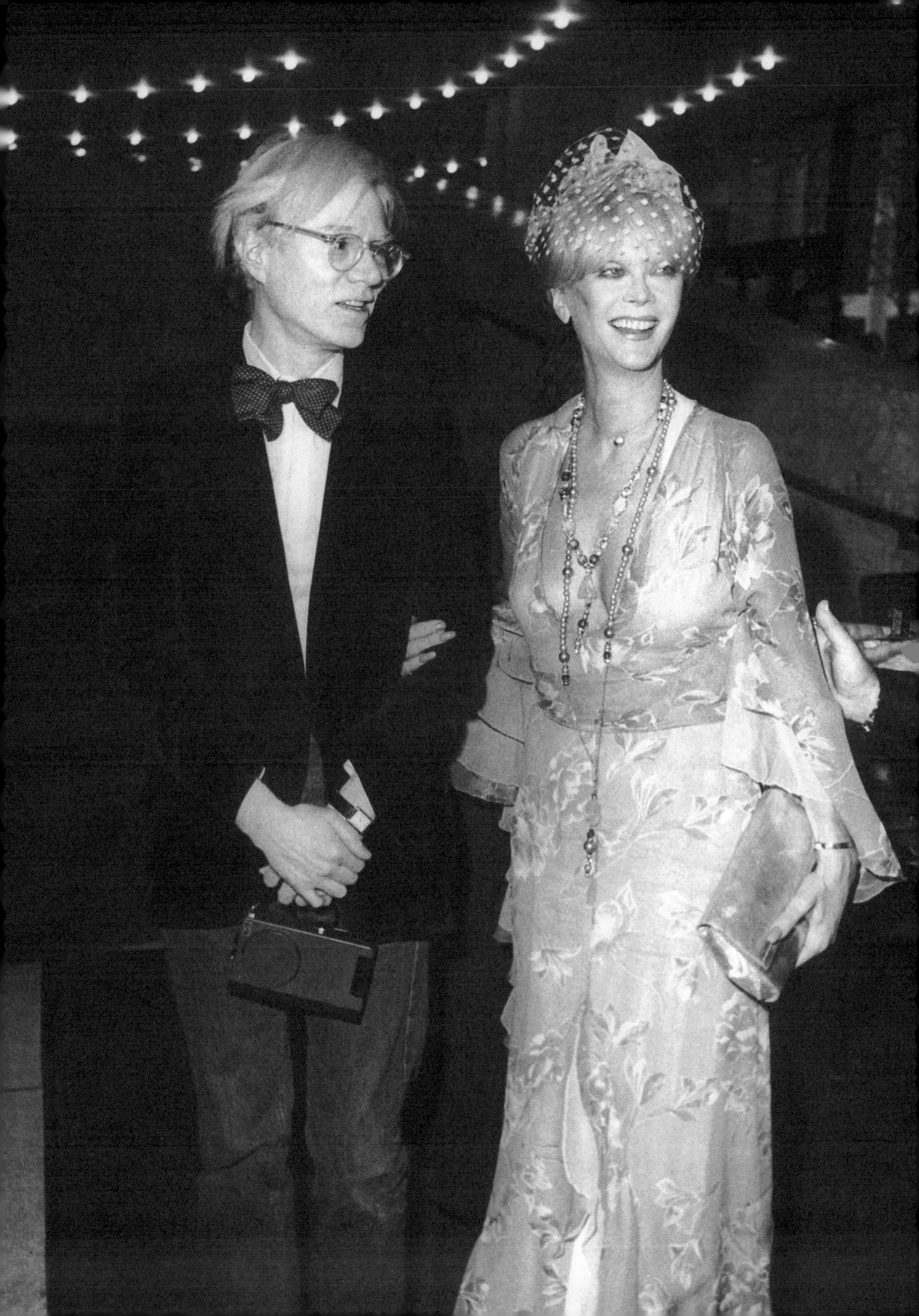

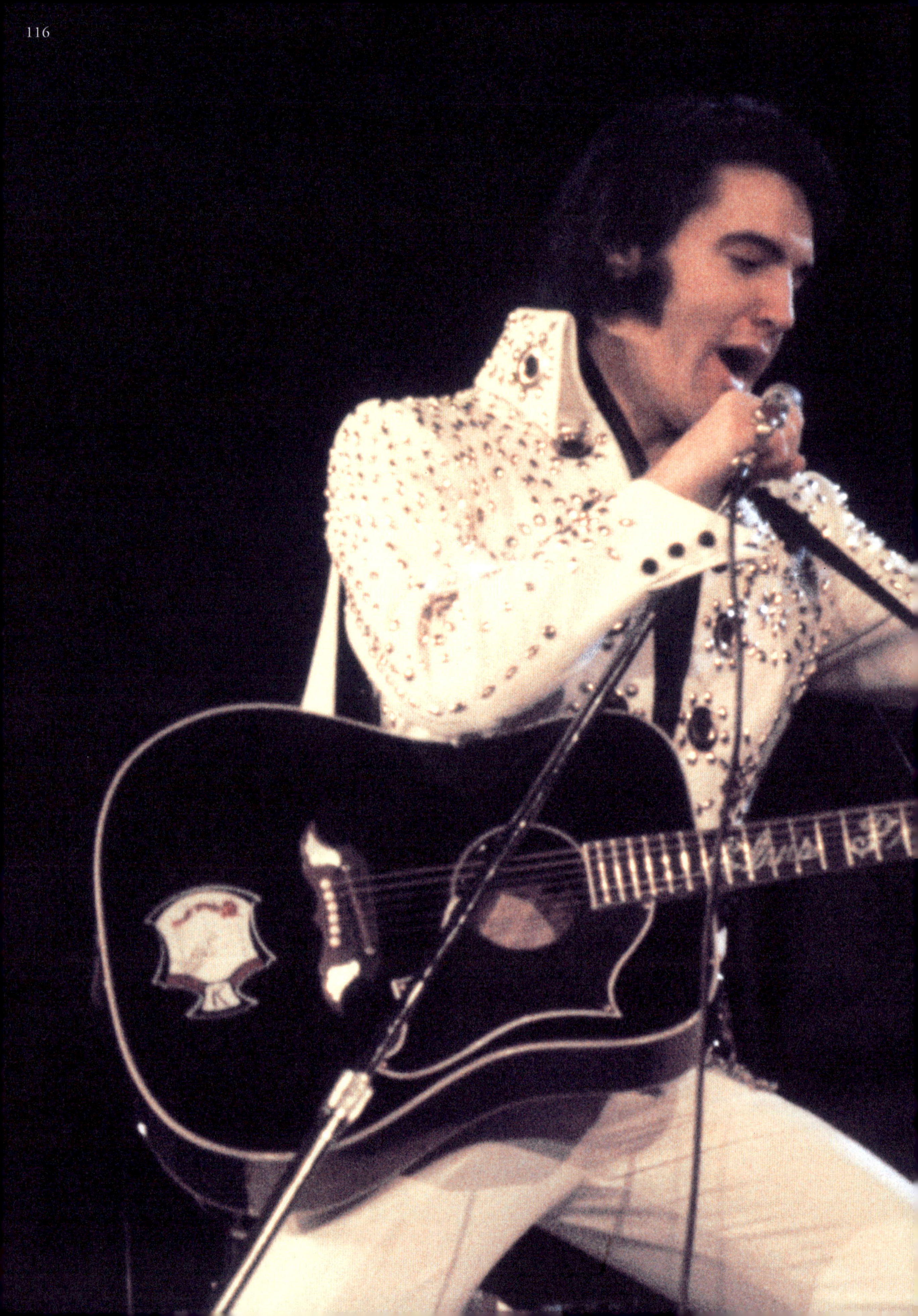

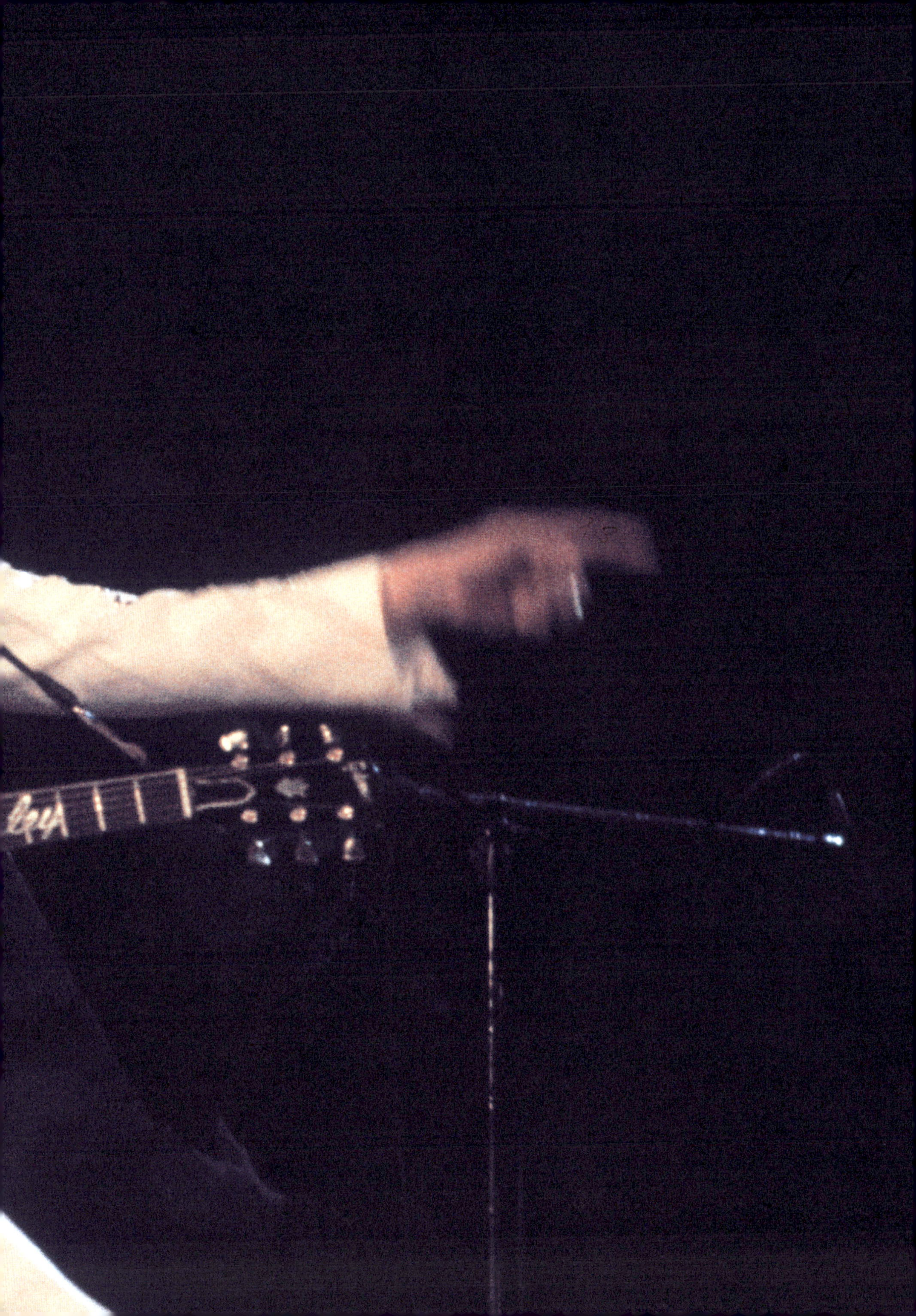

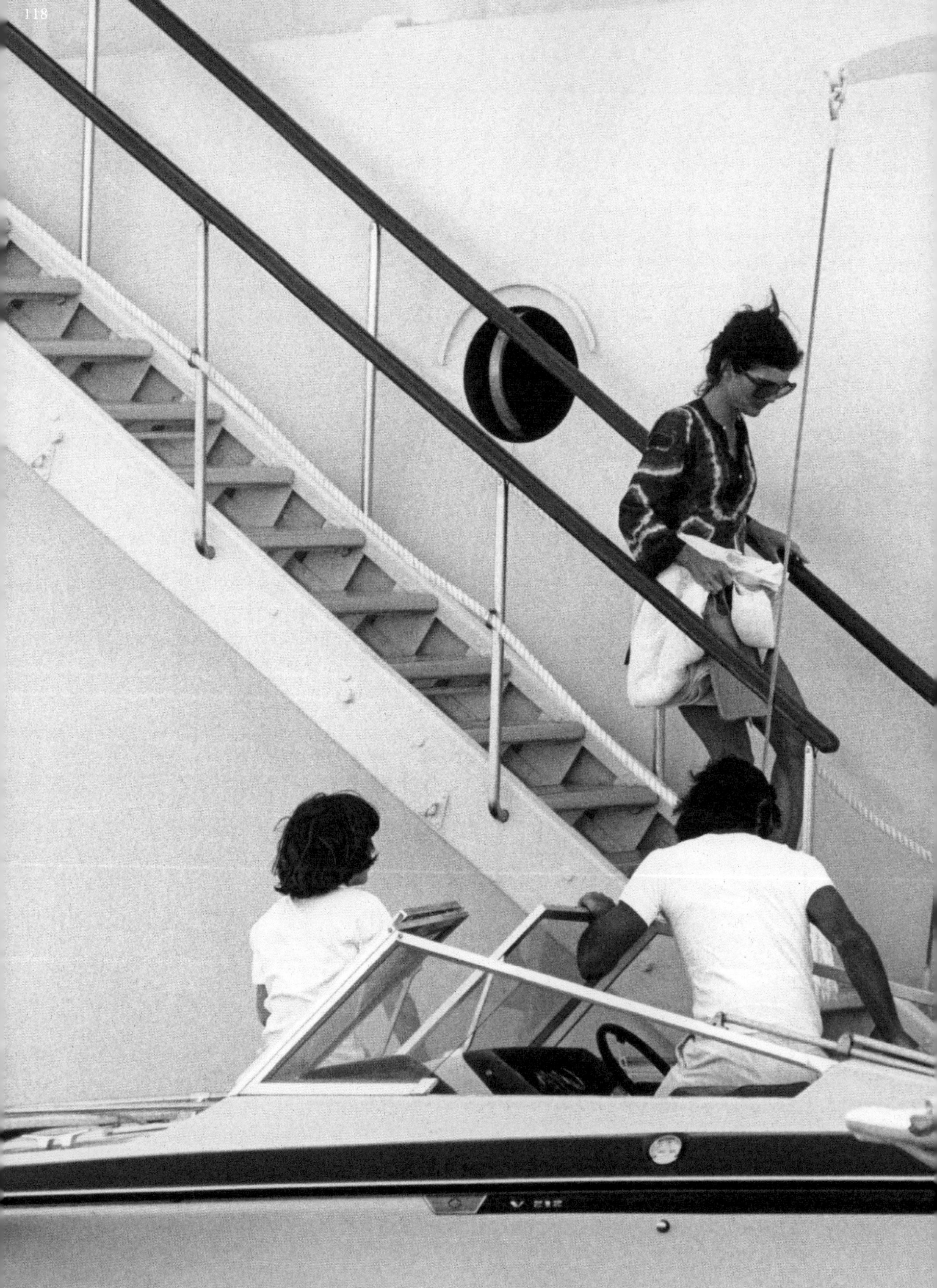

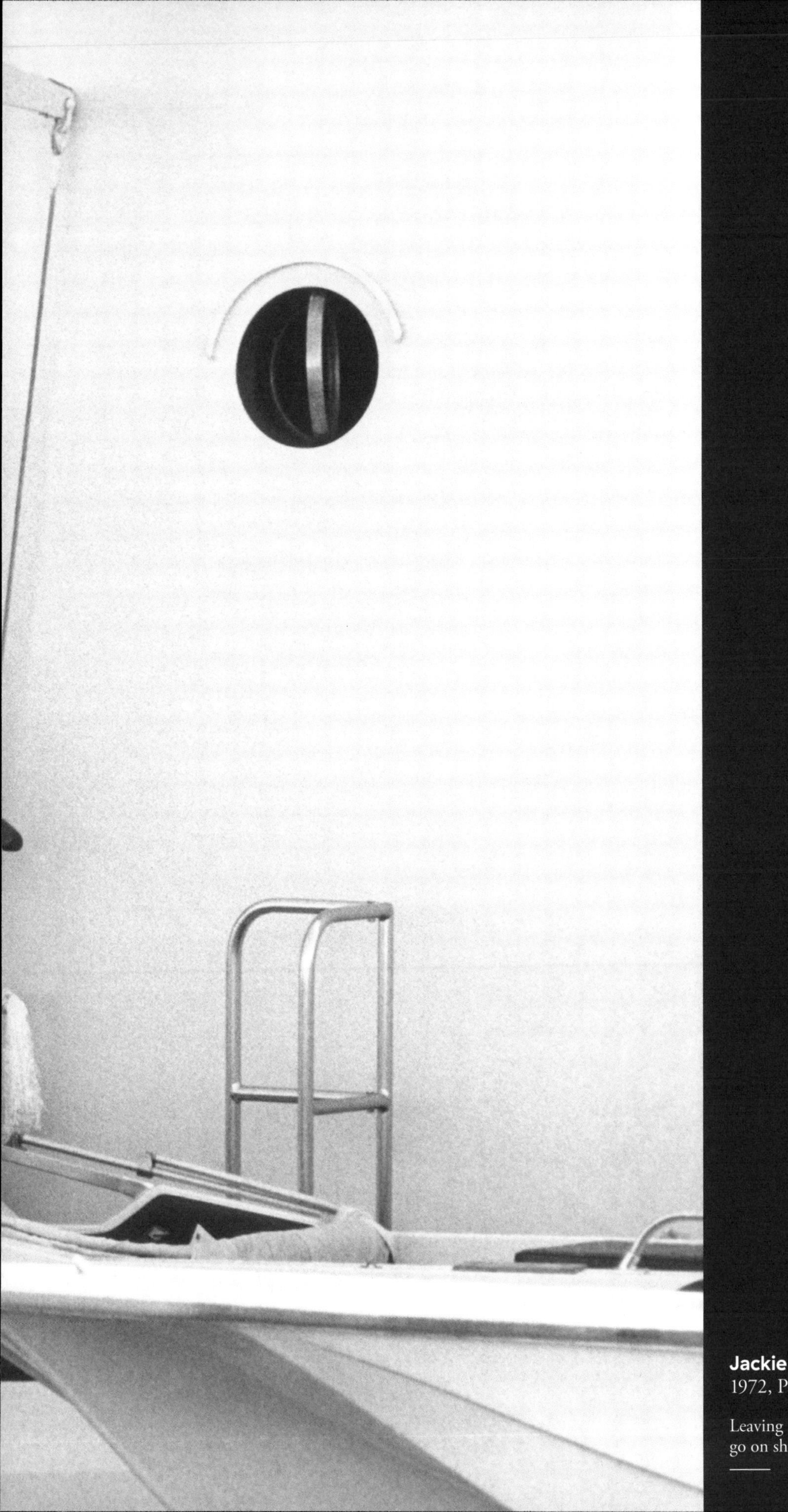

Jackie Kennedy Onassis
1972, Palm Beach

Leaving the *Christina* to take the dinghy to go on shore at the Palm Beach Yacht Club.

Sammy Davis Jr.
1966, New York City

Introducing his movie *A Man Called Adam*.

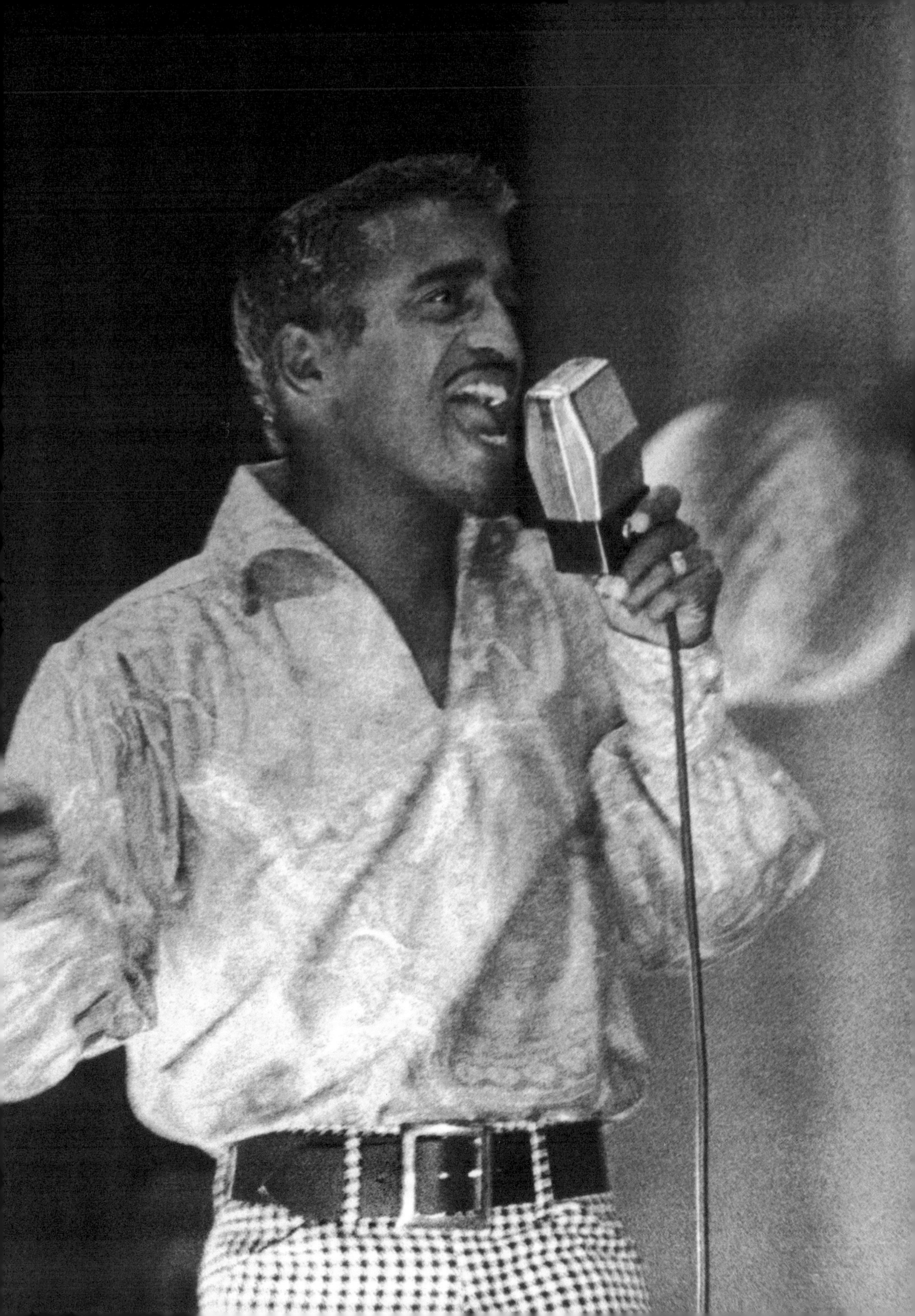

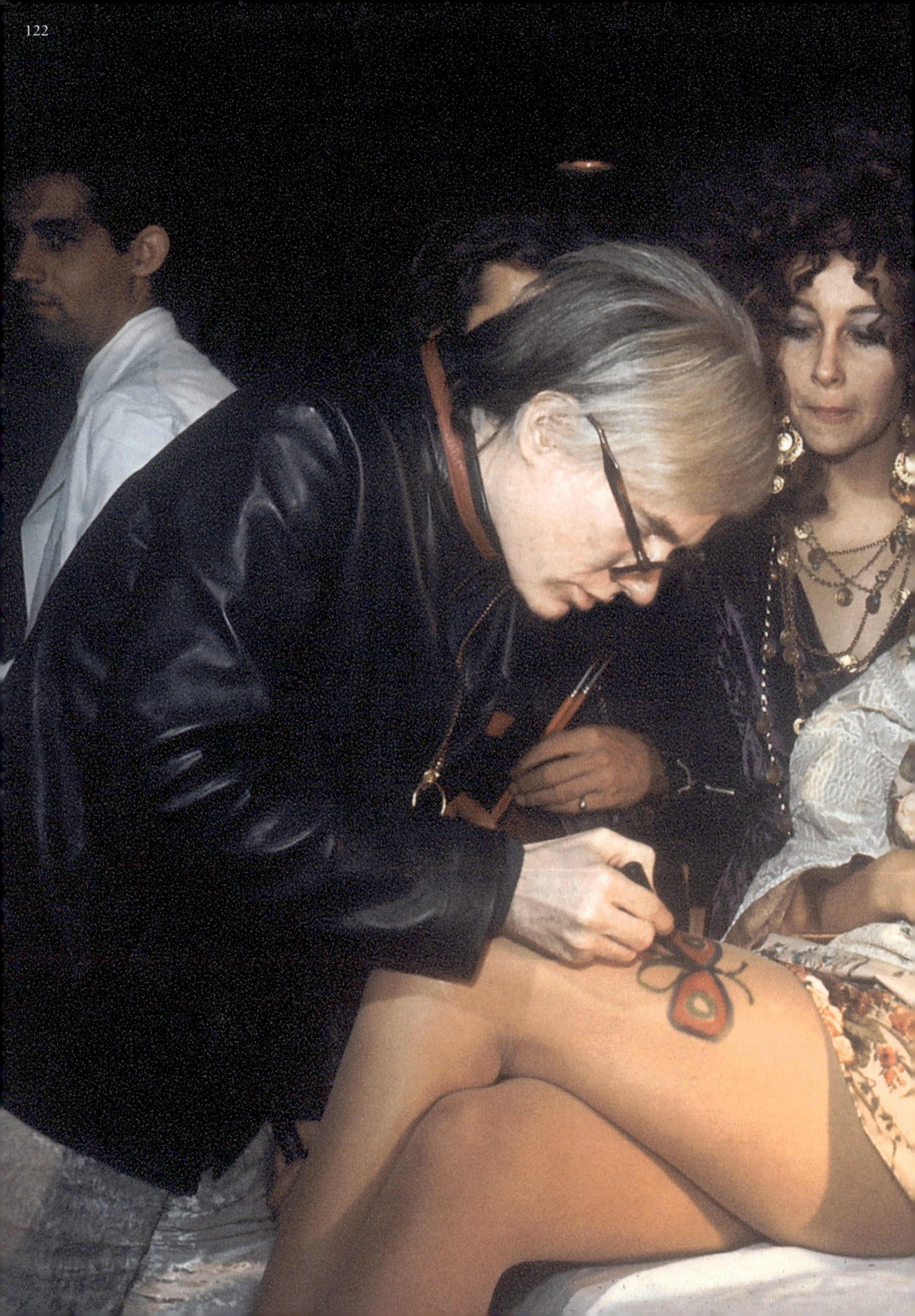

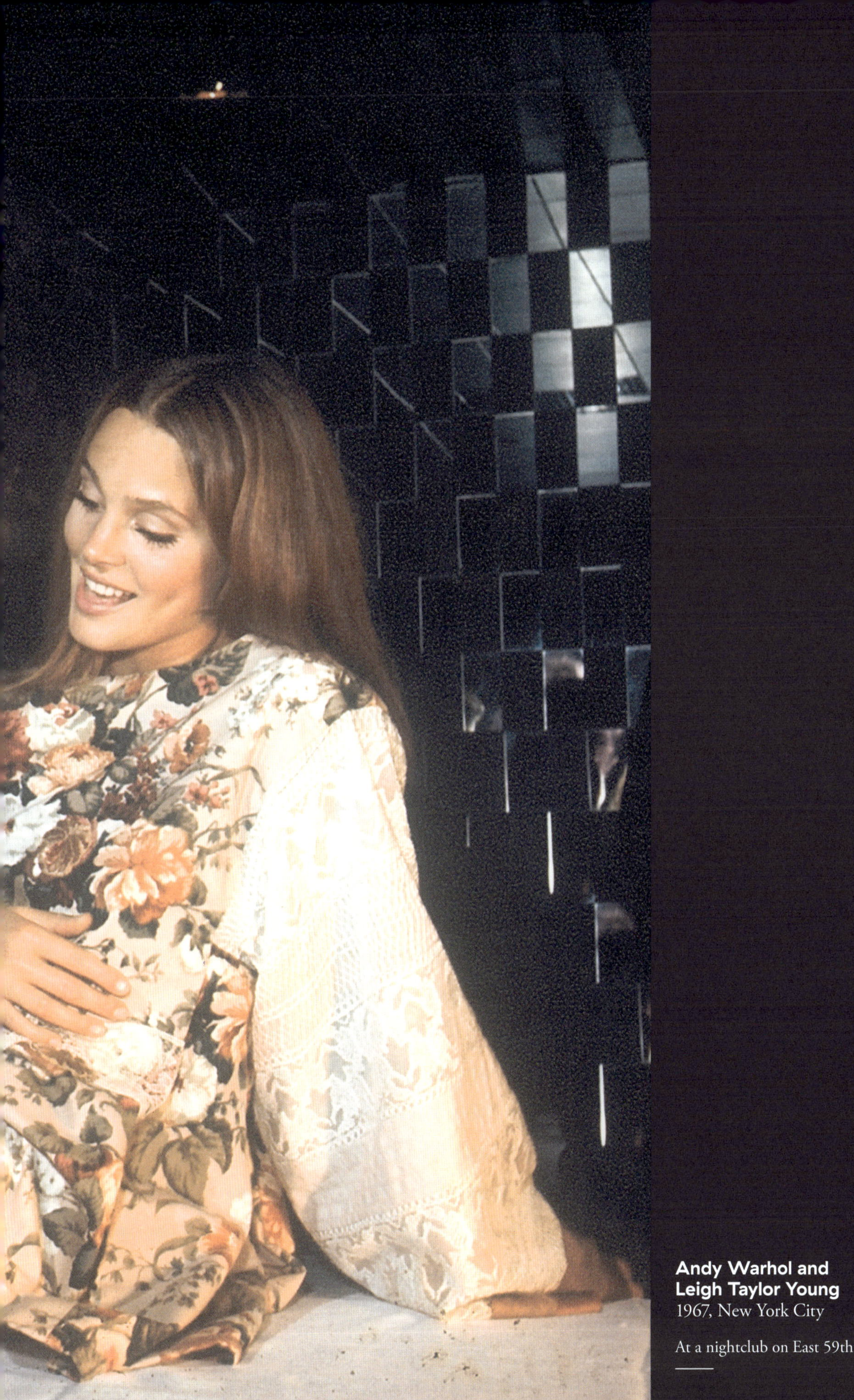

**Andy Warhol and
Leigh Taylor Young**
1967, New York City

At a nightclub on East 59th Street.

The Beatles
1965, New York City

At their first press conference at
the Warwick Hotel with their manager
Brian Epstein, at left in the photo.
——

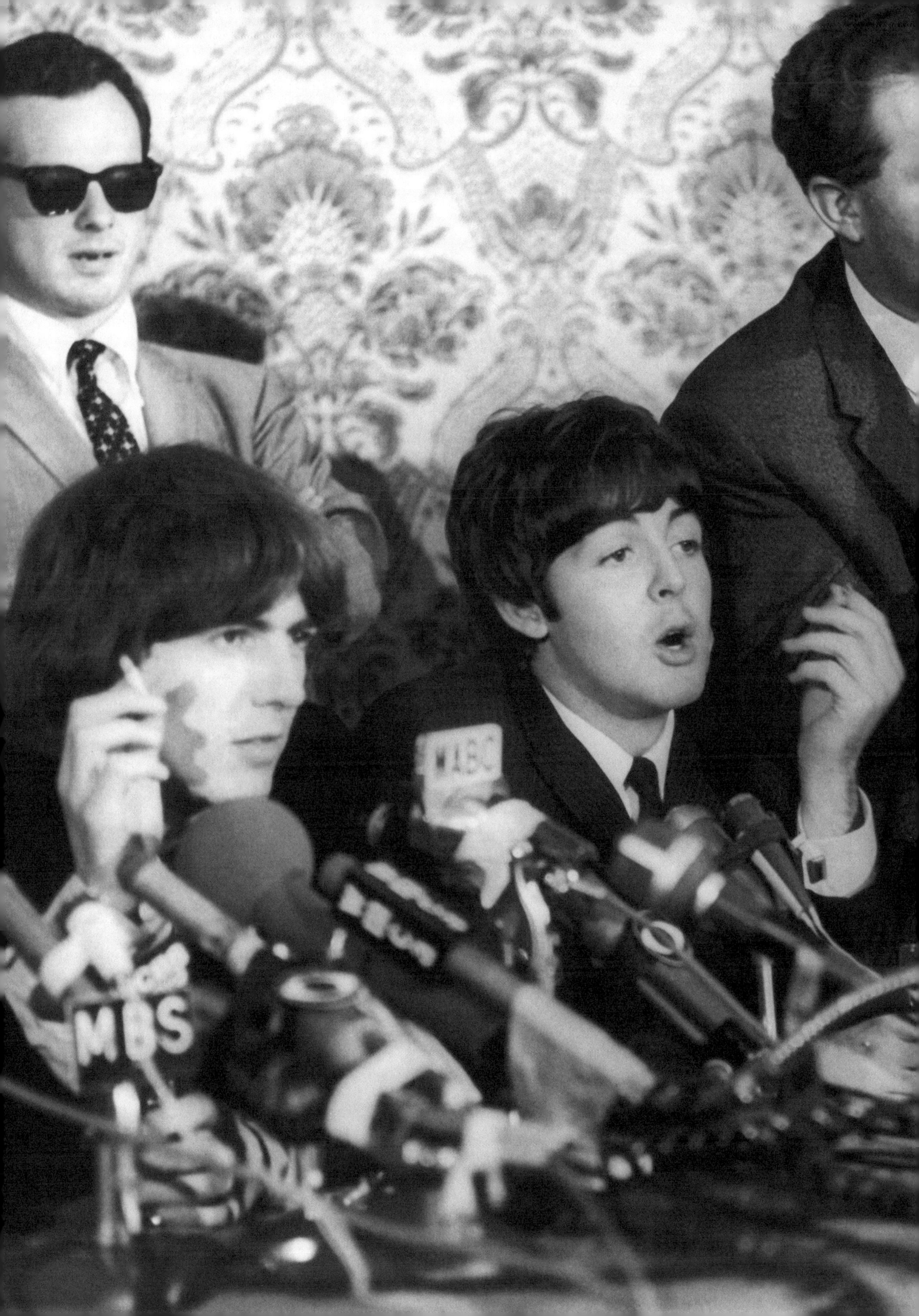

Madonna
1986, New York City

On the movie set of *Who's That Girl*.

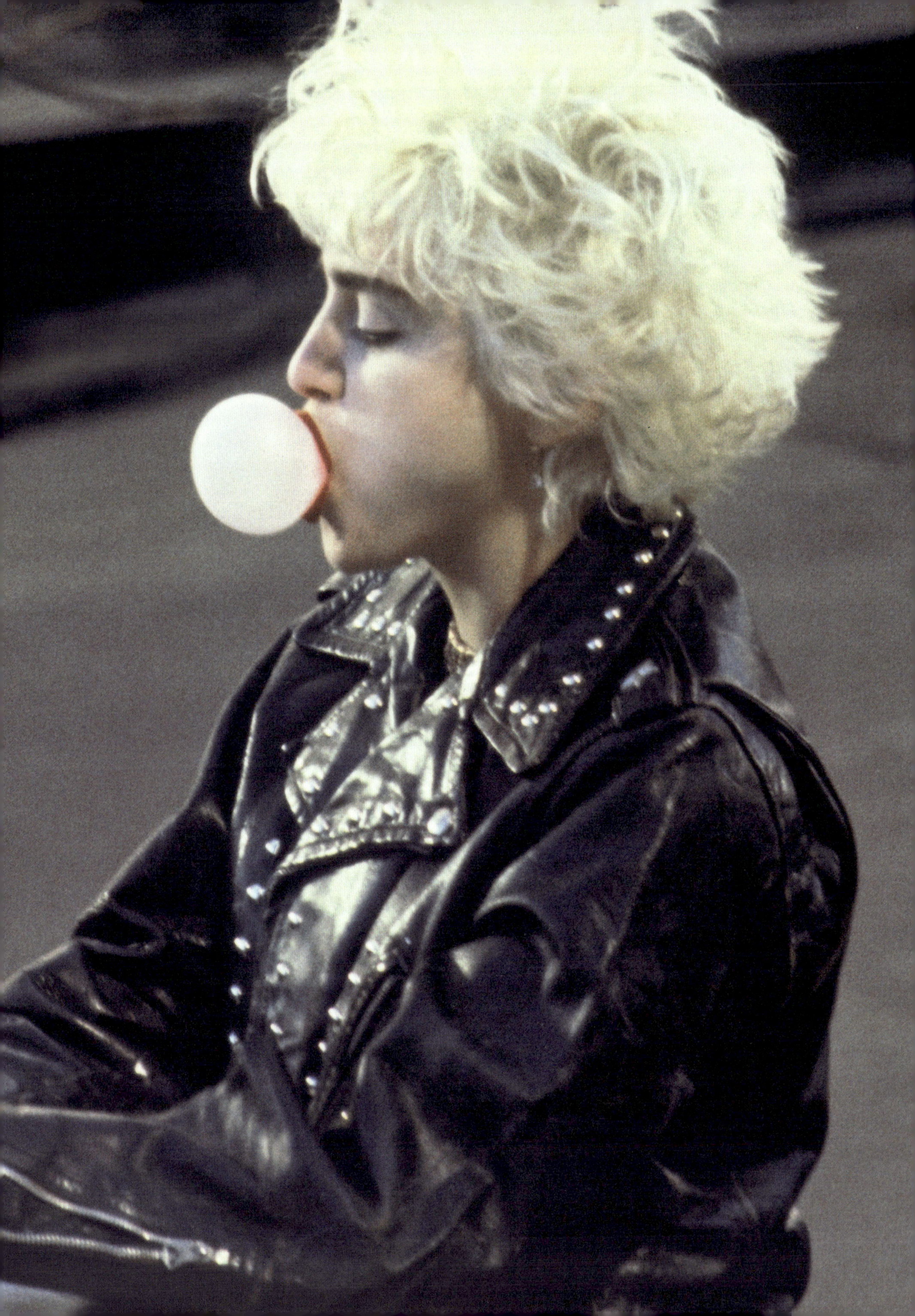

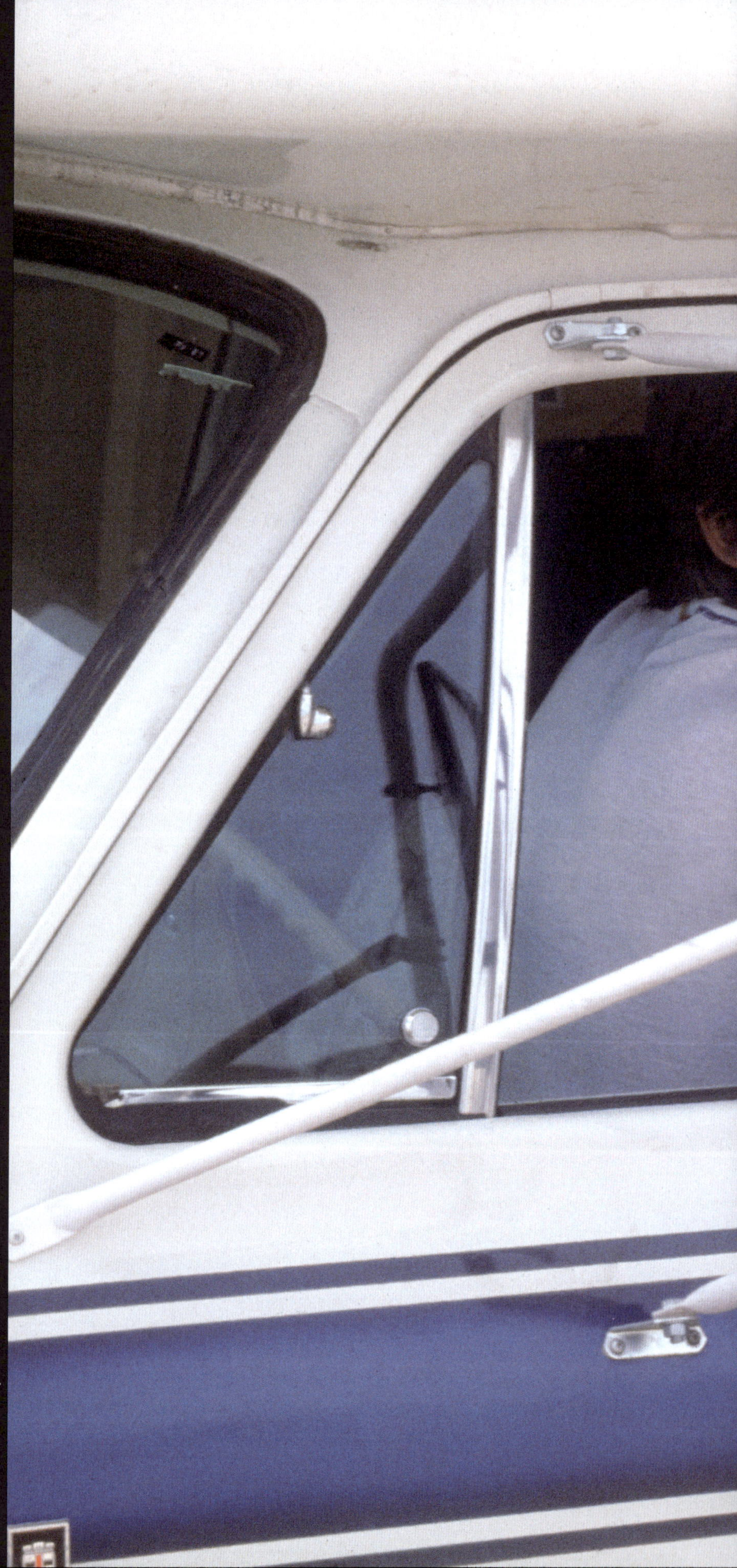

Sylvia Kristel
1981, New Mexico

On the set of the movie
Private Lessons.

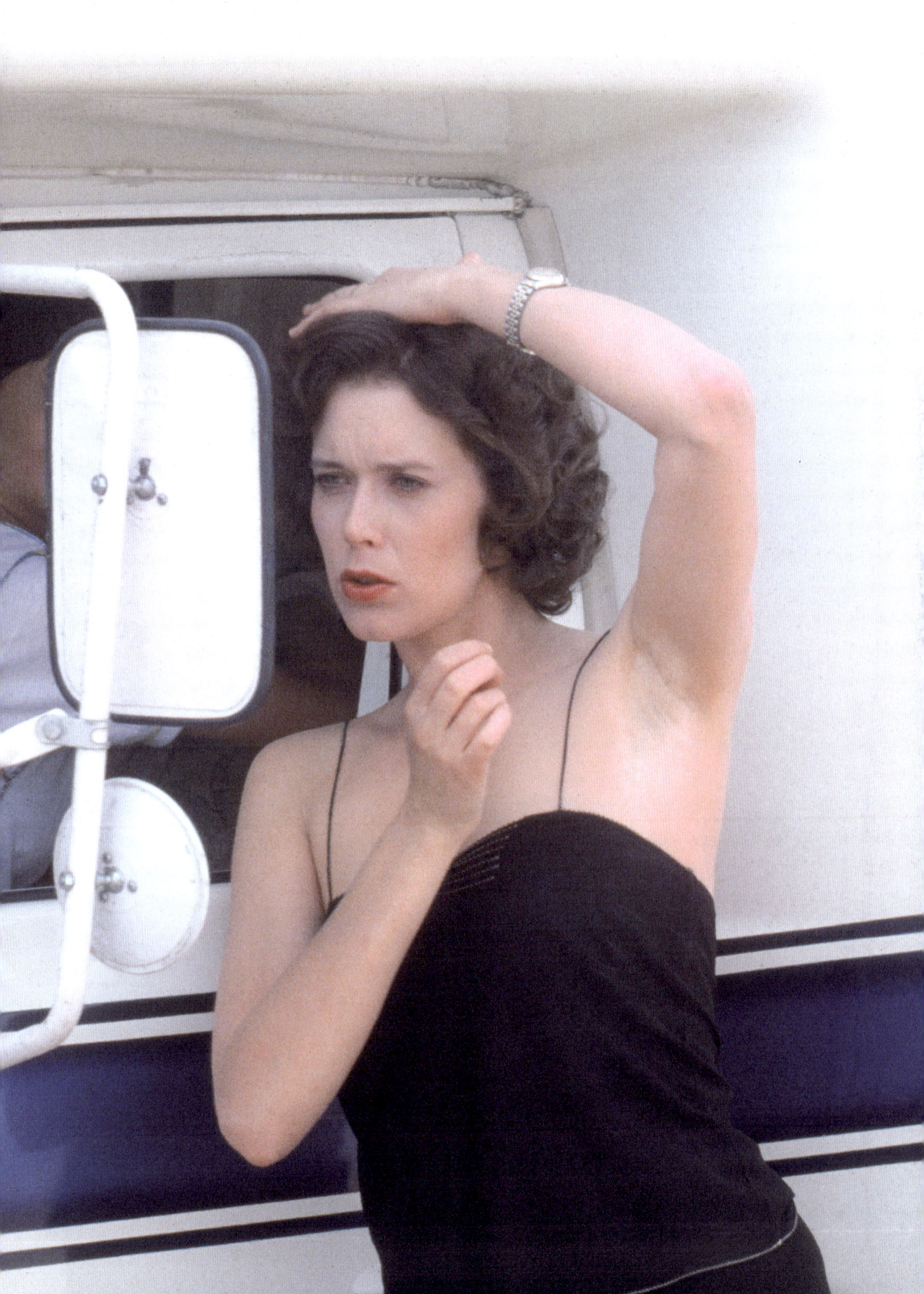

Robert Redford
1977, Arnhem (The Netherlands)

Playing football on the movie set of
A Bridge Too Far.

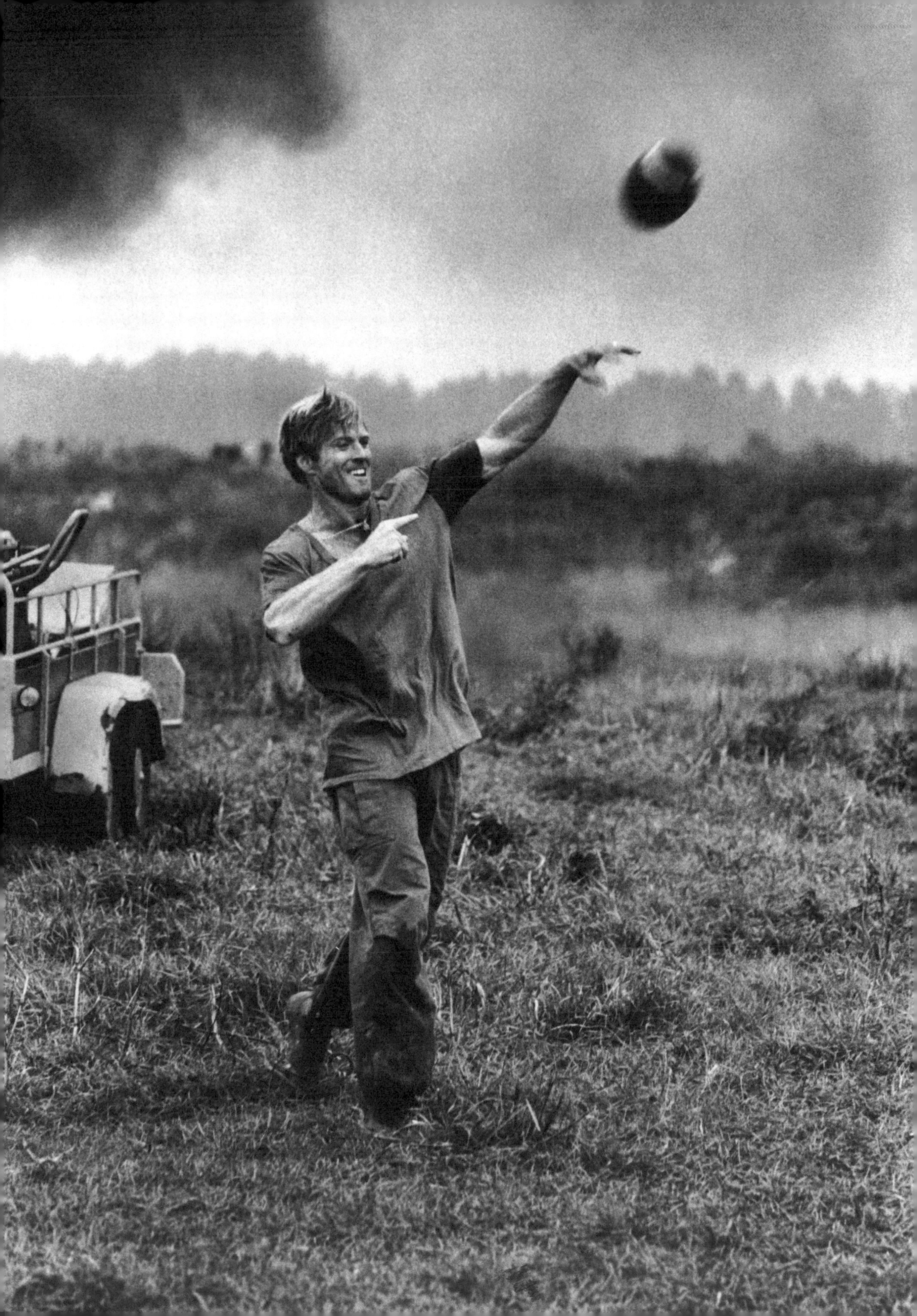

John Lennon
1965, New York City

At a press conference at
the Warwick Hotel.

———

Following double page

Mick Jagger
1977, New York City

In a car outside the Pierre Hotel.

———

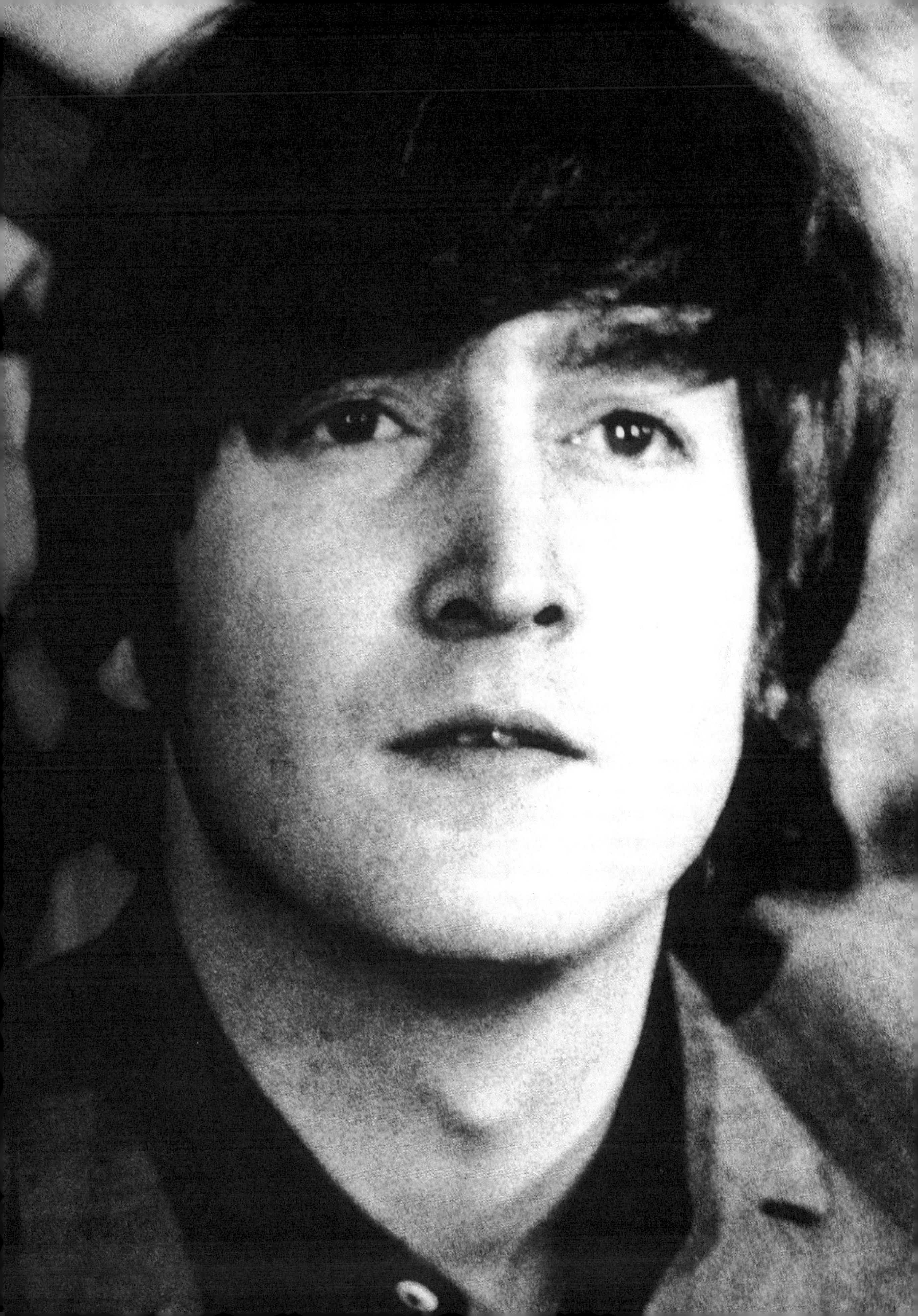

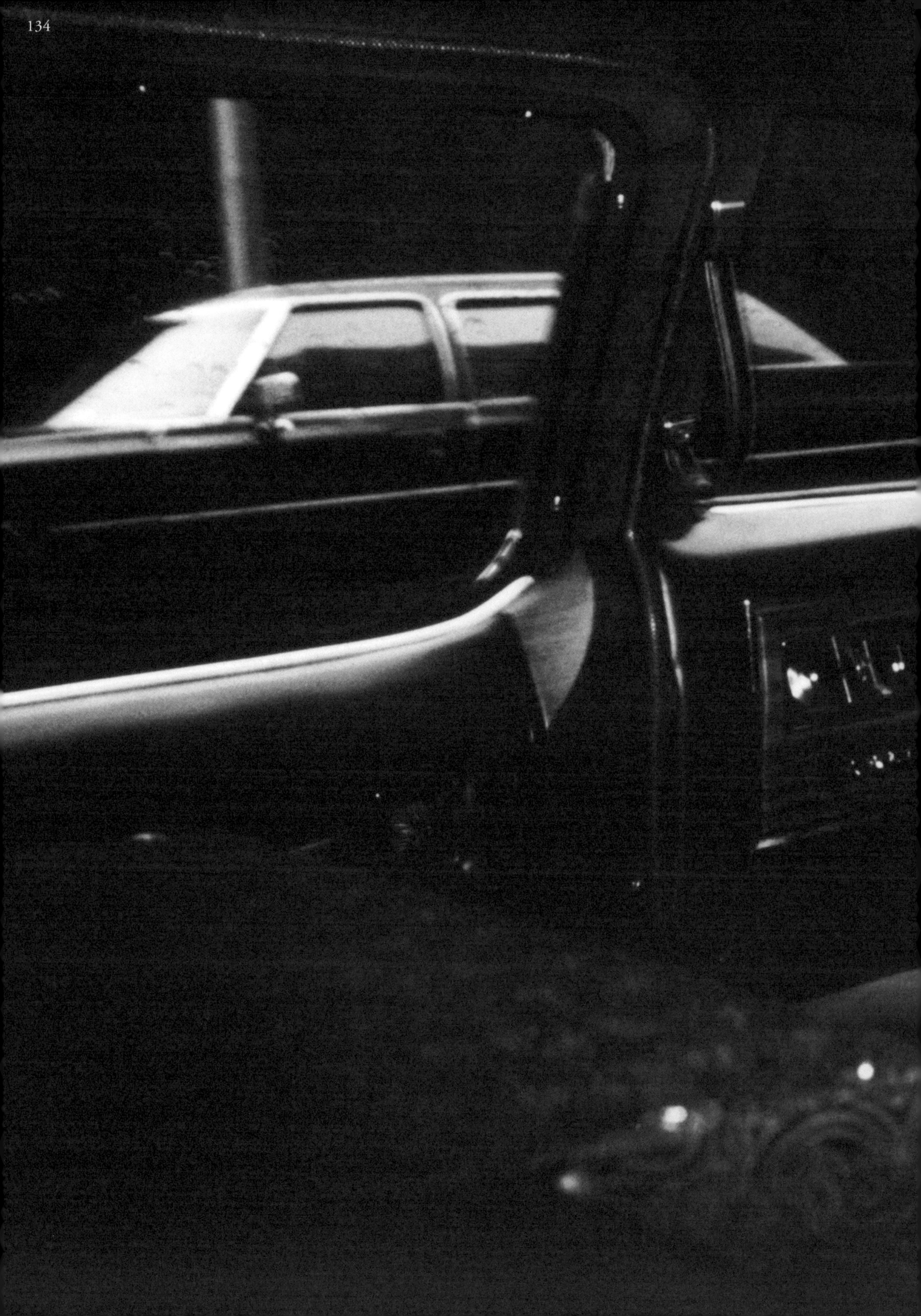

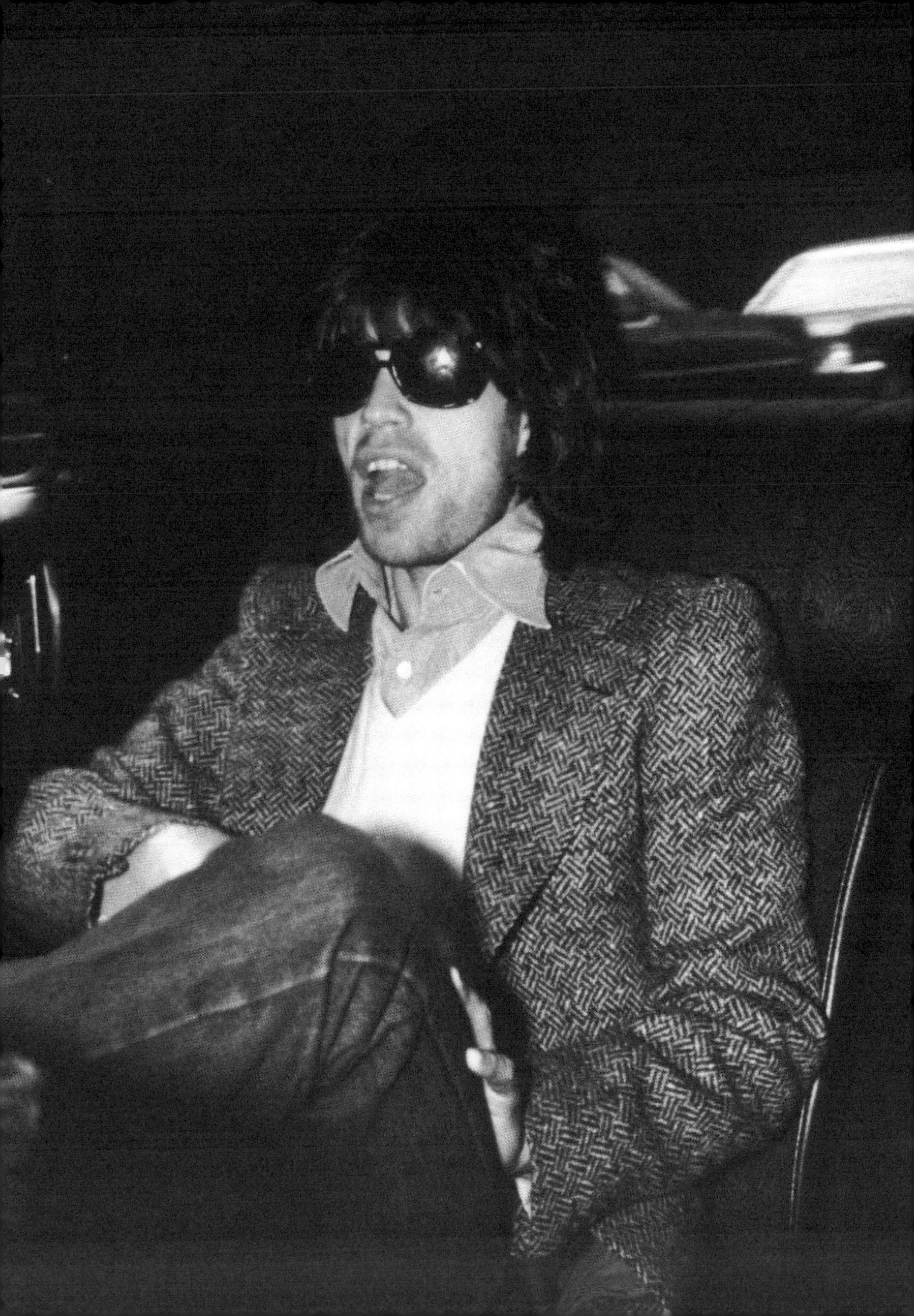

Julio Iglesias
1986, New York City

Celebrating New Year's Eve
at the Essex House Hotel.

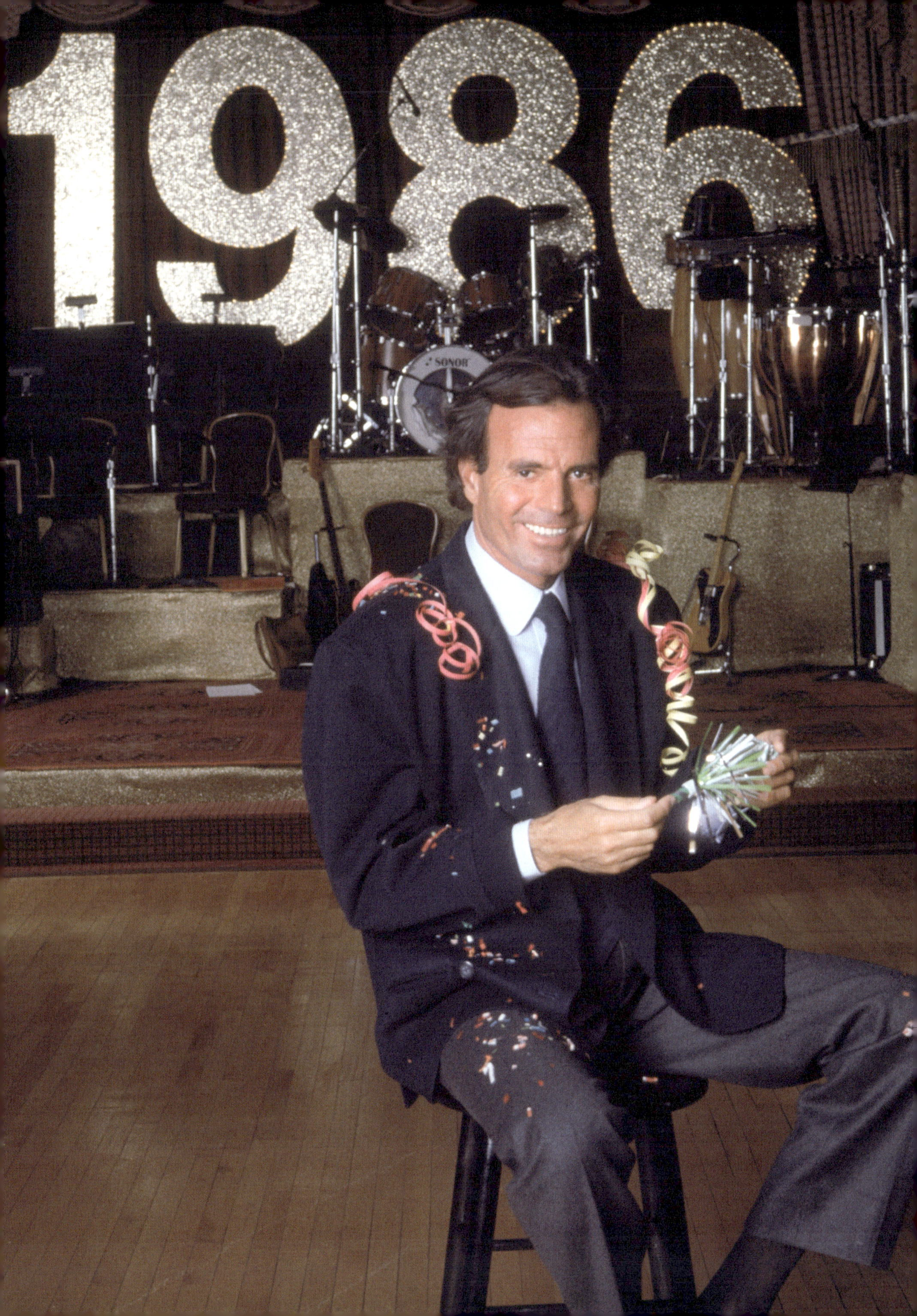
1986

"The excitement is palpable, smoke and drinks everywhere."

I have spent the last couple of weeks in Los Angeles as a "guest" photographer backstage at the *Johnny Carson Show*.

The show is usually taped in New York, but to break things up and get new talent, the whole show picks itself up and goes to LA, where there is a totally different vibe.

Rudy Tellez, the producer of the show, likes me, so for the past couple of years he has invited me to come along, which in itself is a great honor, but also a huge opportunity to photograph some of the world's greatest showbiz personalities and celebrities.

It is tense backstage when Johnny Carson is in the building, but every now and then things lighten up, as when Perry Como (who used to be a barber) gets a haircut by comedian Buddy Hackett, or when Mama Cass stands waiting to go on while knitting a sweater.

It's also a great opportunity to make contacts, and when I meet a freelance writer who has several assignments and is looking for a photographer, I jump at the chance. One of her assignments is the Golden Door Spa in Mexico.

She also has a magazine assignment to interview Nancy Sinatra, who is opening at the International Hotel in Las Vegas, and she invites me along to take some pictures.

I had been at the International just about 10 days earlier for Elvis Presley 's opening, so I know the routine. One star closes, and introduces the next act.

I had some amazing luck getting pictures of Elvis Presley, but the closing of his show with the introduction of Nancy Sinatra could be equally fantastic, so I readily agree to come with her.

In the hotel, rumors are flying everywhere. Is Frank Sinatra going to be there for his daughter and will Elvis show up at Nancy's party? The excitement is palpable, smoke and drinks everywhere. It is beginning to look like a real Vegas event.

And finally it happens, Frank is in the room. Elvis arrives and goes over to greet him and Fred Astaire jumps in to complete this unique photo. This combination of Sinatra, Astaire and Elvis will never happen again. I was truly blessed that evening.
___

Elvis Presley
1969, Las Vegas

On his way to be introduced
on stage by Barbra Streisand
at the International Hotel.

———

Following double page

**Elvis Presley, Frank Sinatra
and Fred Astaire**
1969, Las Vegas

At opening night party for Nancy
Sinatra in the International Hotel.

———

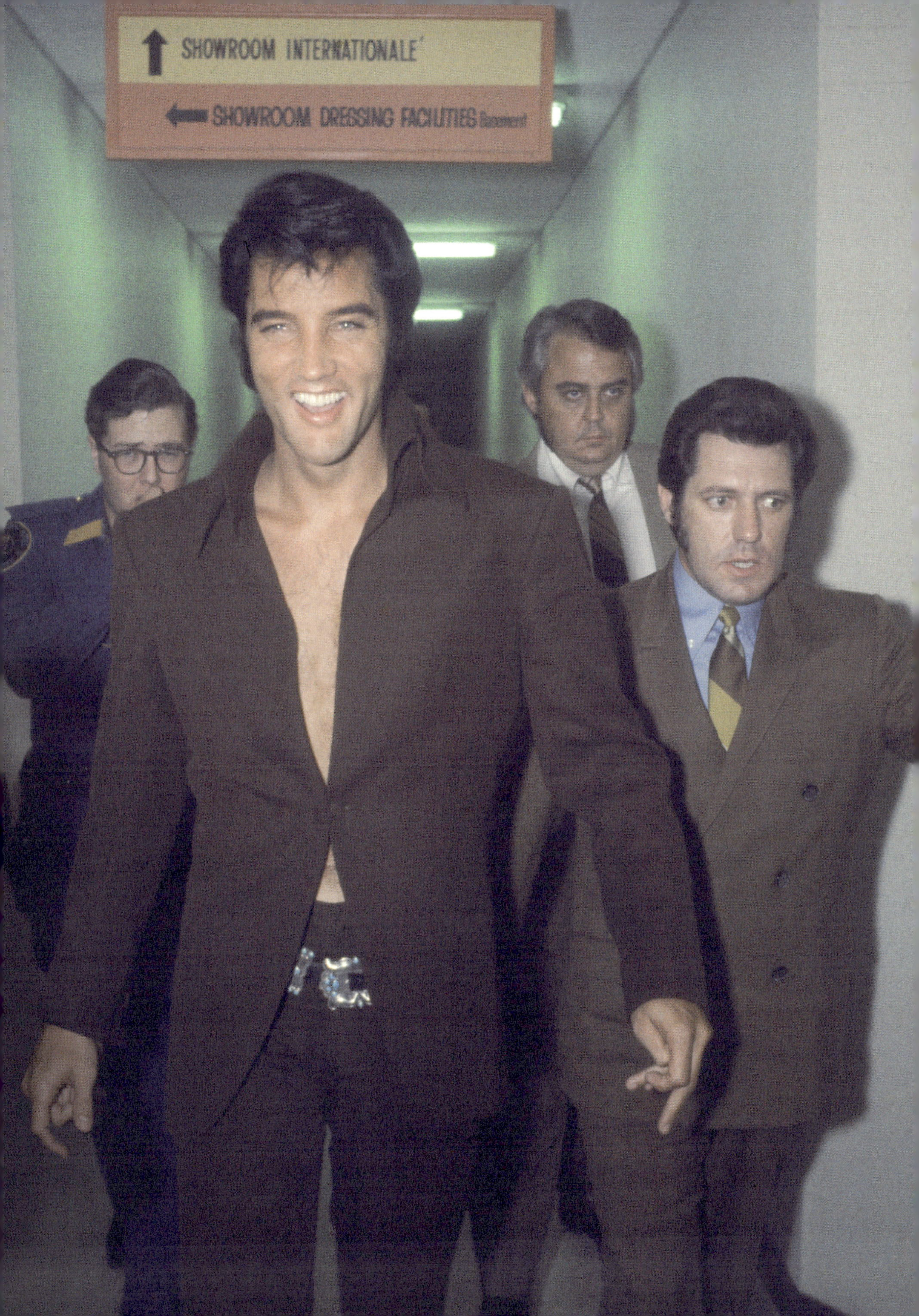
↑ SHOWROOM INTERNATIONALE'
← SHOWROOM DRESSING FACILITIES Basement

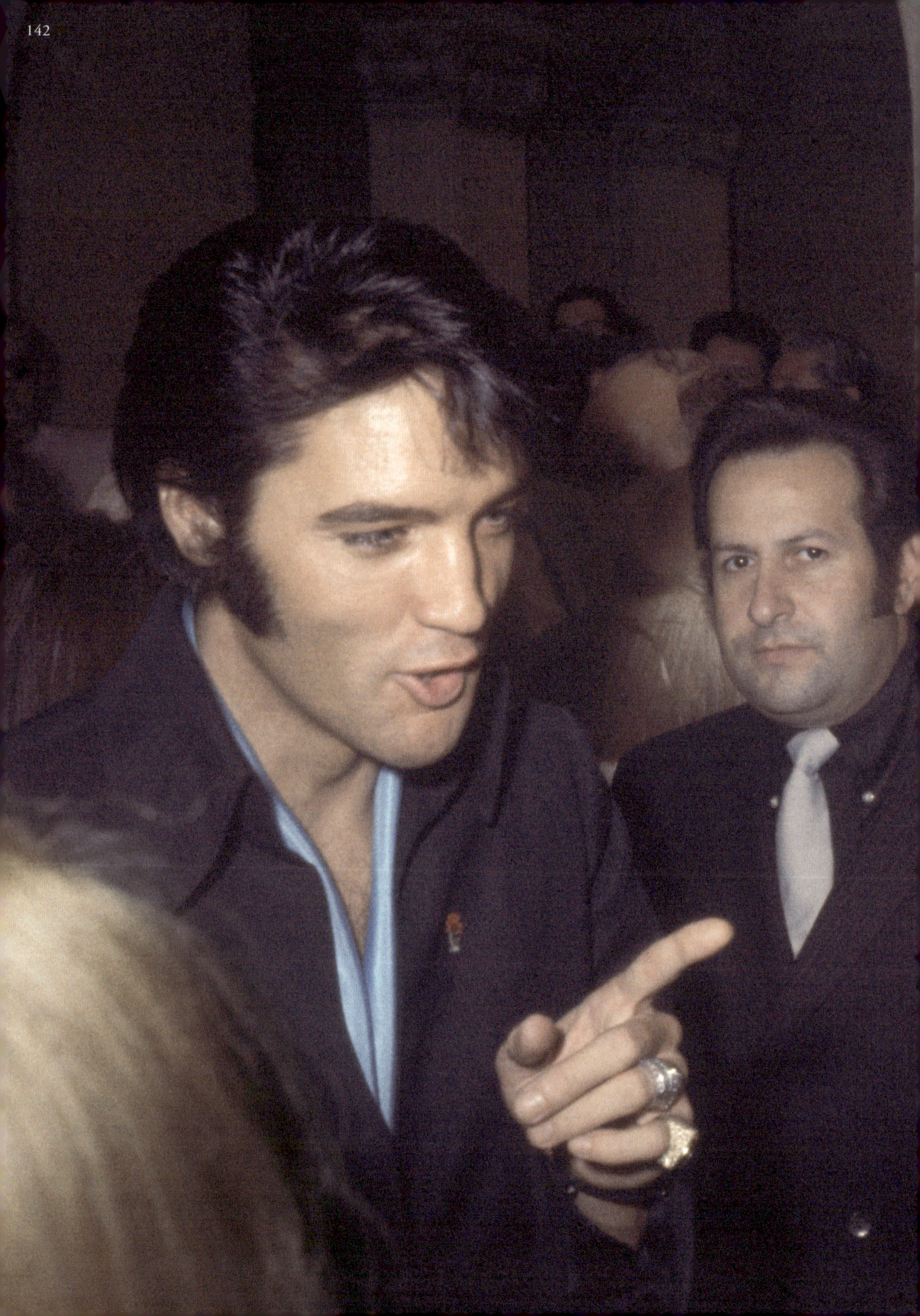

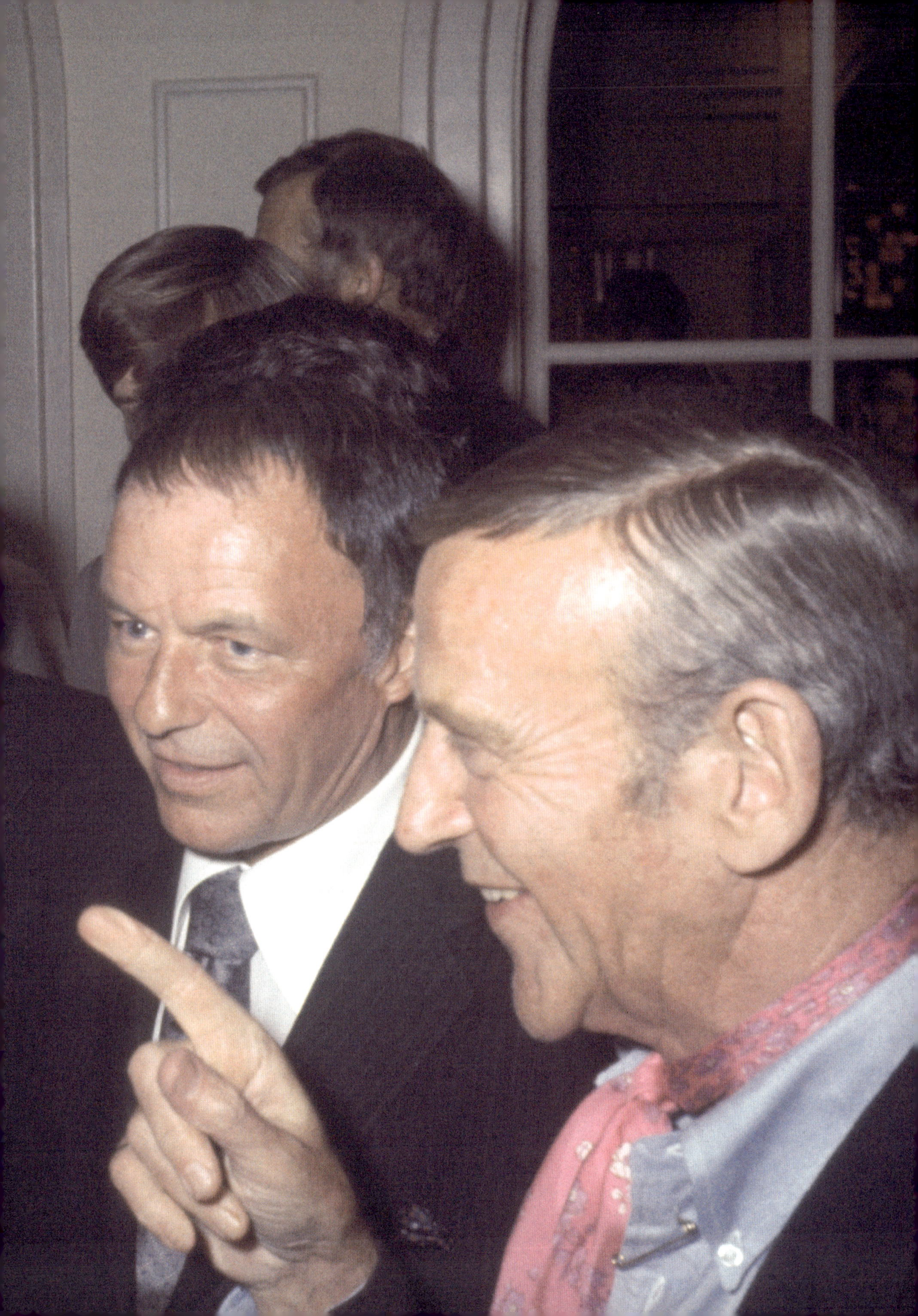

Ari Onassis
1972, New York City

Leaving his favorite New York
restaurant *The 21 Club*.

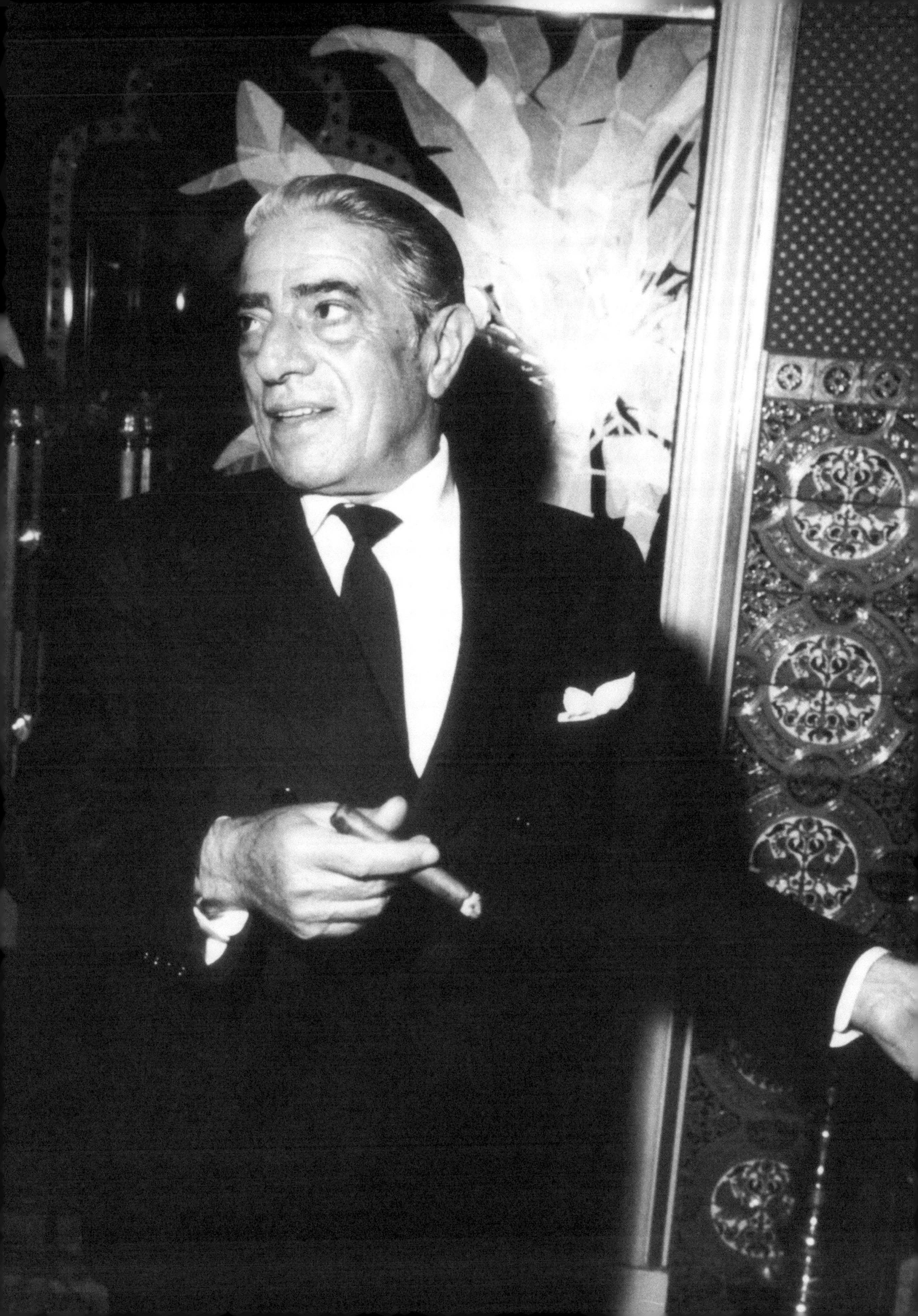

B.B. King
1979, New York City

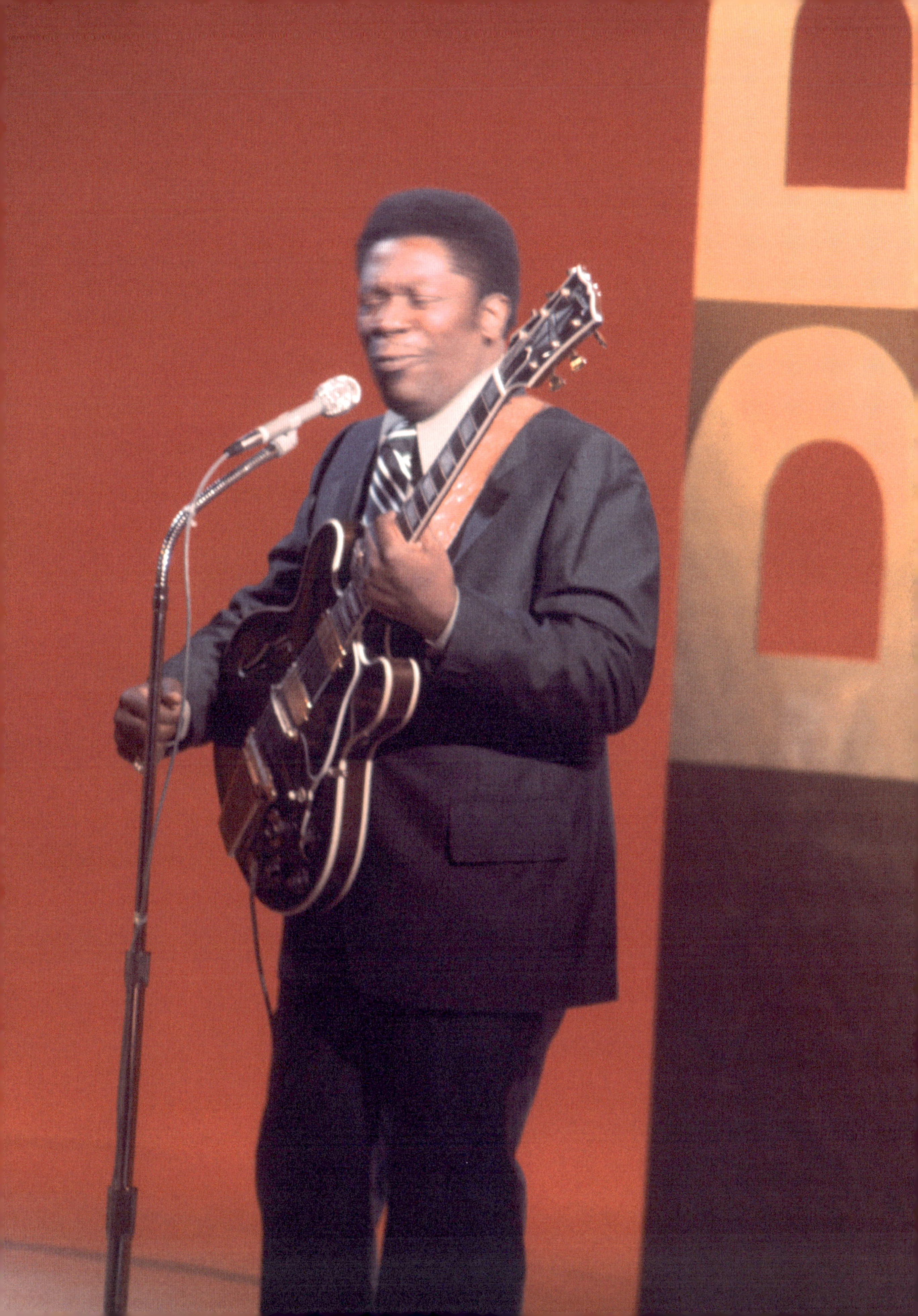

Charles Bronson
1974, New York City

On the movie set of *Deathwish*.
———

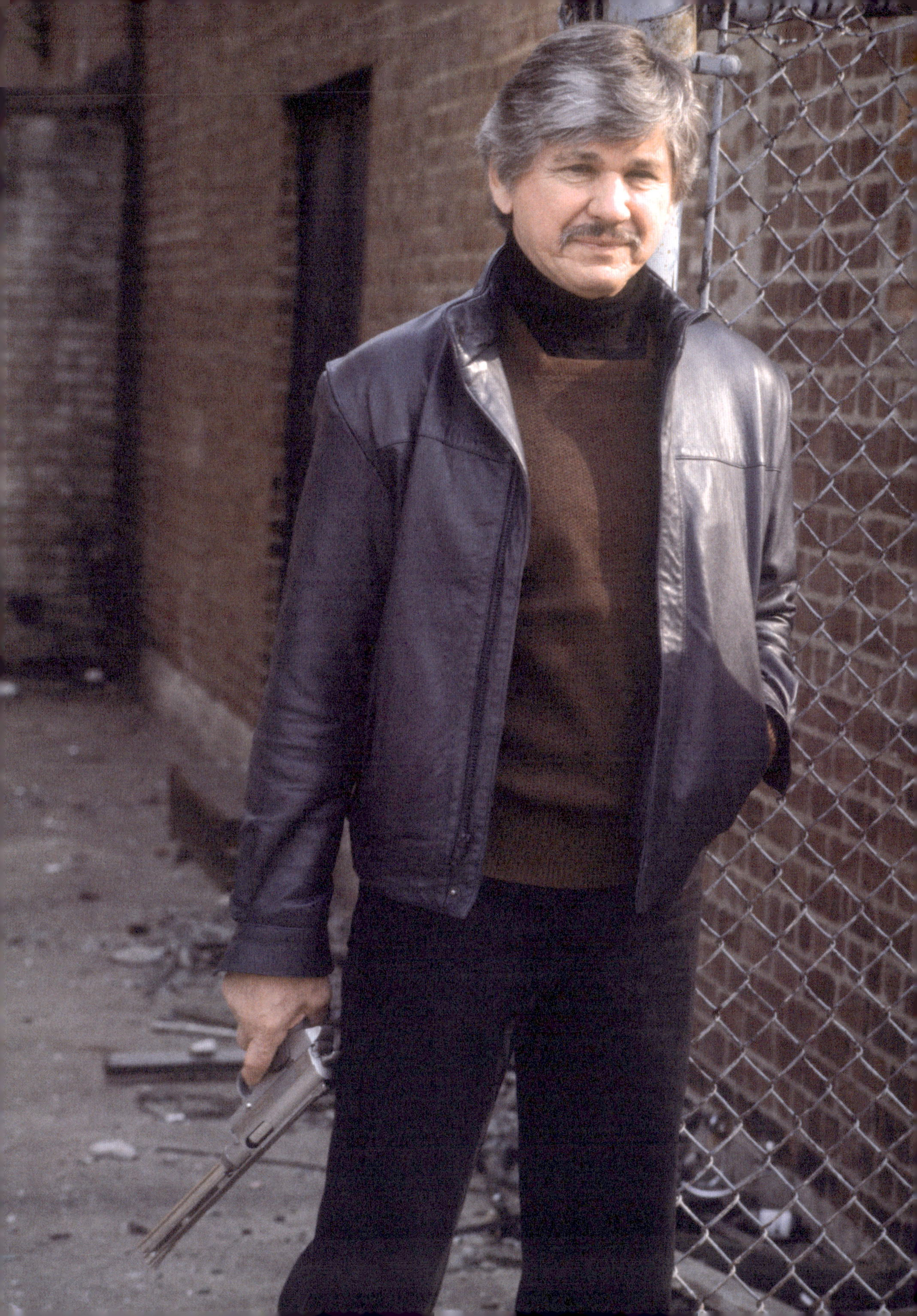

King Kong
1976, New York City

———

Following double page

Lucille Ball
1968, Los Angeles

Backstage at Johnny Carson's
Tonight Show with with her mother
standing in the doorway.

———

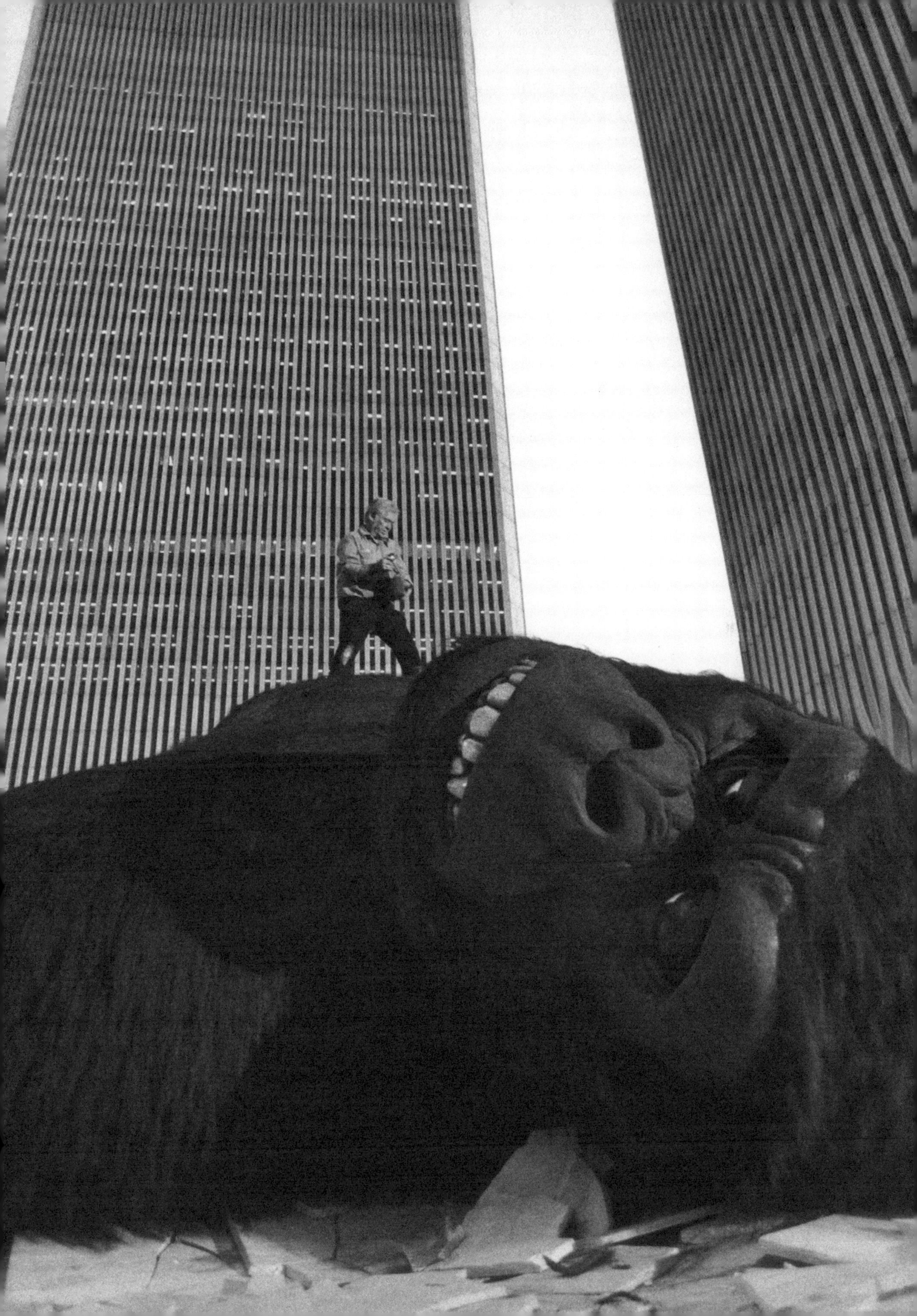

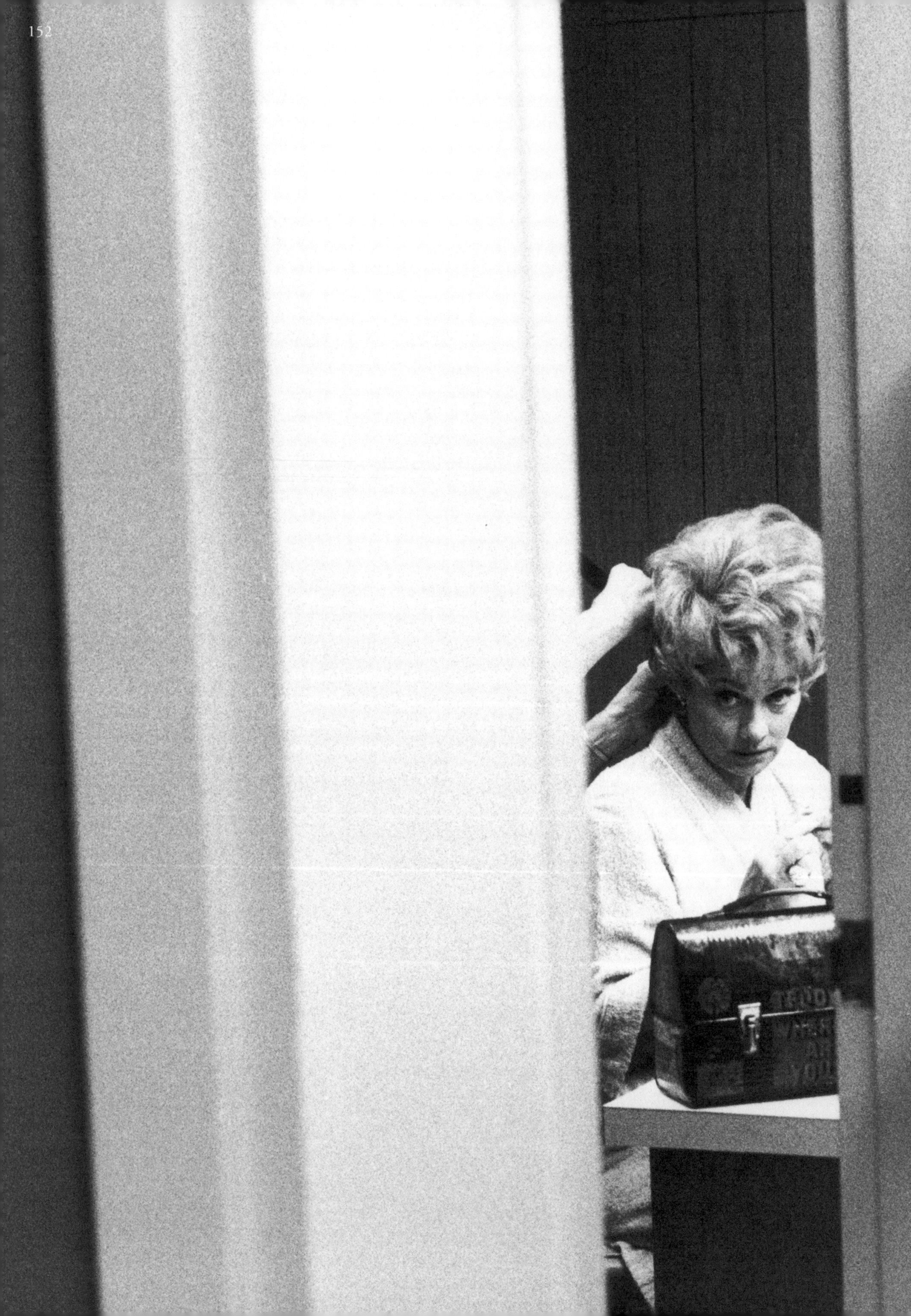

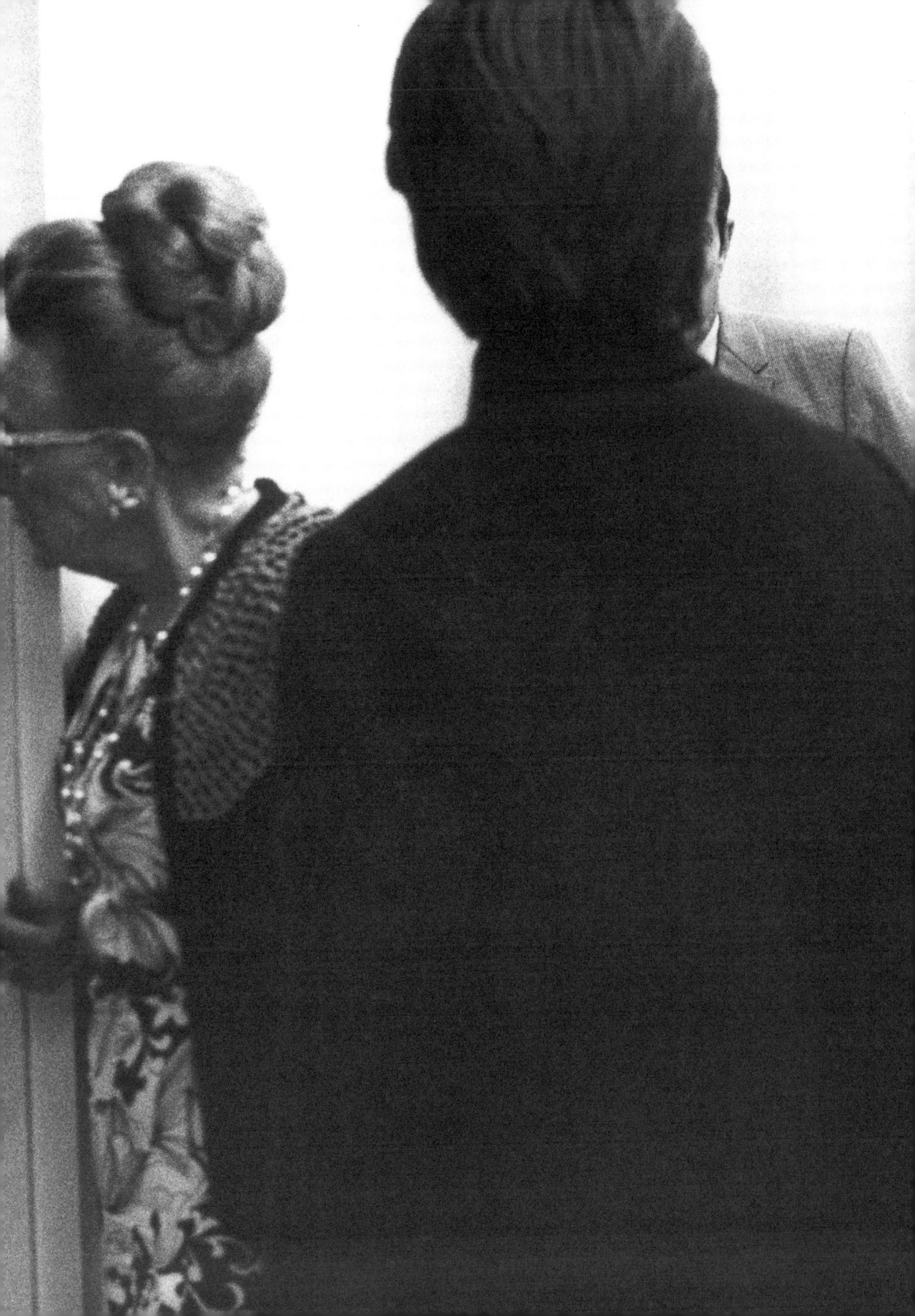

On the movie set of *Cuba*.

Sean Connery
1979, Cadiz (Spain)

On the movie set of *Cuba*.

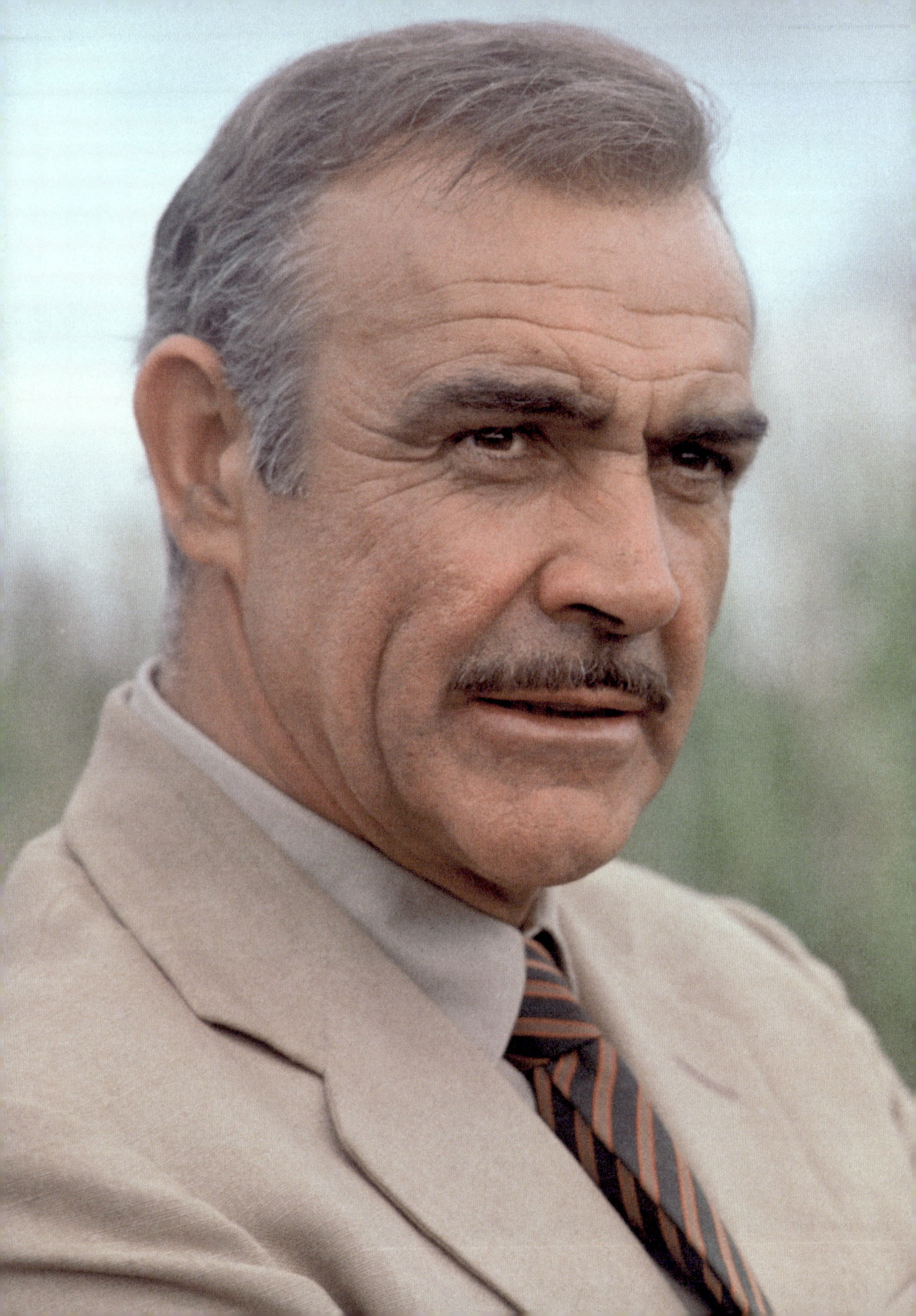

Jack Nicholson
1969, New York City

With a friend at a Halloween Party.

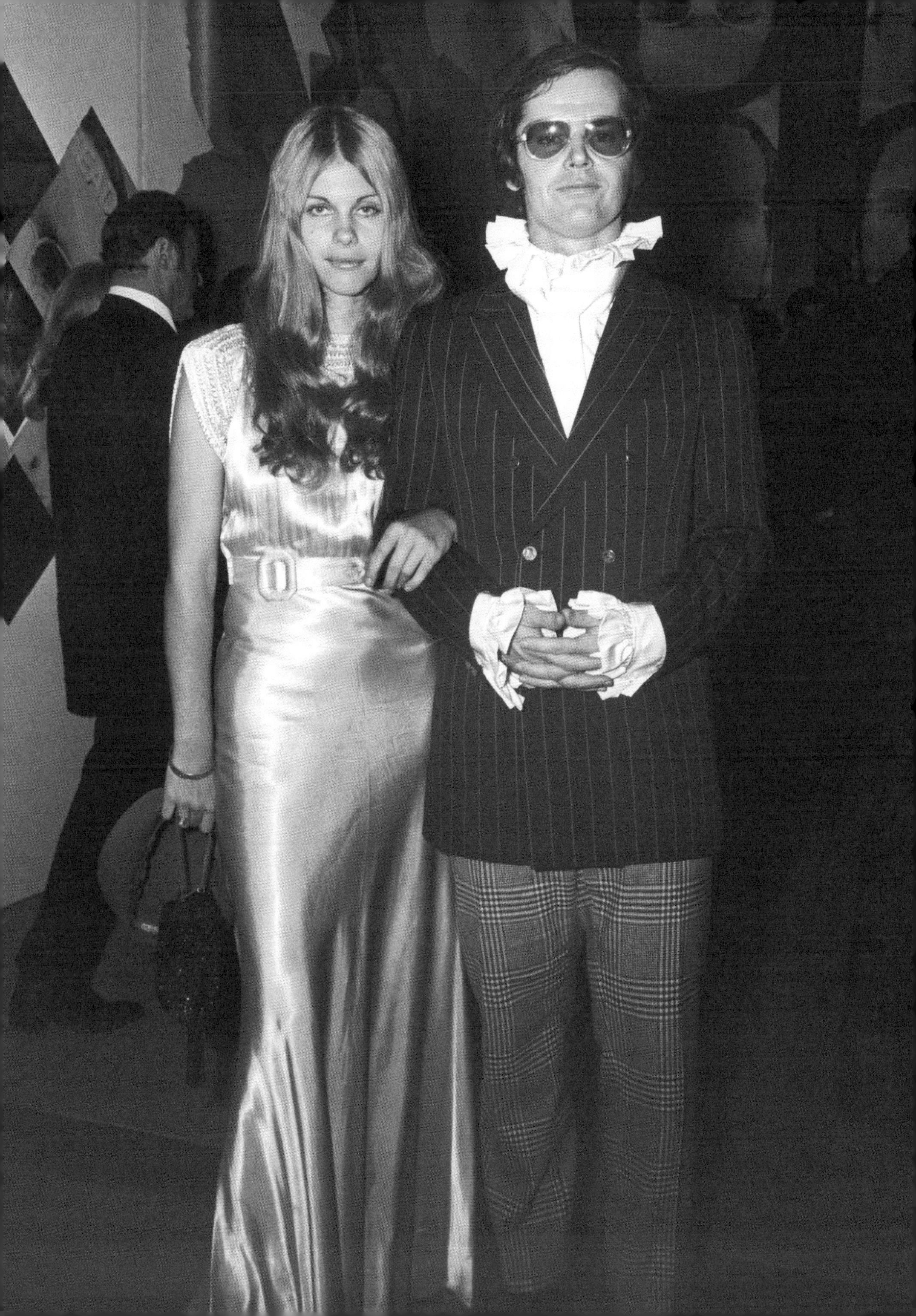

Faye Dunaway
1967, New York City

On her way to the movie premiere
of *Hurry Sundown,* and in the background
the world famous *Latin Quarters.*

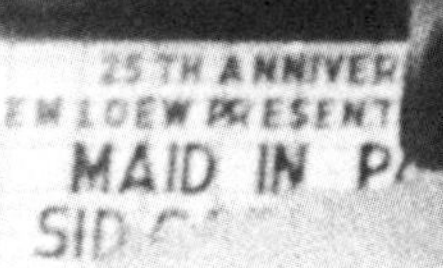
25 TH ANNIVER
EM LOEW PRESENT
MAID IN P
SID C
Paradise Bootery

Dean Martin
1969, Los Angeles

On the *Tonight Show*
with Johnny Carson.

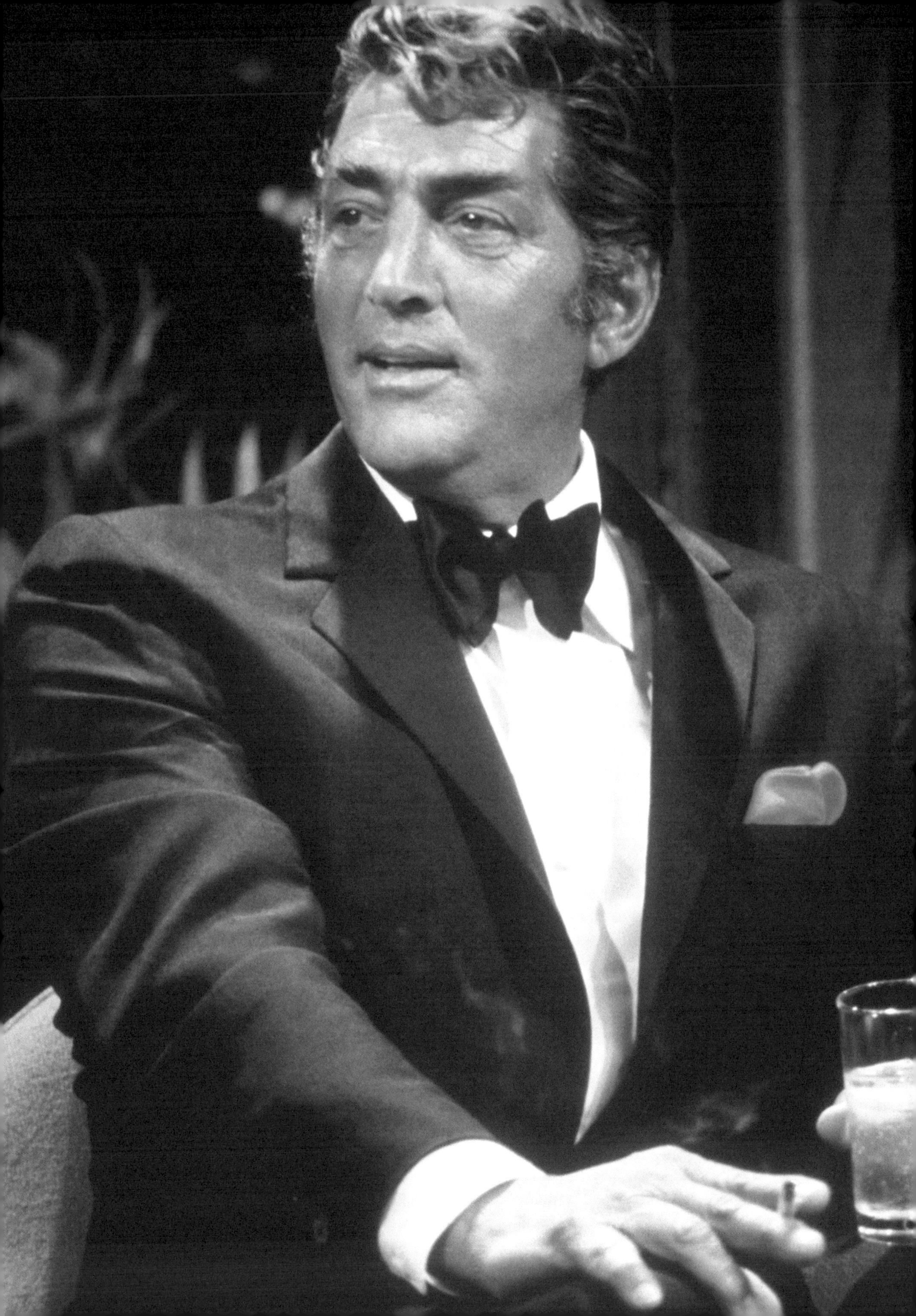

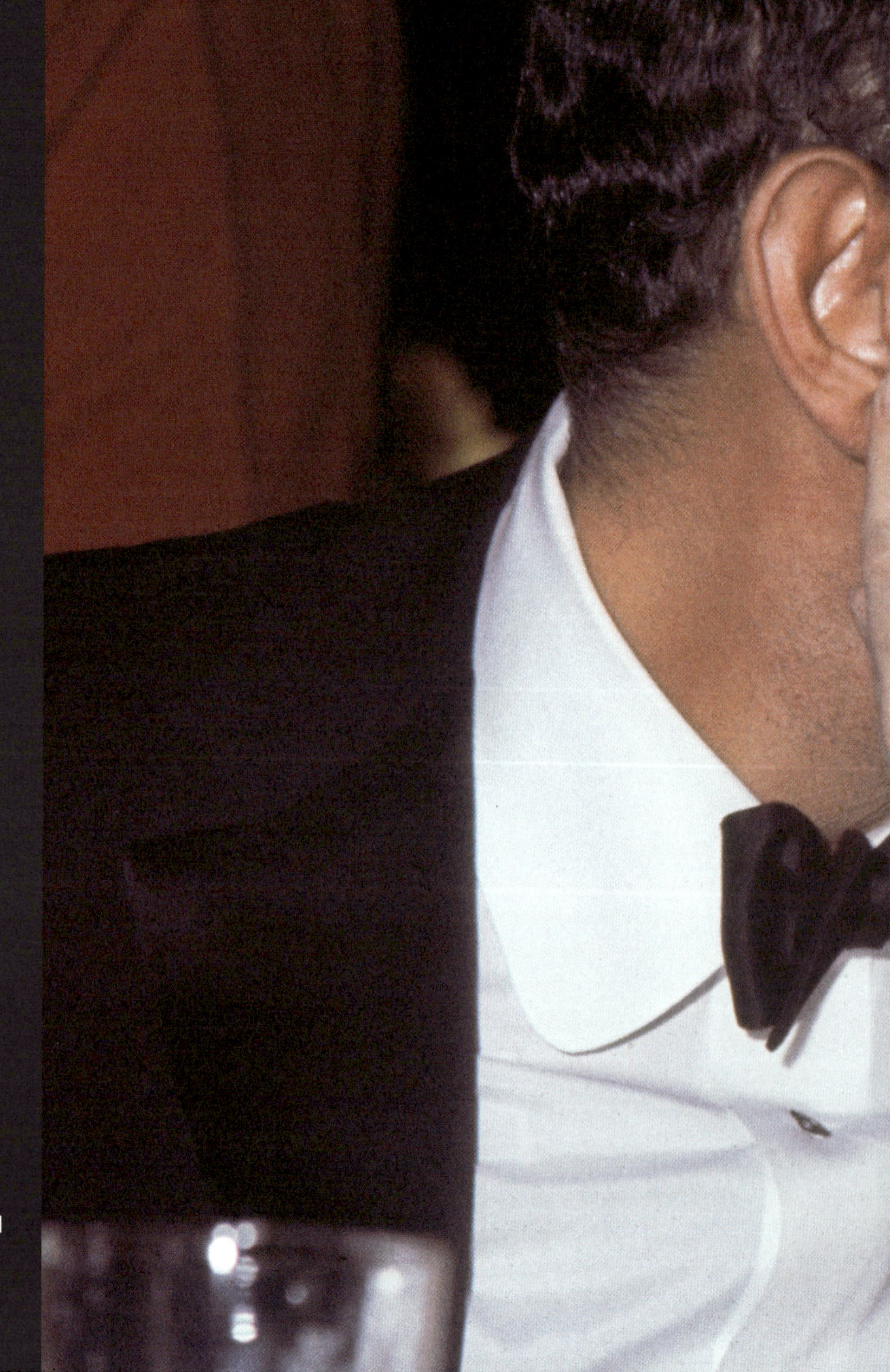

Tony Bennett and Judy Garland
1968, New York City

At the Americana Hotel.

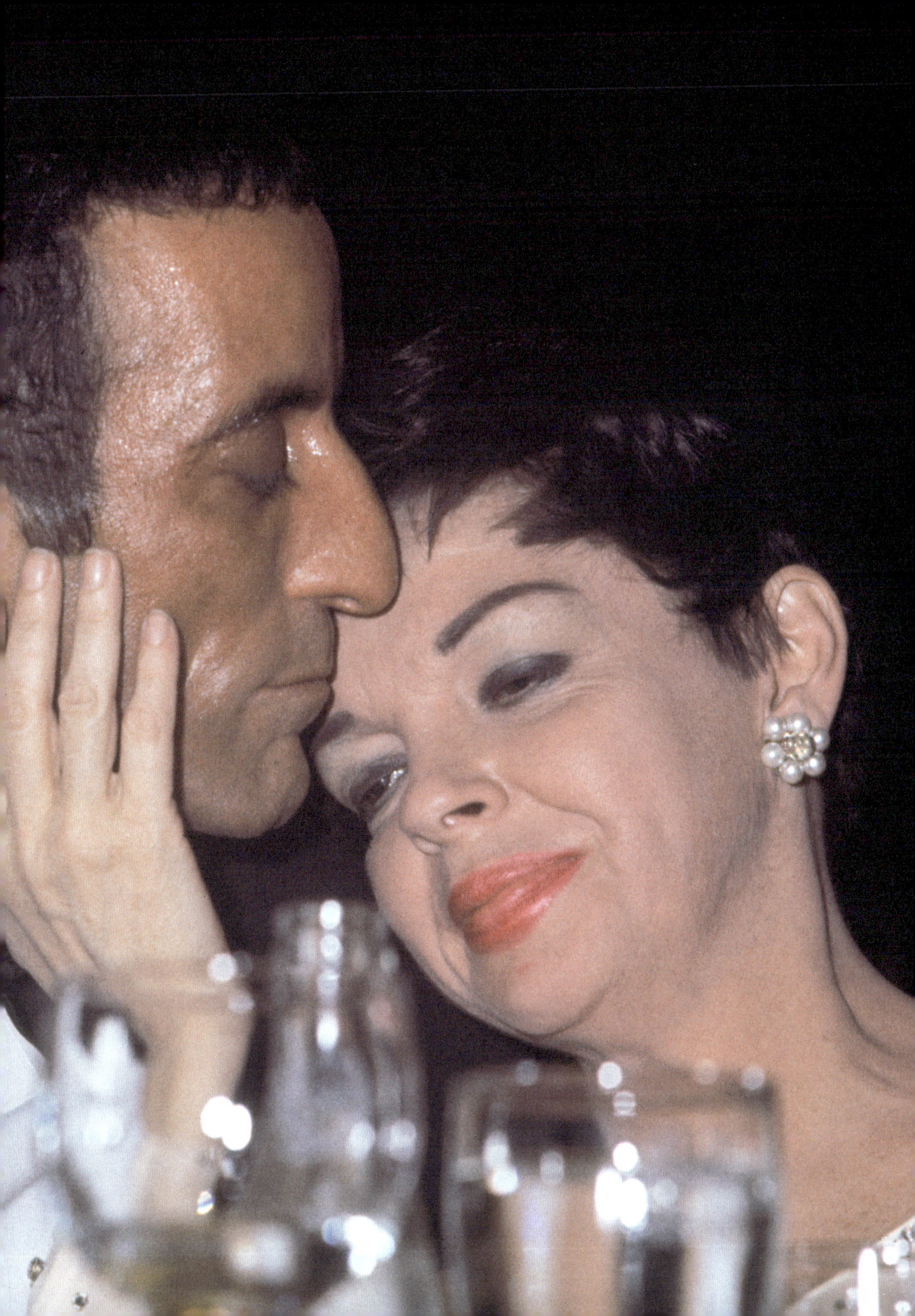

Whoopi Goldberg
1984, New York City

At the Hard Rock Café.

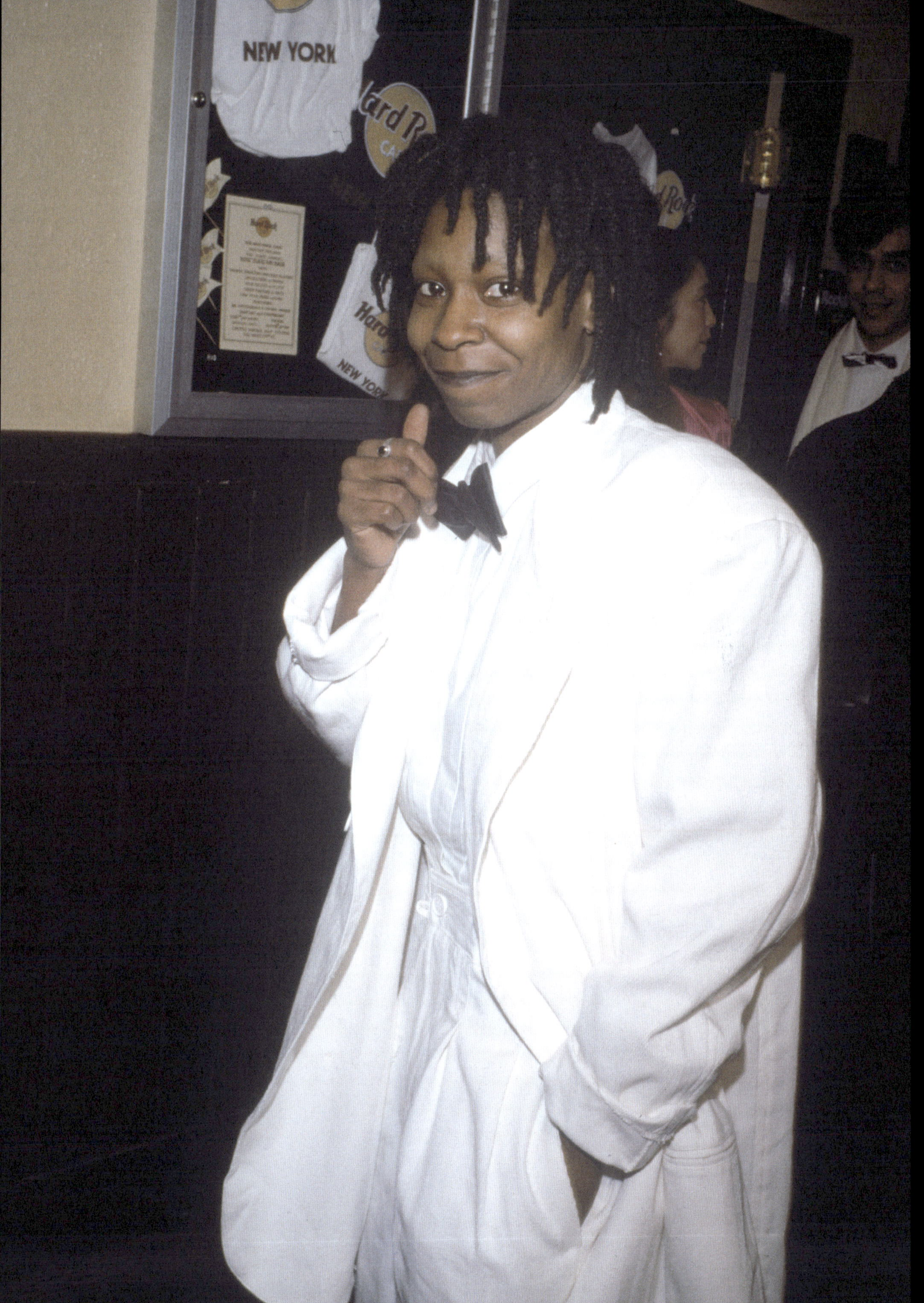
NEW YORK
Hard Rock
CAFE
NEW YORK

Cher
1968, New York City

Backstage at Madison Square Garden
for a Martin Luther King benefit.

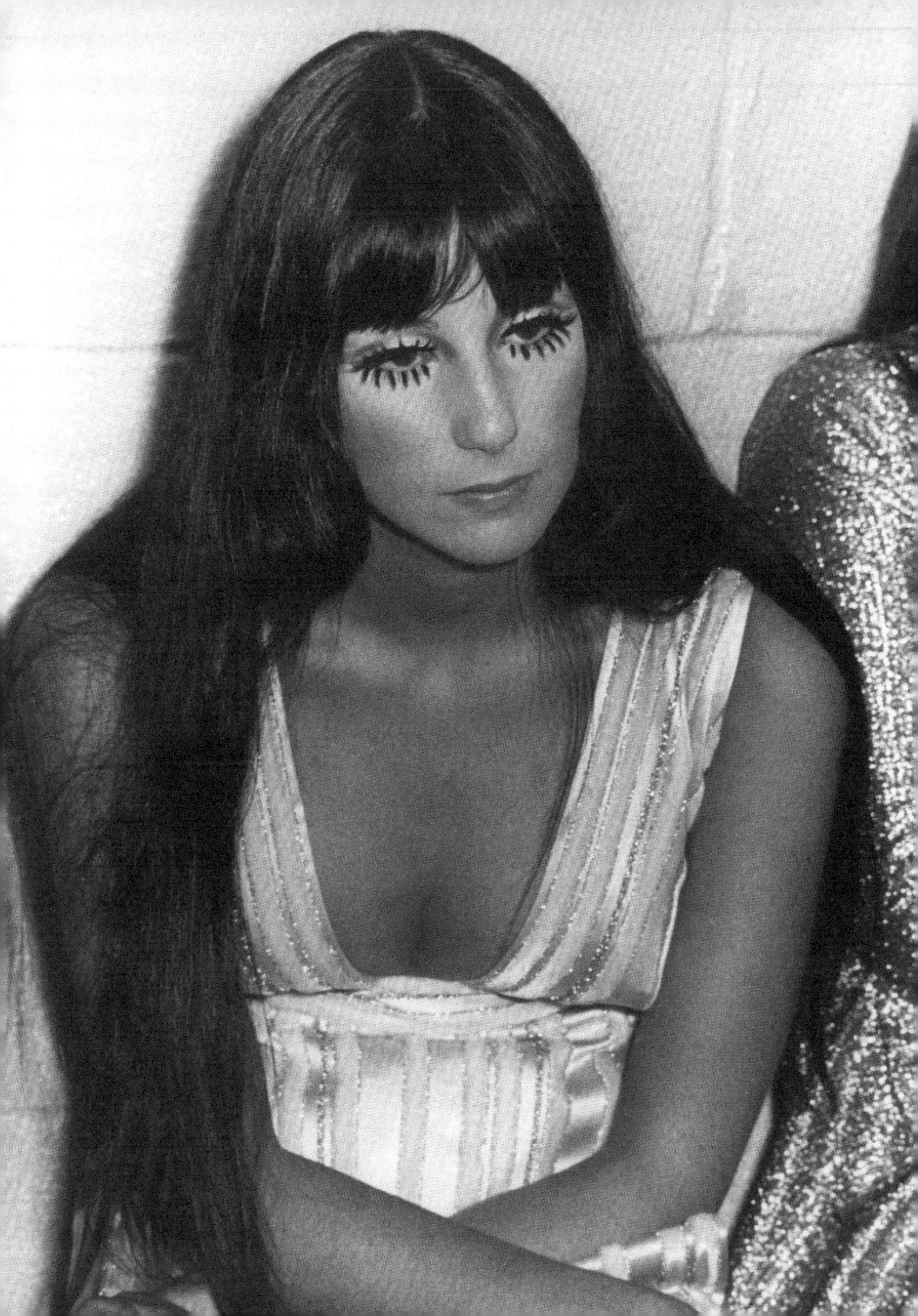

Audrey Hepburn
1982, New York City

At a tribute to Hubert Givenchy,
Fashion Institute of Technology.
——

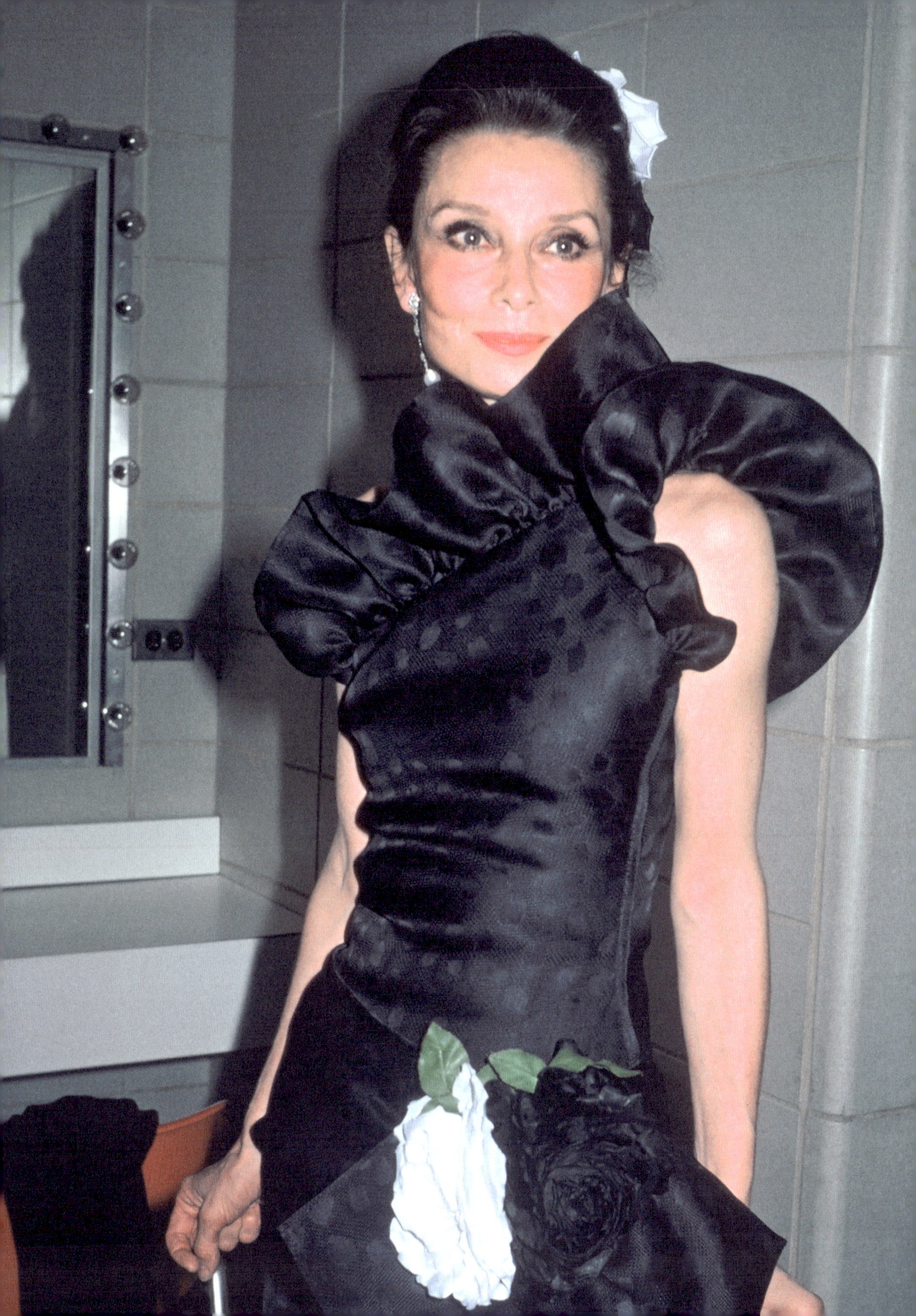

Sidney Poitier
1969, New York City

At the *New York Film Critics Circle Awards,*
at Sardi's.
———

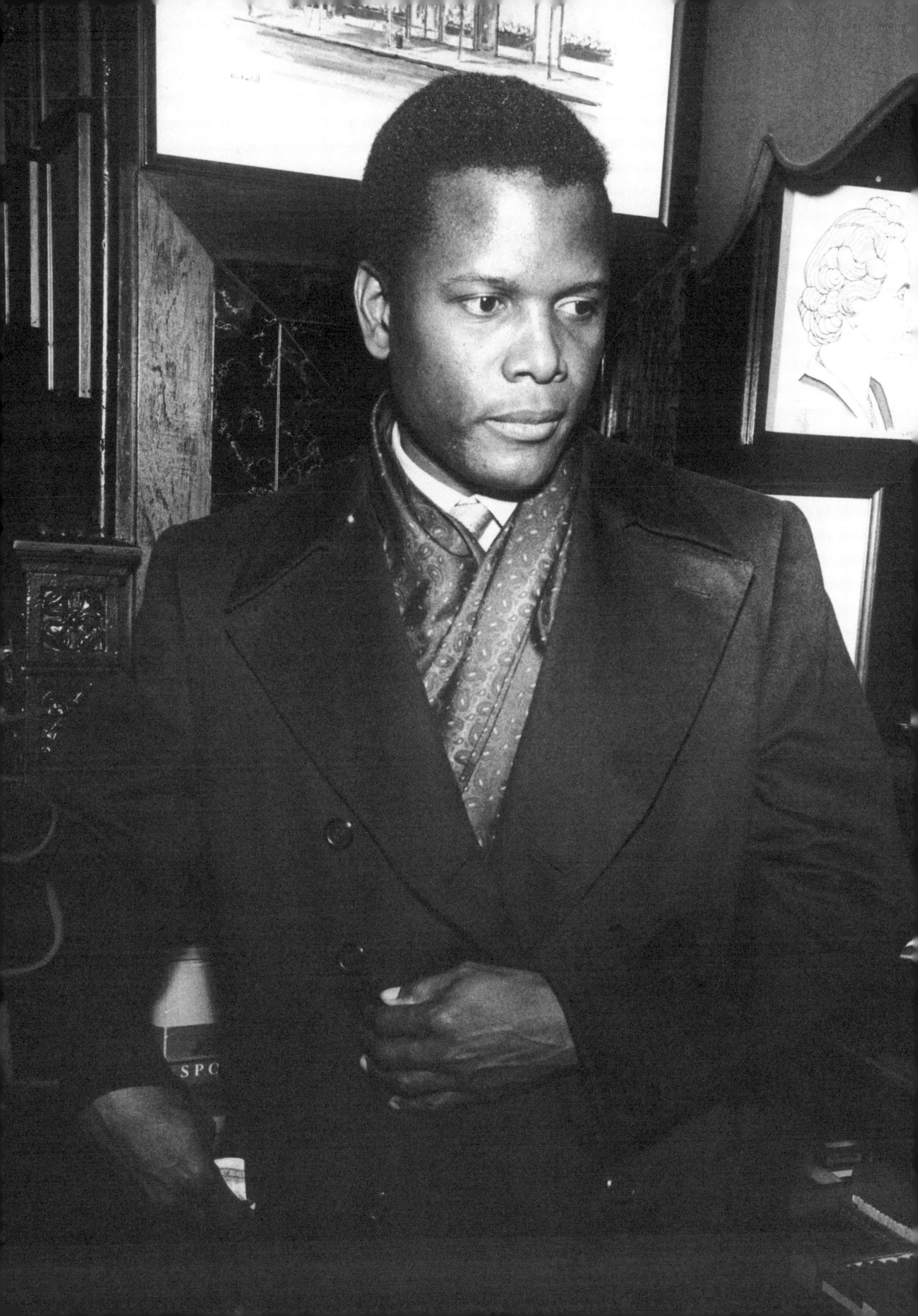

Brad Pitt
1997, New York City

In New York filming *Meet Joe Black*.

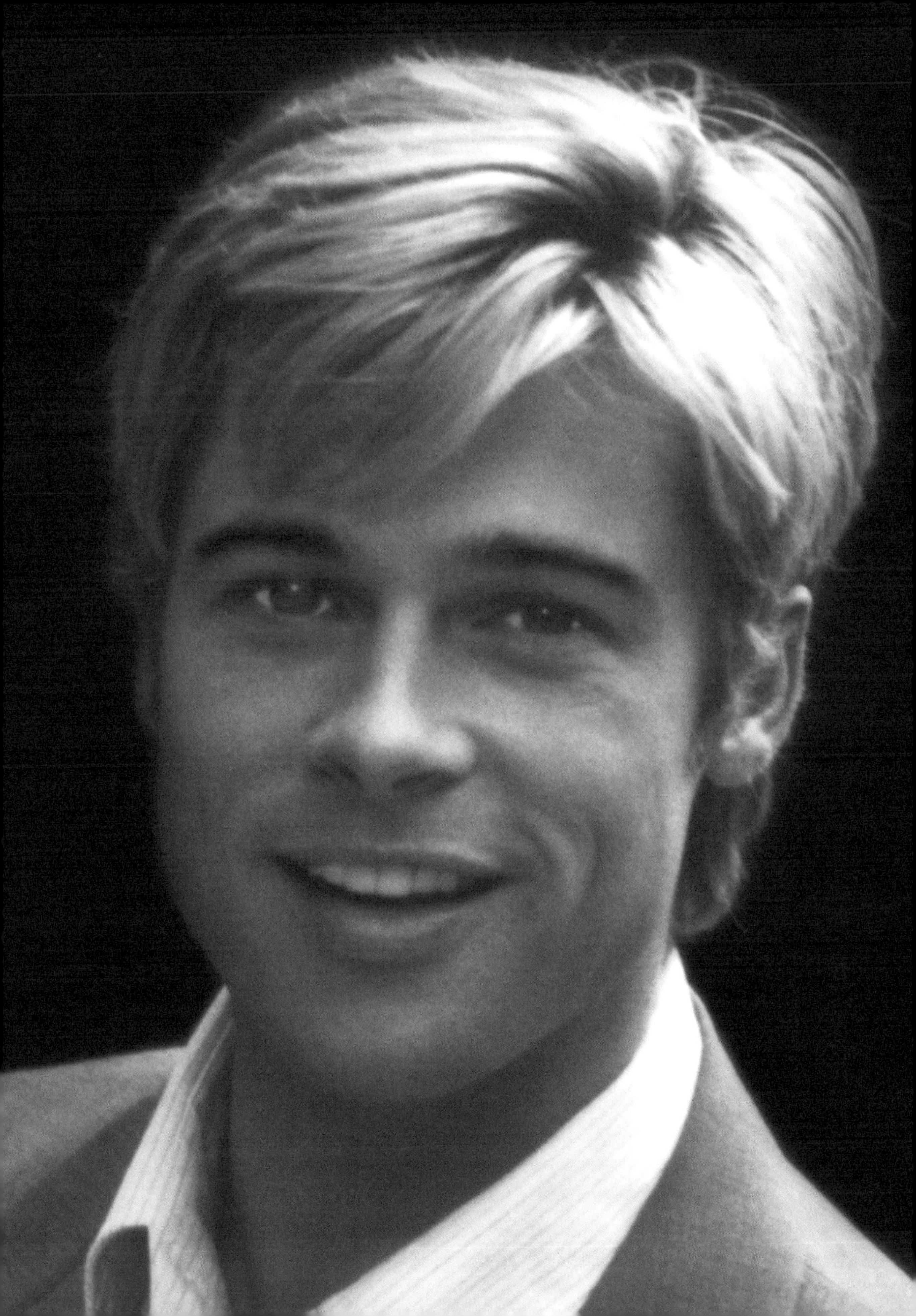

Woody Allen
1990, New York City

At Carnegie Hall.
—

Following double page

Elton John and Ann–Margret
1975, New York City

In town to promote the
movie *Tommy*.
—

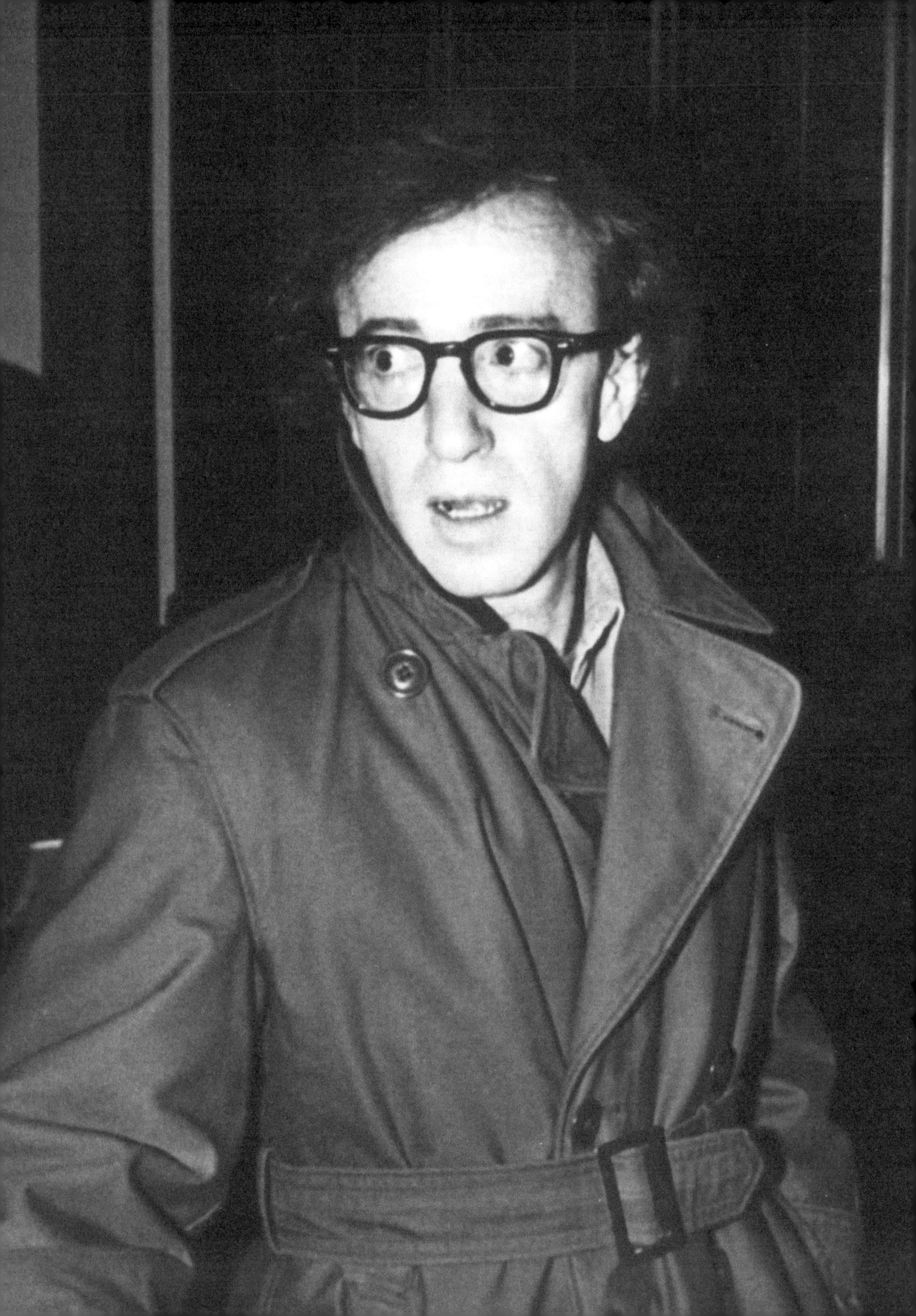

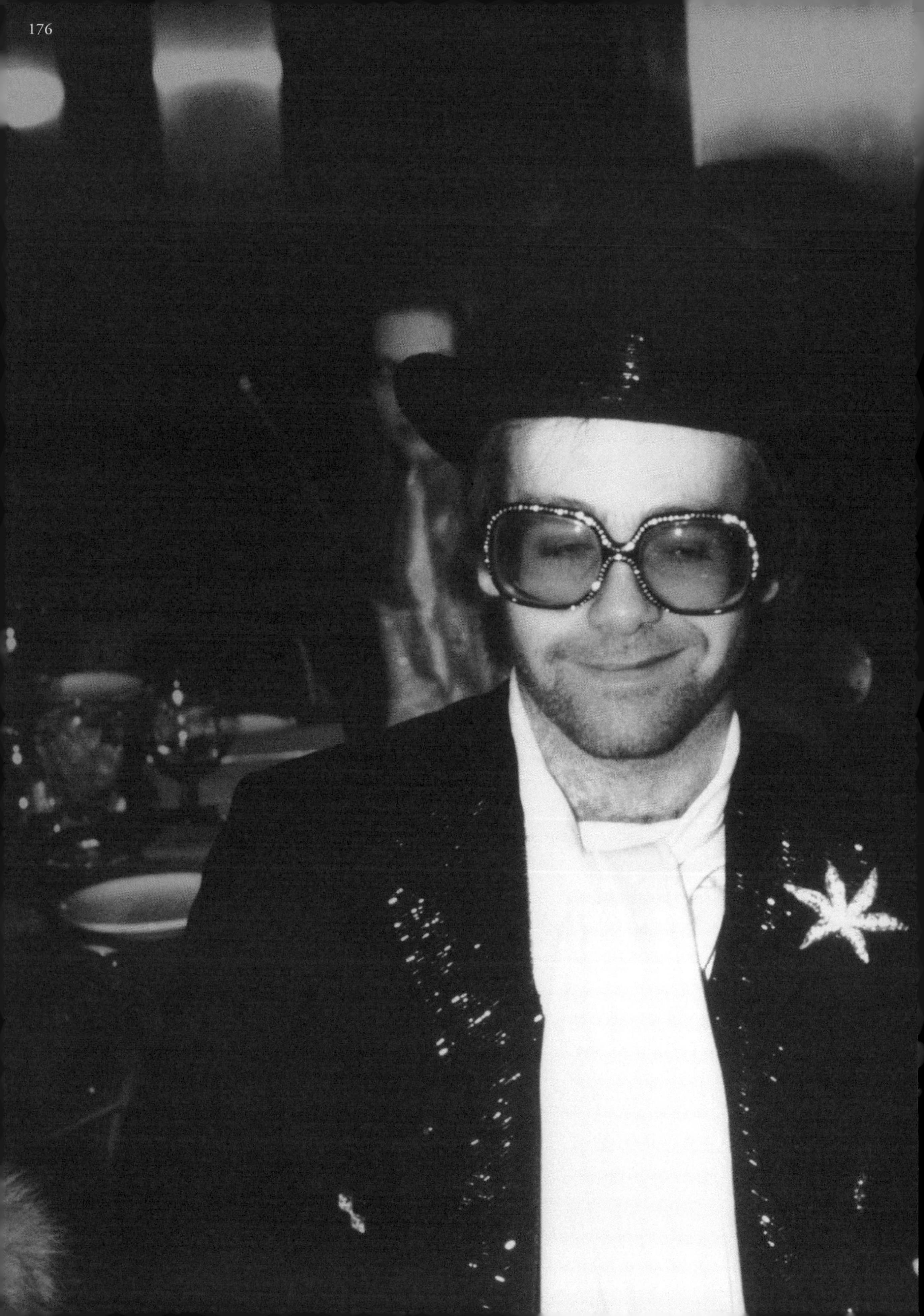

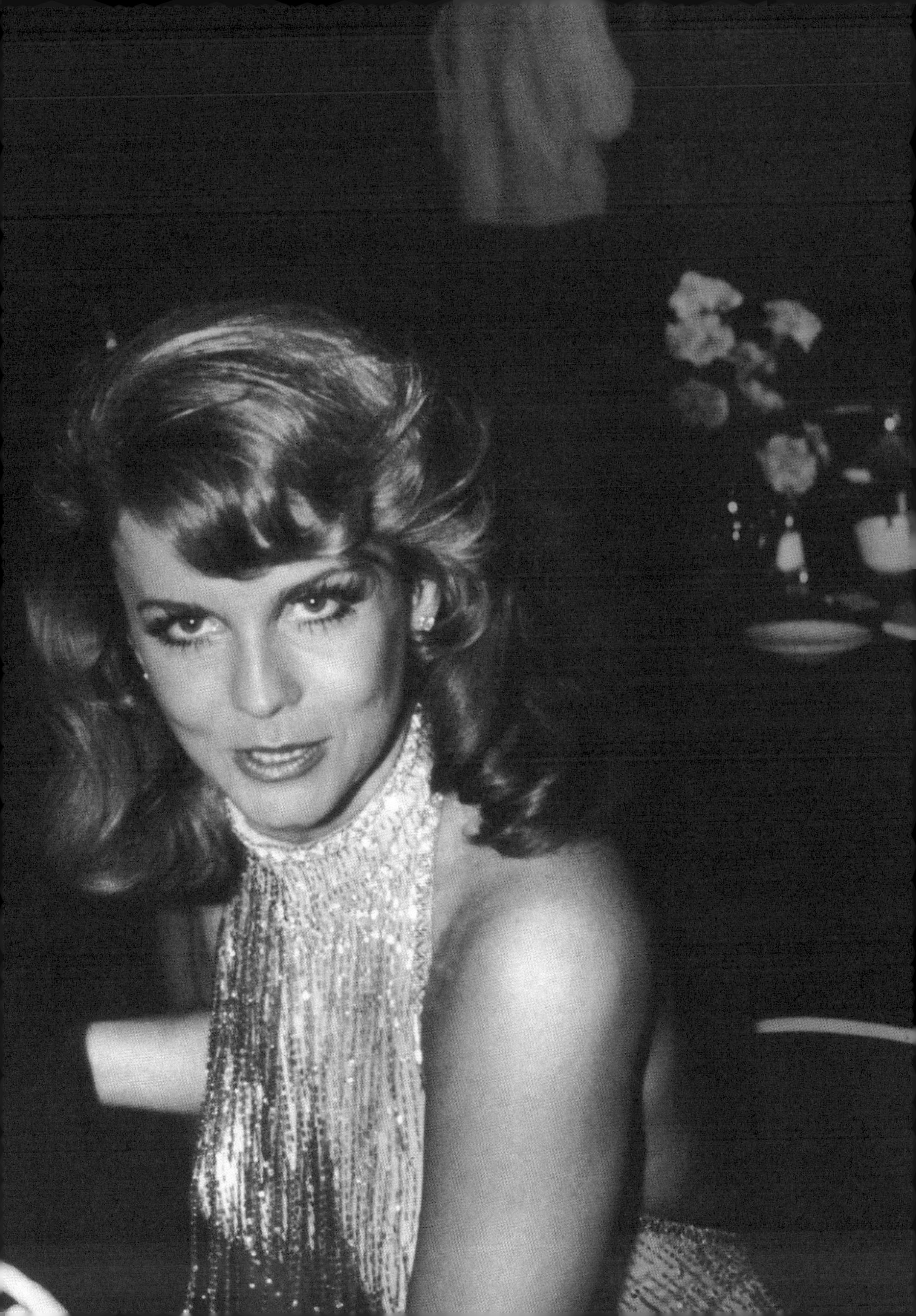

Stevie Wonder
1967, New York City

At the Americana Hotel.

———

Following double page

Mick Jagger and Stevie Wonder
1974, New York City

At a party honoring Stevie Wonder.

———

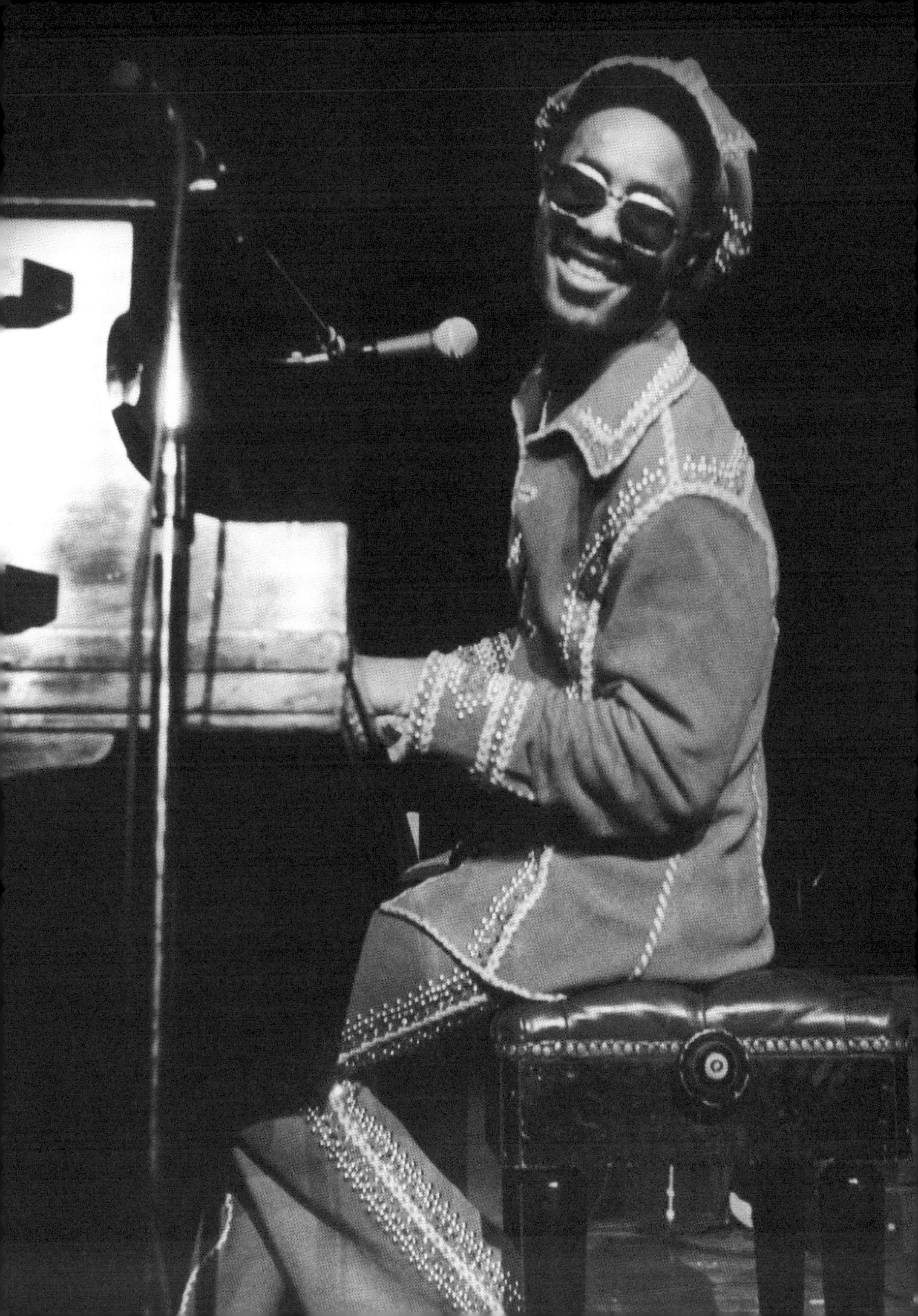

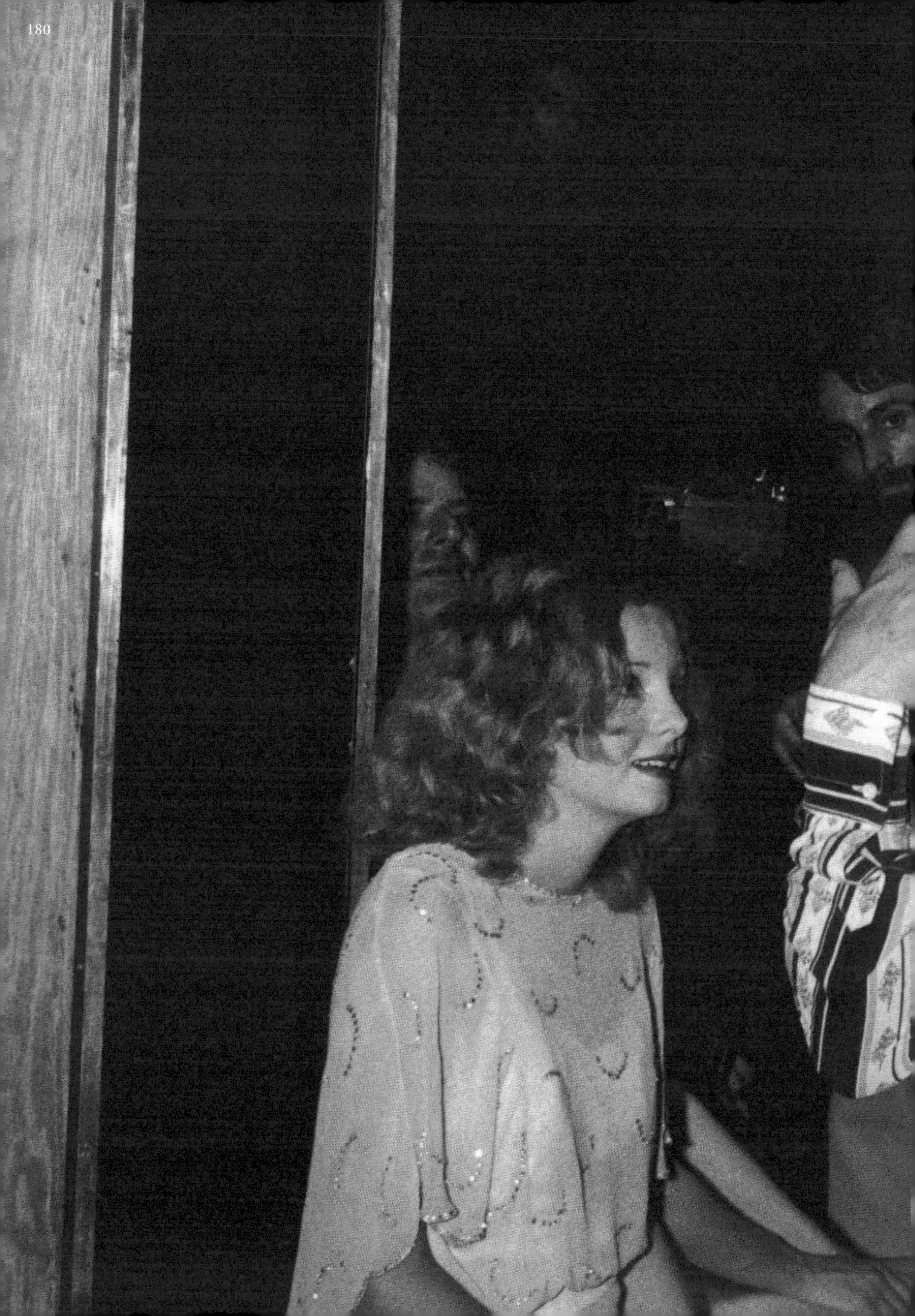

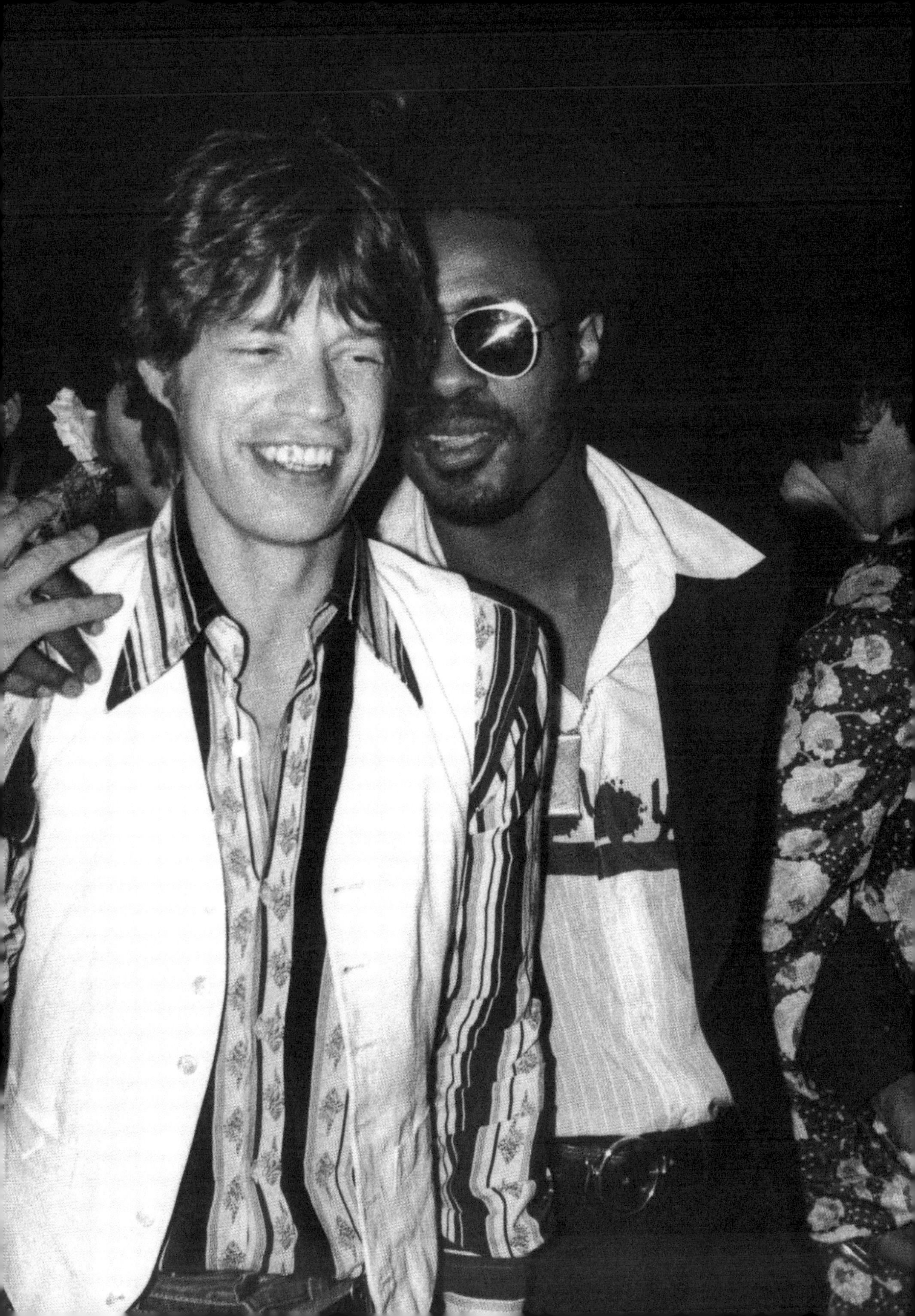

At the *Golden Plate Awards.*

Steven Spielberg
1986, Washington DC

At the *Golden Plate Awards.*
——

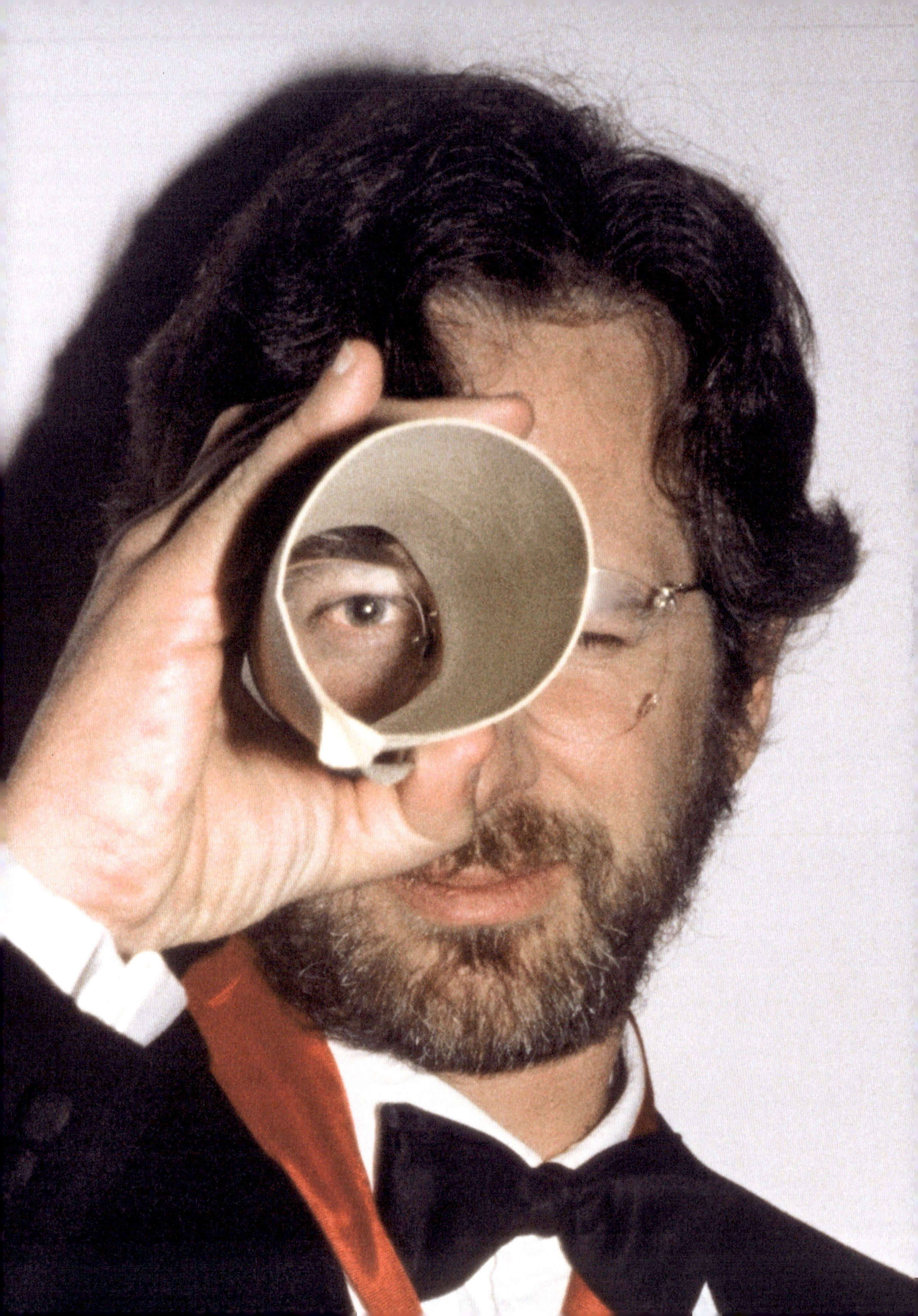

Farrah Fawcett
1977, Los Angeles Beach

On a horse filming a Fabergé shampoo
TV commercial.

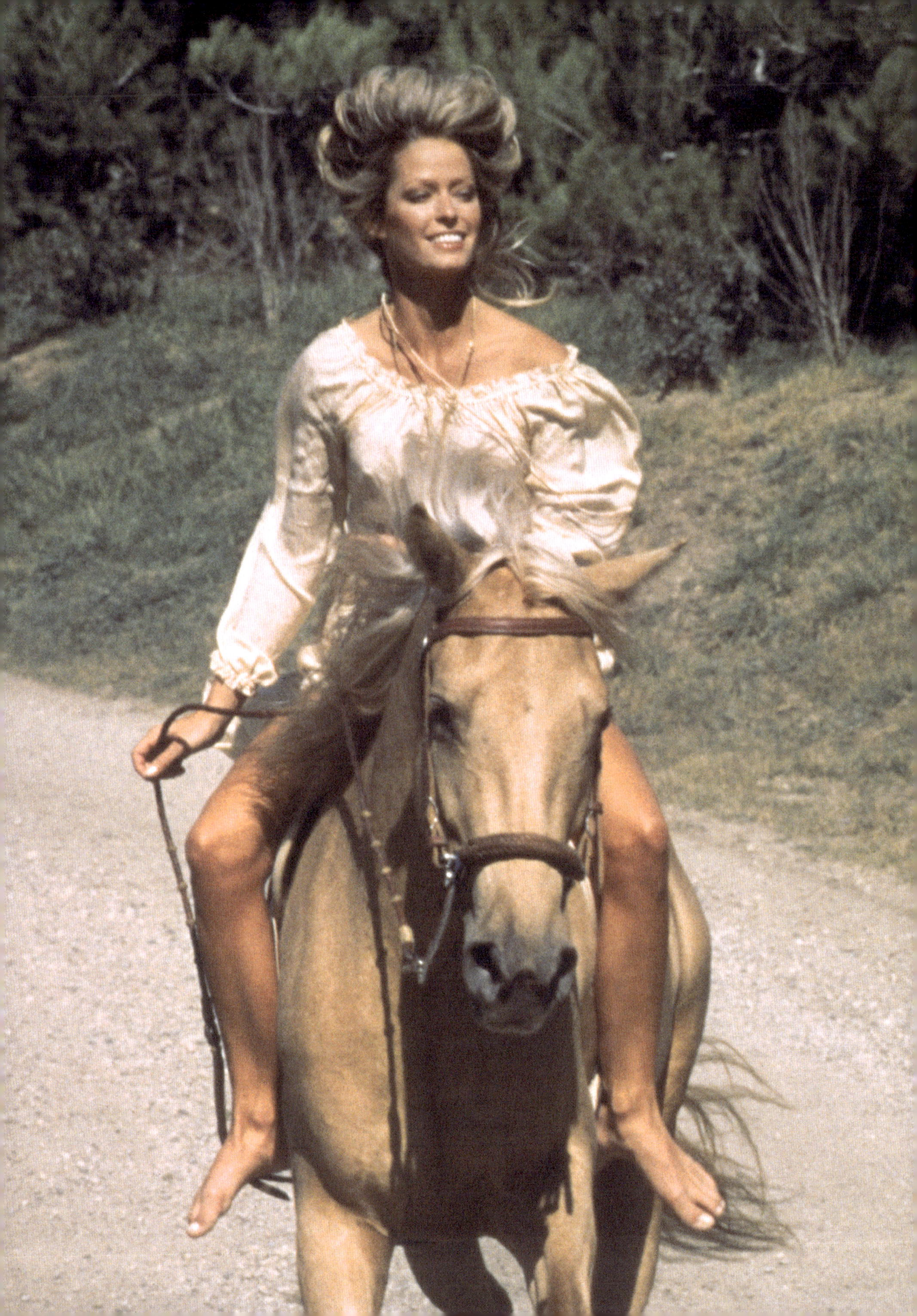

Sophia Loren
1970, New York City

Outside the Essex House in New York while
promoting her latest movie *Sunflower*.

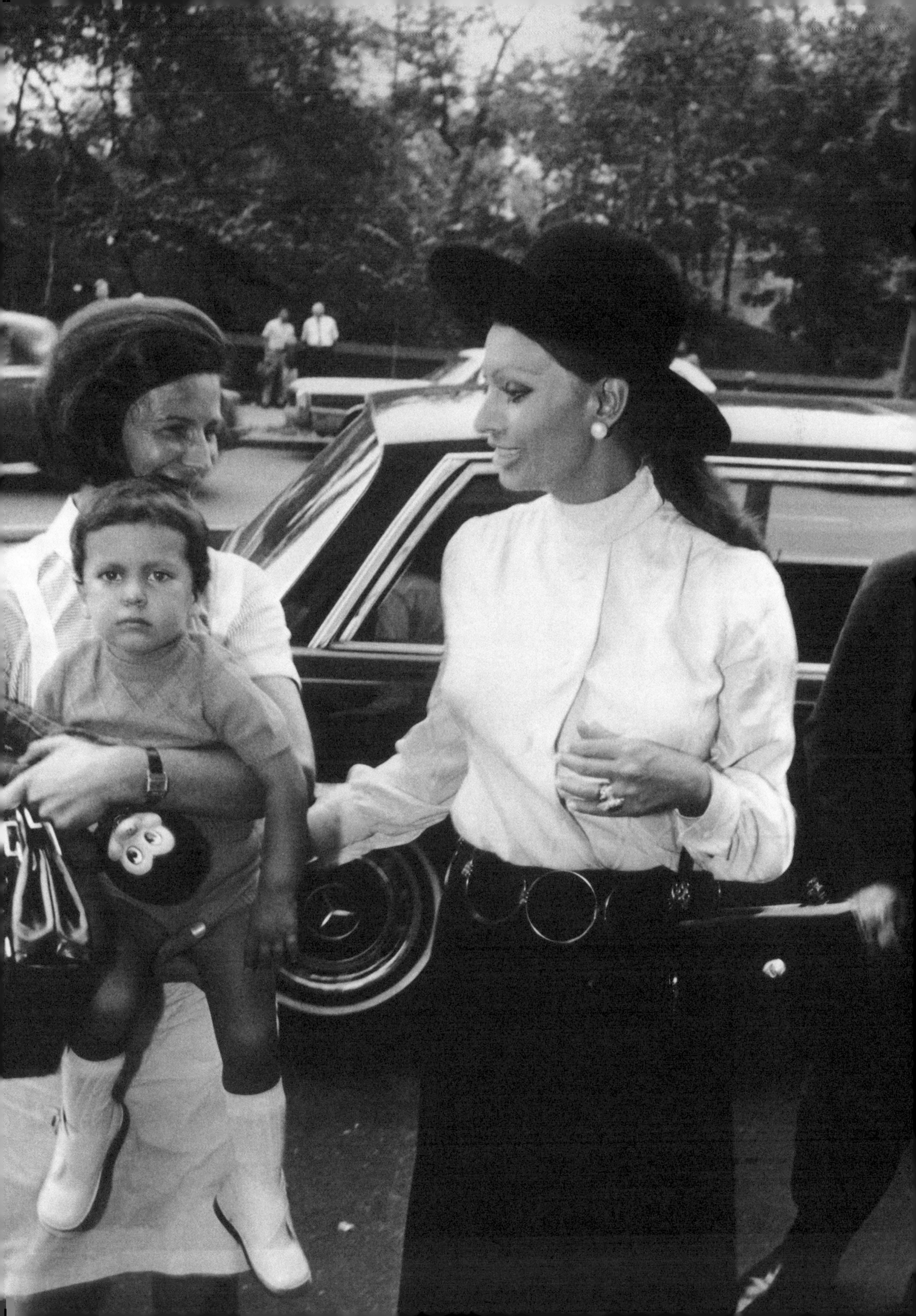

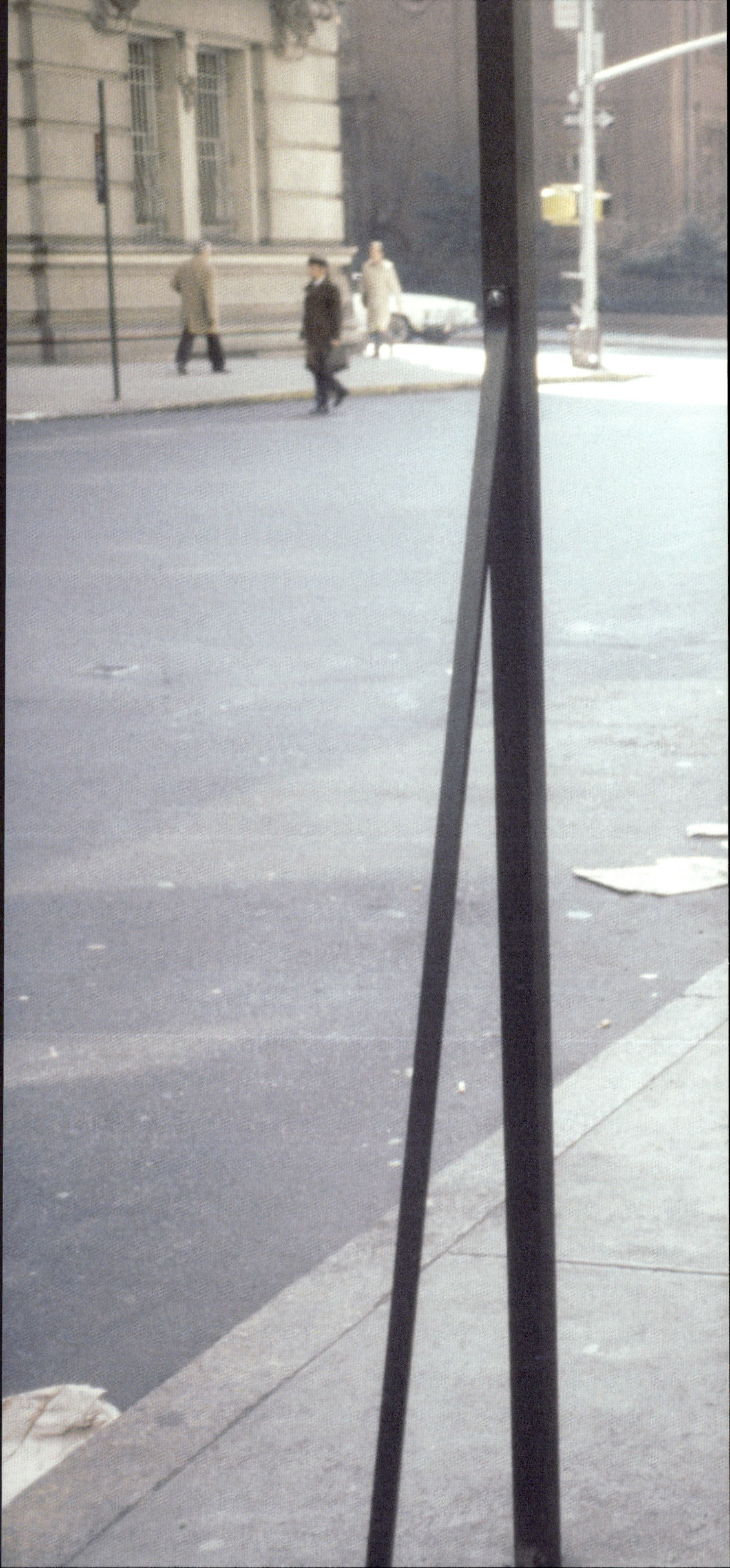

Rutger Hauer
1980, New York City

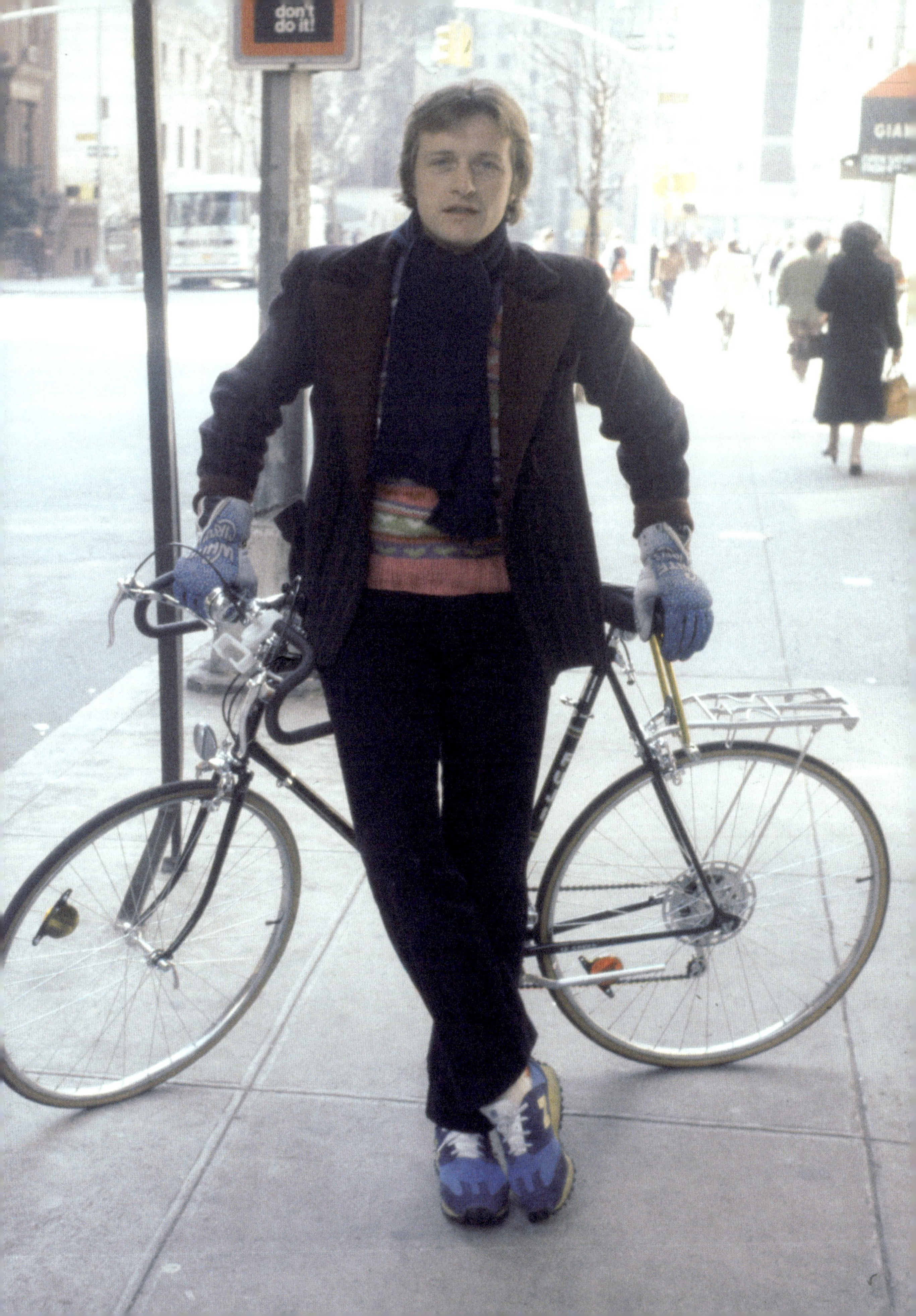

don't
do it!

Meryl Streep
1979, West Virgina

Filming *The Seduction of Joe Tynan*
with Alan Alda.
———

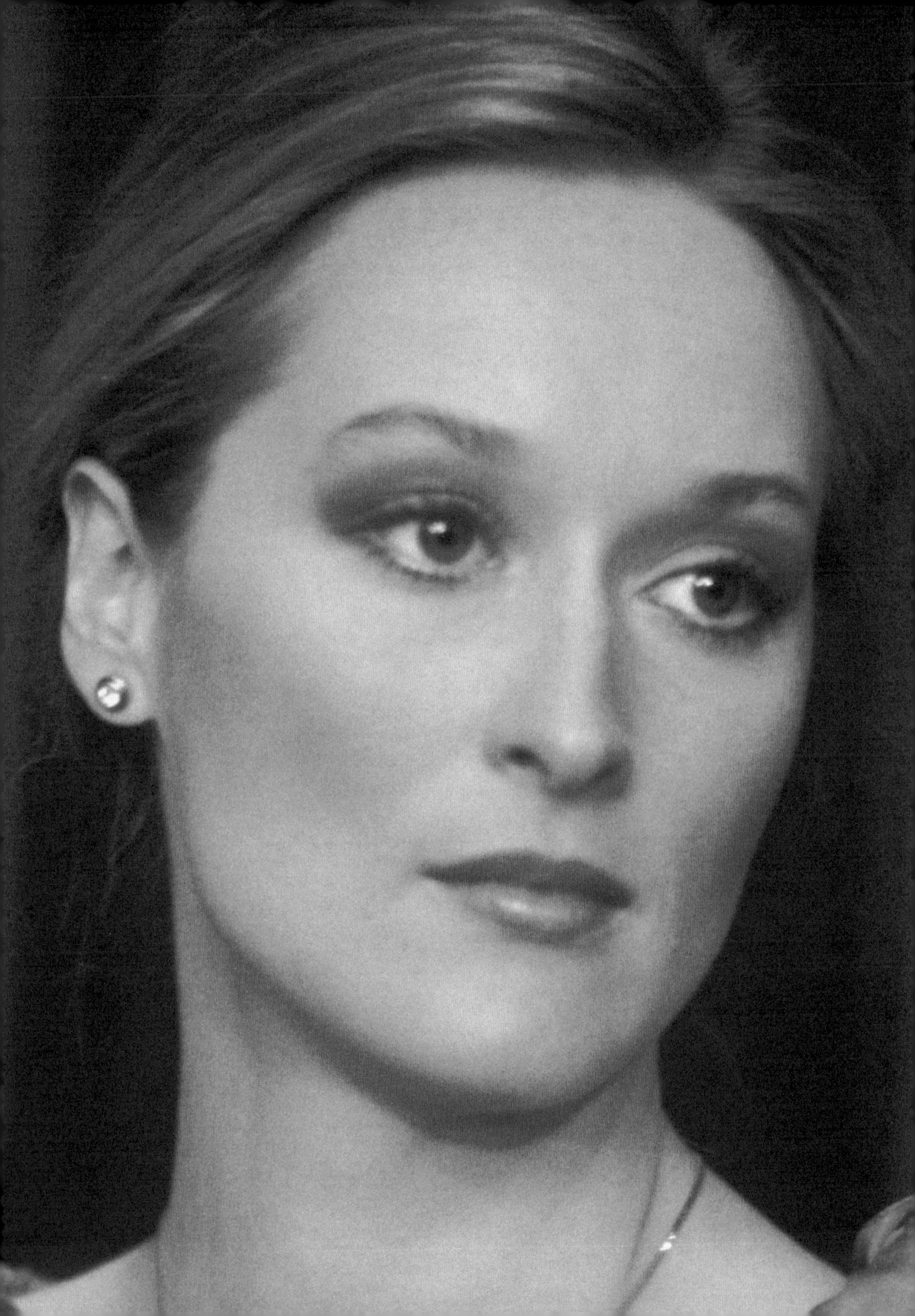

Sammy Davis Jr.
1966, New York City

In *Golden Boy*, backstage in dressing
room of the Majestic Theatre.

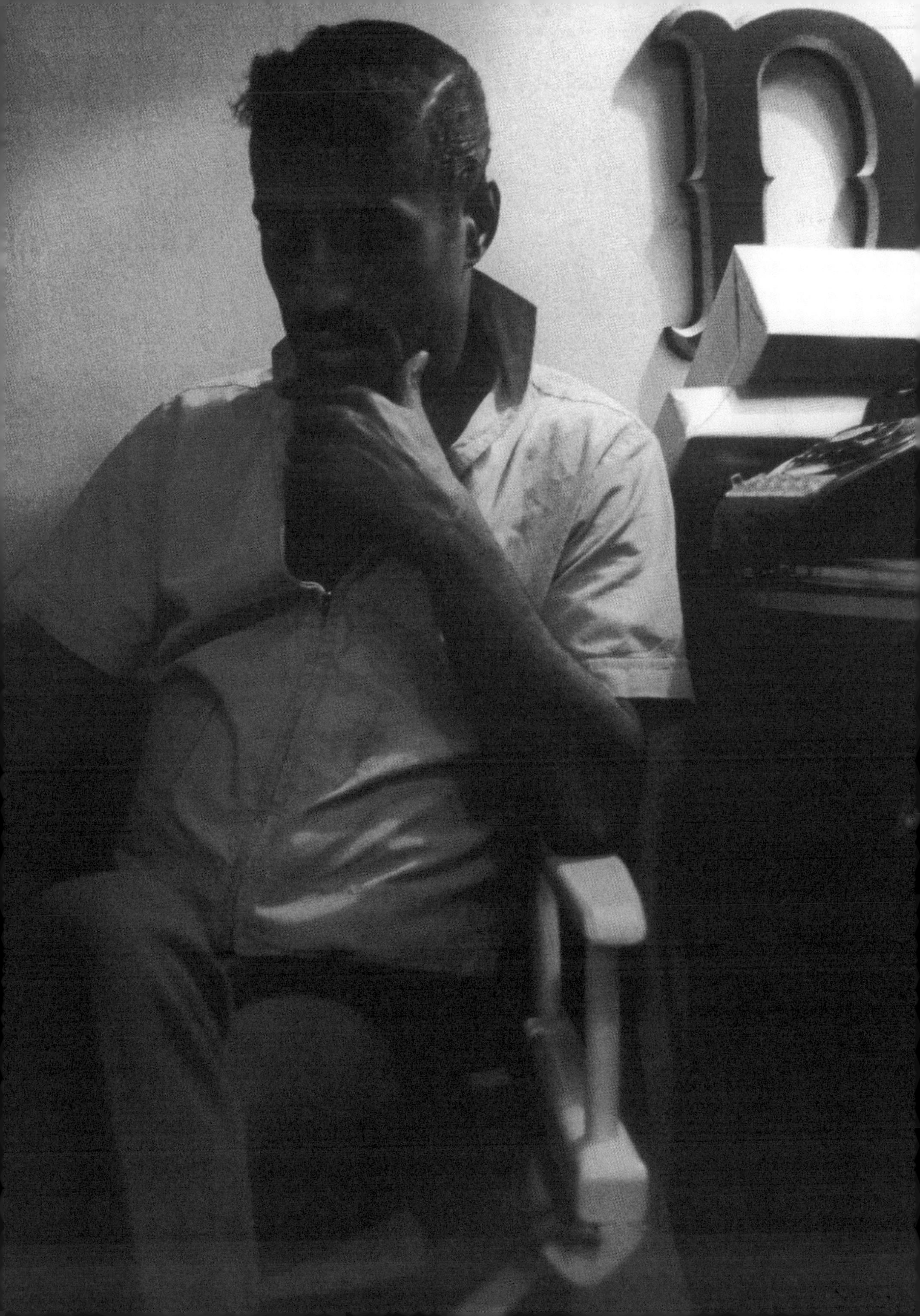

"She is not a subject I like to go after, but I need to."

I have many photographs of Jackie Kennedy Onassis in my files, but to stay current and relevant, I need to get some more pictures of her. She is not a subject I like to go after, but I need to.

Not some run-of- the- mill paparazzi shot, such as running in and out of a car or building-no, I need to get something more exclusive.

Jackie is very much a New York socialite. Her comings and goings are pretty well documented, almost predictable, so I have to make the moment count when she does show up at some event or benefit.

I'm at the New York State Theater at Lincoln Center in late June of 1975 where Rudolph Nureyev will be dancing at the American Ballet Theatre Gala. This a huge social event and after all the guests have arrived, the rumors start flying that Jackie

Onassis is in the building. However, not through the front doors. No one has seen her arrive. If she is here, she is staying well in the background. In fact, she is in the Green Room with no access for anyone.

But readiness and patience are my friends again and when the door opens ever so slightly to let a waiter in, I see my moment. No time to think, and instinct takes over. But did I catch what I was seeing through my viewfinder?

Later that night I bring my color film to the lab to have it developed. I can't even wait to pick it up the next morning, so I just stay there for hours. With anticipation I open the box with the photos. There is my shot of a lifetime. Jackie with an elegant cigarette holder in her mouth smoking a cigarette!
———

Jackie Kennedy Onassis
1975, New York City

In the Greenroom at the American
Ballet Theater at Lincoln Center.

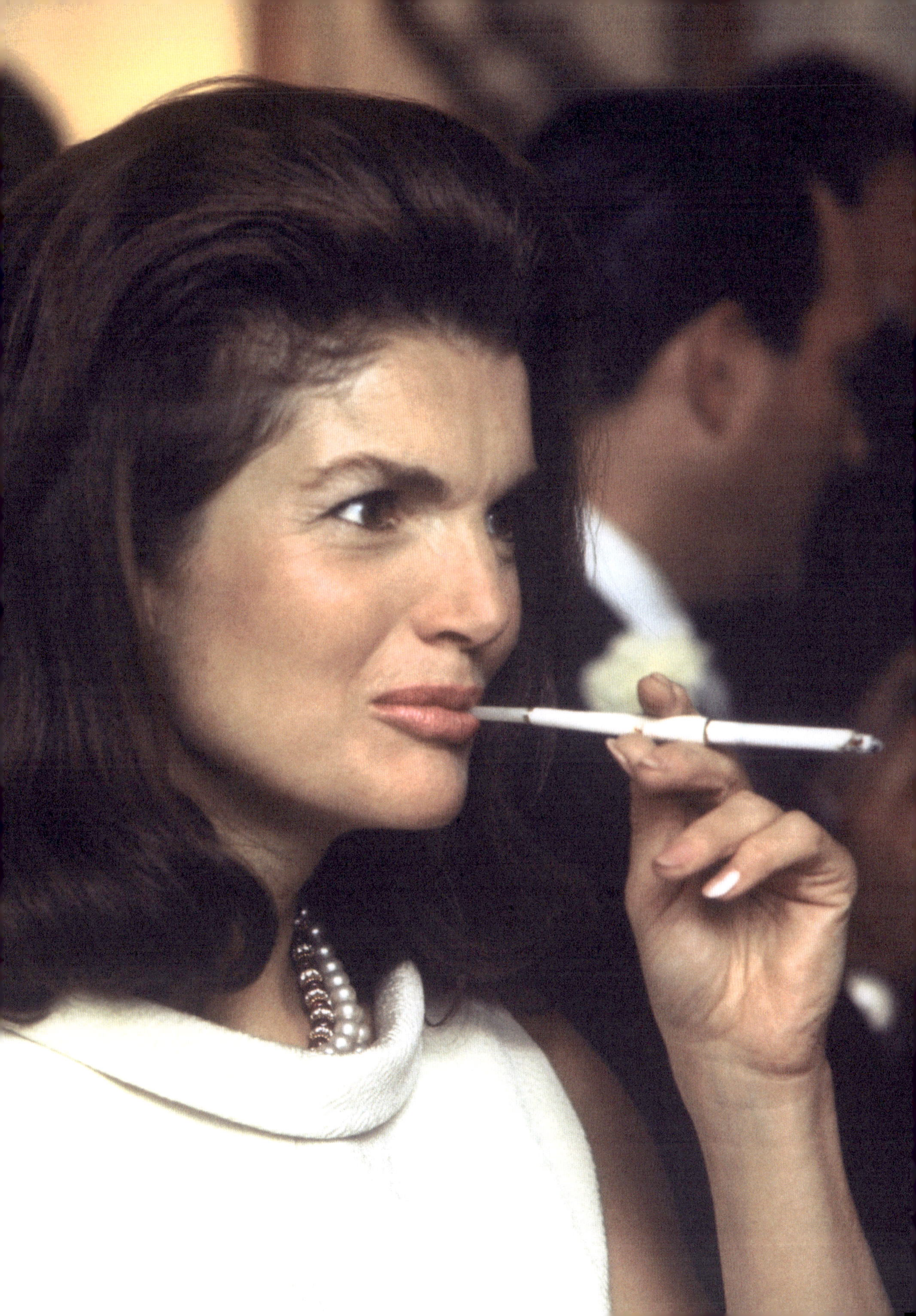

1978, New York City

Jackie Kennedy Onassis
1978, New York City

At a Broadway show.

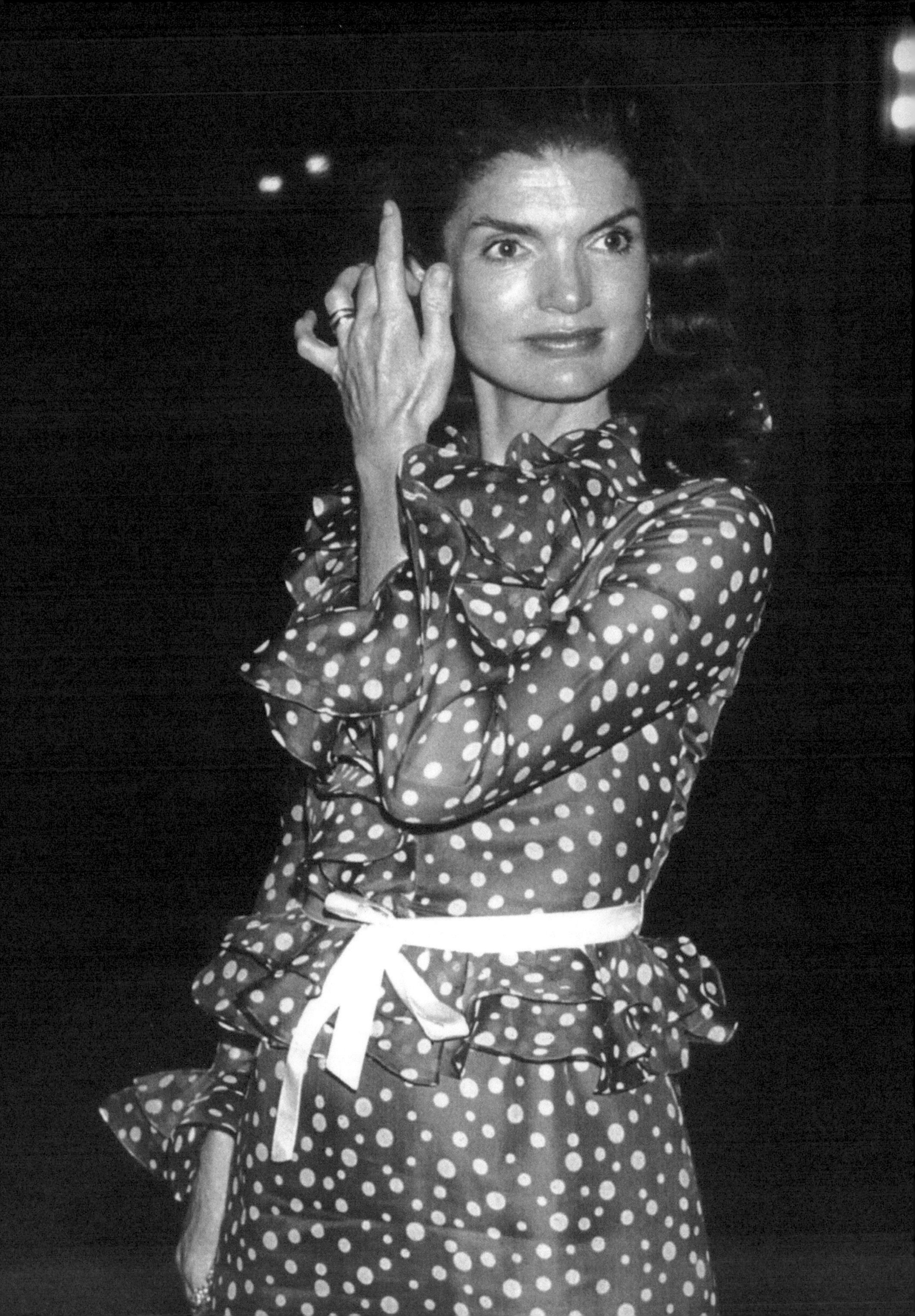

Robert Redford
1977, Arnhem (The Netherlands)

Playing football on the movie set of
A Bridge Too Far.
——

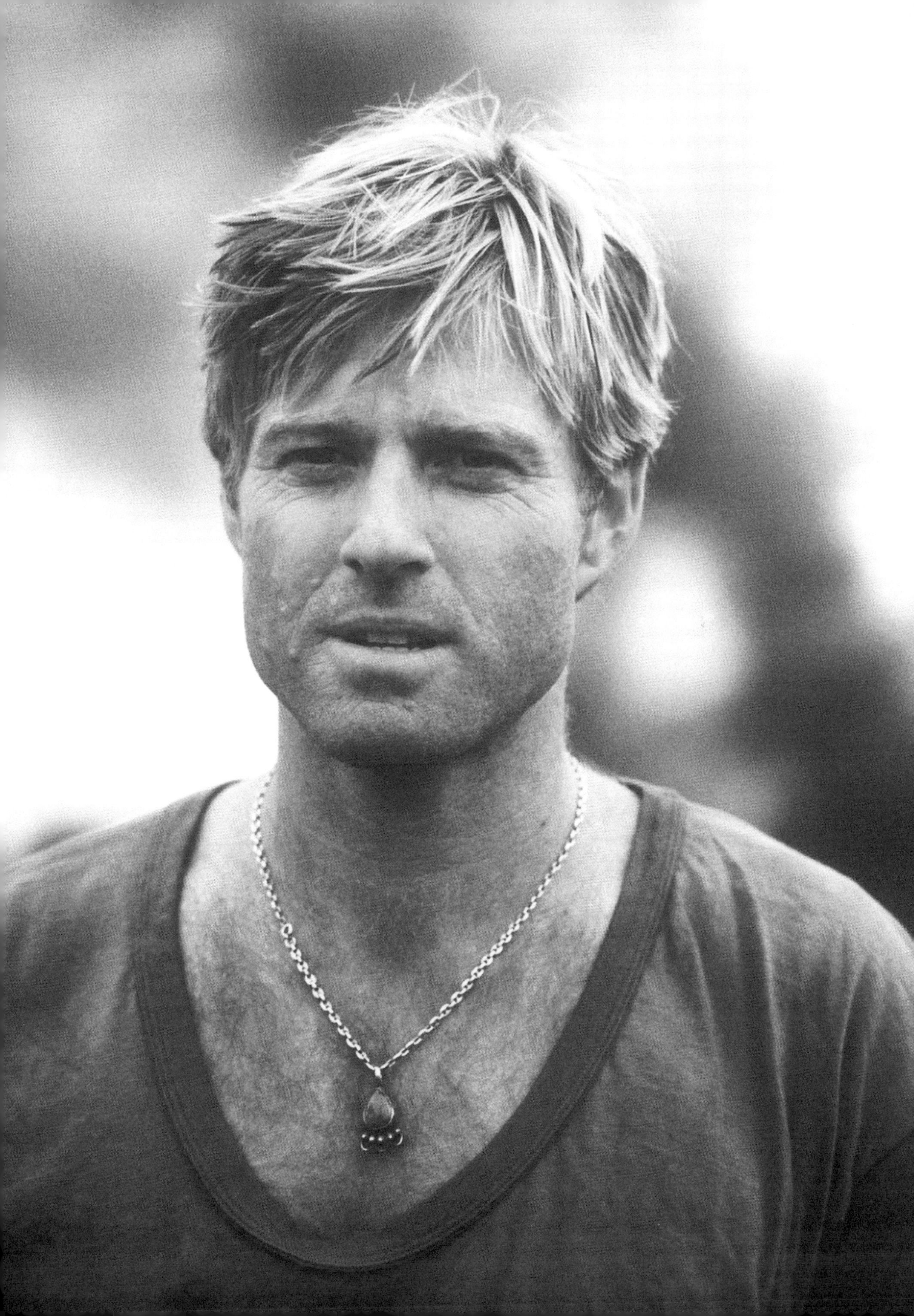

Jim Morrison and Pamela Courson
1968, New York City

At the Cheetah Club.

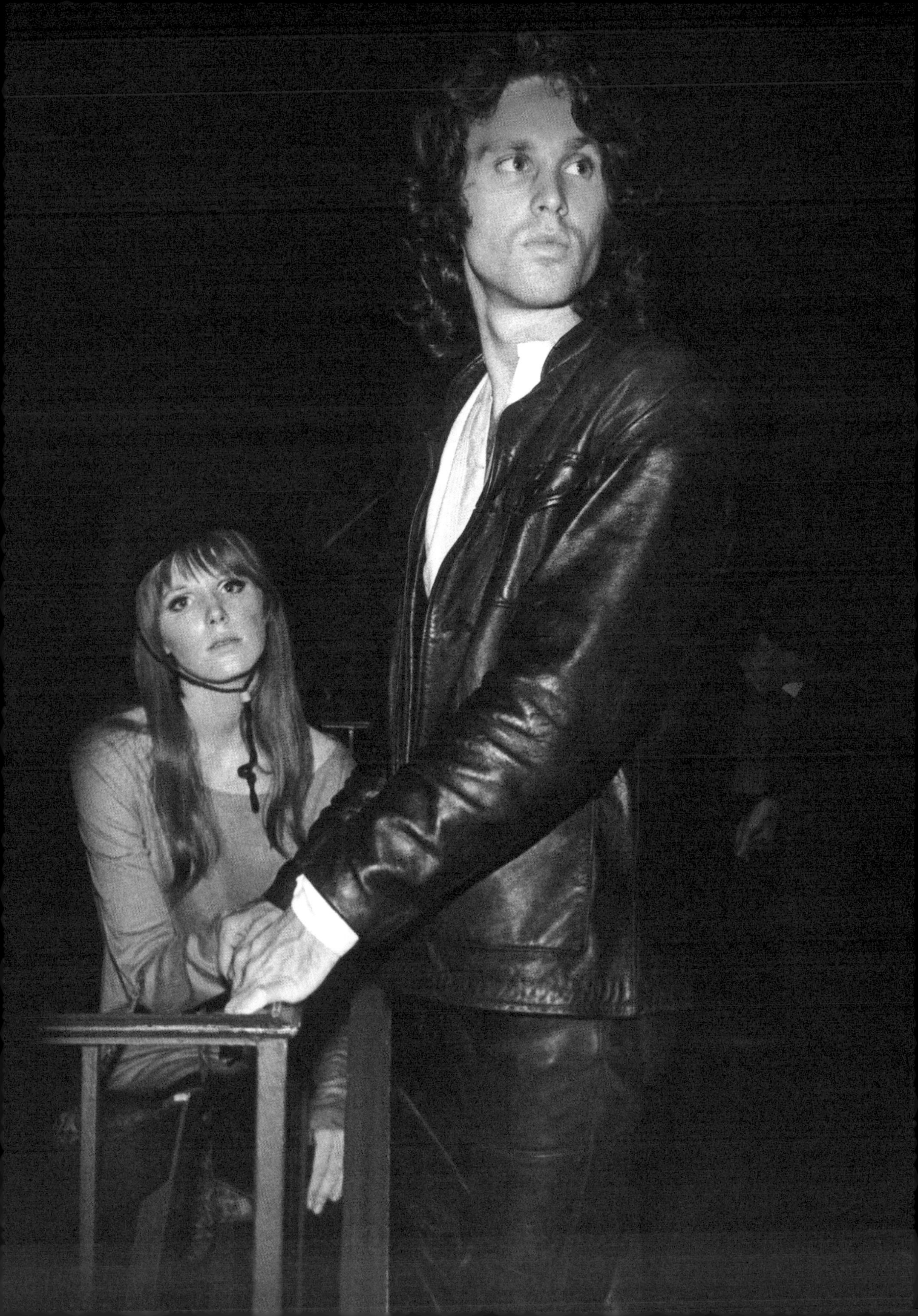

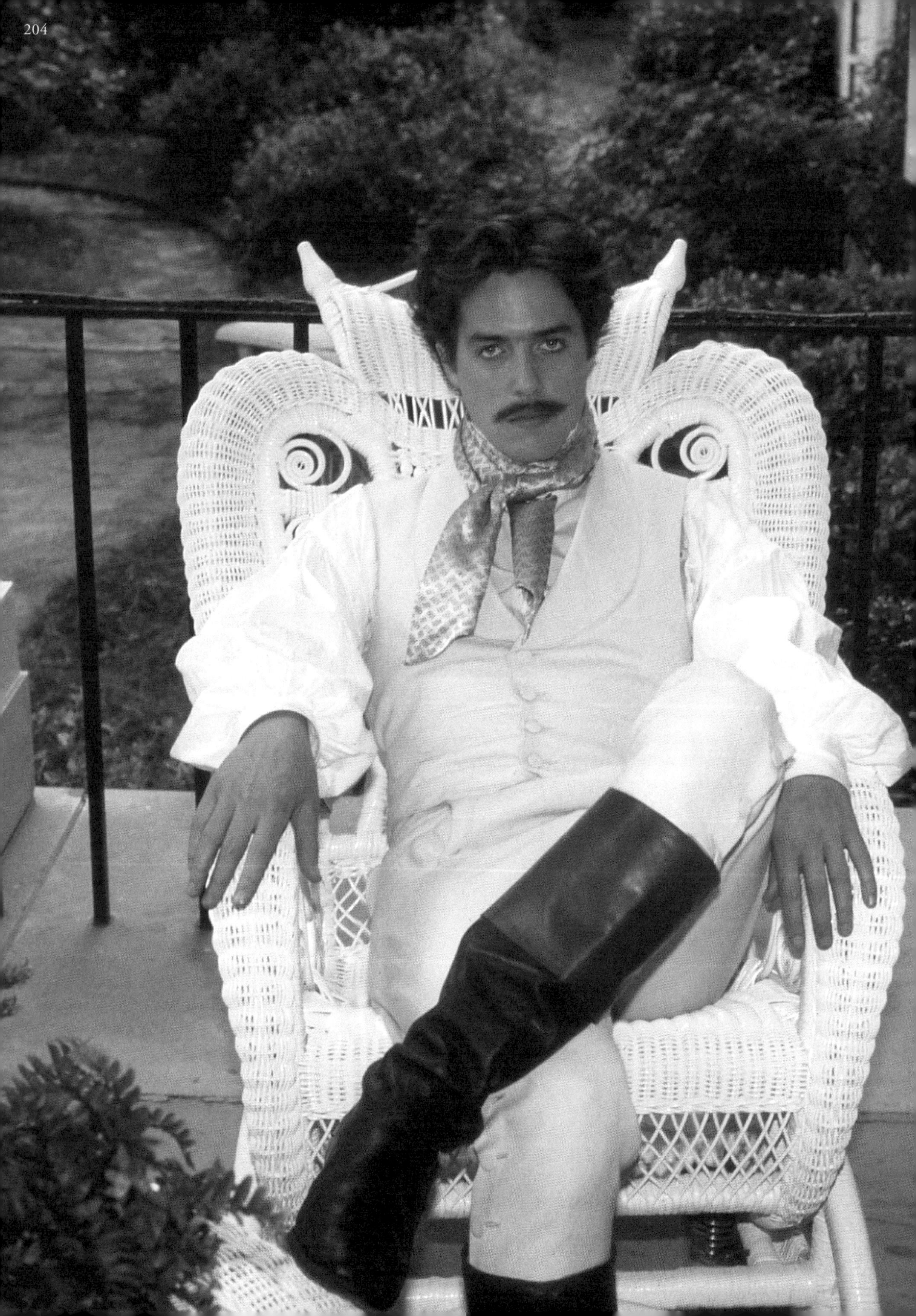

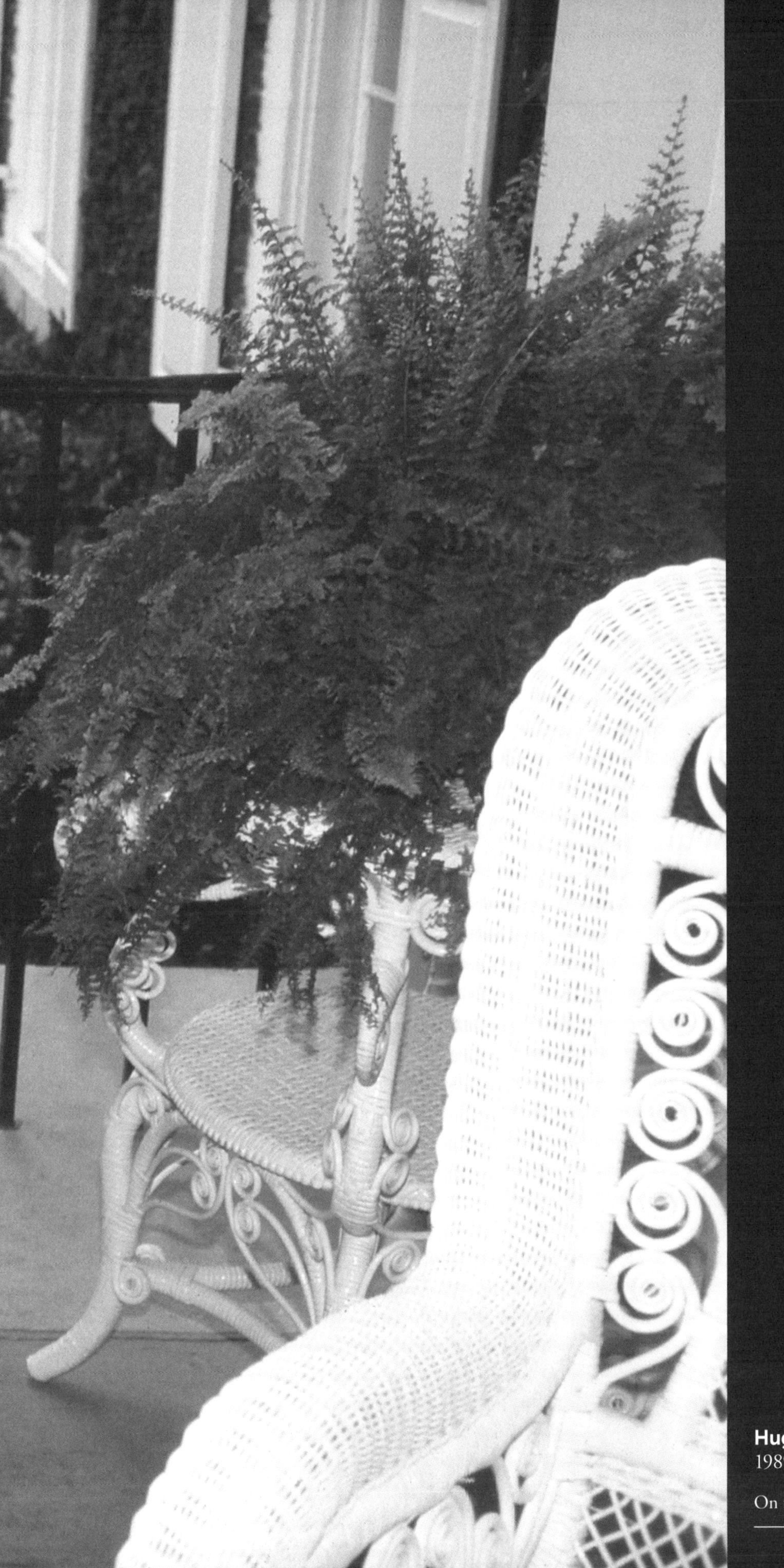

Hugh Grant
1989, Charleston (South Carolina)

On the movie set of *Champagne Charlie*

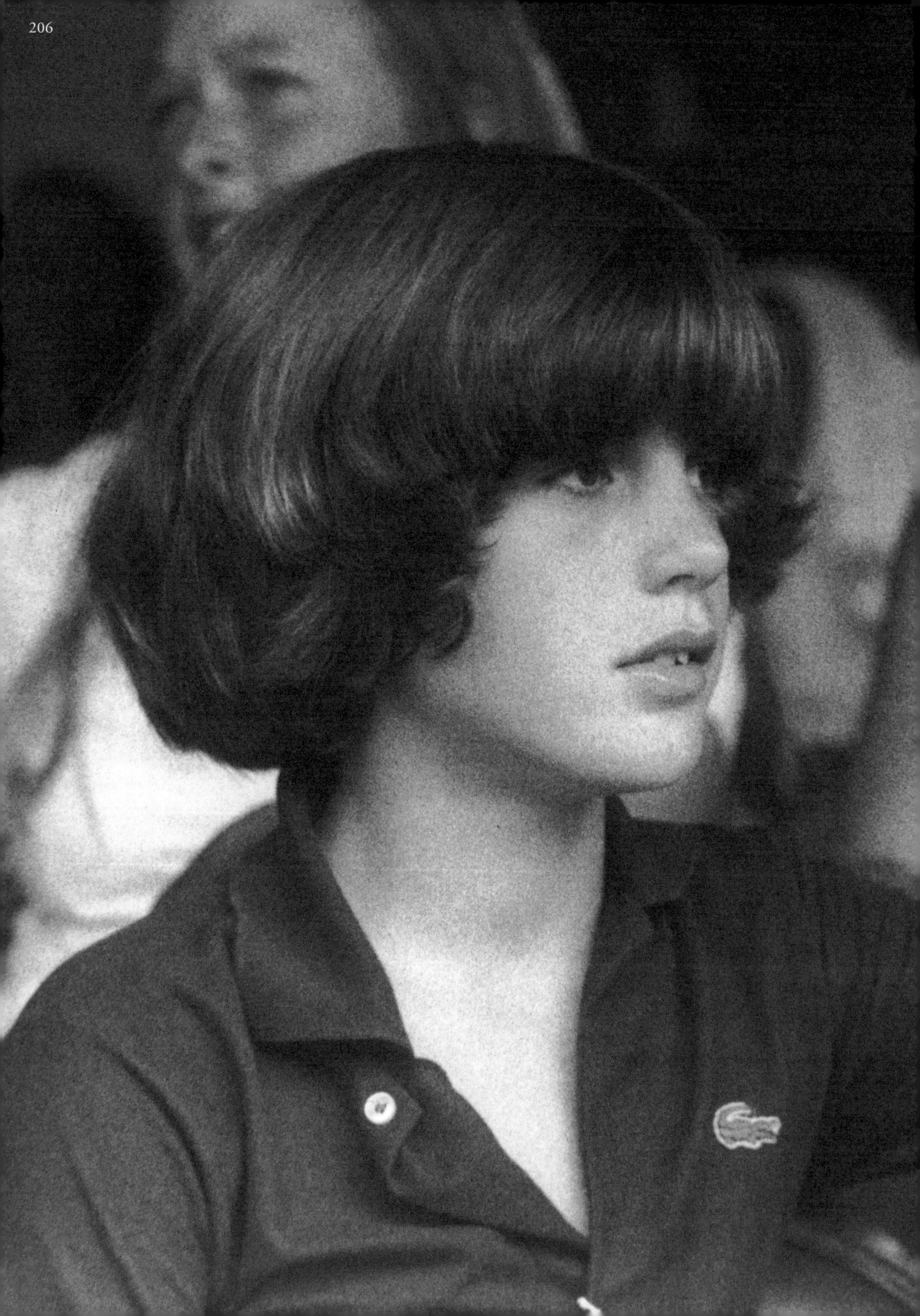

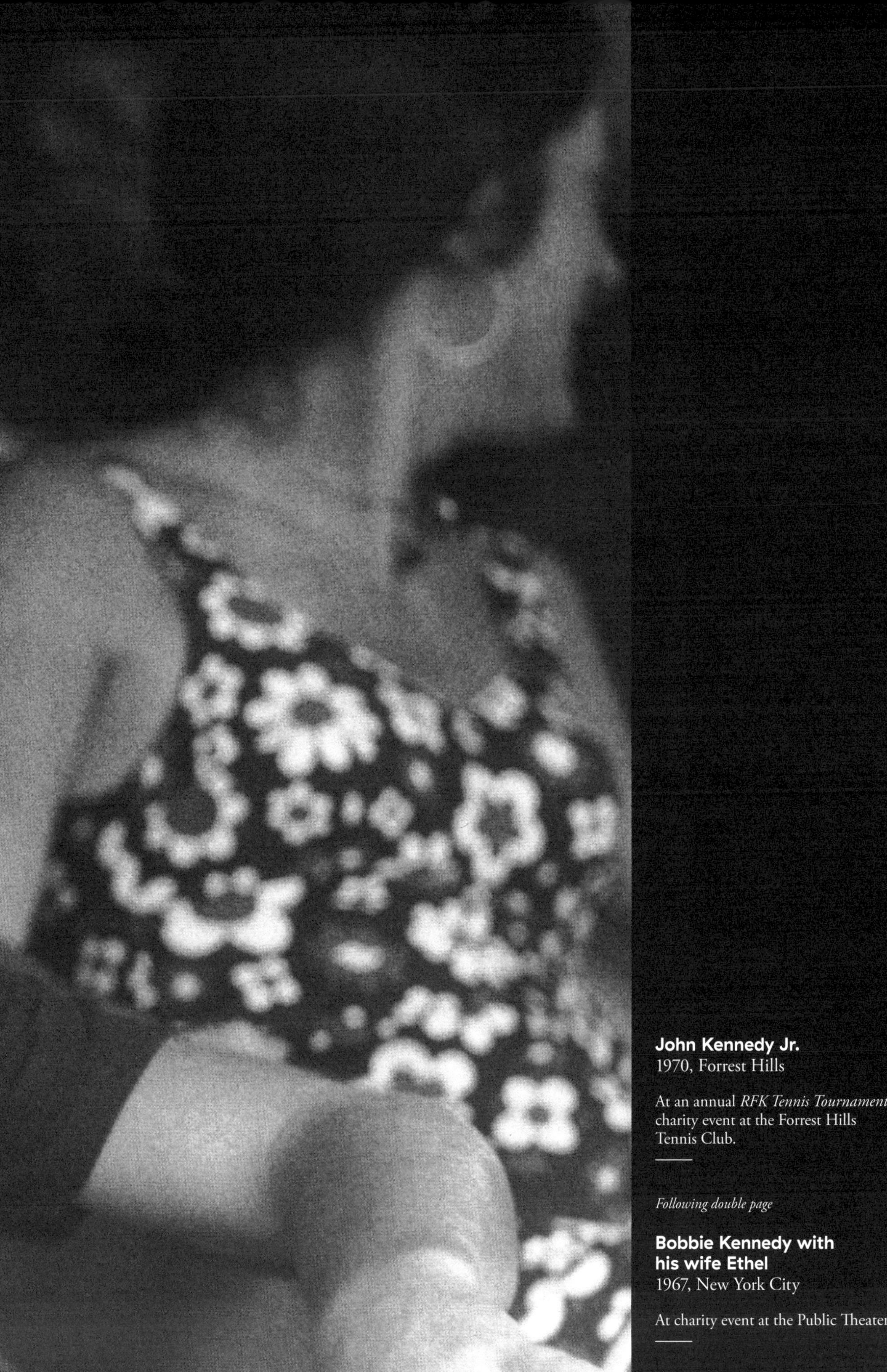

John Kennedy Jr.
1970, Forrest Hills

At an annual *RFK Tennis Tournament*
charity event at the Forrest Hills
Tennis Club.

———

Following double page

**Bobbie Kennedy with
his wife Ethel**
1967, New York City

At charity event at the Public Theater.

———

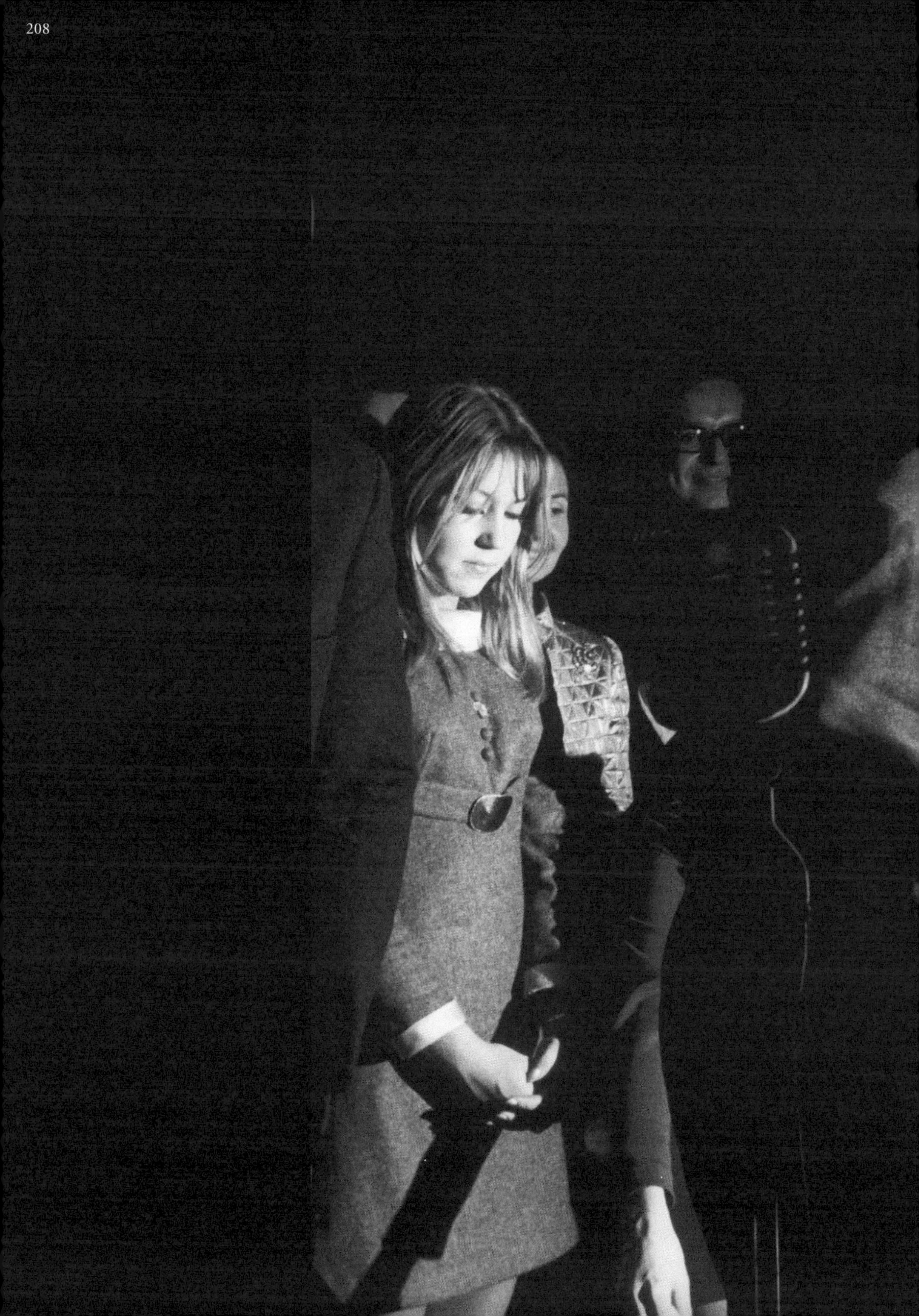

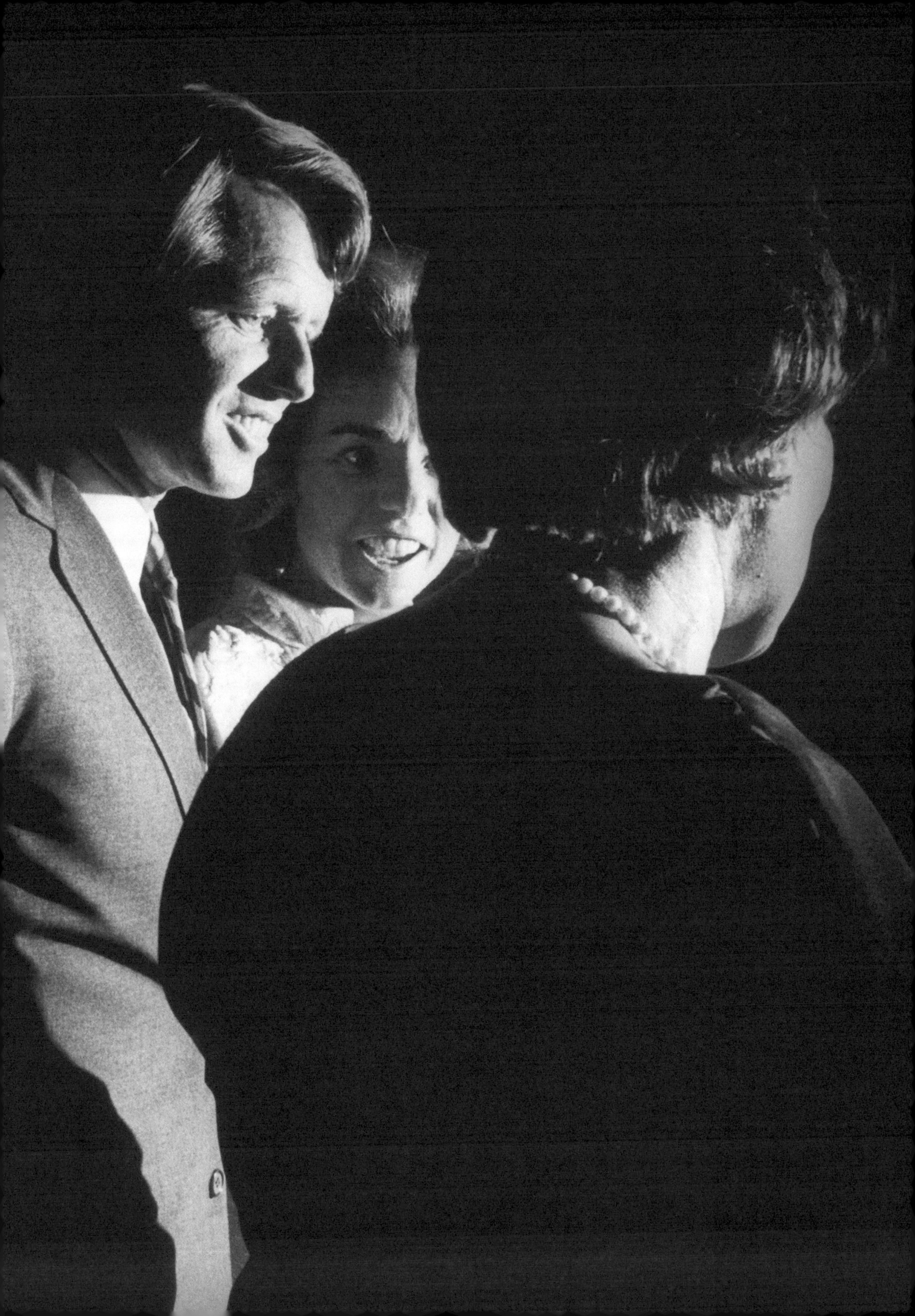

Richard Nixon
1968, New York City

At the Pierre Hotel before returning to
Washington D.C to be sworn in as president.
———

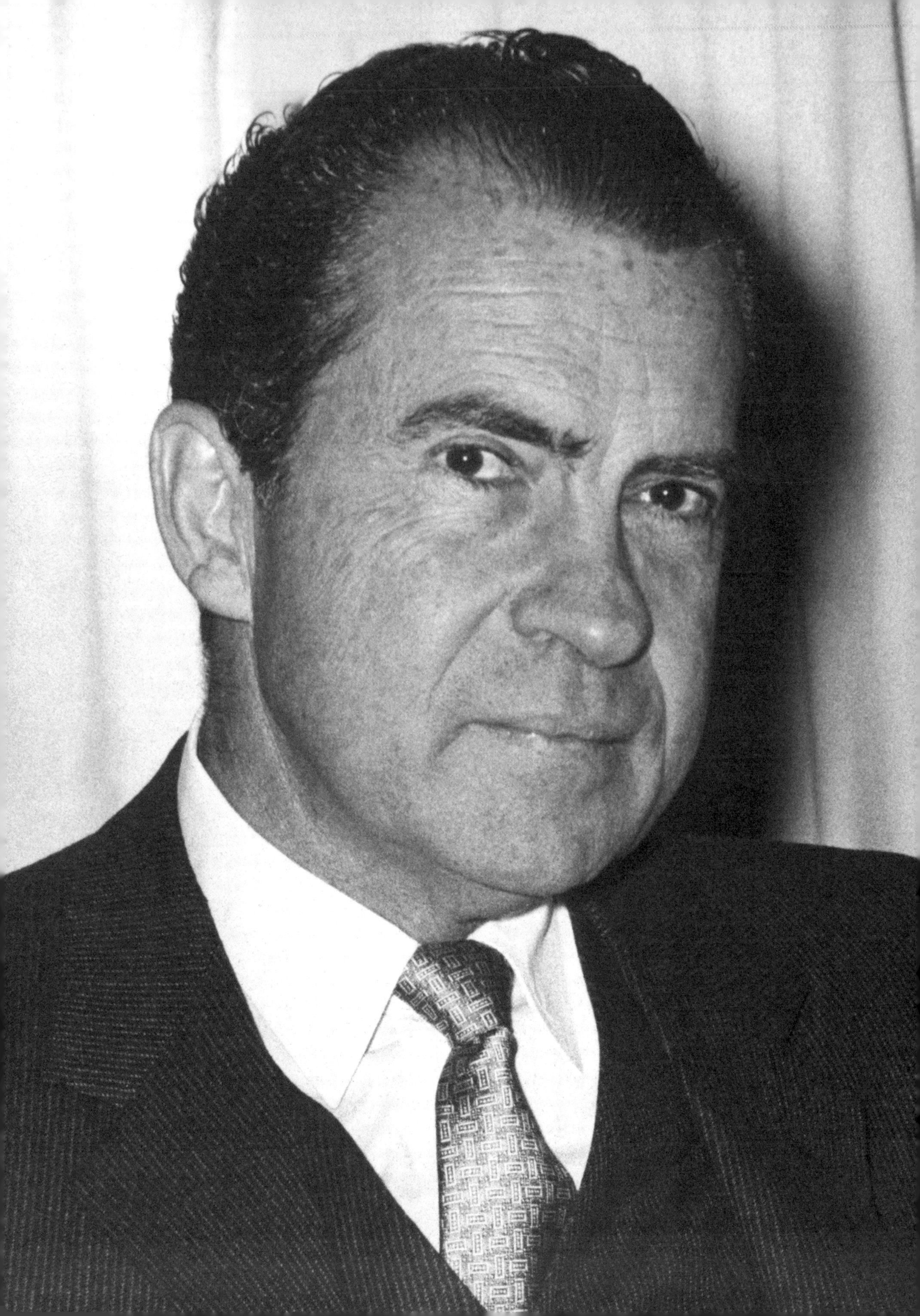

Paul McCartney
1965, New York City

At a press conference at
the Warwick Hotel.
———

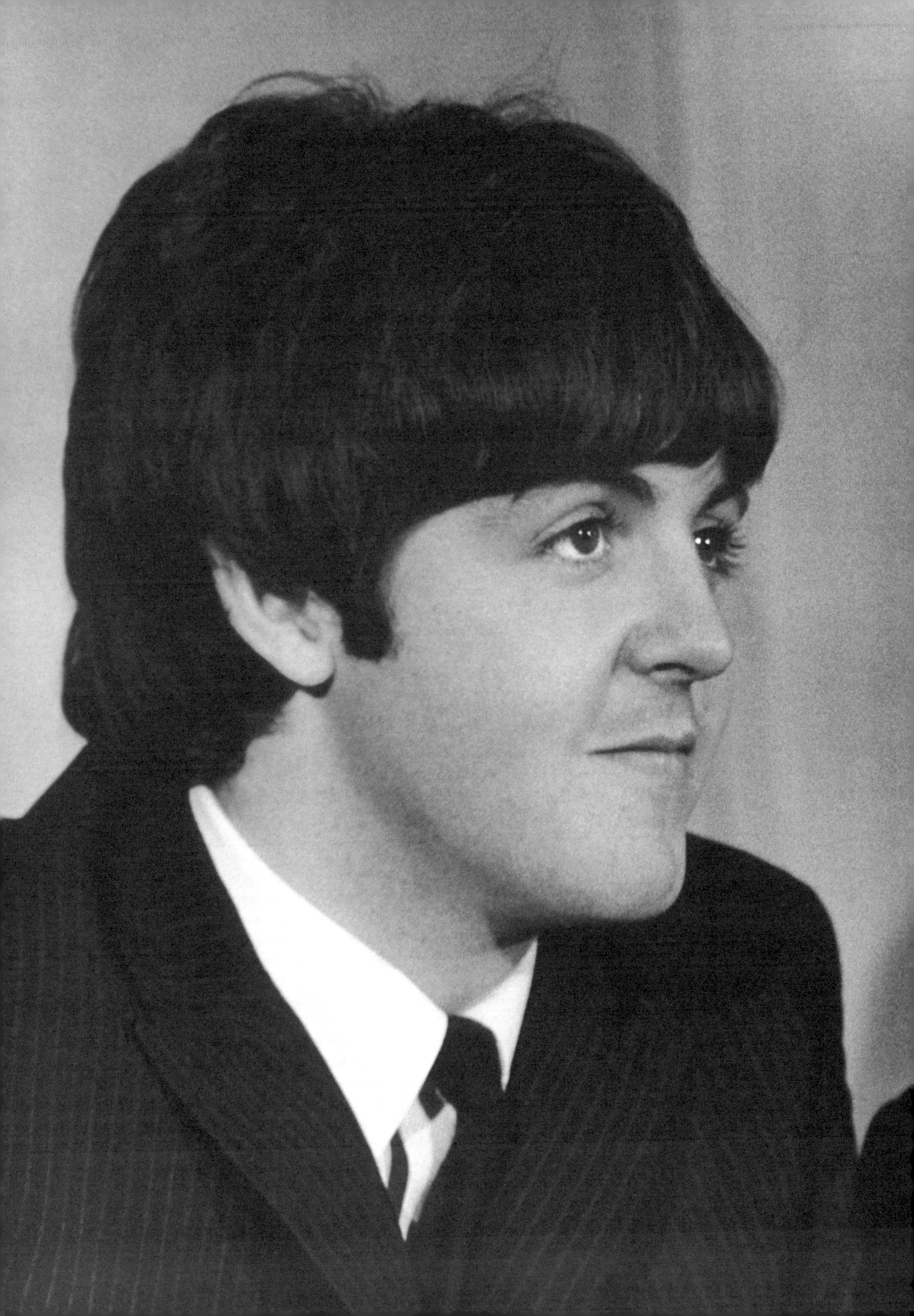

On the movie set of *Rosemary's Baby*.

Mia Farrow
1968, New York City

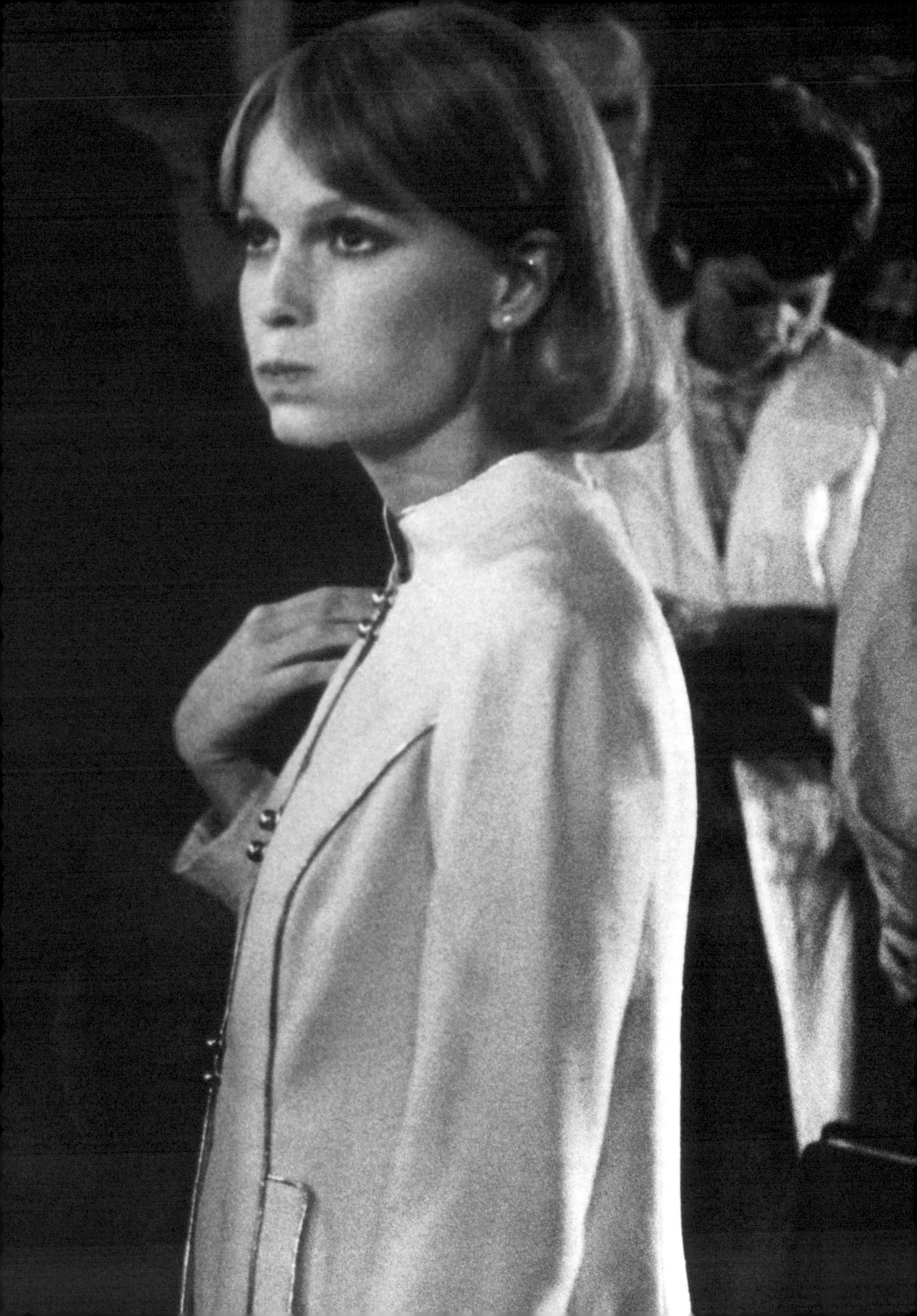

Jack Nicholson
1970, New York City

After winning an award for *Easy Rider*
at the *New York Film Critics Circle Awards*,
at Sardi's.

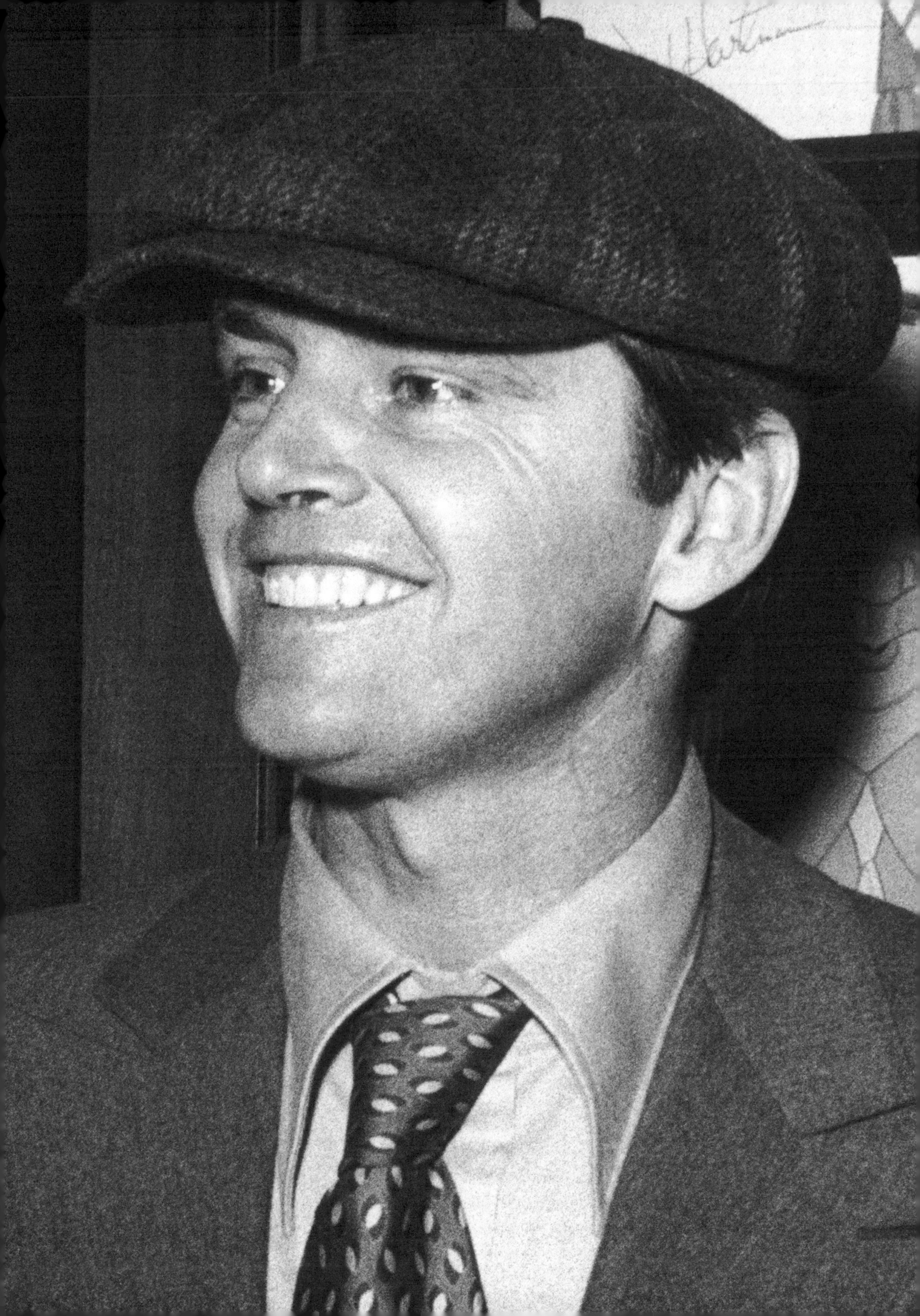

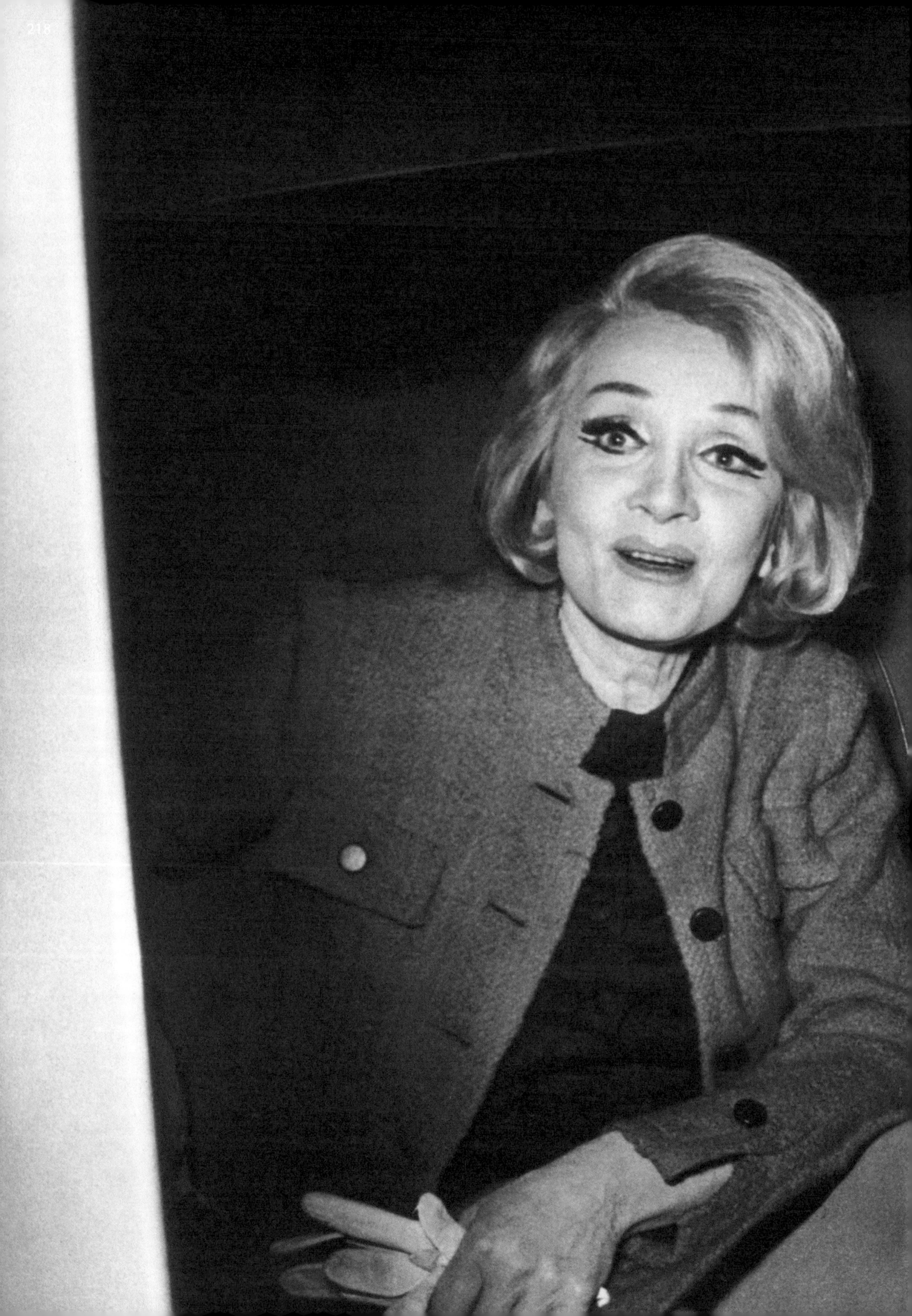

Marlene Dietrich
1969, New York City

Going to a Broadway Theater

Michael Jackson
1978, New York City

At *Studio 54*.

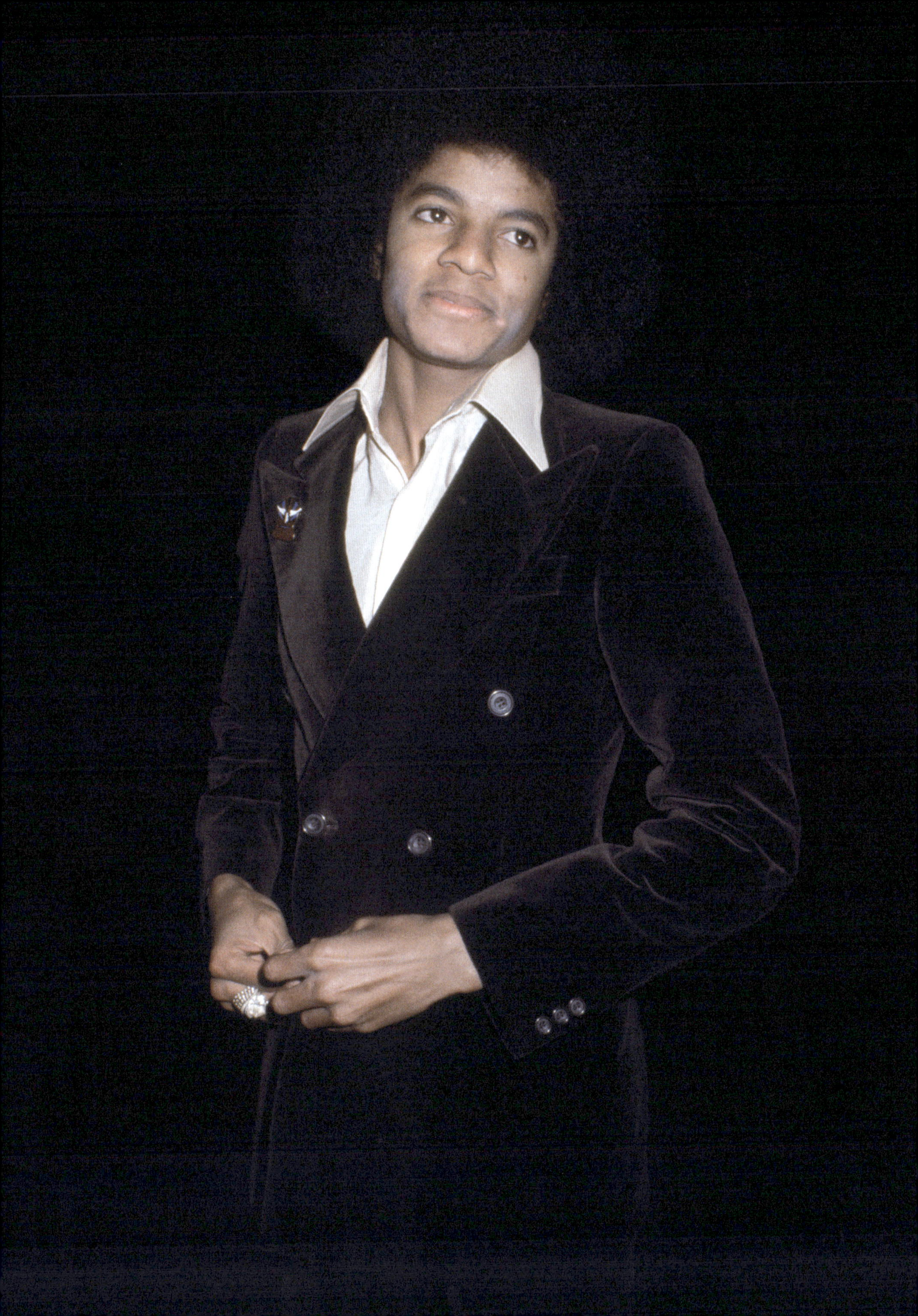

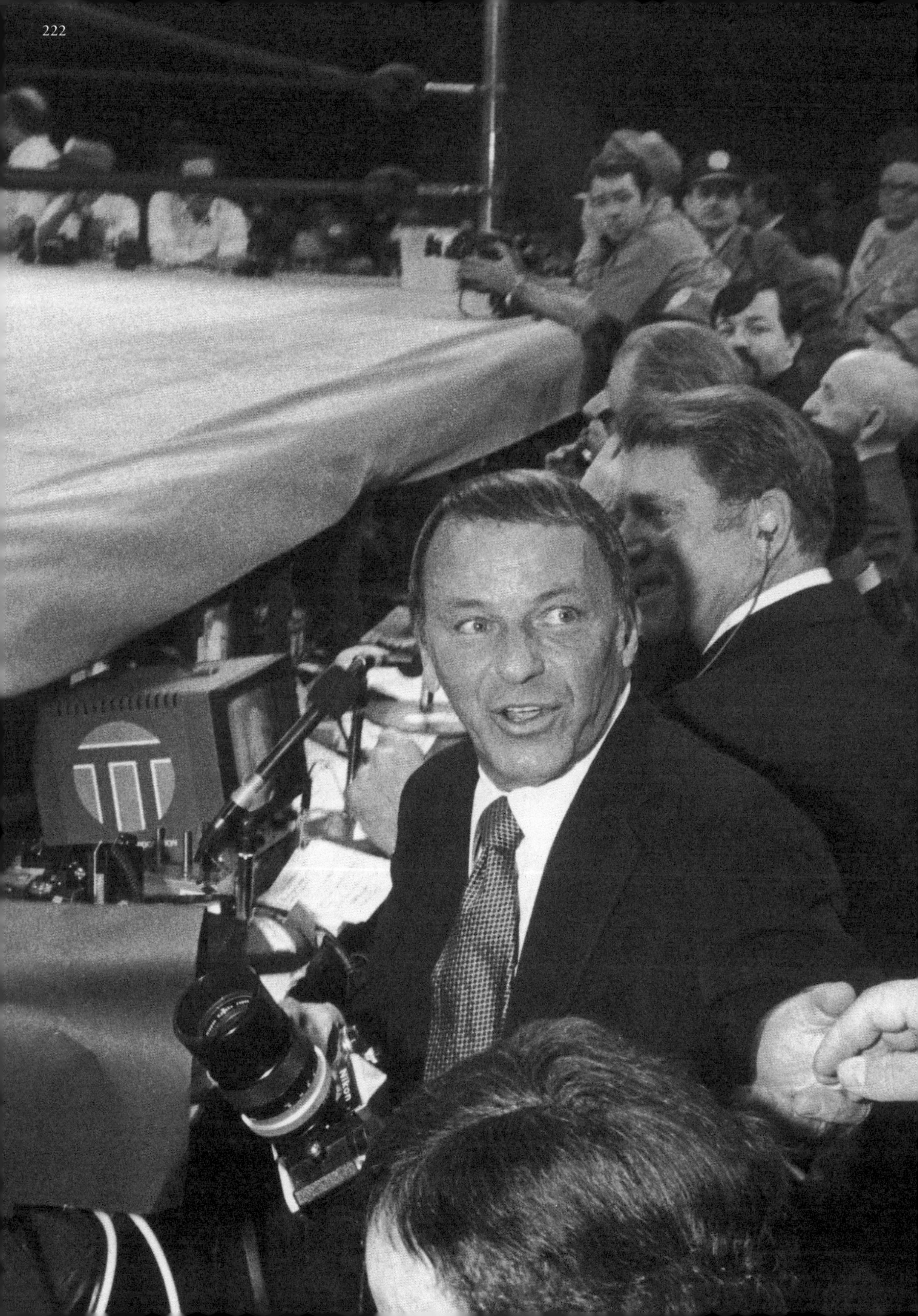

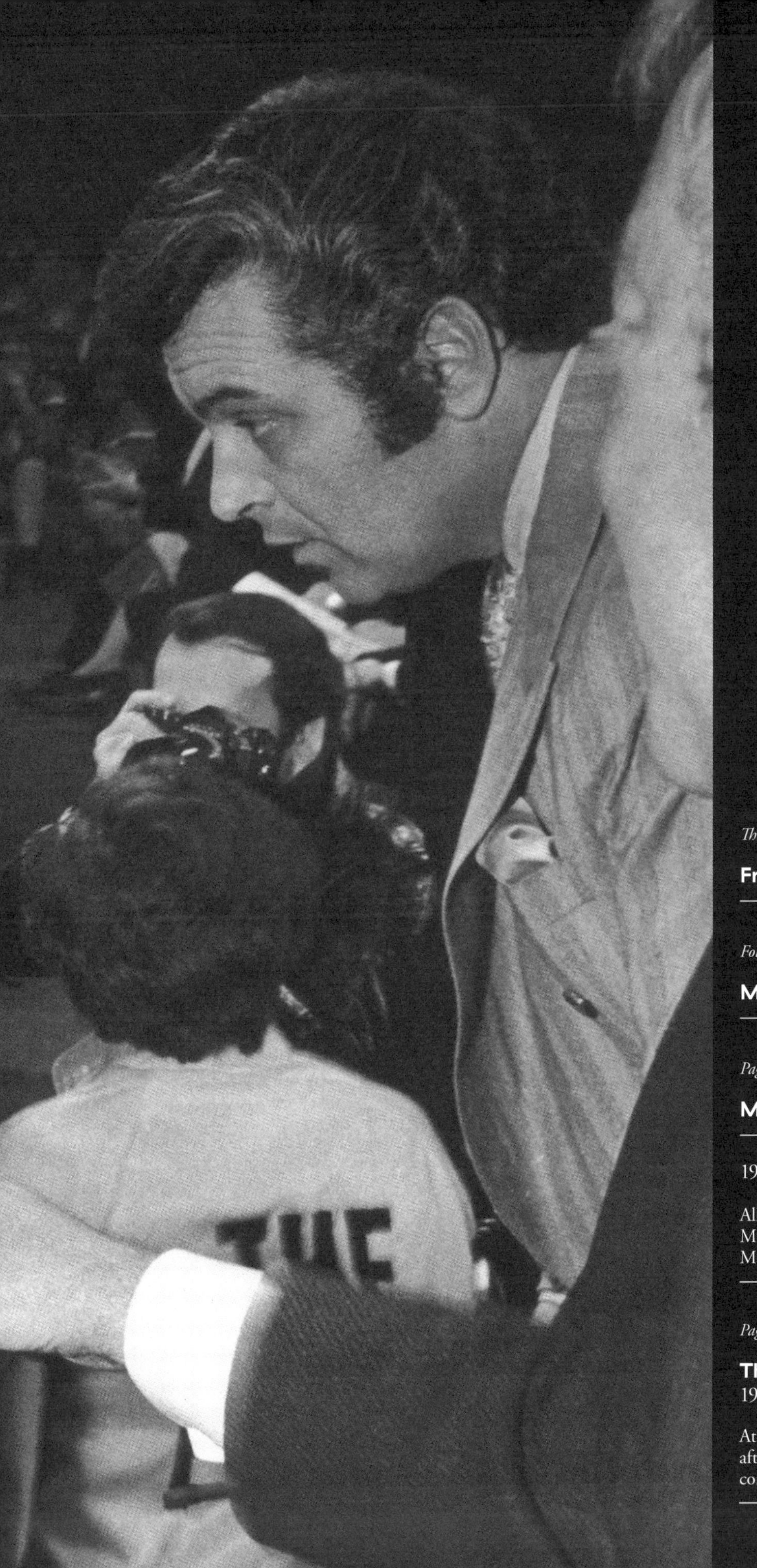

THE

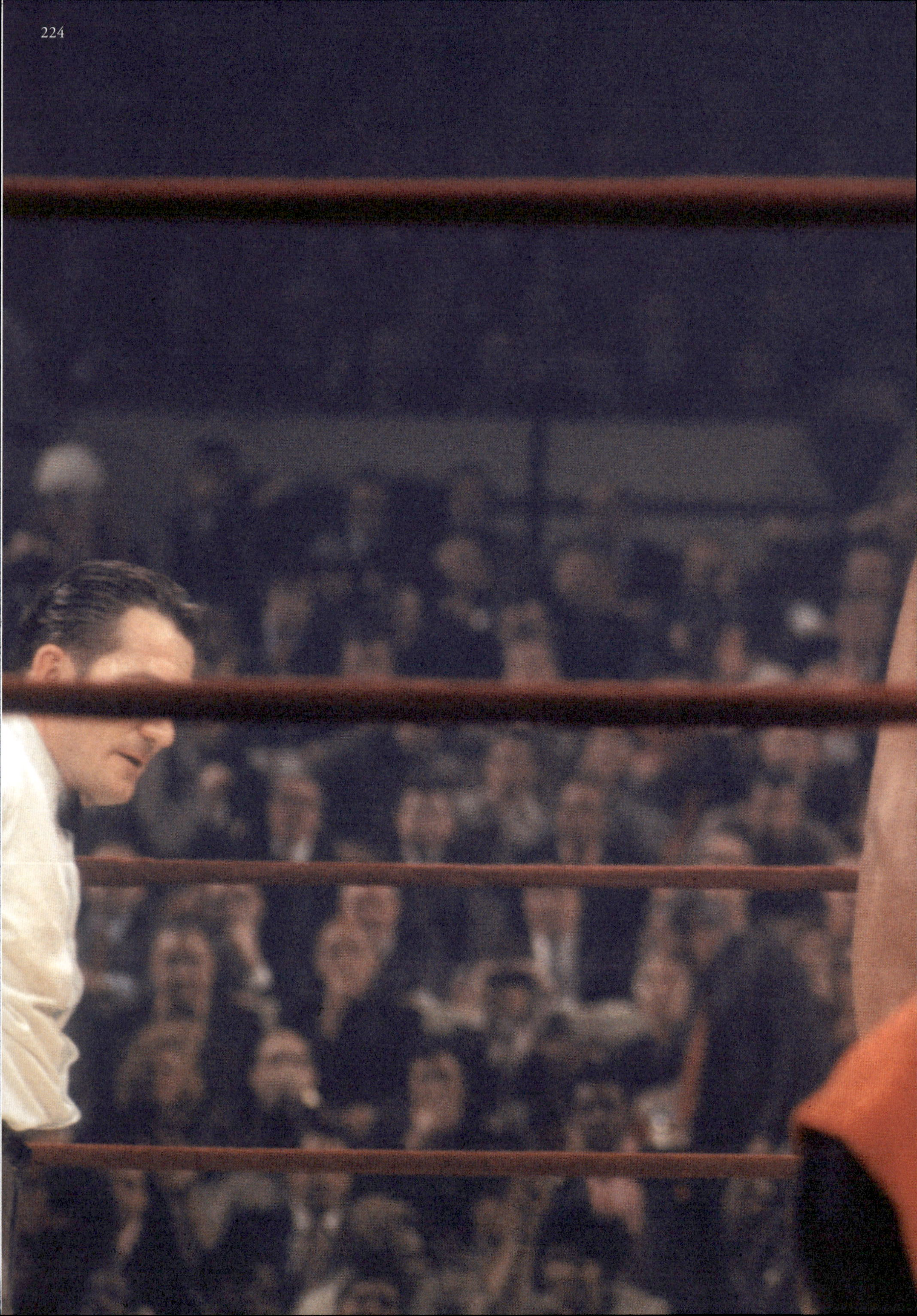

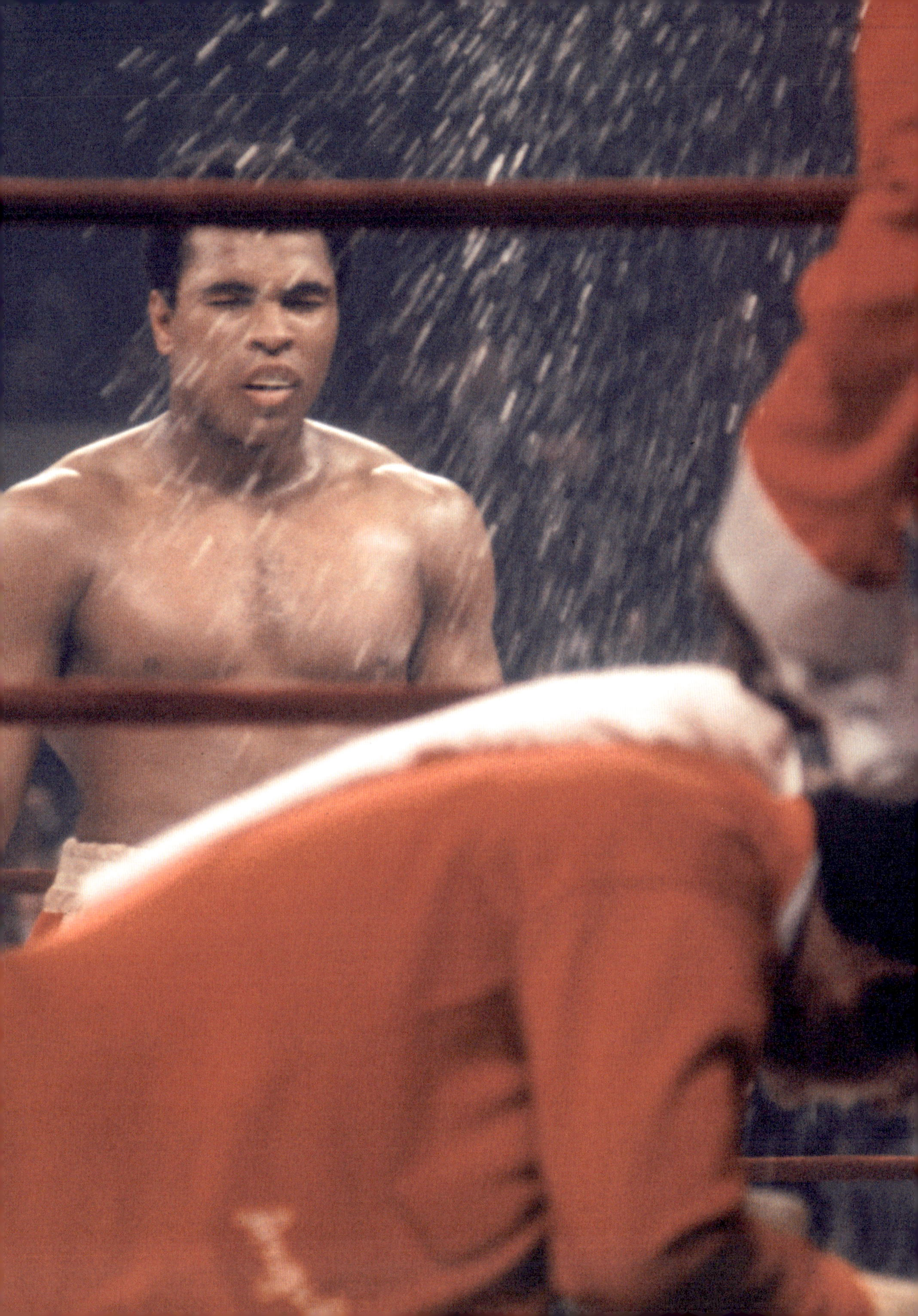

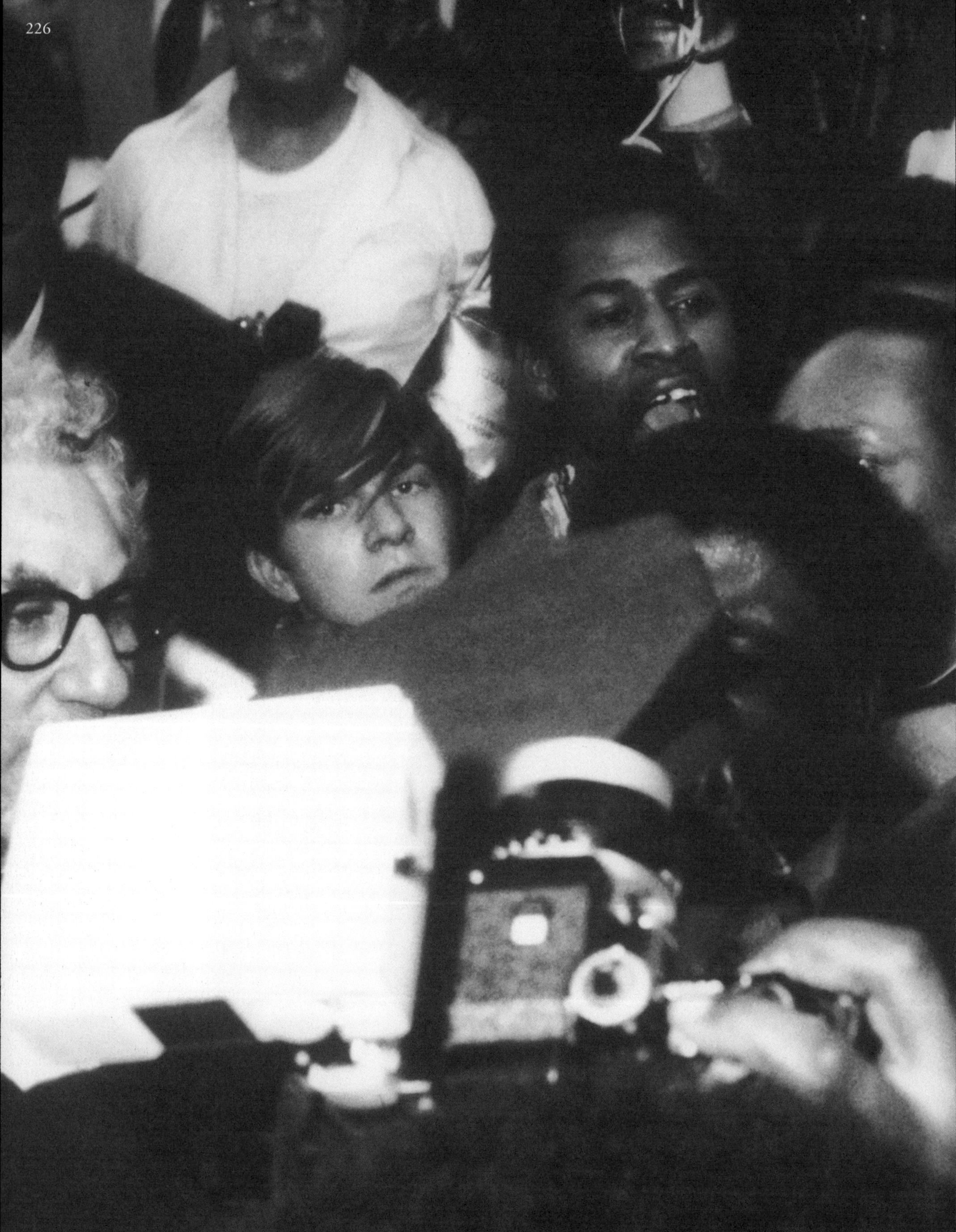

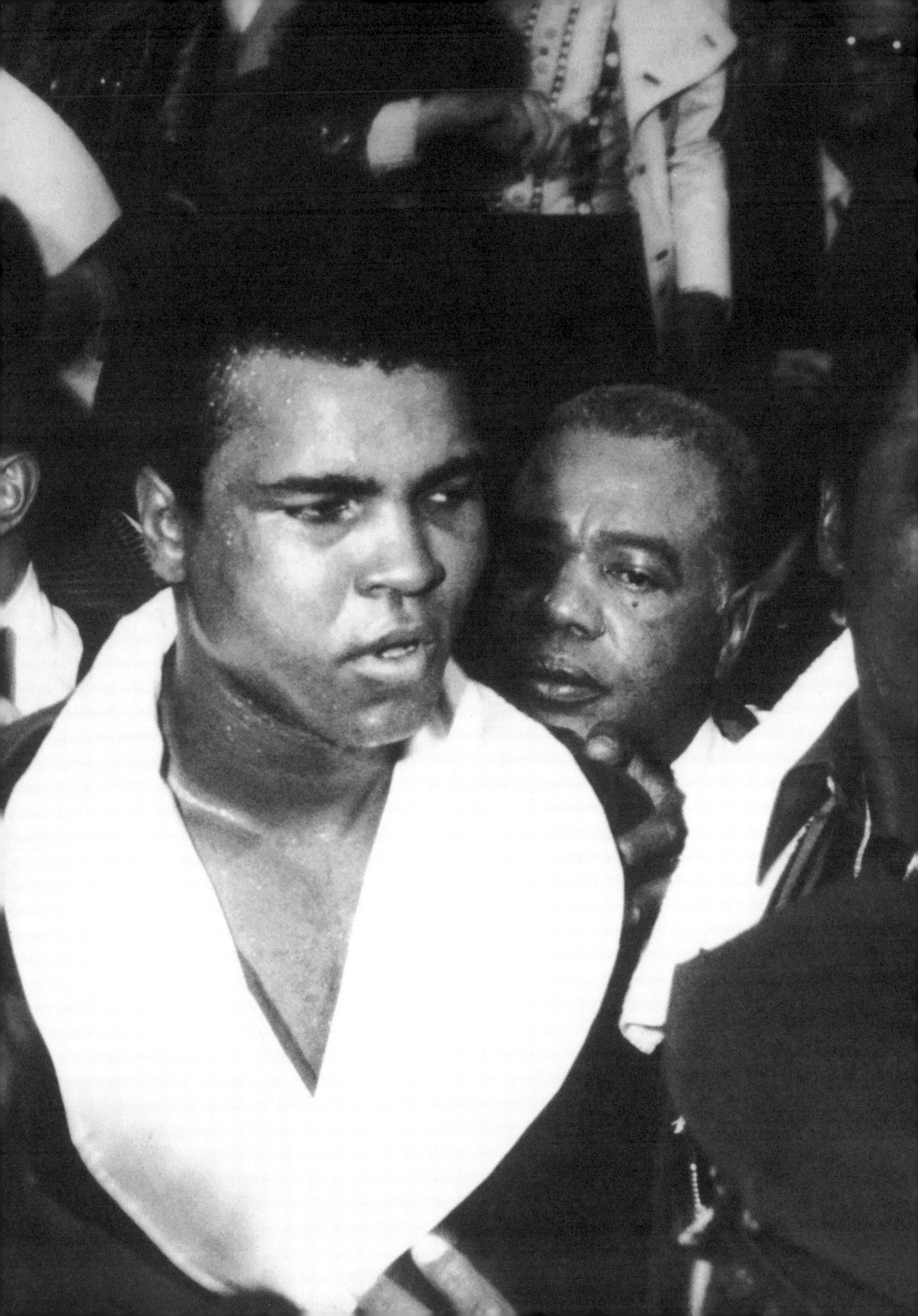

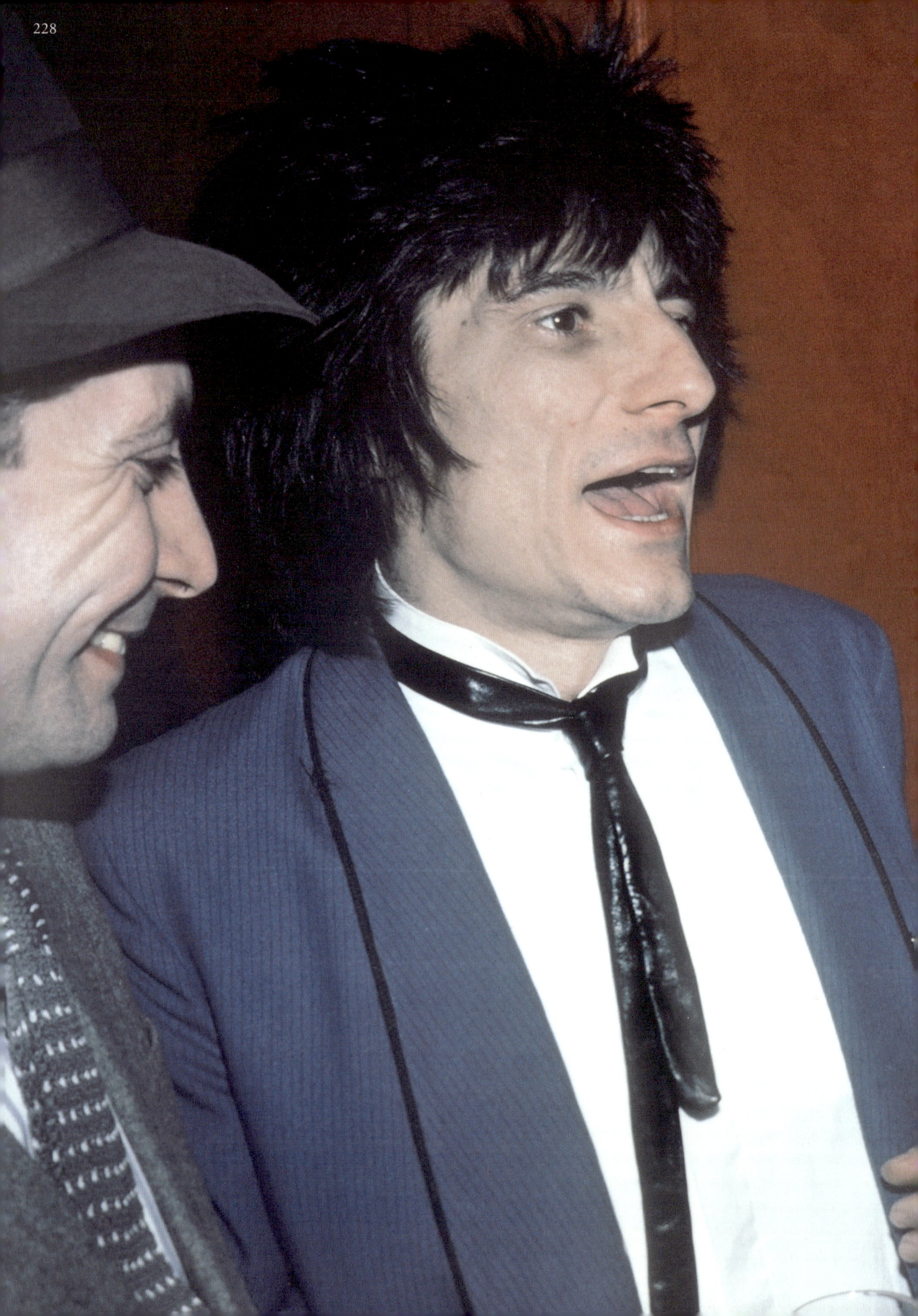

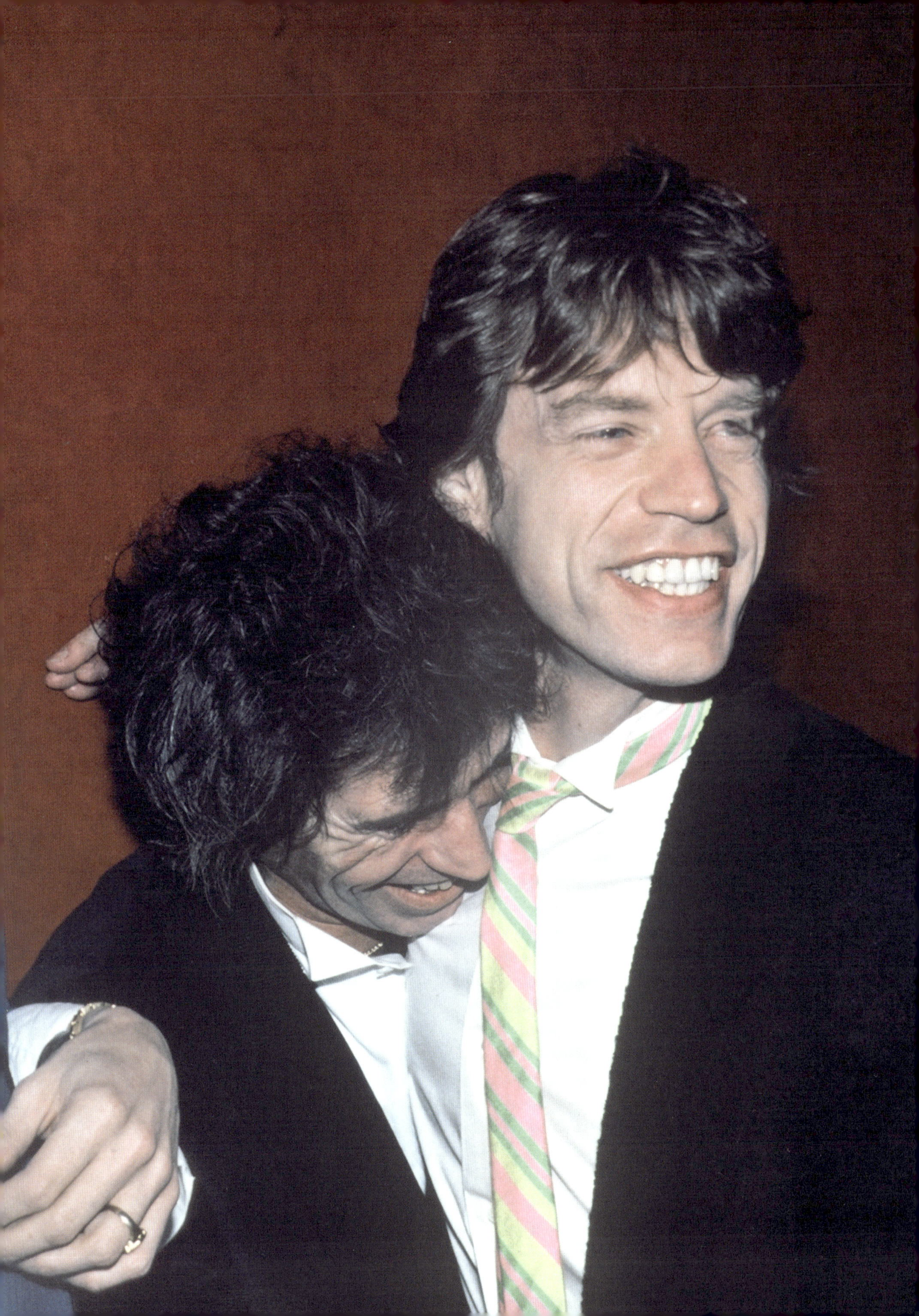

1974, New York City

At the post-premiere party for
her last film *Mame*.

Lucille Ball

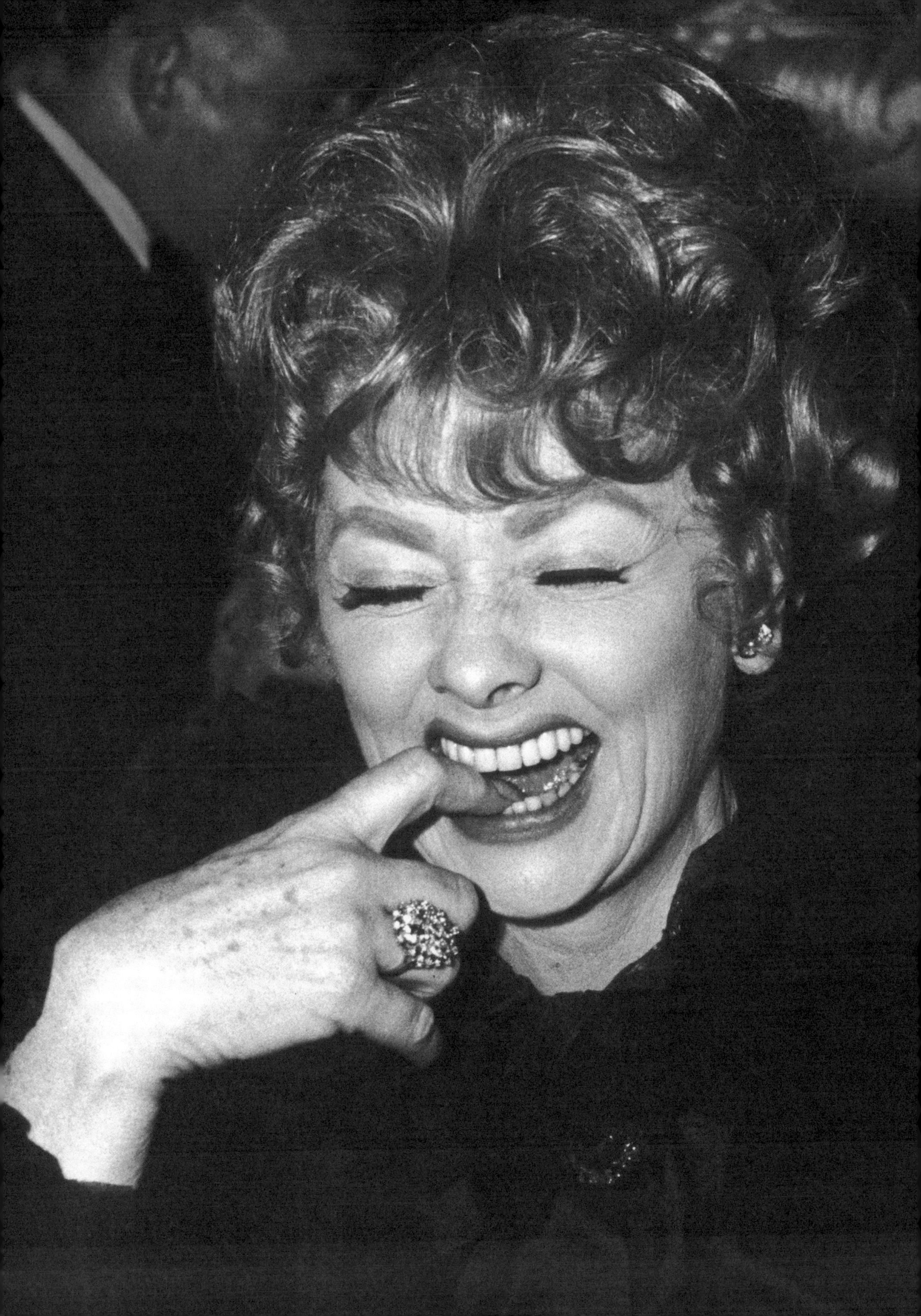

Johnny Cash
1969, Nashville

During rehearsels for his show
at the Grand Ole Opry.
——

Following double page

Roger Moore
1968, Paris

On the set of the James Bond
movie, *Moonraker*.
——

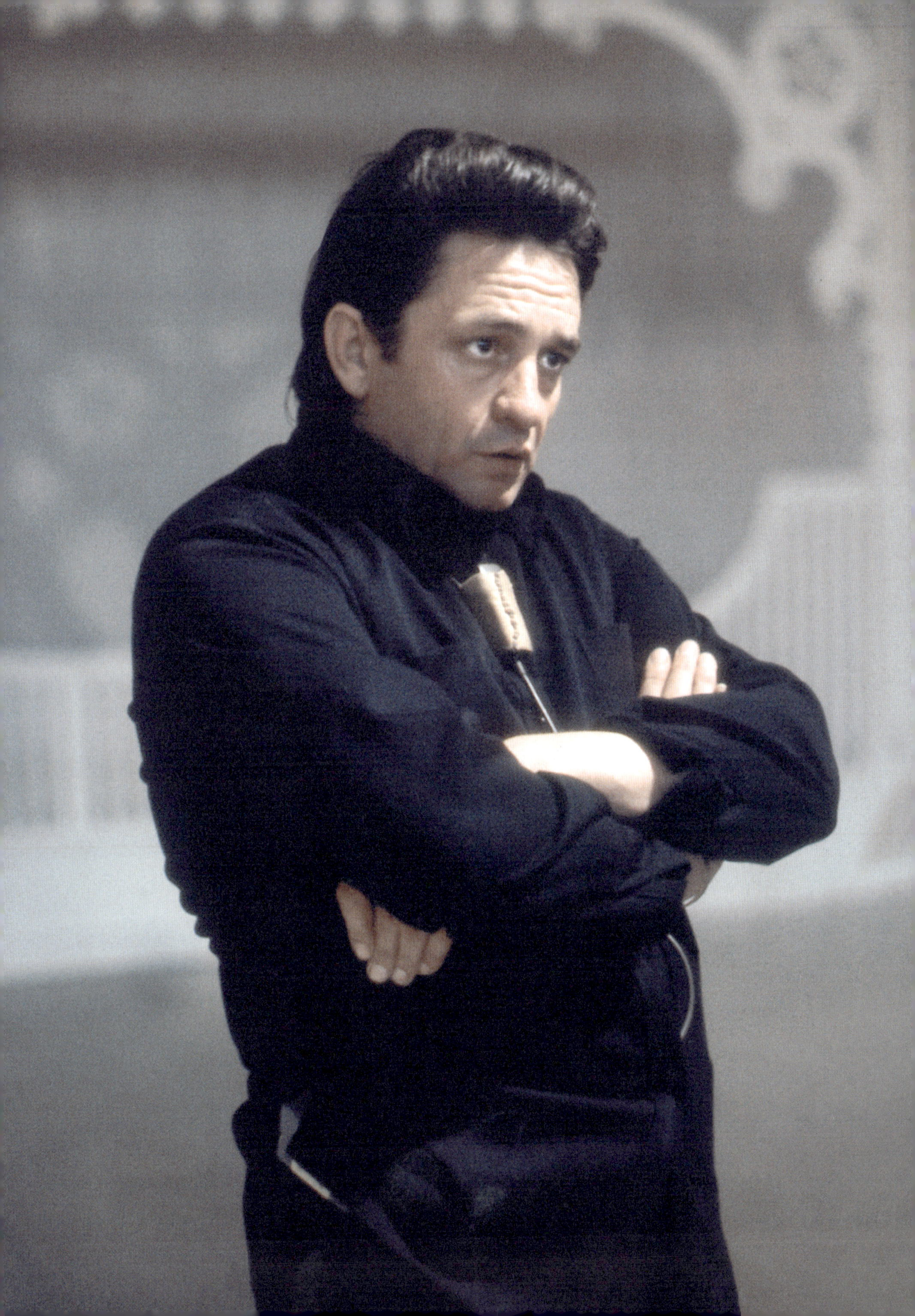

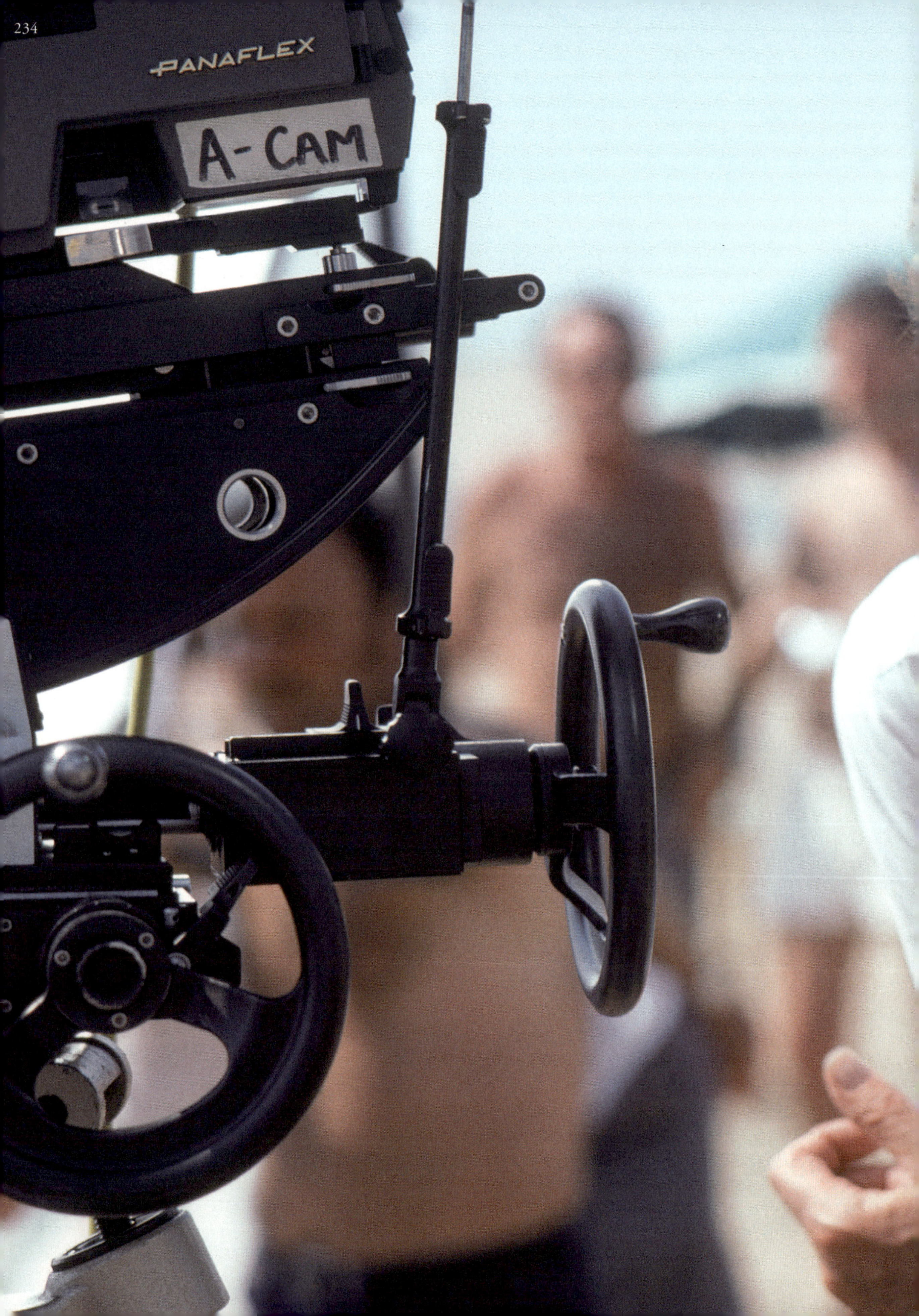
PANAFLEX
A-CAM

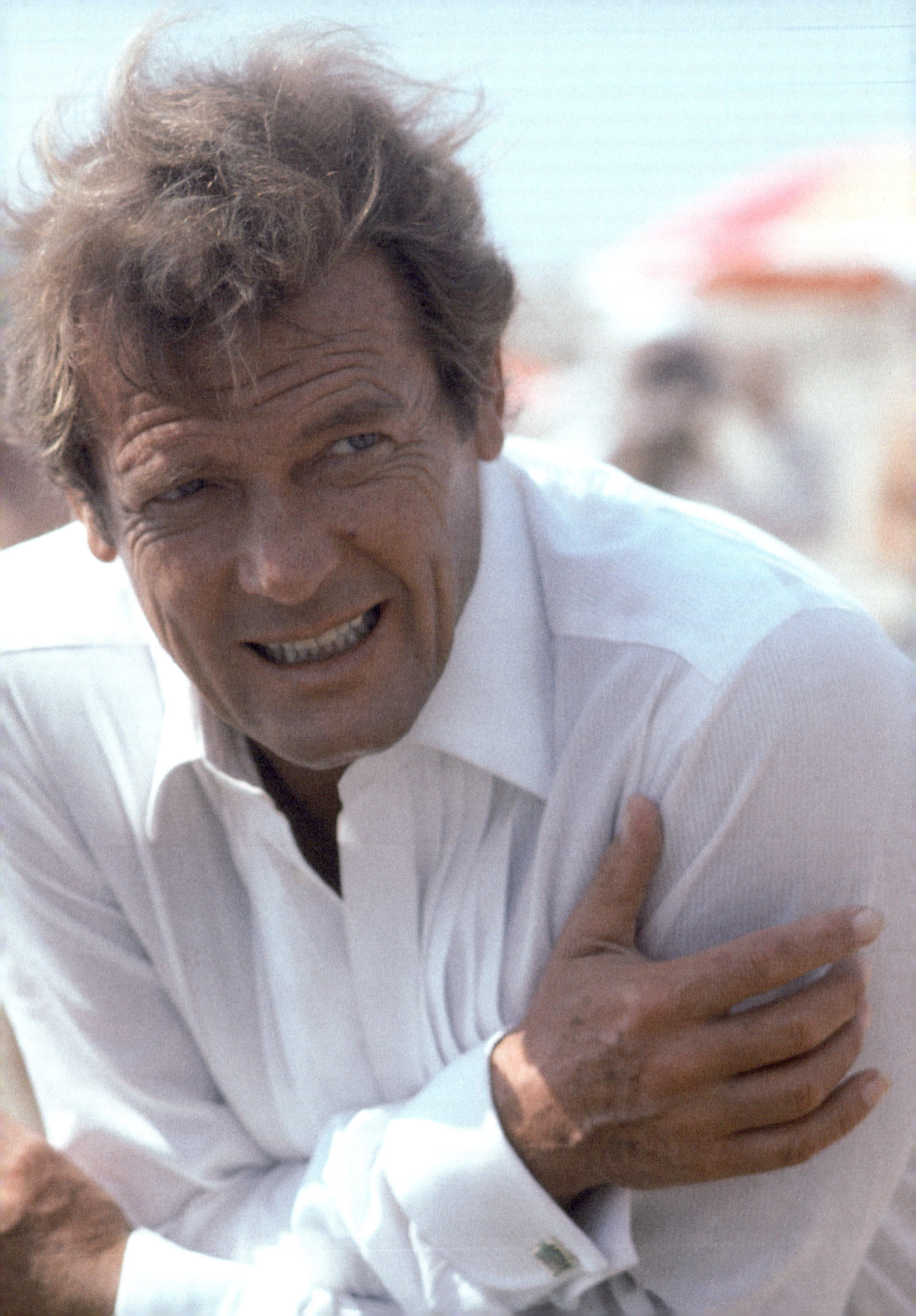

Janis Joplin
1969, New York City

At the Fillmore East Theater.

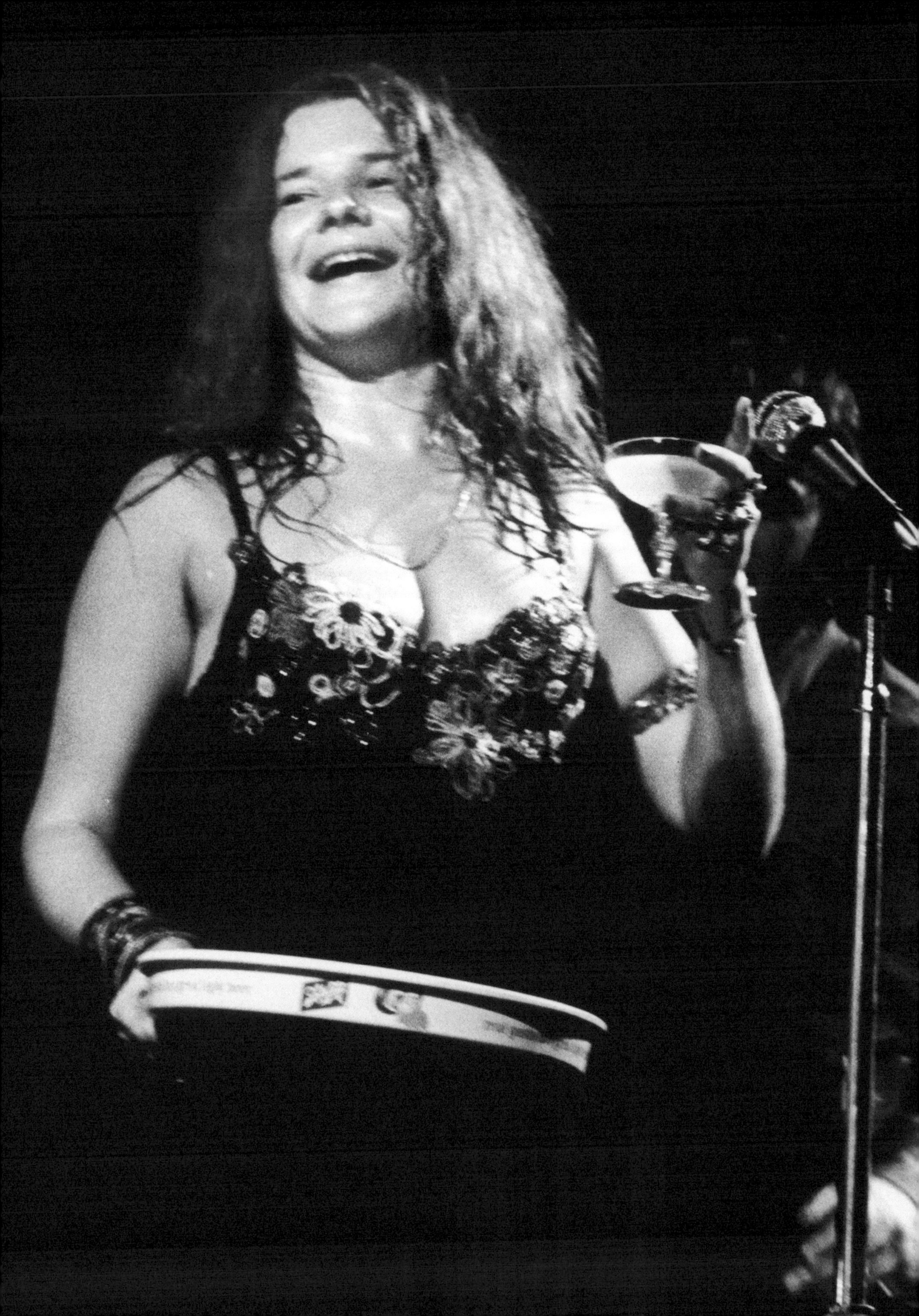

Arnold Schwarzenegger
1982, New York City

At the premiere of his movie *Conan the Barbarian*.

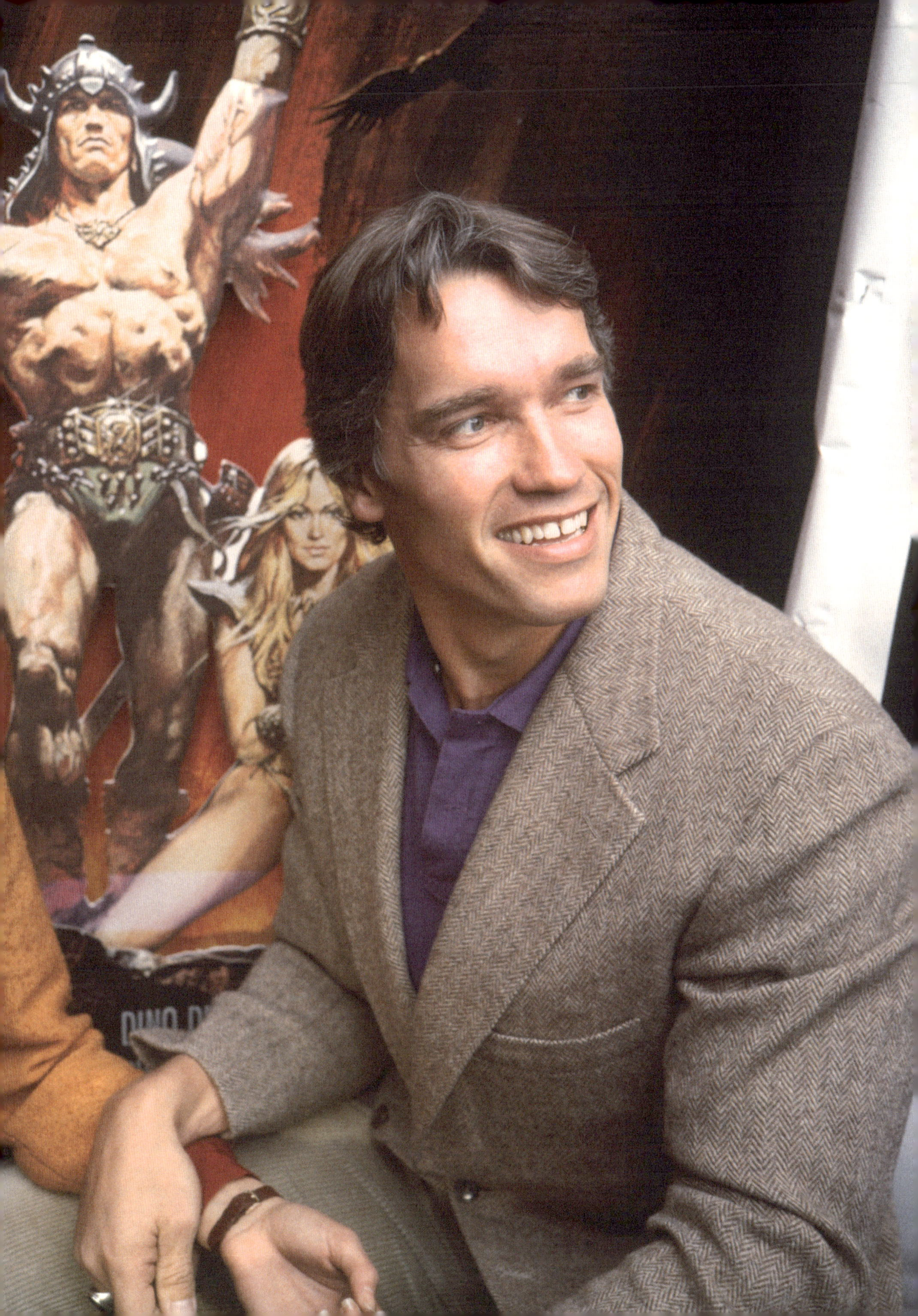

Visiting the Winter Garden.

Ginger Rogers
1970, New York City

Visiting the Winter Garden.
—

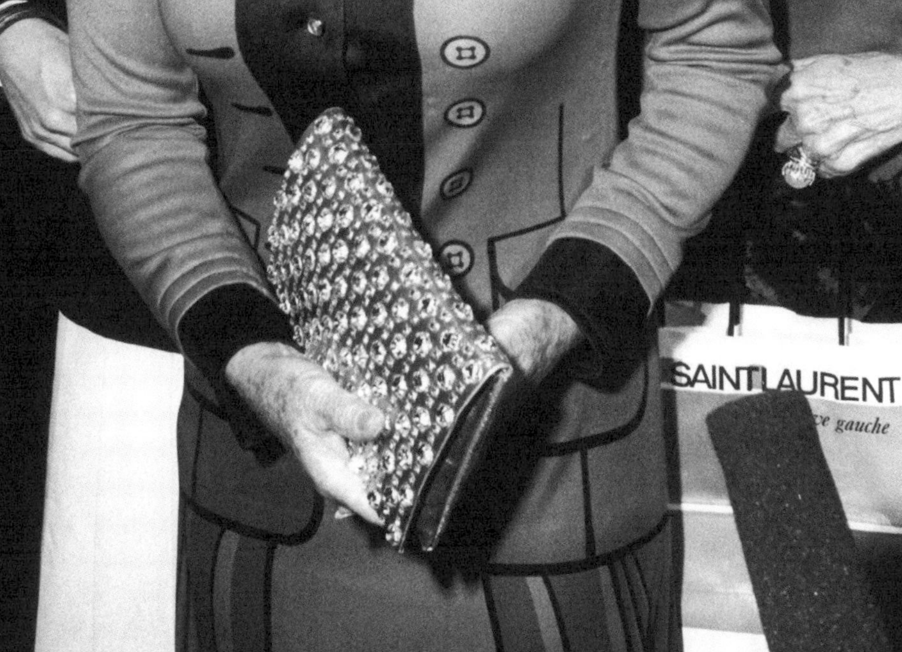

SAINT LAURENT
rive gauche

Albert Finney
1982

On location for the movie *Annie*..

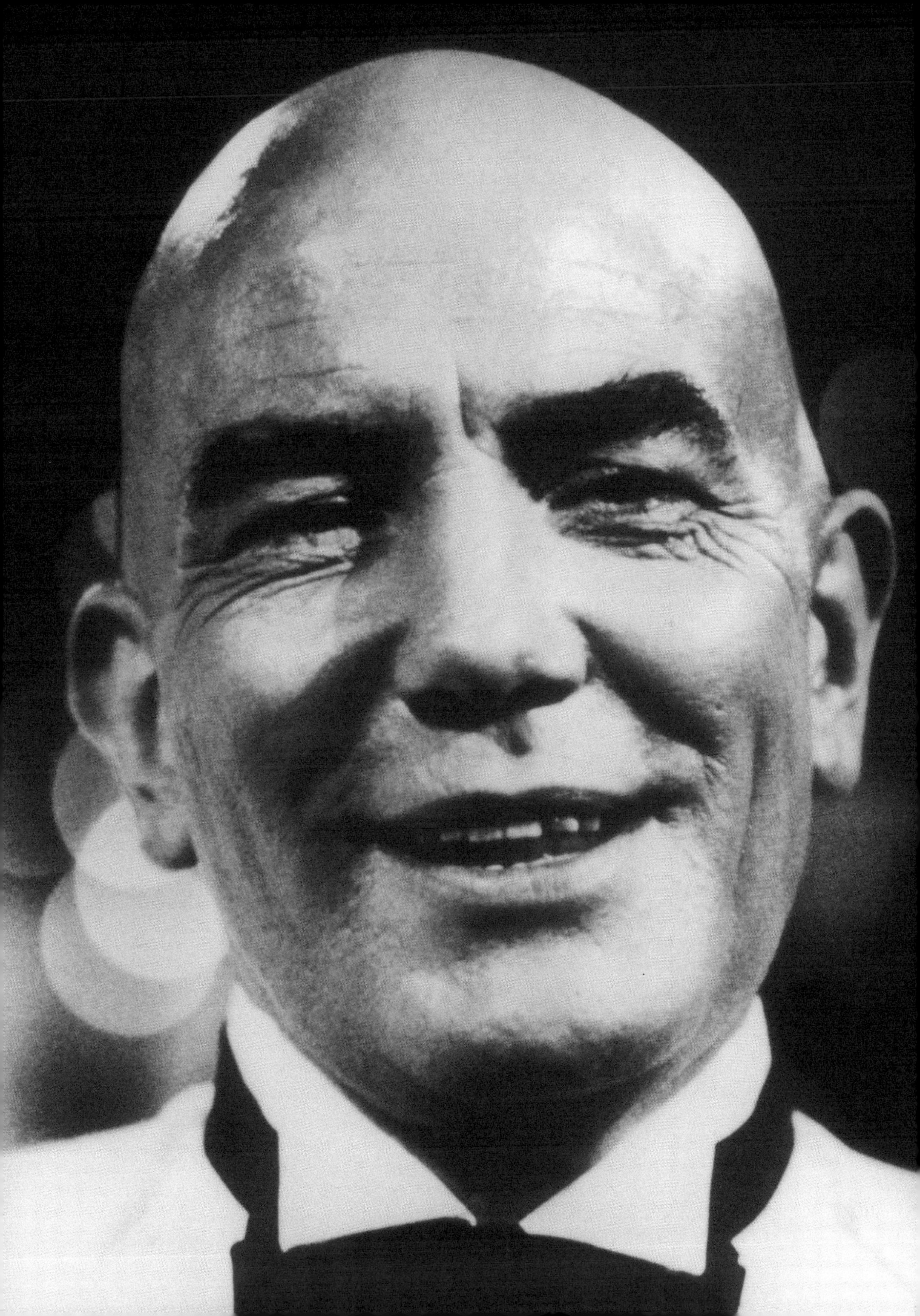

Faye Dunaway
1967, New York City

At the movie premiere of *Bonnie and Clyde*.

———

Following double page

**Jerry Lewis, George Shearing,
Sammy Davis Jr. and Frank Sinatra**
1987, Atlantic City

———

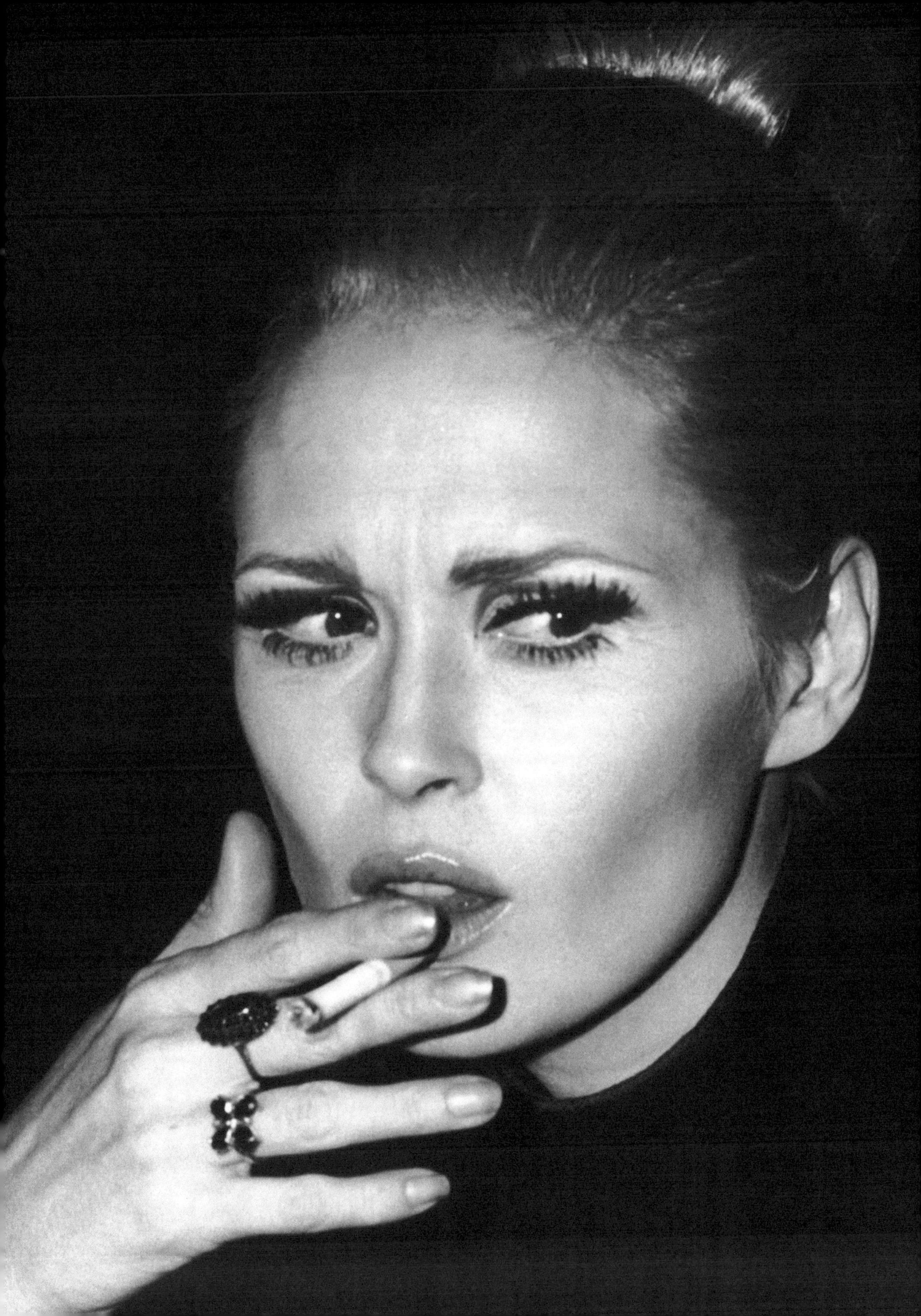

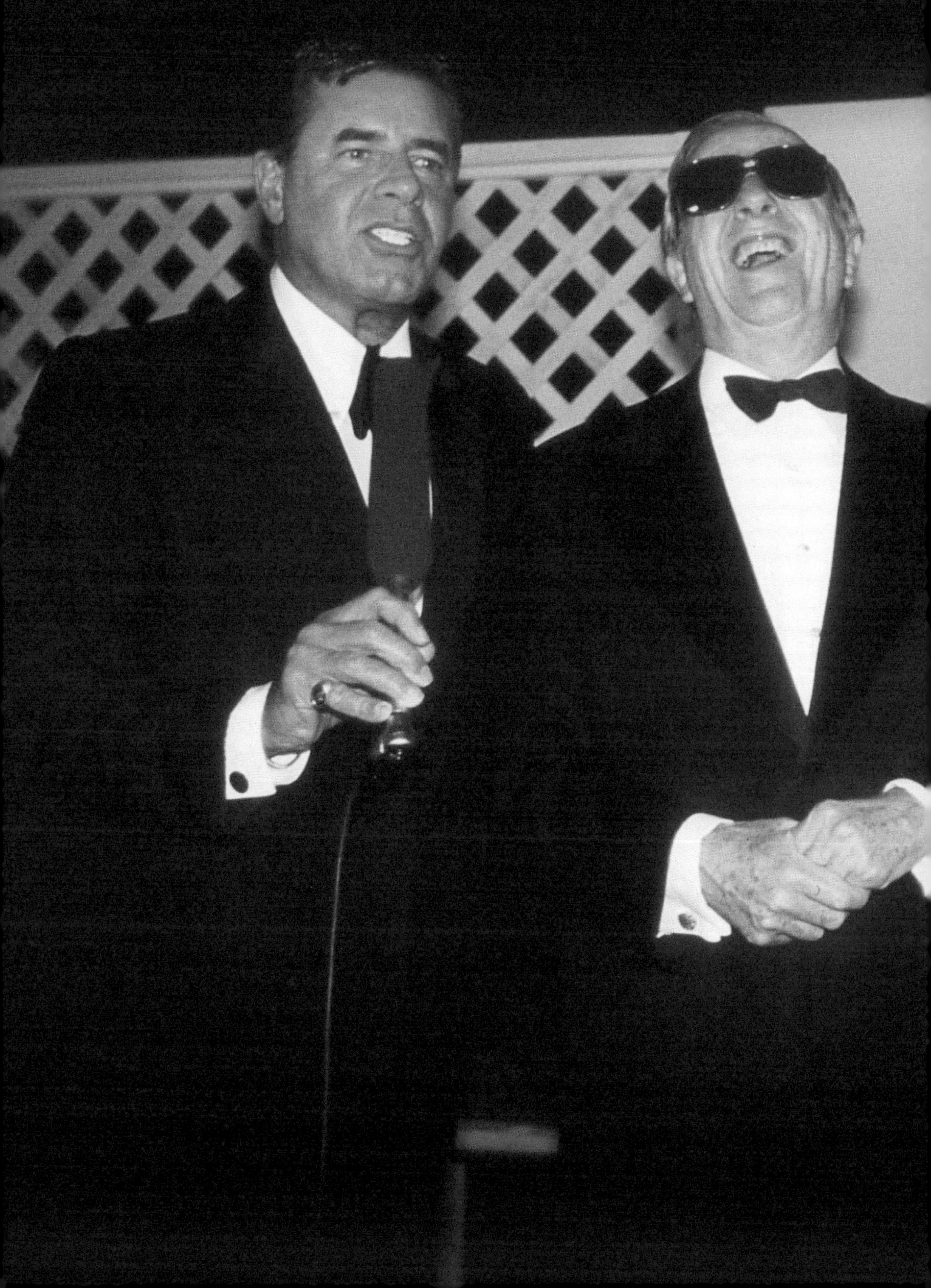

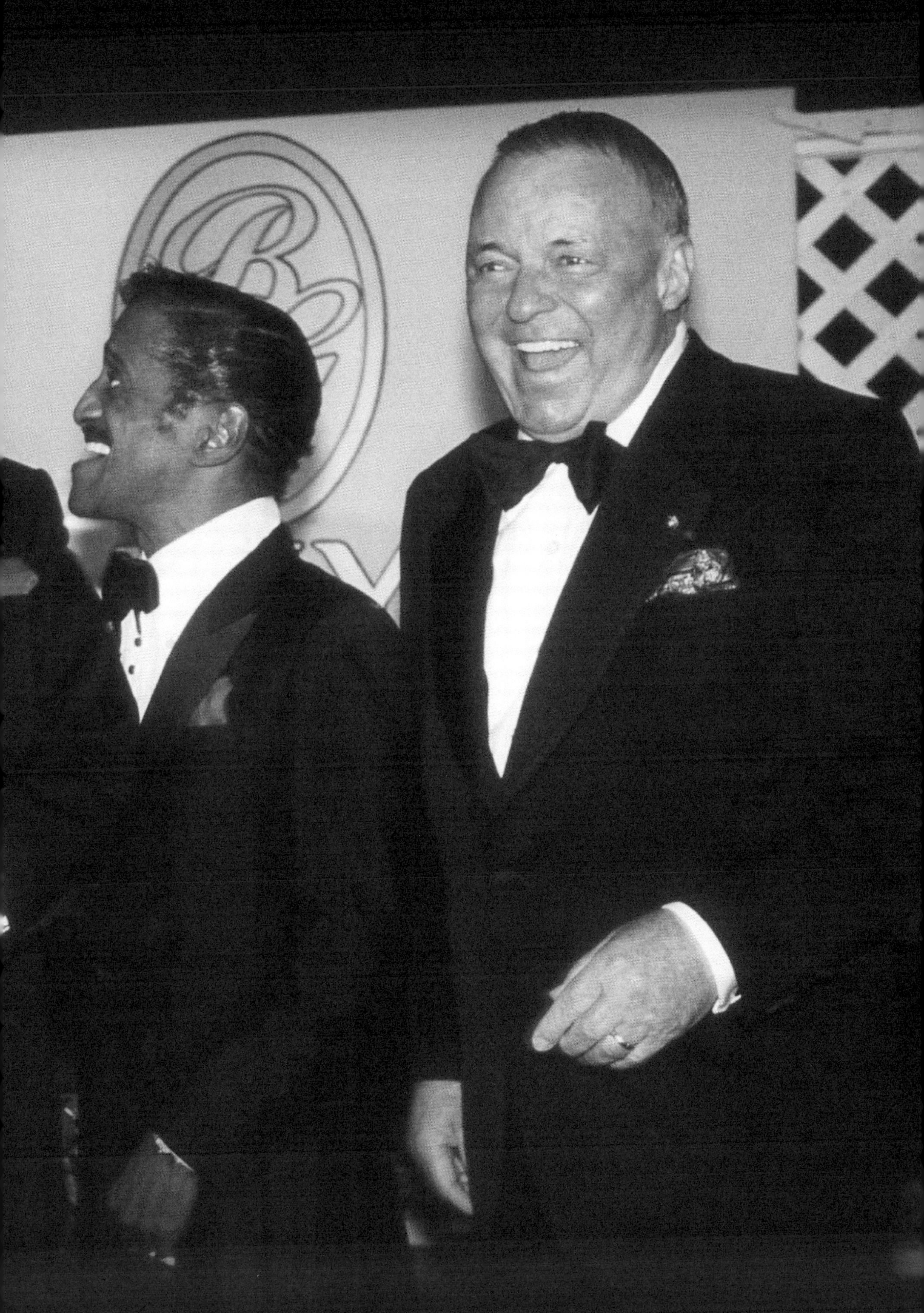

Dustin Hoffman
1967, New York City

At a Madison Square Garden benefit event.

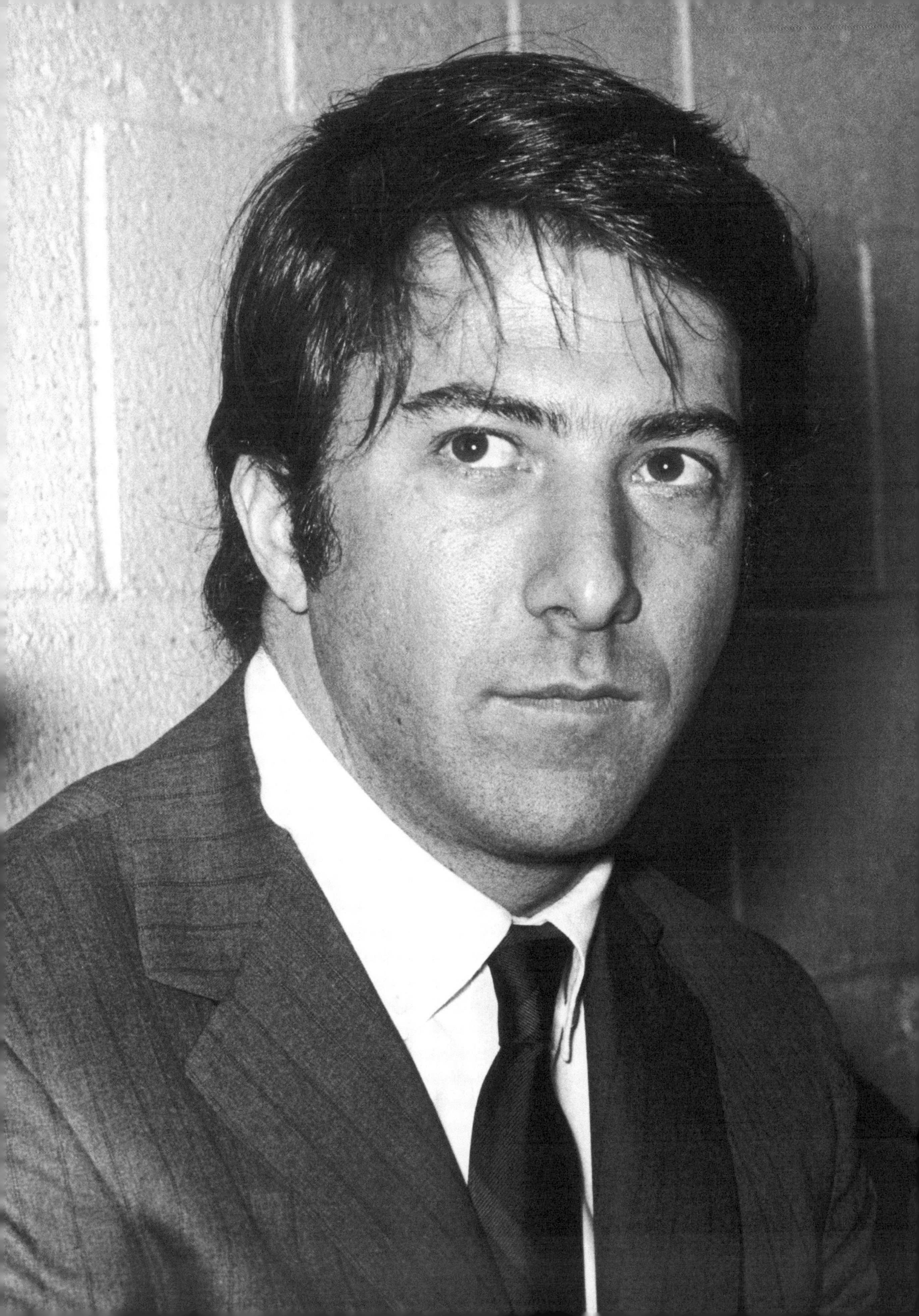

Duke Ellington
1965, New York City

At Lincoln Center.

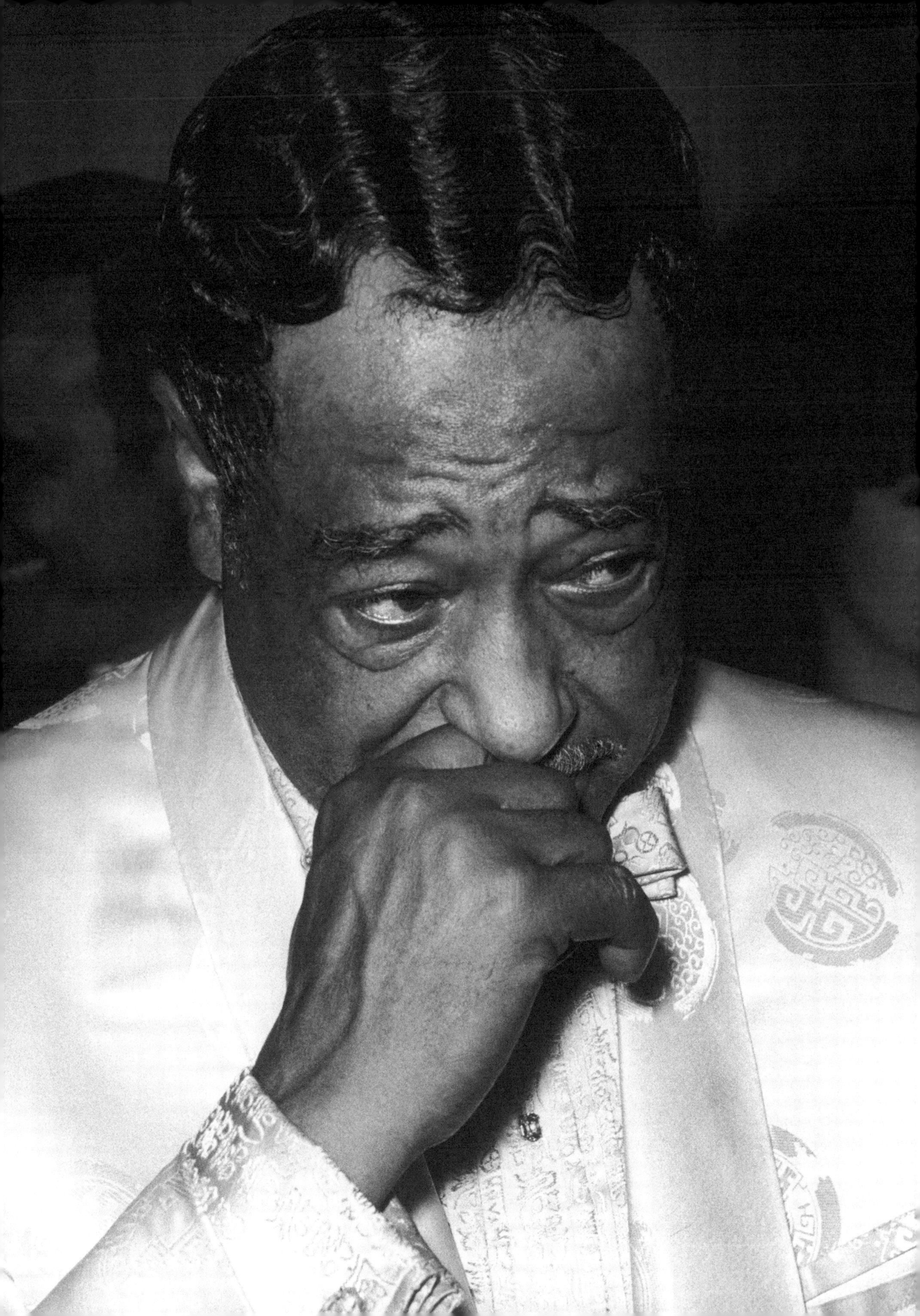

Andy Warhol
ca. 1989, New York City

With camera at the Metropolitan
Museum of Art, at the Costume Institute gala.

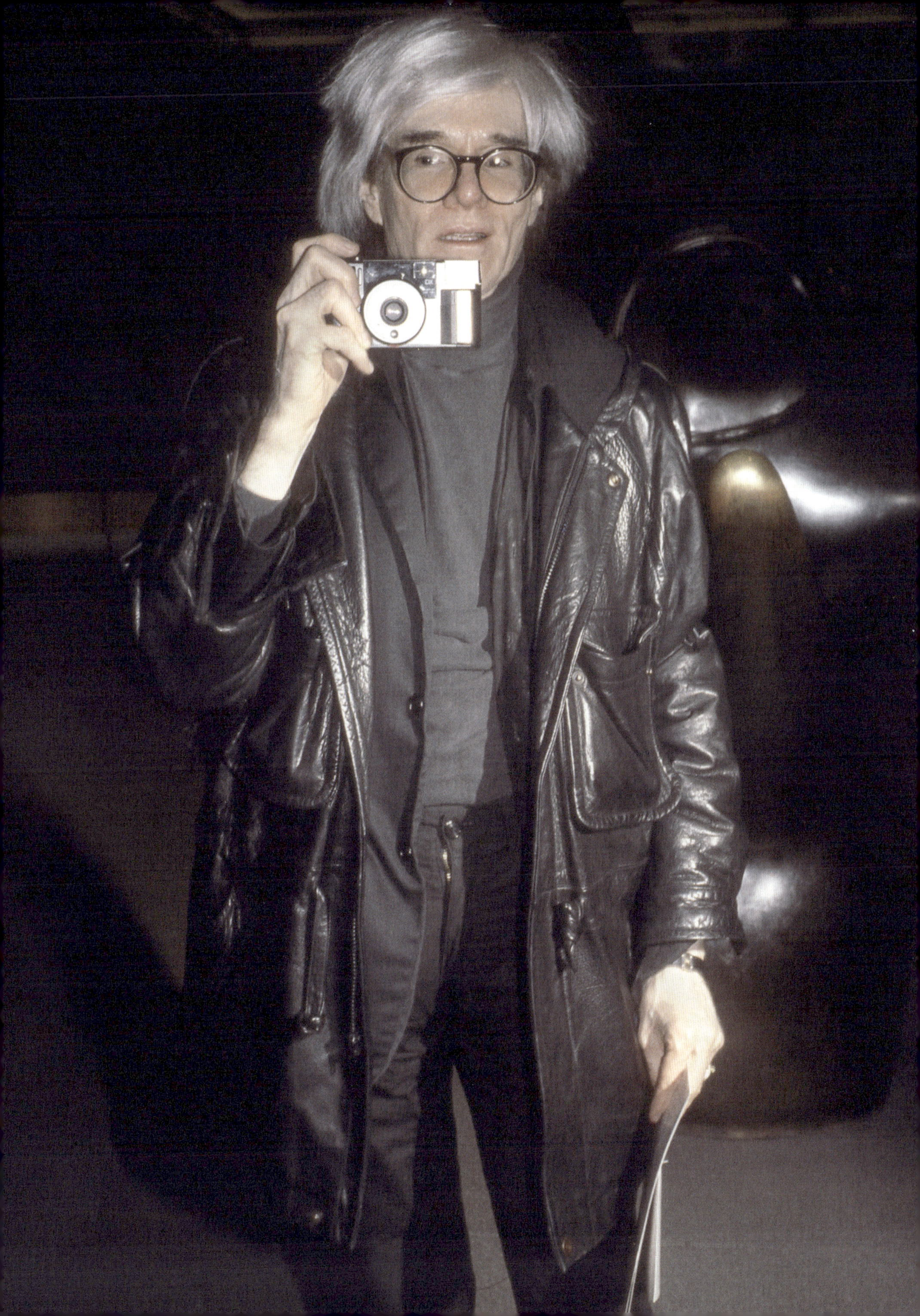

Diana Ross
1969, New York City

At a charity event at the
Waldorf Astoria Hotel.

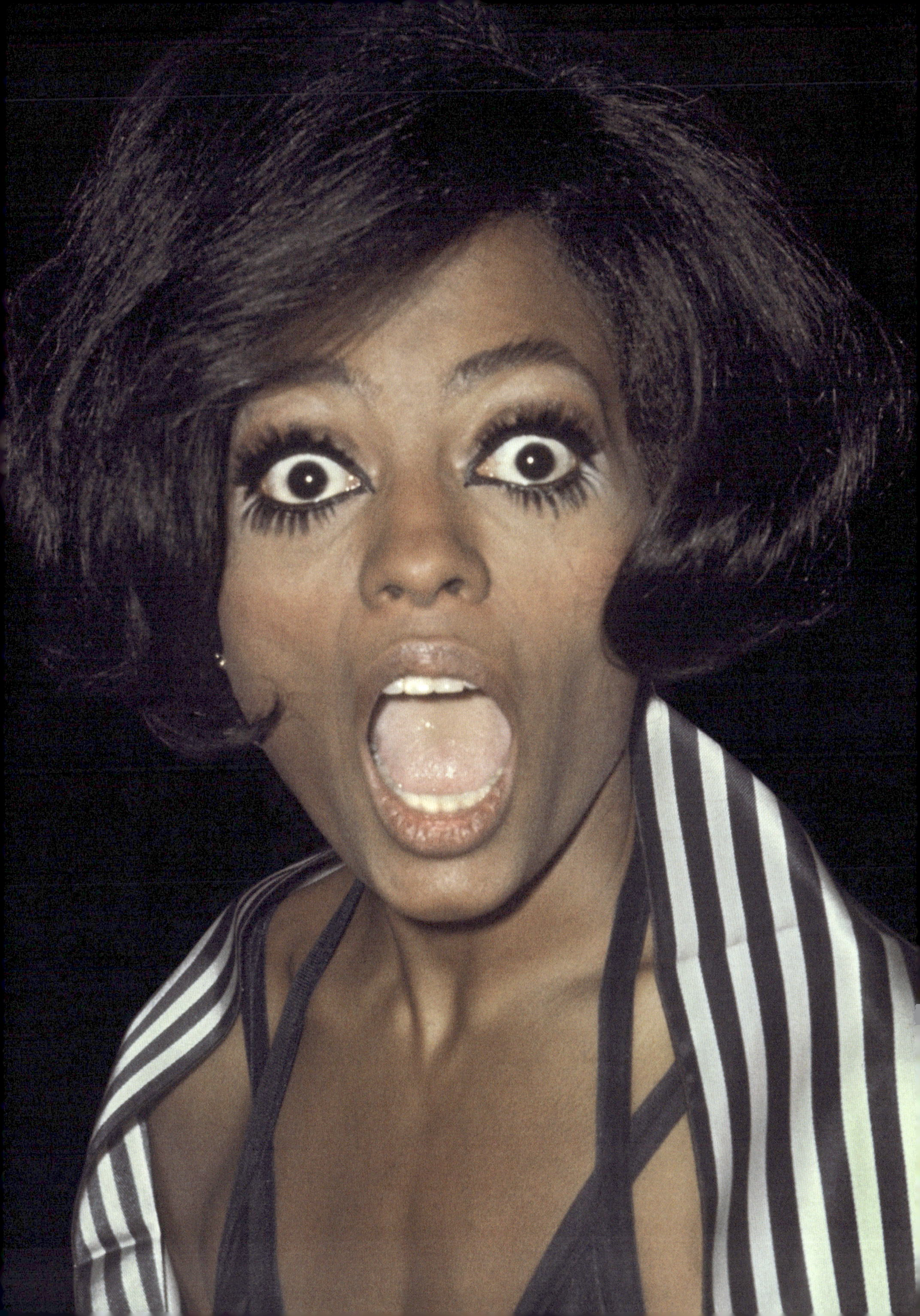

Priscilla Presley
1984, Dallas

On her first day of filming, on the
set of the TV show *Dallas*.

———

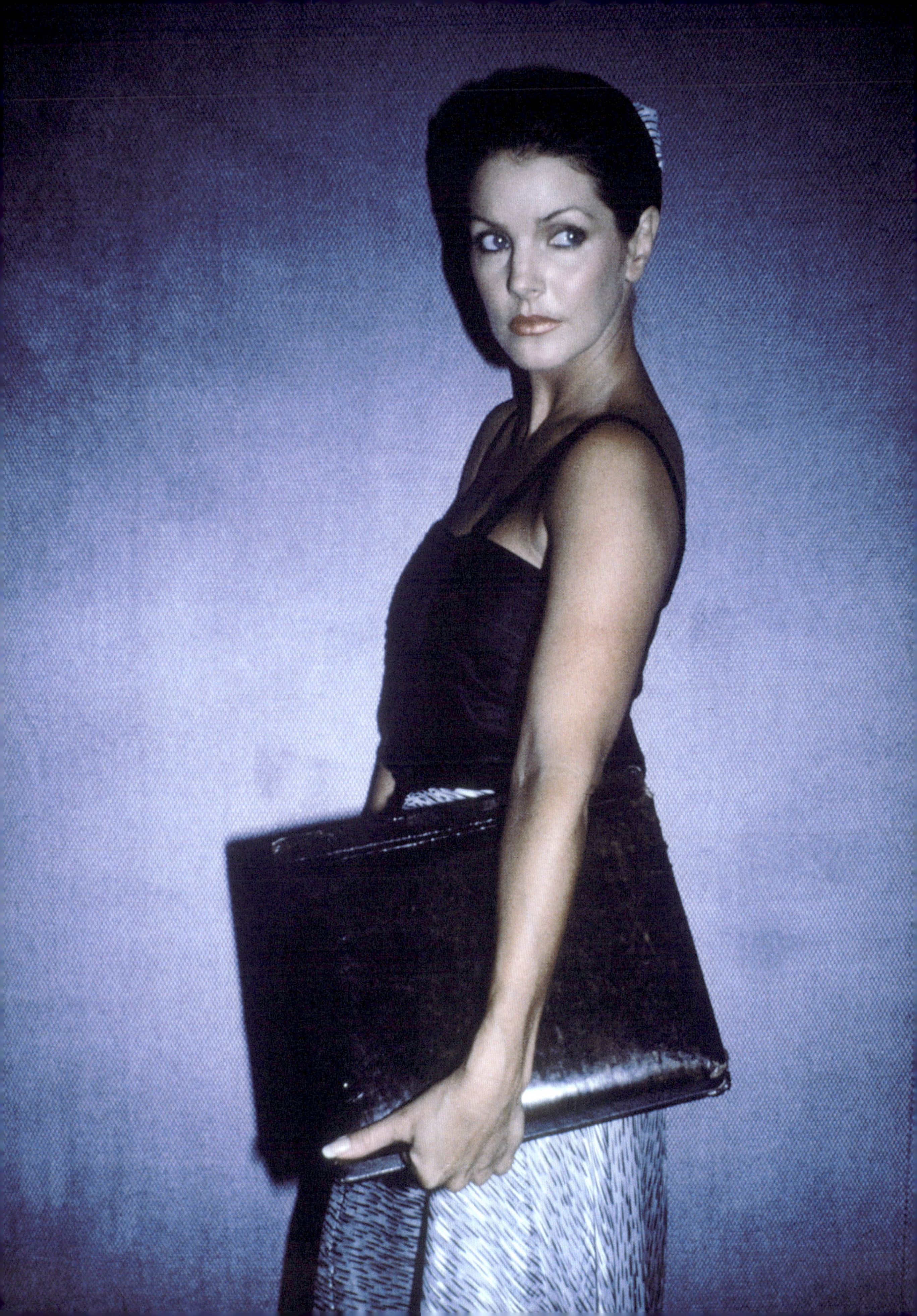

Charlie Chaplin
1972, New York City

Being honored by the Film Society
of Lincoln Center. This was his
first time back after two decades.

———

Following double page

Oprah Winfrey
1987, New York City

At the *Emmy Awards*.

———

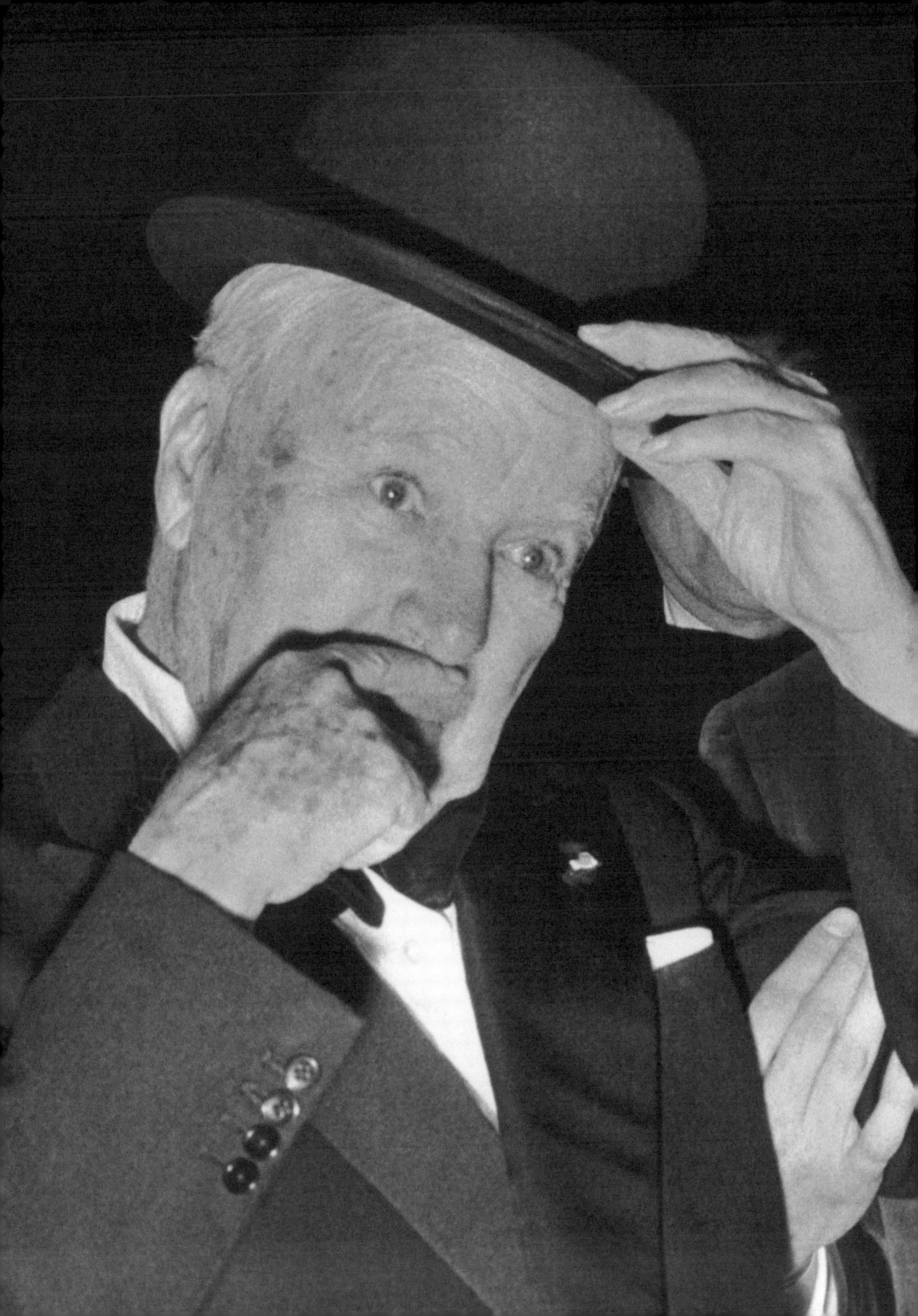

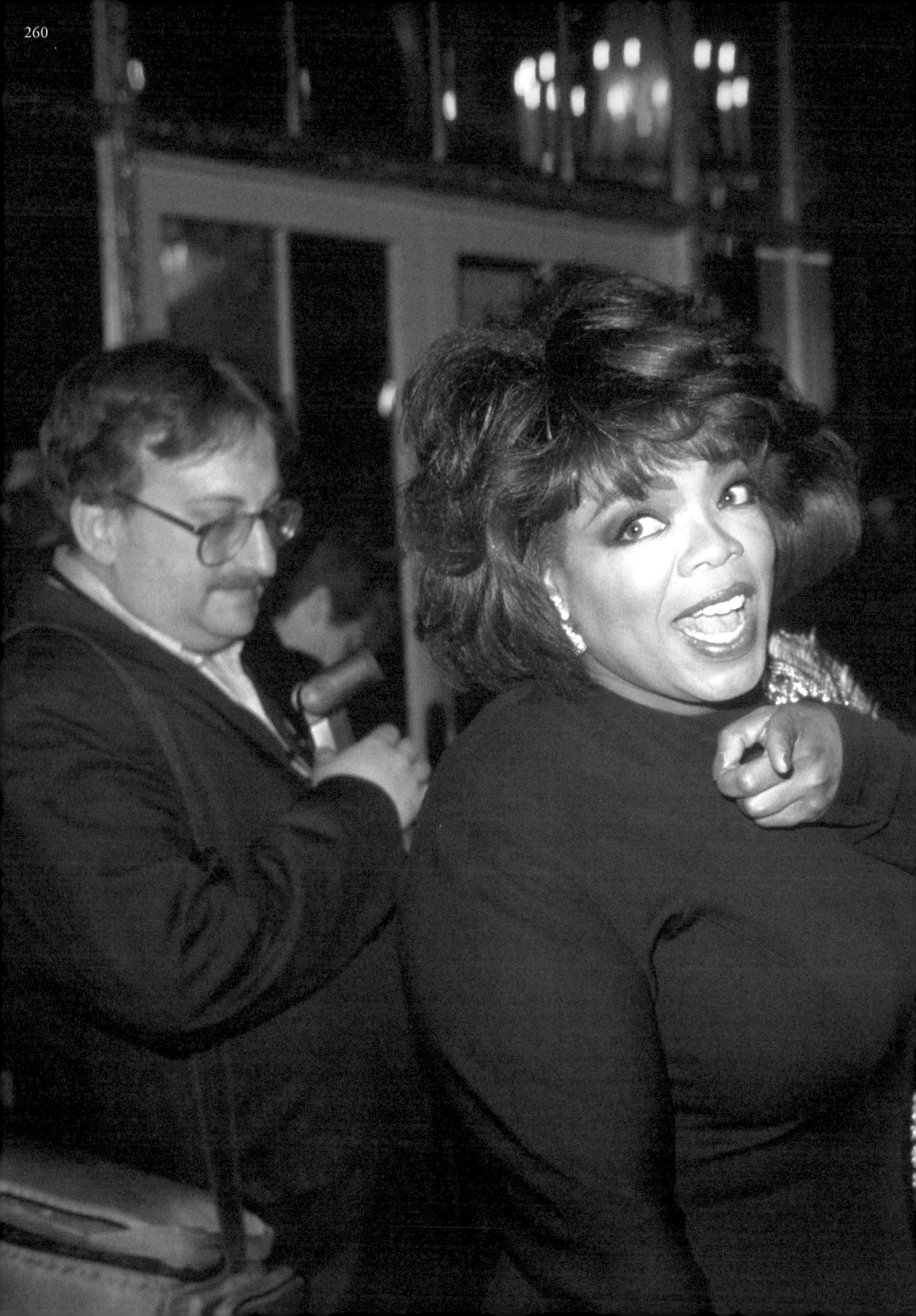

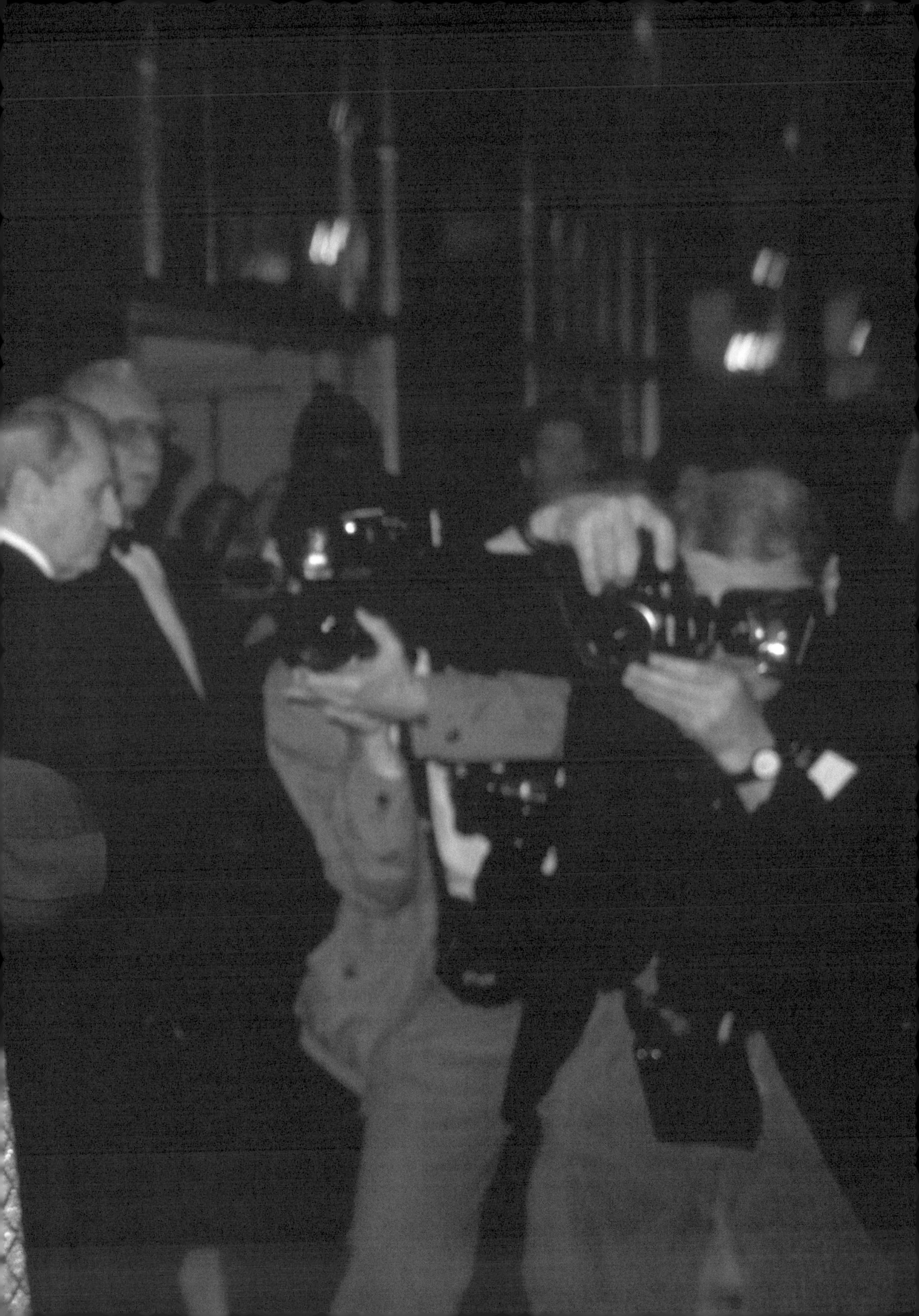

David Bowie
1987, New York City

At the press conference
for his Glass Spider Tour.

____

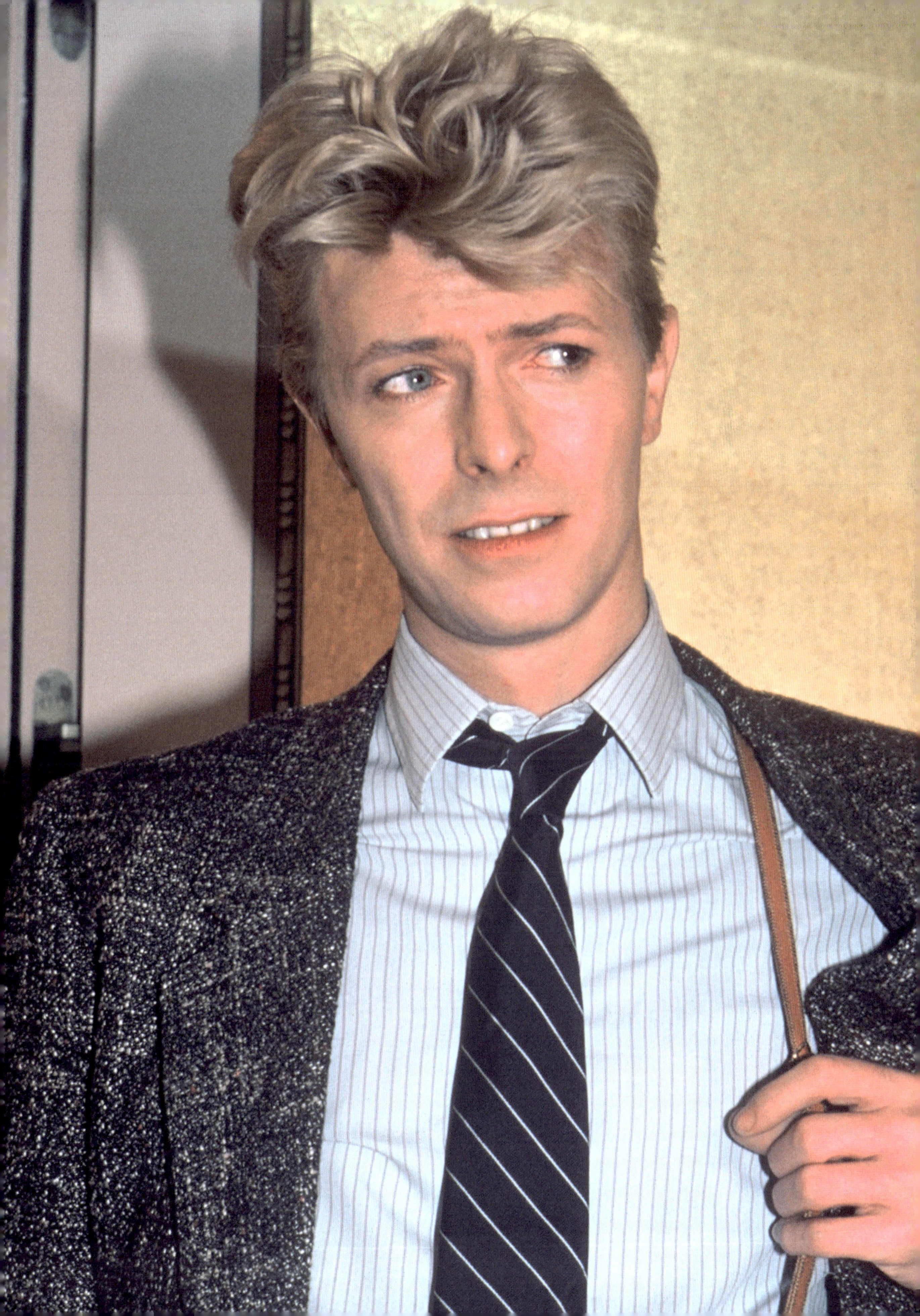

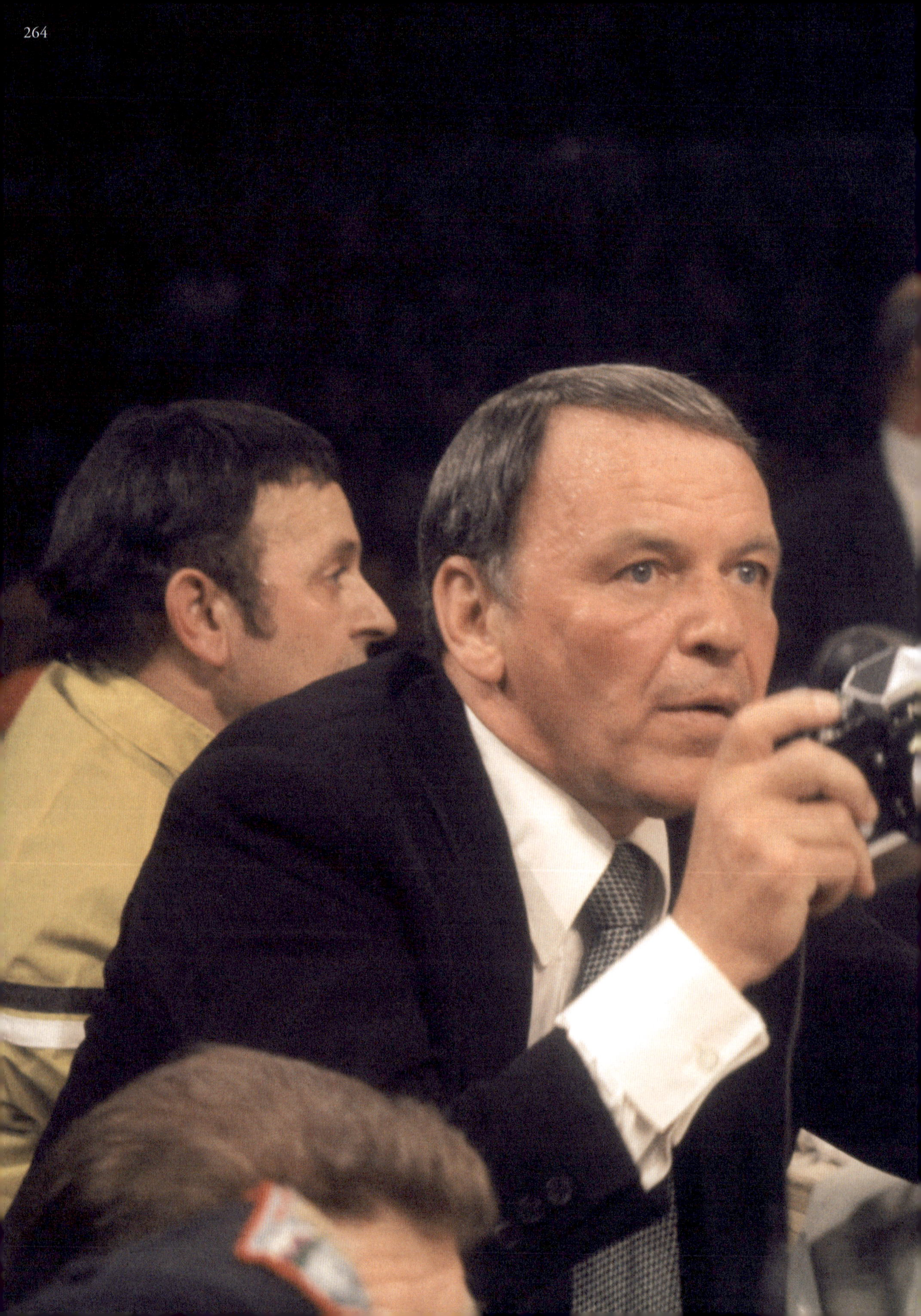

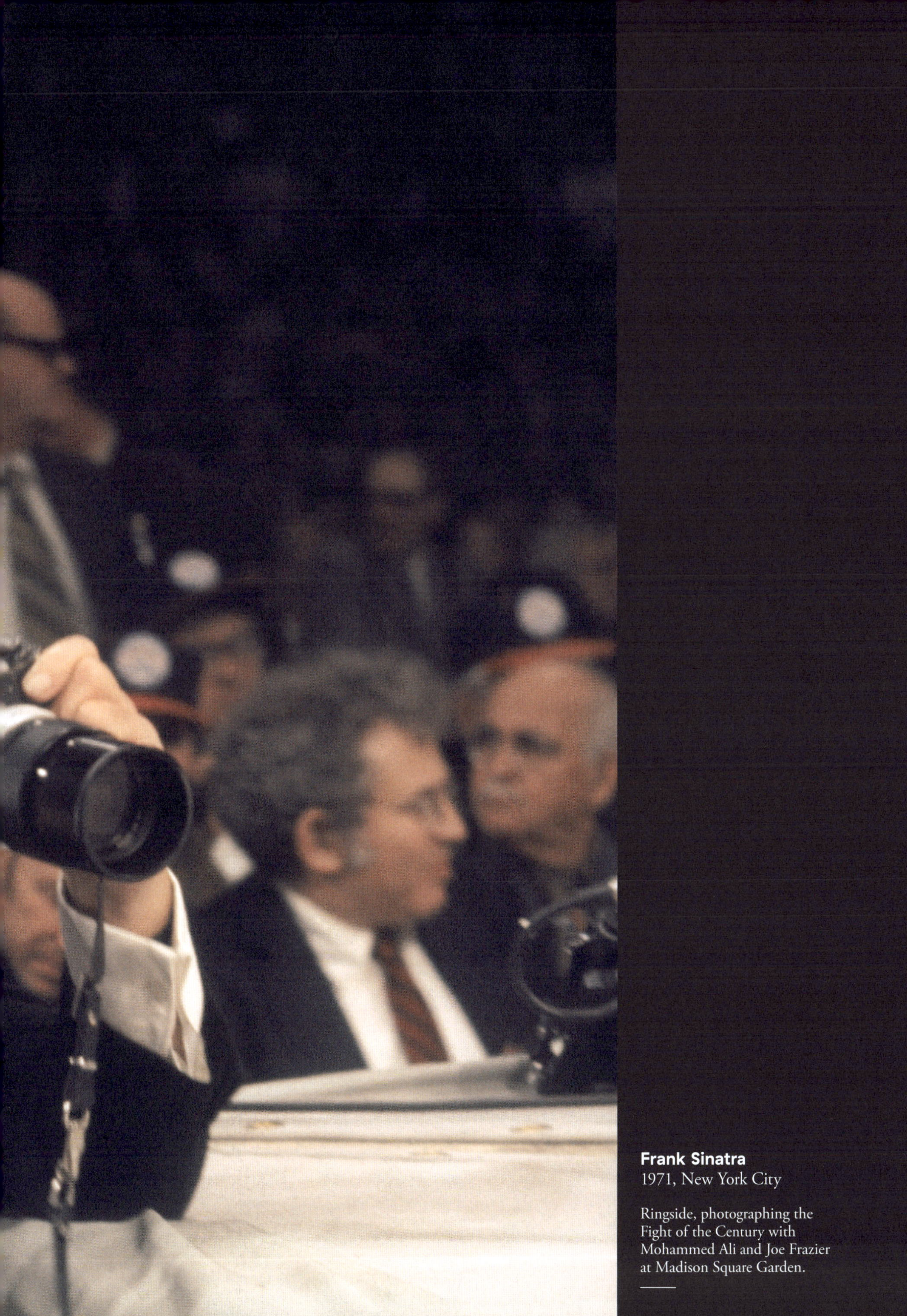

Frank Sinatra
1971, New York City

Ringside, photographing the
Fight of the Century with
Mohammed Ali and Joe Frazier
at Madison Square Garden.

———

Bette Midler
1973, New York City

At the Palace Theatre before going
on stage for her show *Bette at the Palace*.

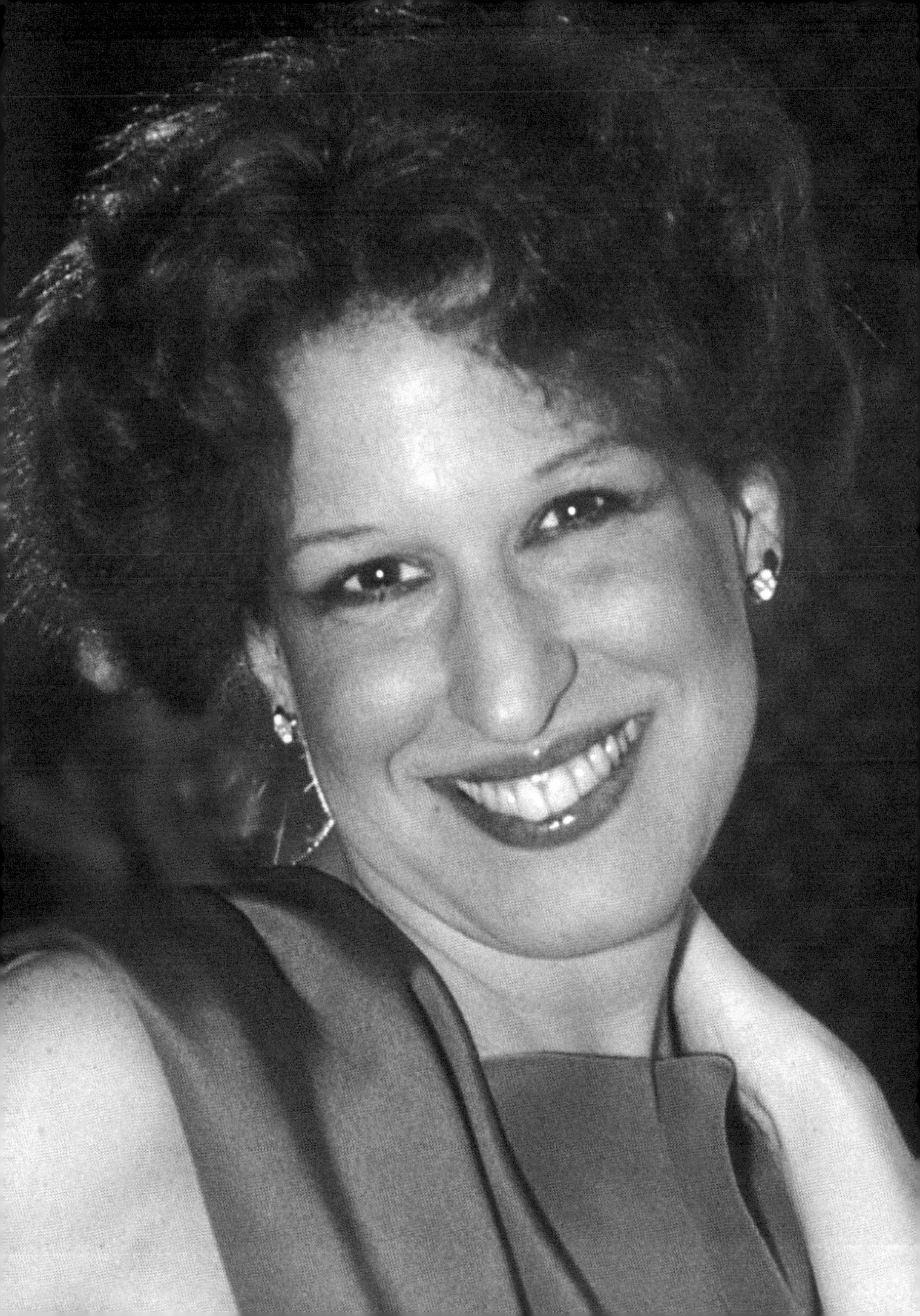

Christina Onassis
1972, Palm Beach

At the Palm Beach Yacht Club.

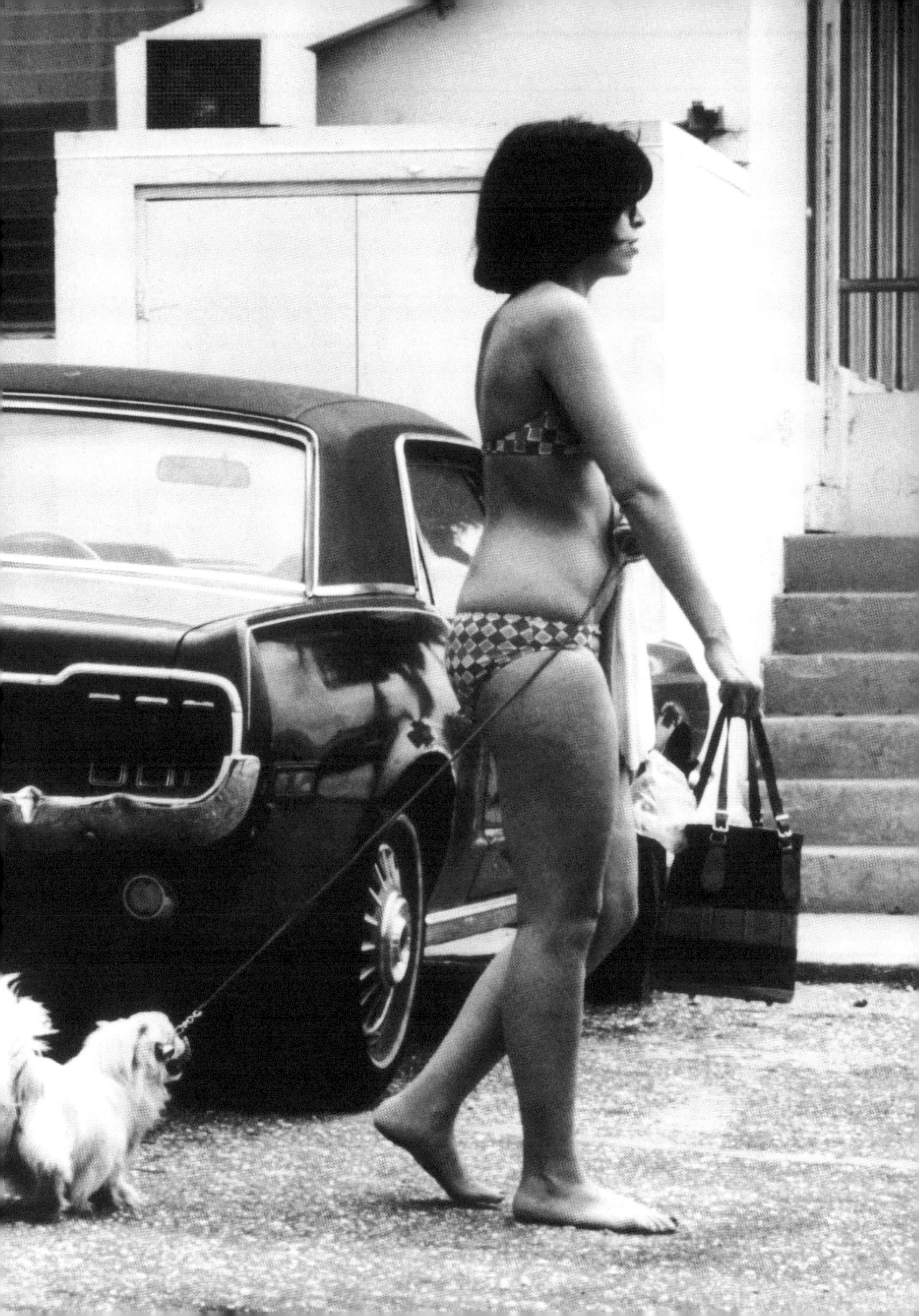

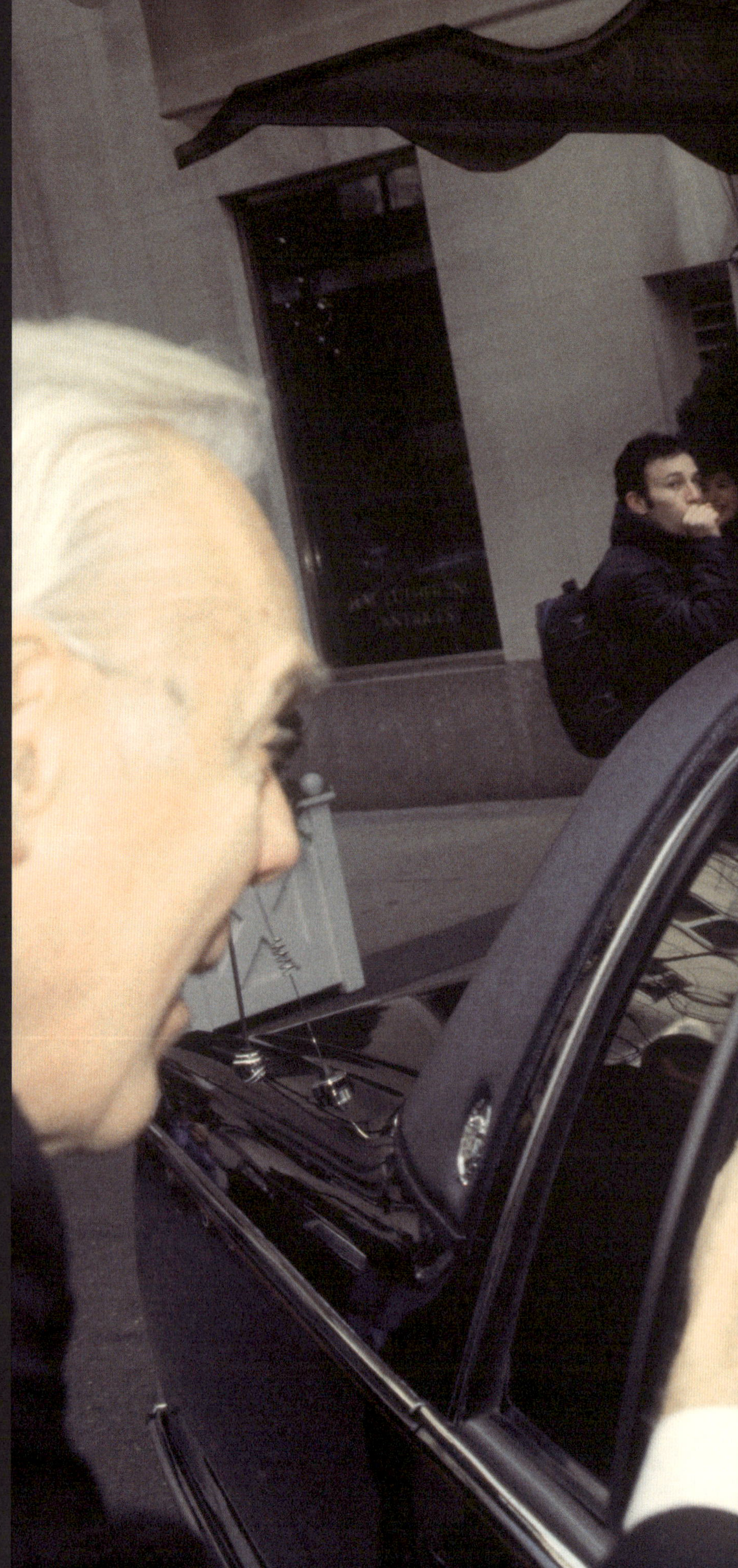

Princess Diana
1995, New York City

Leaving New York (the Carlyle Hotel) to
go back to England for the last time.

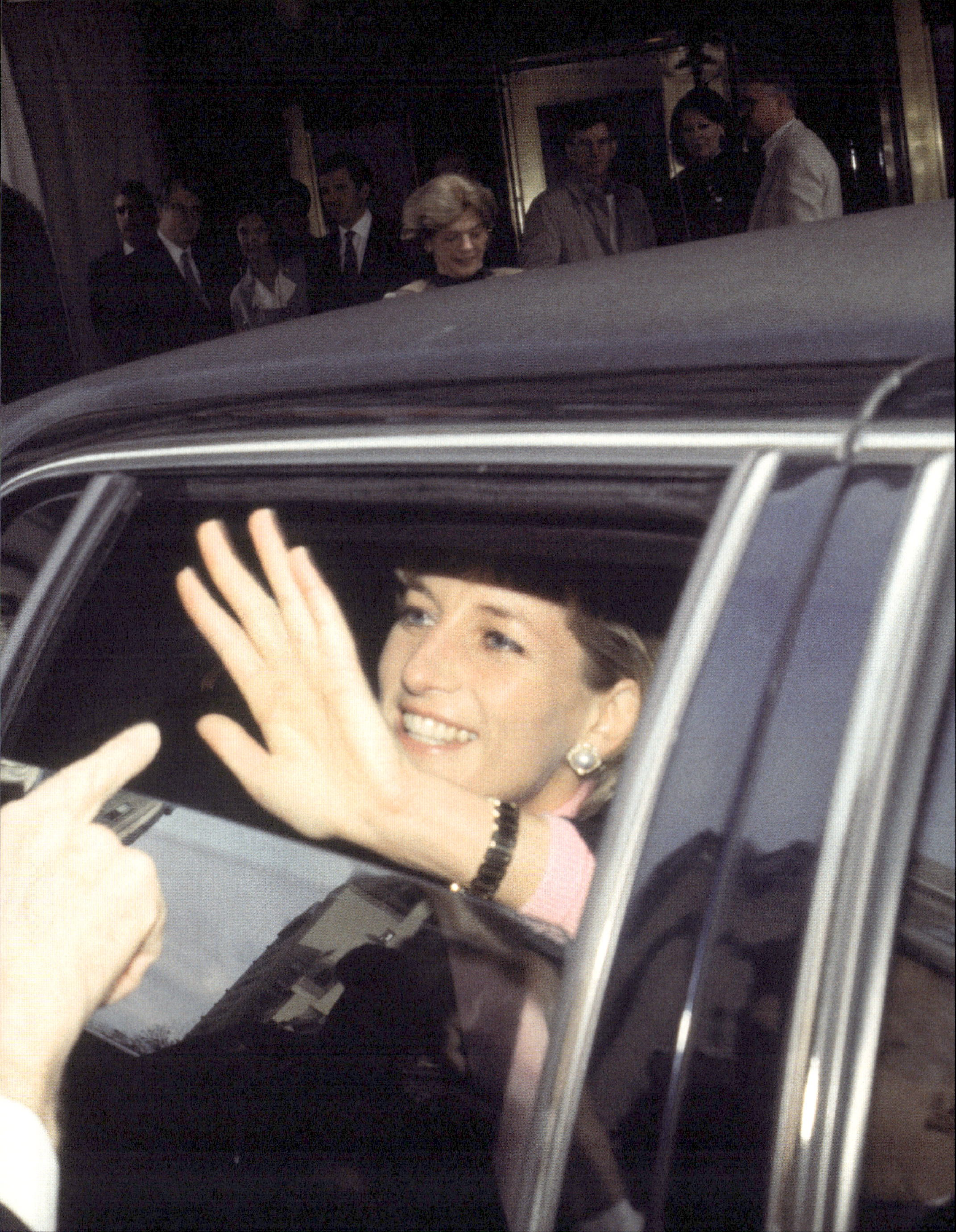

"Oscar, Oscar. That was the middle name of my first husband."

The name alone! Bette Davis! It almost strikes fear in my being! I'm thinking of the movies *"What Ever happened to Baby Jane"* and *"Jezebel"* just to name a few. This is a movie star in every sense of the word, so when I read that she will be appearing at Town Hall to talk about her career, I jump at the chance.

Her publicist John Springer is at the theater. We have known each other for a long time and there is a mutual respect between us, so when he tells me that his star, Miss Davis, is nervous and apprehensive, he suggests that maybe I should go backstage and just talk to her and try to keep her occupied while waiting. I promise I'll try.

When I see Miss Davis I introduce myself, and when I say my name is Oscar, her whole demeanor changes. In her distinctive voice, she exclaims several times: "Oscar, Oscar! That was the middle name of my first husband."

She is clearly delighted and mentions she has a story to tell. She has forgotten she's backstage, and recalls the time when a committee got together to organize an event to honor movies and movie stars. They showed her a statuette that would be presented to the winners, but which was still nameless. Looking at the backside she exclaimed, "Just like my Oscar's ass!" The name stuck.

She lights a cigarette, it is almost time to go on stage. She allows me to take some pictures.
She is Bette Davis again!
———

Bette Davis
1973, New York City

Smoking in the Rainbow Room
in Rockefeller Center.
———

Following double page

Bette Davis
1973, New York City

Surrounded by fans,
outside Town Hall.
———

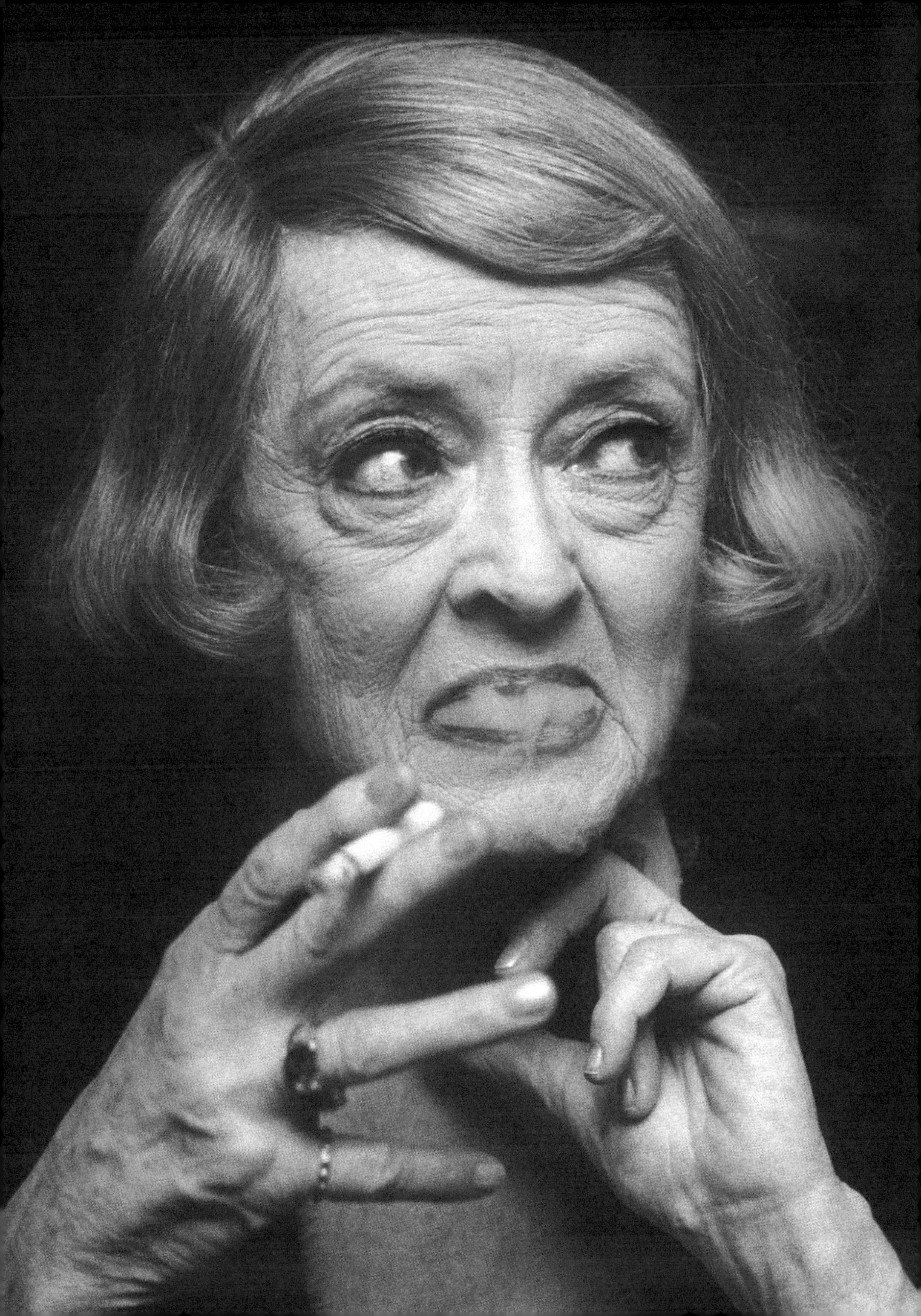

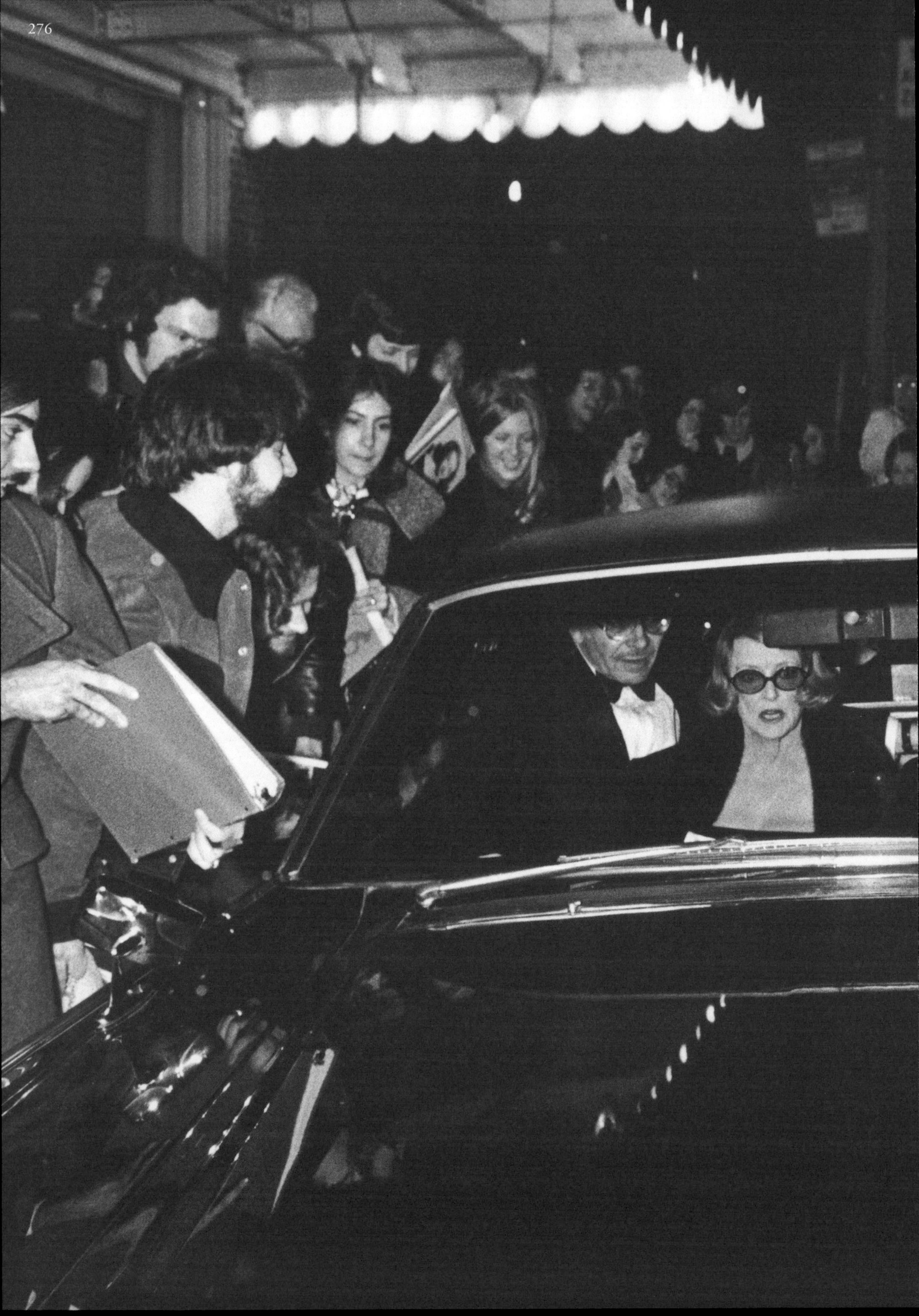

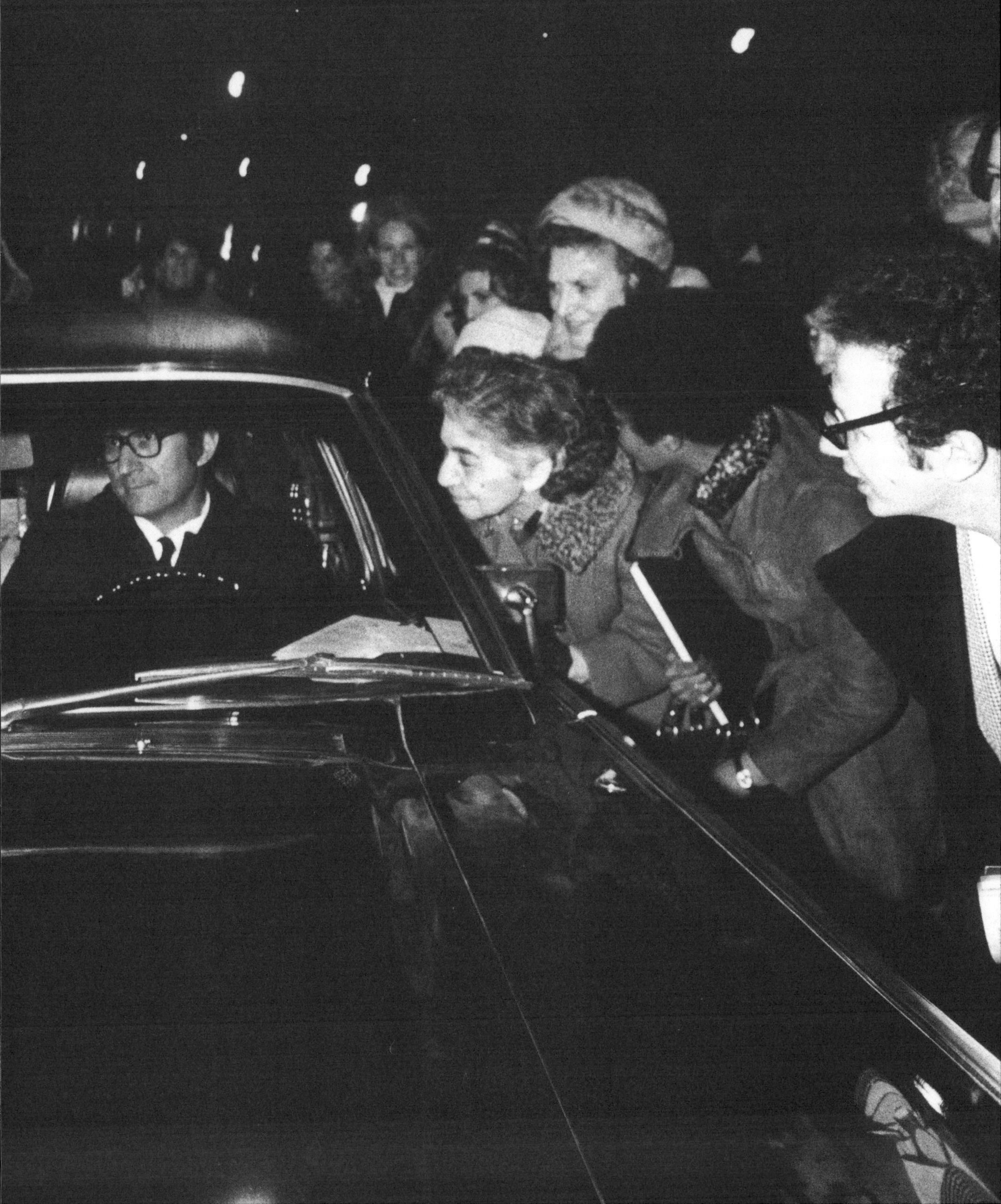

Charles Aznavour
1967, New York City

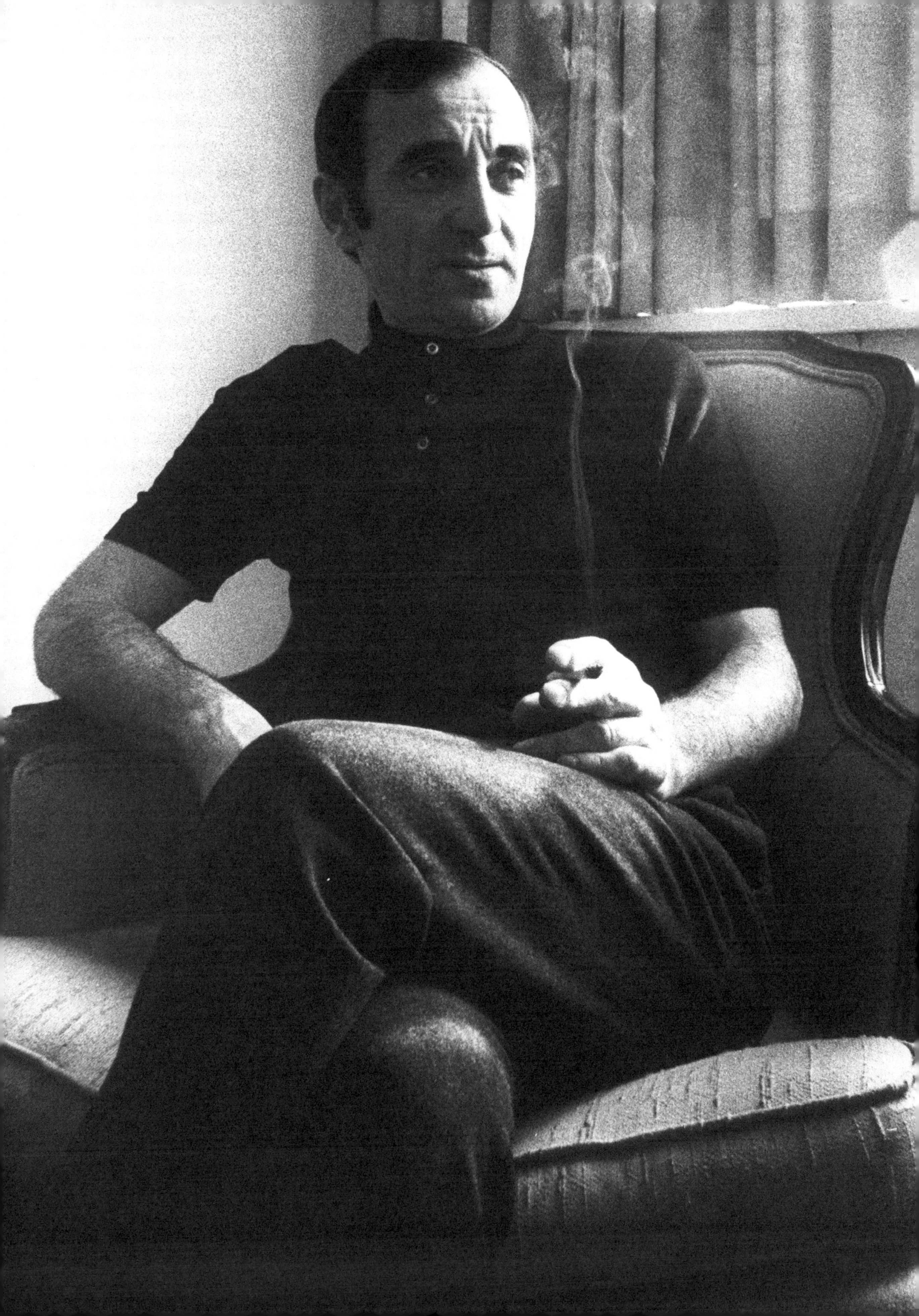

Aretha Franklin
1967, New York City

Backstage at Madison Square Garden
for a charity event.

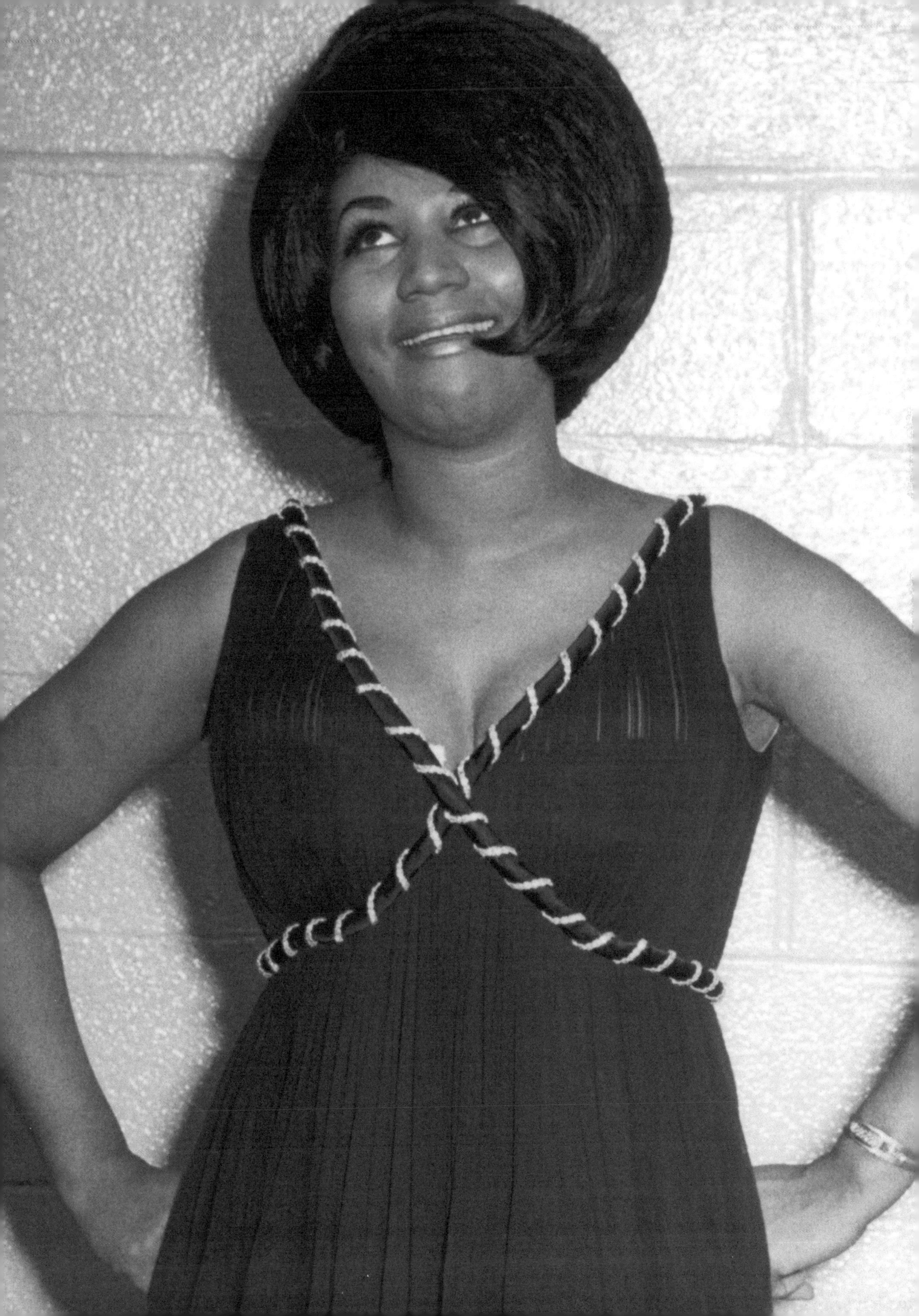

Elvis Presley
1969, Las Vegas

At the International Hotel.

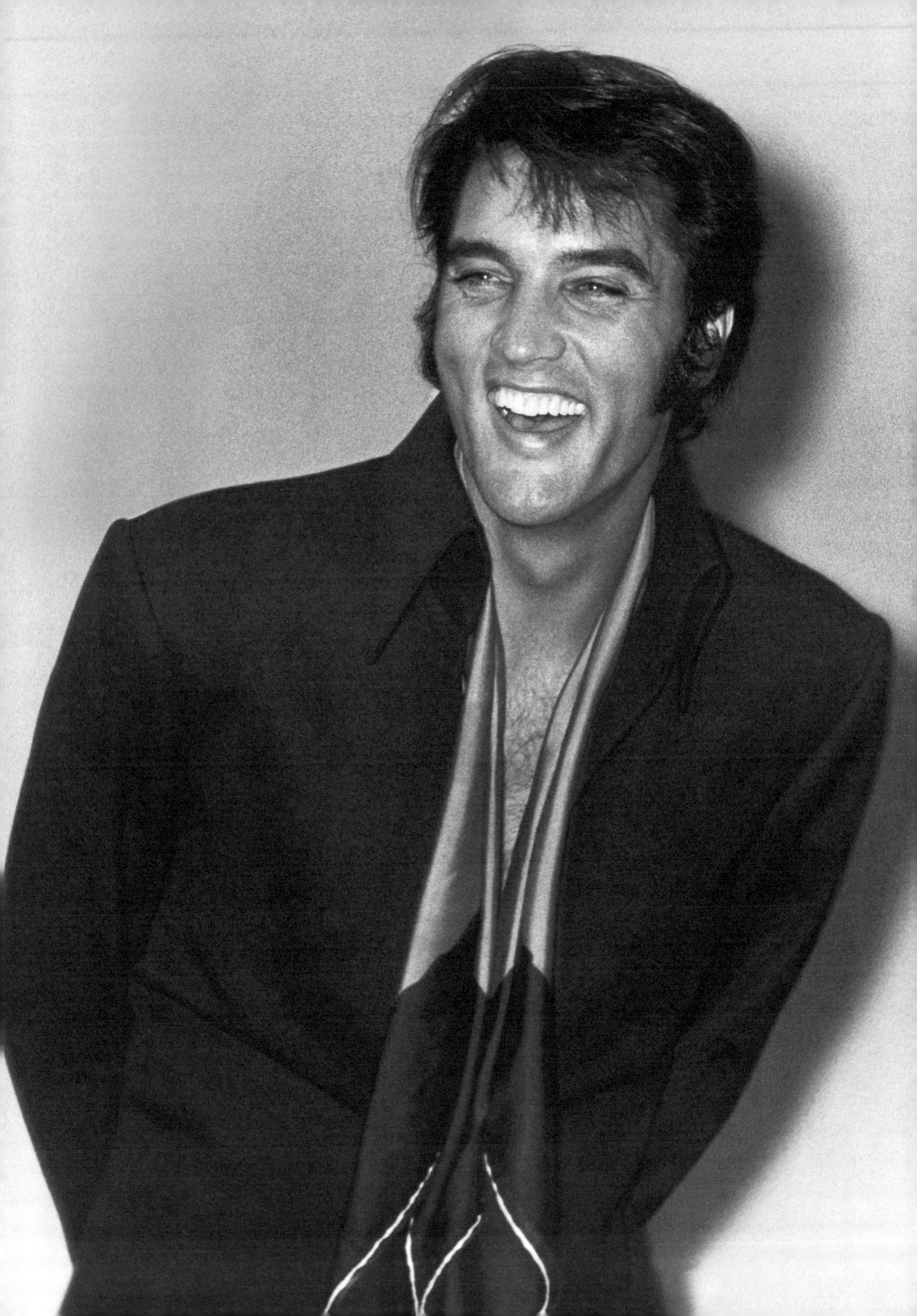

David Bowie
1987, New York City

Rehearsing for his Pepsi Cola sponsored concert tour.

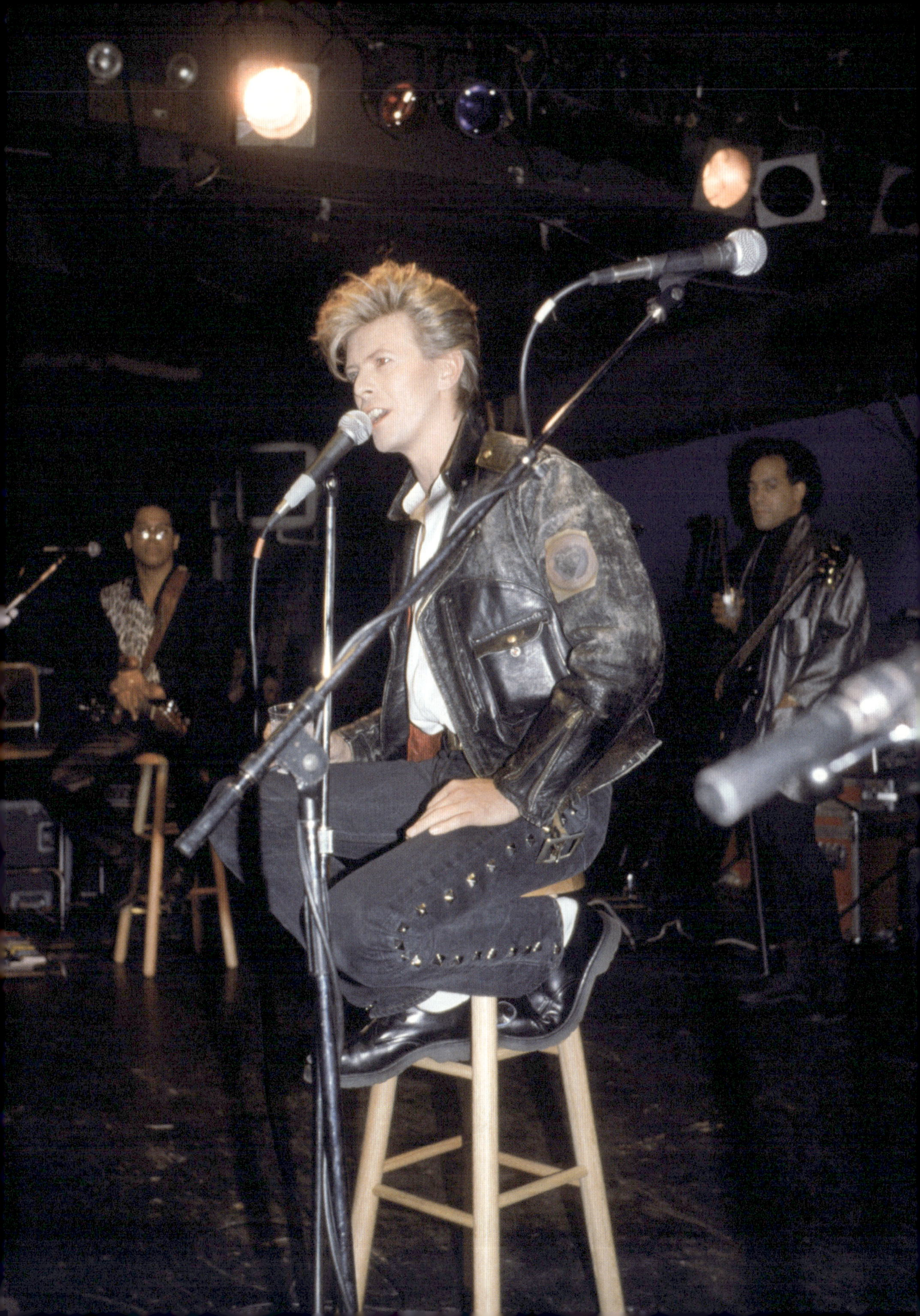

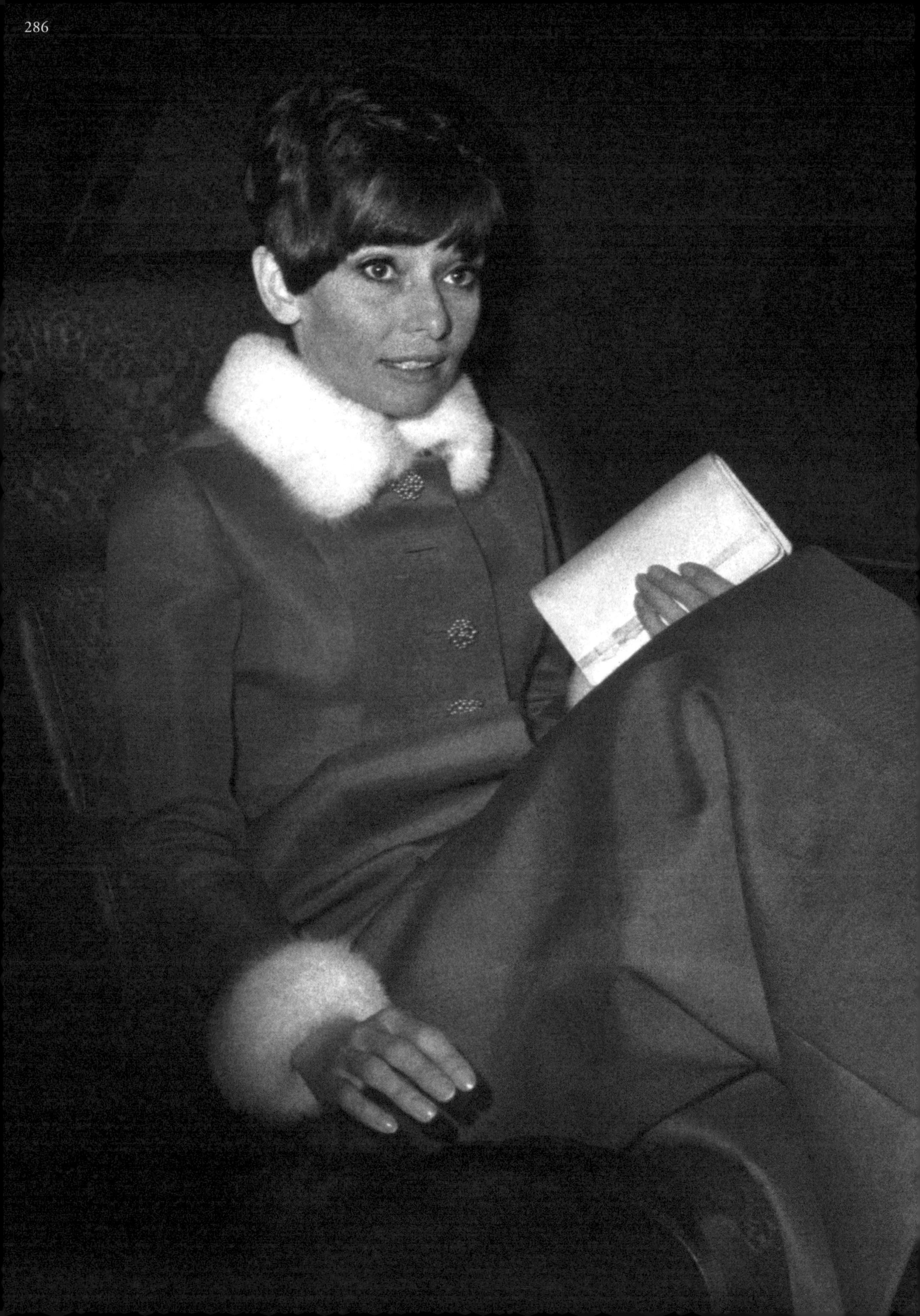

Audrey Hepburn
1968, New York City

Leaving *New York Film Critics
Circle Awards* at Sardi's, for the film
Wait Until Dark.
——

Paul Newman
1968, New York City

Backstage at the *Tonight Show*
with Johnny Carson.

———

Following double page

Johnny Carson
1968, Los Angeles

———

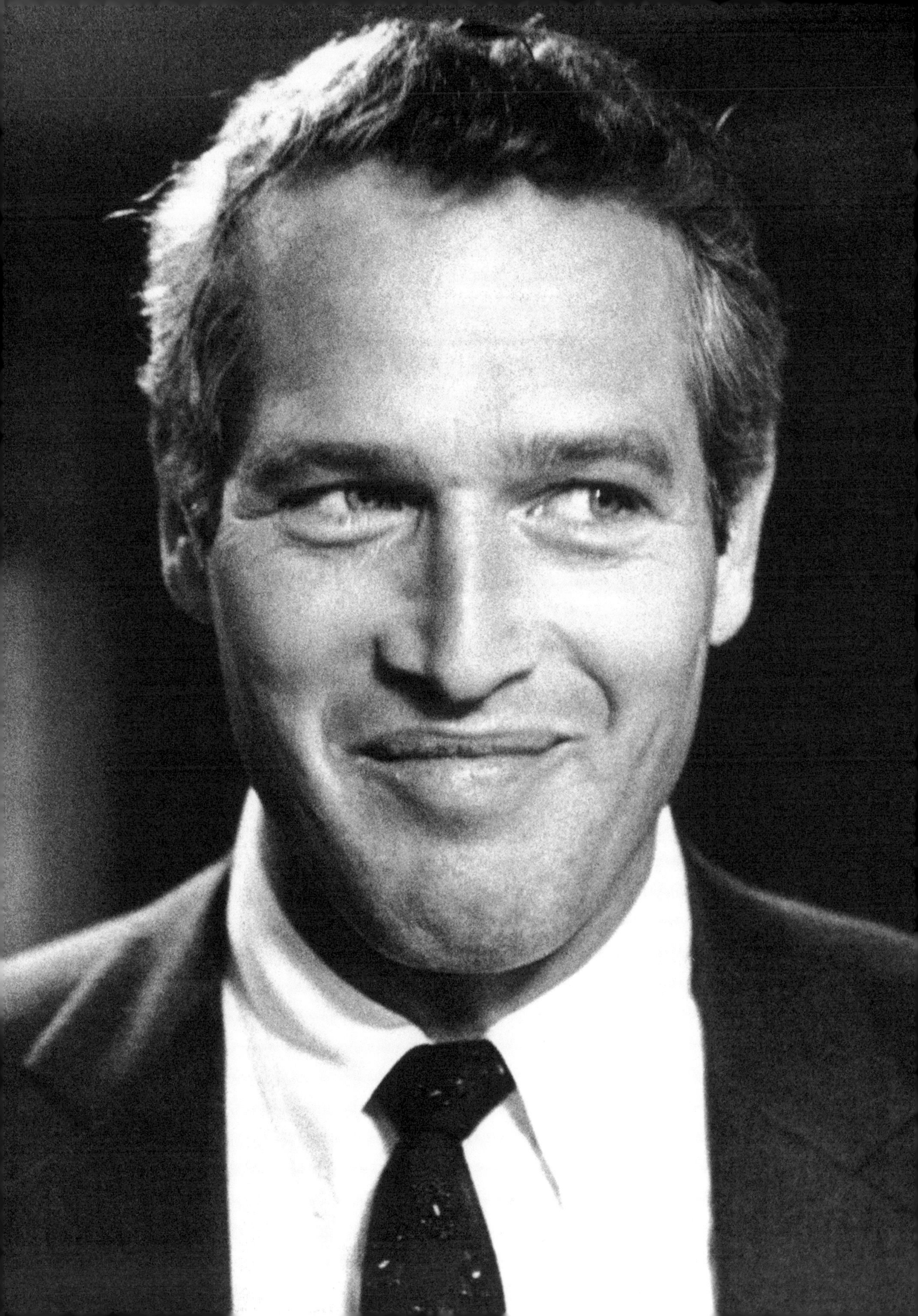

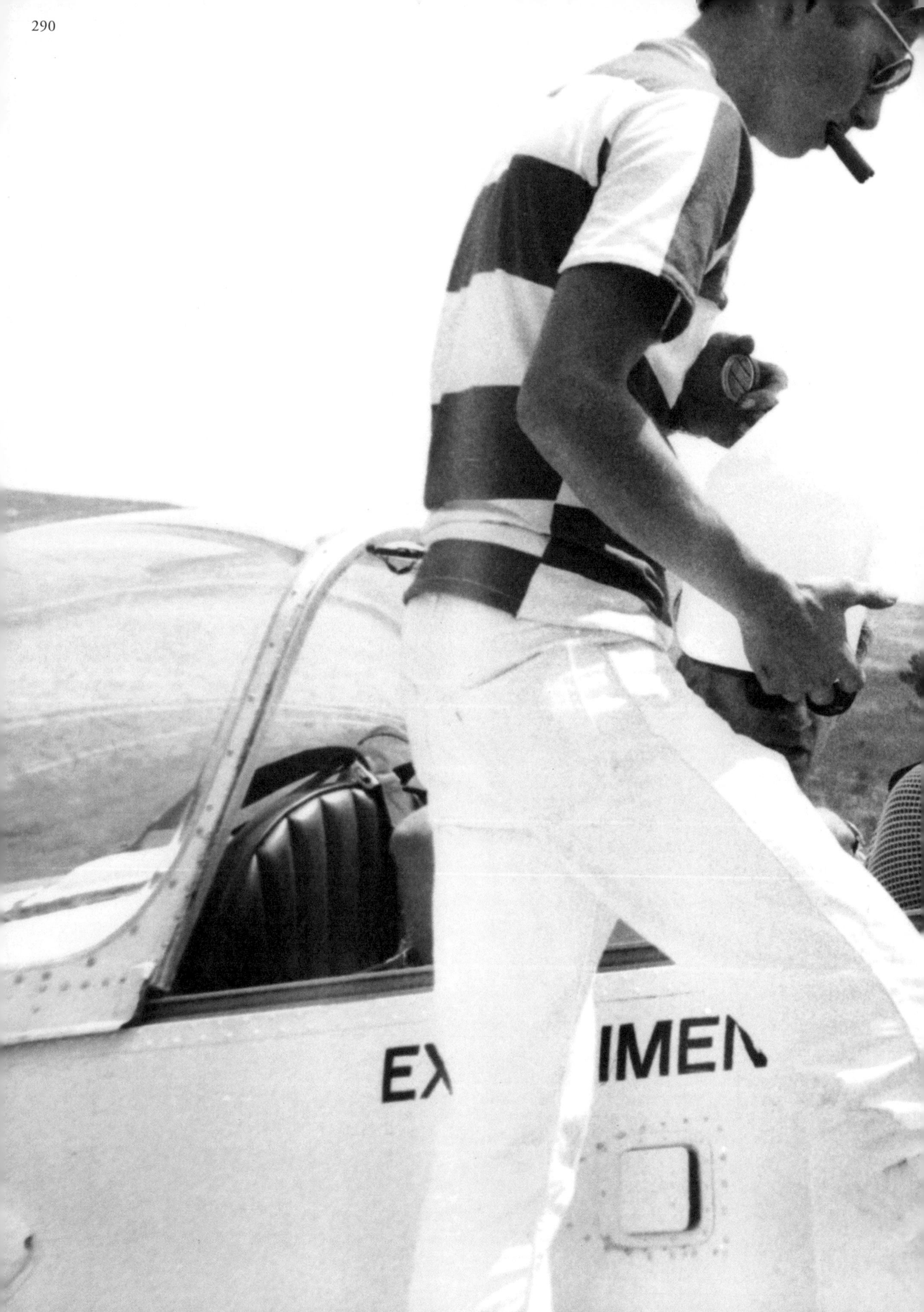
EX   IMEN

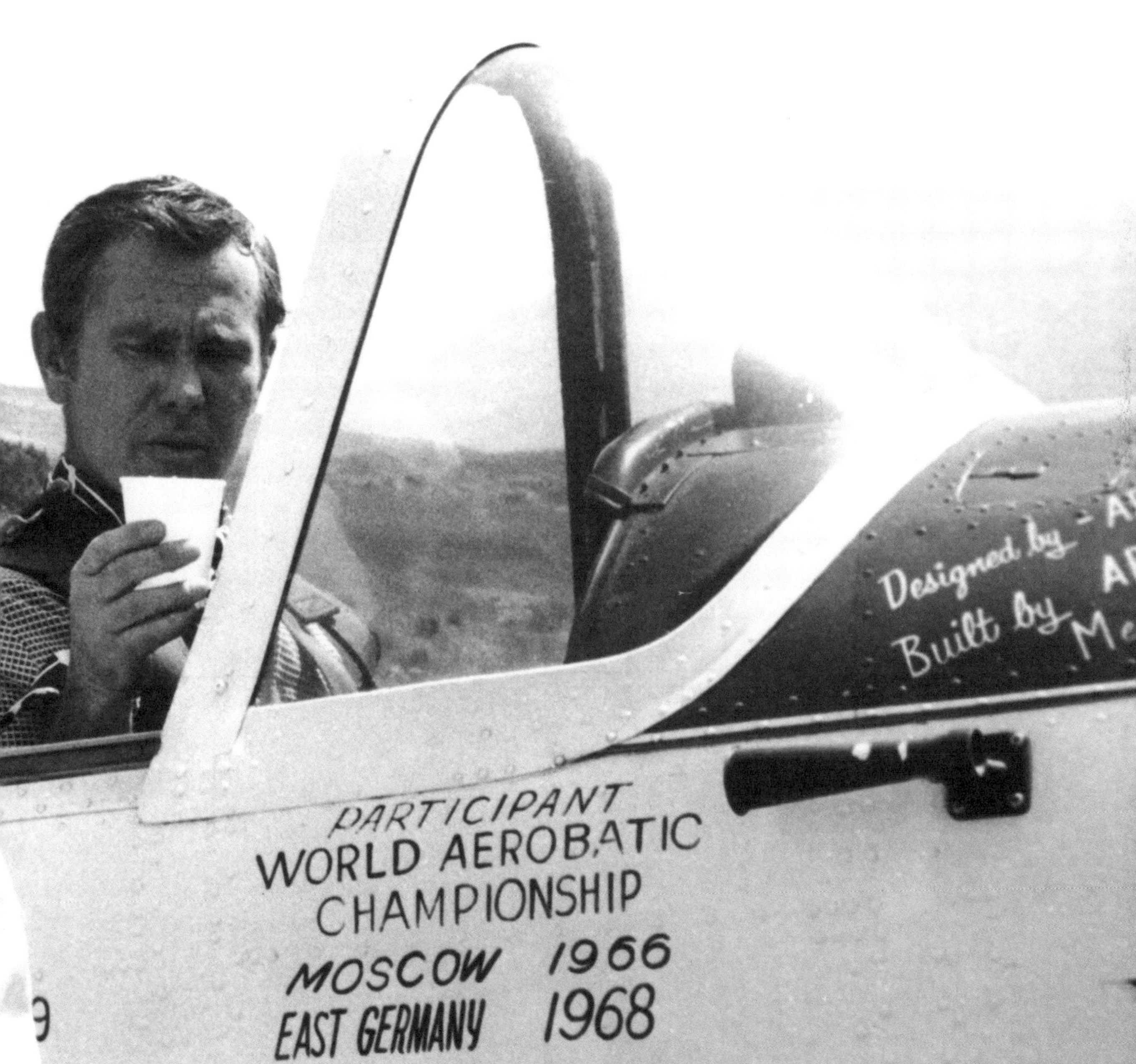

Designed by - A
Built by - A
M
PARTICIPANT
WORLD AEROBATIC
CHAMPIONSHIP
MOSCOW 1966
EAST GERMANY 1968

Debbie Harry
1987, New York City

In the Greenroom at the American
Ballet Theatre Lincoln Center.

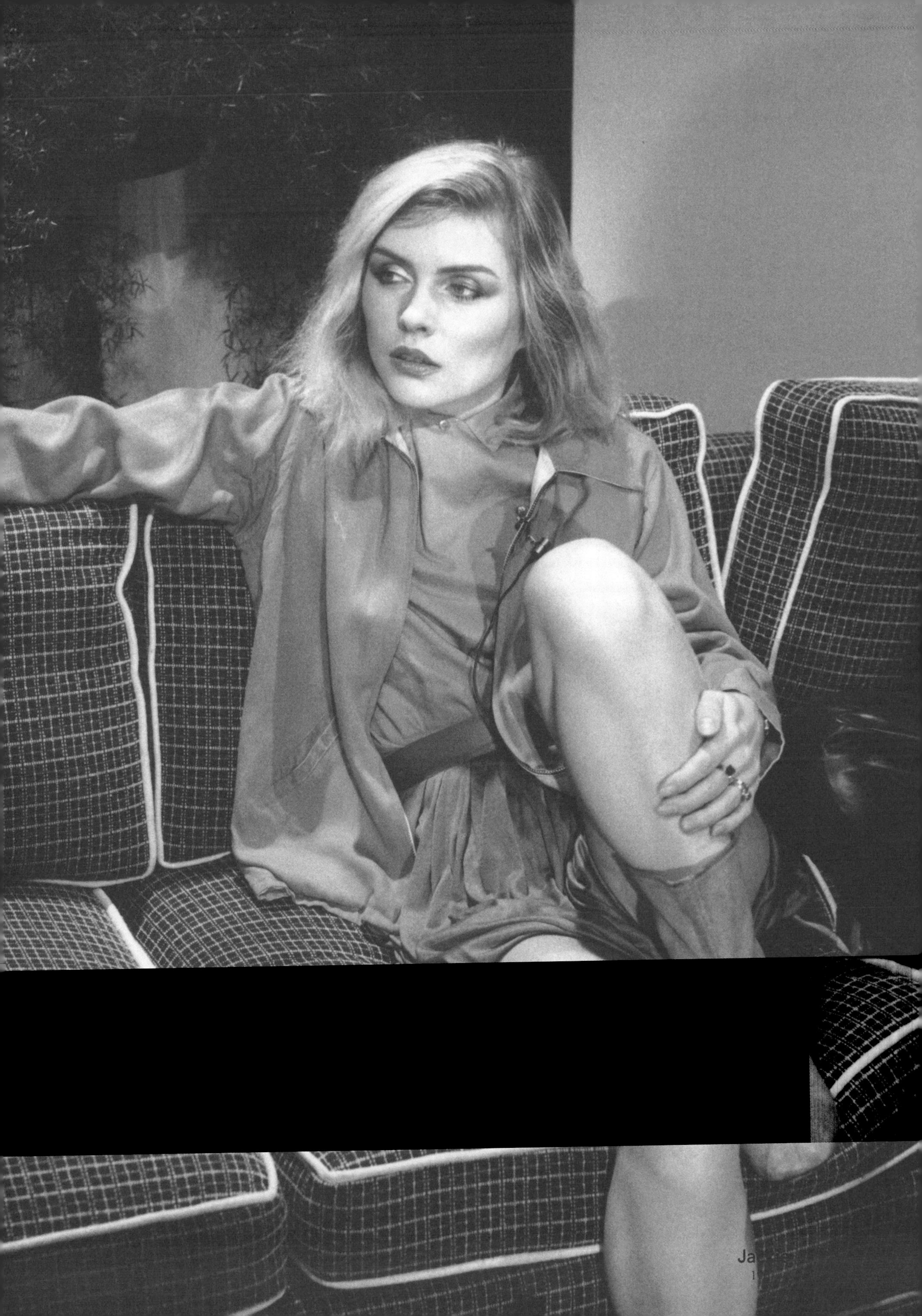
Ja

Jimi Hendrix
1967, New York City

On his way to the *Monterey Pop Festival.*
———

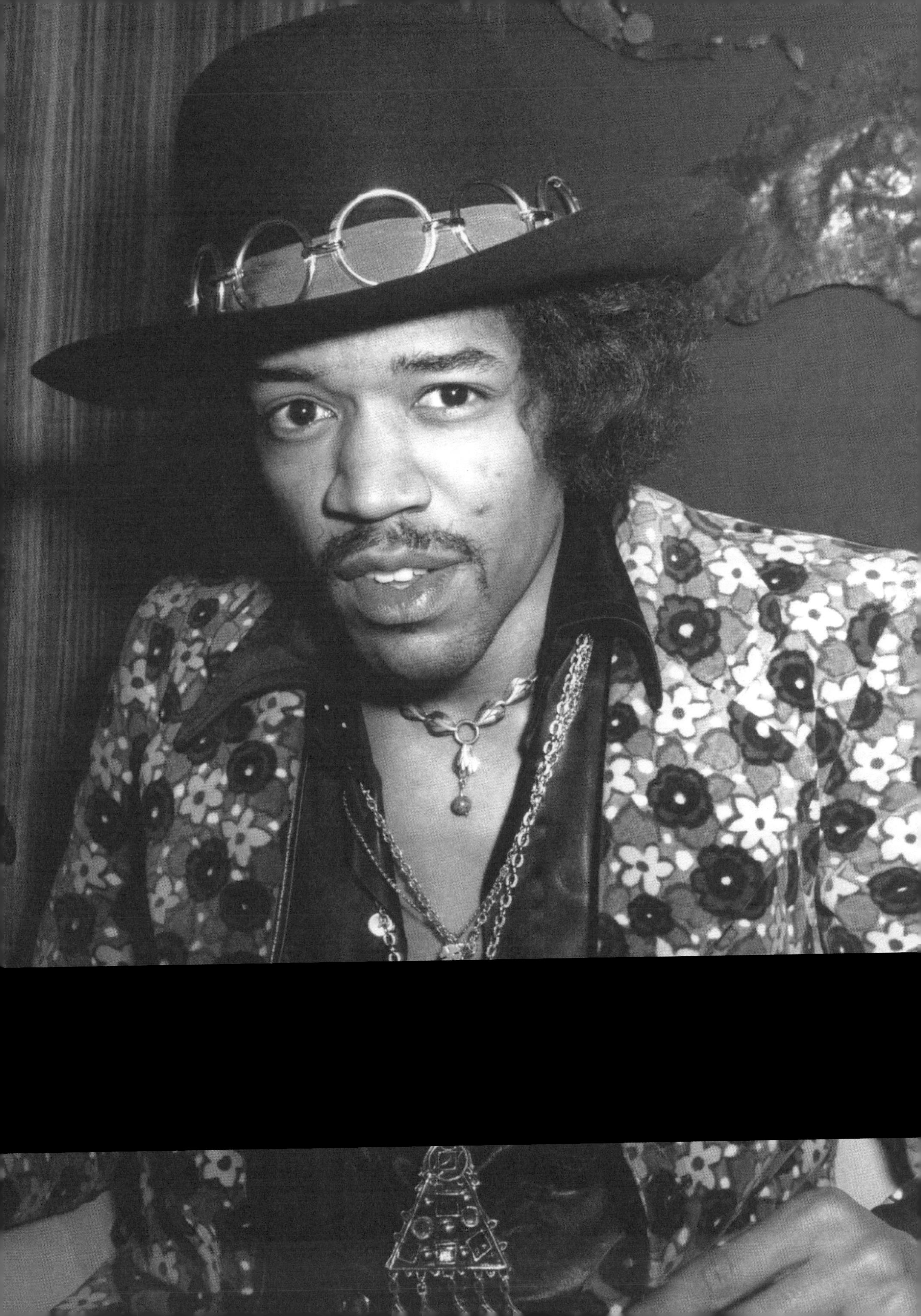

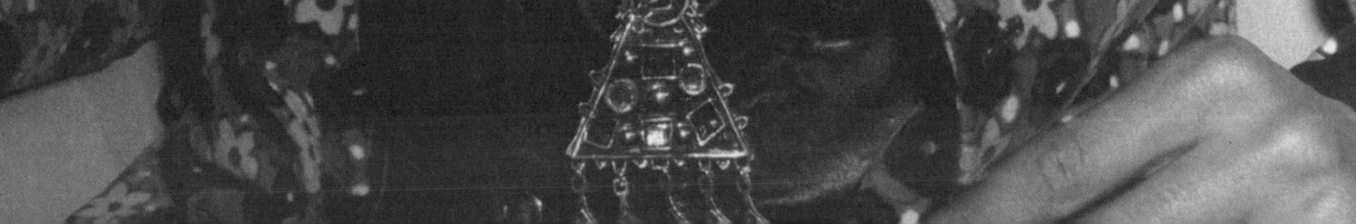

Index

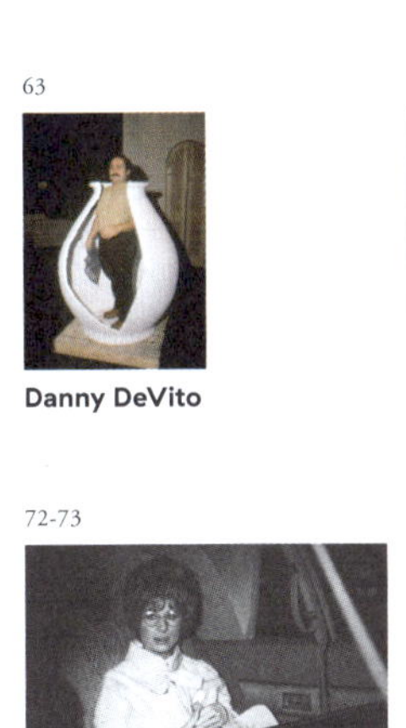

63
Danny DeVito

65 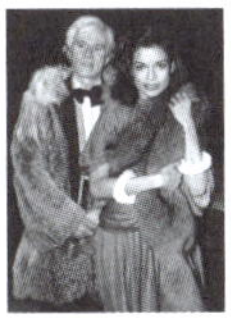
Andy Warhol and
Bianca Jagger

67 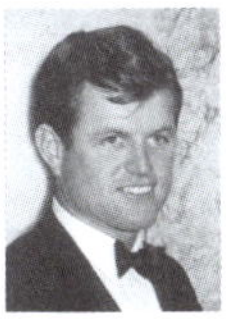
Ted Kennedy

68-69
John Lennon and Yoko Ono

71
Charles Aznavour

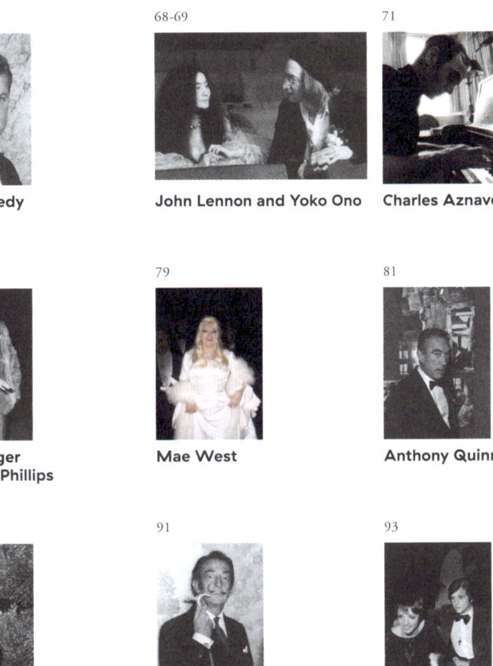

72-73 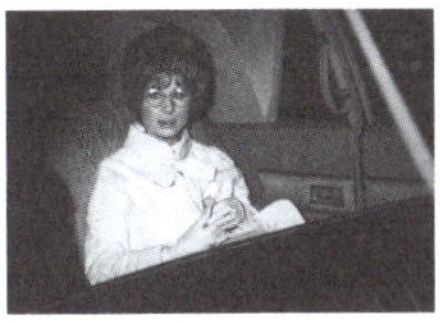
Barbra Streisand

75 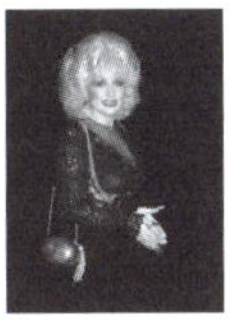
Dolly Parton

77 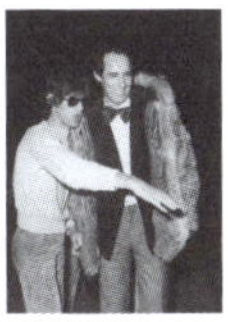
Mick Jagger
and John Phillips

79
Mae West

81
Anthony Quinn

83 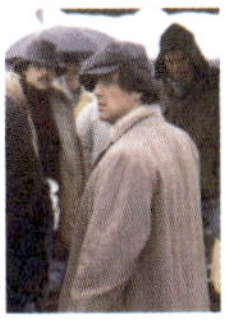
Sylvester Stallone

85 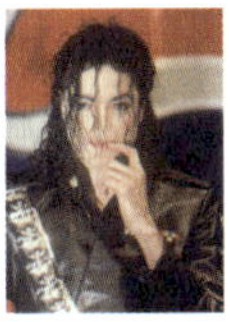
Michael Jackson

89 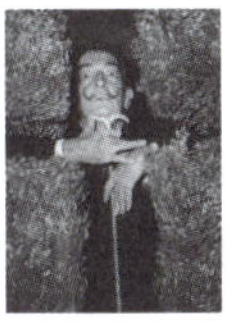
Salvador Dalí

91
Salvador Dalí

93
Liza Minnelli and
Desi Arnaz Jr.

95

97

98-99

101

103

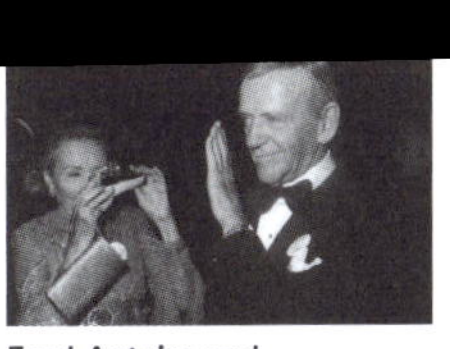
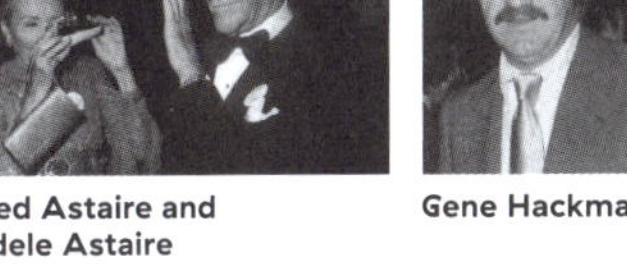

Fred Astaire and
Adele Astaire

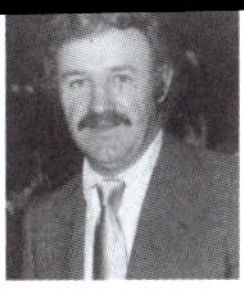

Gene Hackman

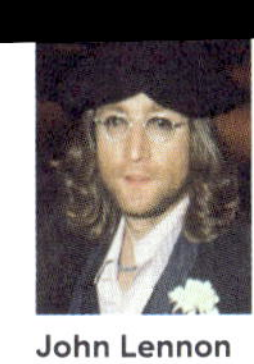

John Lennon

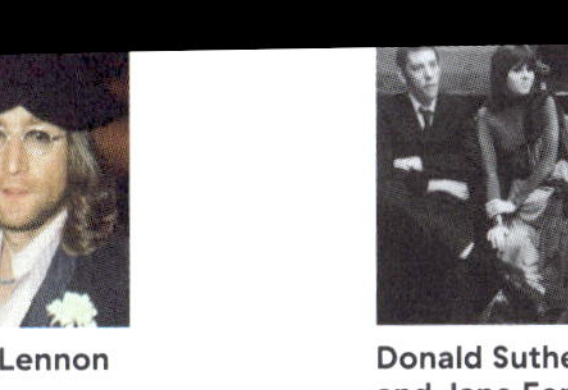

Donald Sutherland
and Jane Fonda

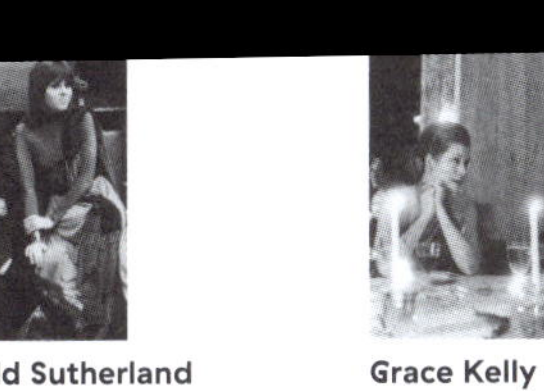

Grace Kelly

Index

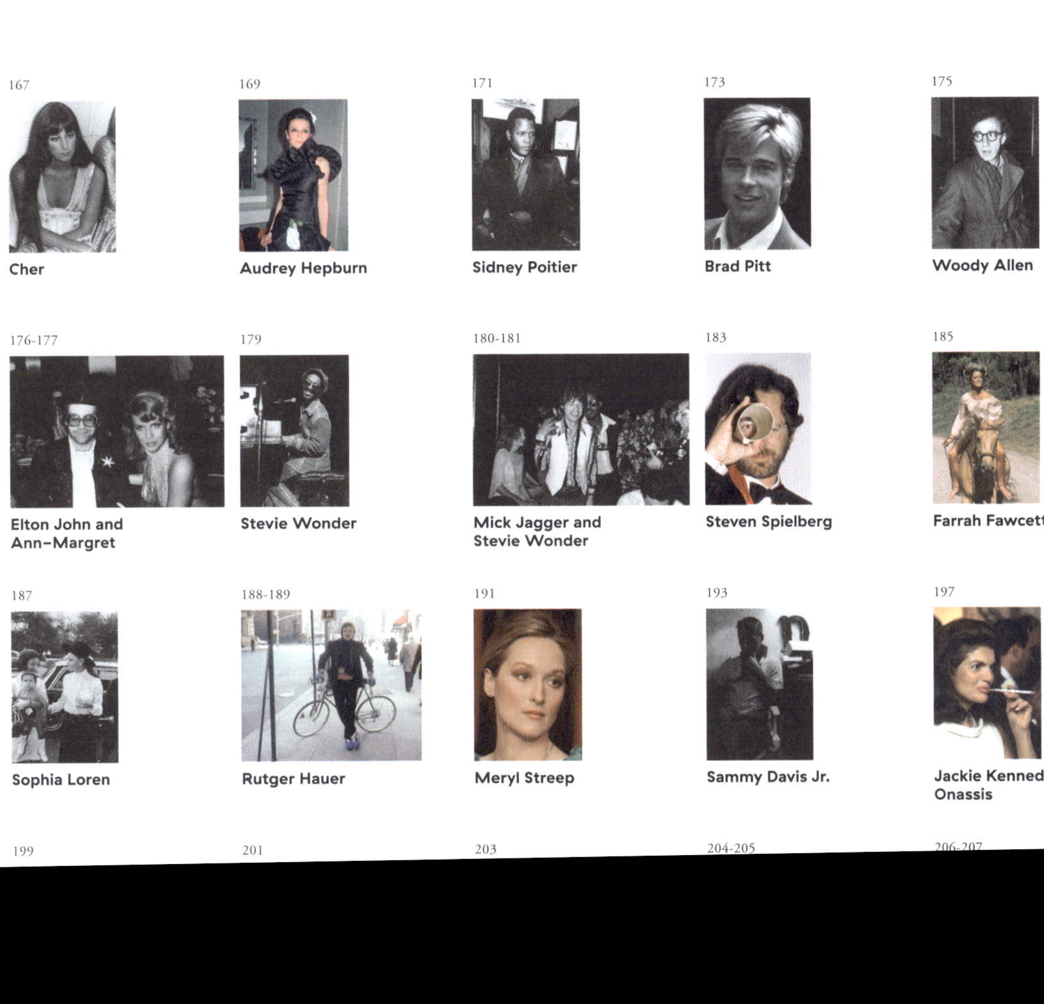

167
Cher

169
Audrey Hepburn

171
Sidney Poitier

173
Brad Pitt

175
Woody Allen

176-177
Elton John and
Ann–Margret

179
Stevie Wonder

180-181
Mick Jagger and
Stevie Wonder

183
Steven Spielberg

185
Farrah Fawcett

187
Sophia Loren

188-189
Rutger Hauer

191
Meryl Streep

193
Sammy Davis Jr.

197
Jackie Kennedy
Onassis

199

201

203

204-205

206-207

Bobbie Kennedy with
his wife Ethel

Richard Nixon

Paul McCartney

Mia Farrow

Jack Nicholson

Index

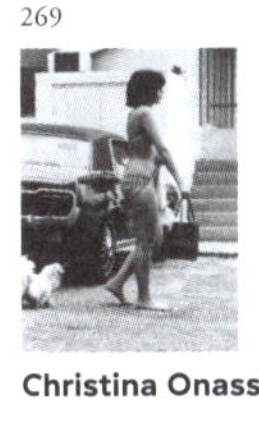

269

Christina Onassis

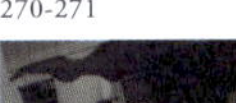
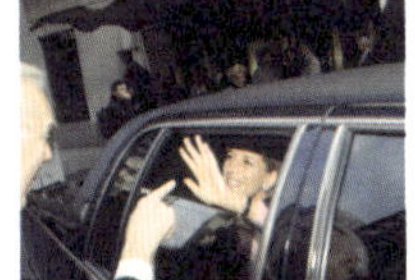

270-271

Princess Diana

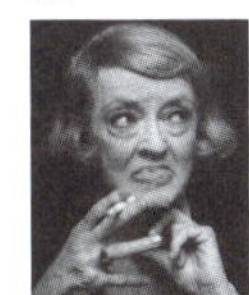

275

Bette Davis

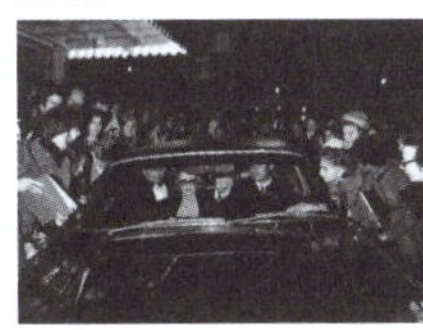

276-277

Bette Davis

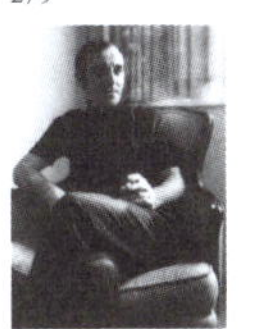

279

Charles Aznavour

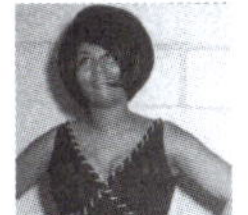

281

Aretha Franklin

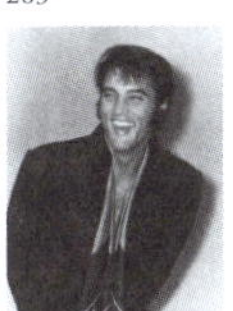

283

Elvis Presley

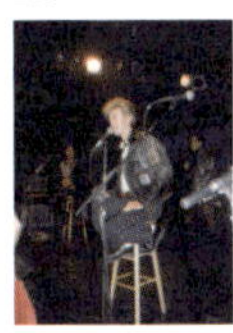

285

David Bowie

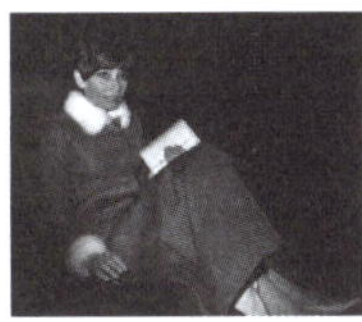

286-287

Audrey Hepburn

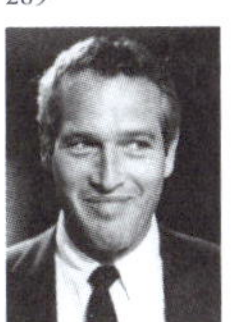

289

Paul Newman

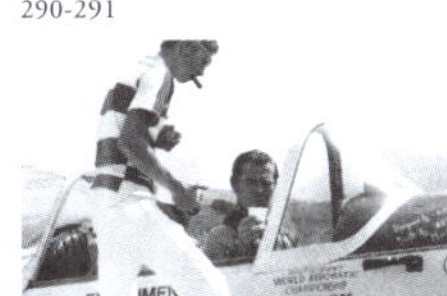

290-291

Johnny Carson

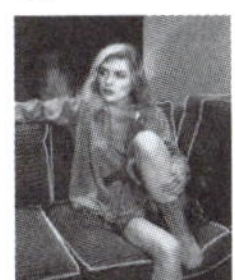

293

Debbie Harry

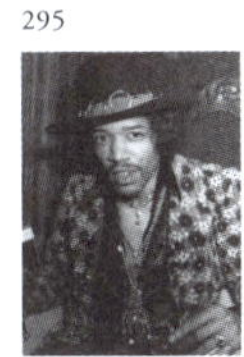

295

Jimi Hendrix

icons by oscar

ISBN 978 90 8989 779 4
NUR 653

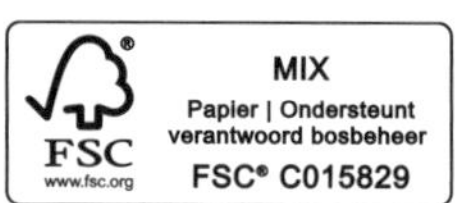

Photography
Oscar Abolafia
www.oscarabolafia.nl

Design
MENDO, Amsterdam
www.mendo.nl
@mendobooks on Facebook,
Twitter, Instagram and Pinterest

Text
Yoke Abolafia - van Berge Henegouwen

Publisher
Uitgeverij TERRA
TERRA is part of TerraLannoo bv
P.O. Box 23202, 1100 DS Amsterdam
The Netherlands
info@terralannoo.nl
www.terra-publishing.com

Special Thanks to
Ellis Kamerling, KAMERLINGVANDERBURGH©
Cees van der Burgh, KAMERLINGVANDERBURGH©
Marcel Salome, Re-Art
Bart de Rooy

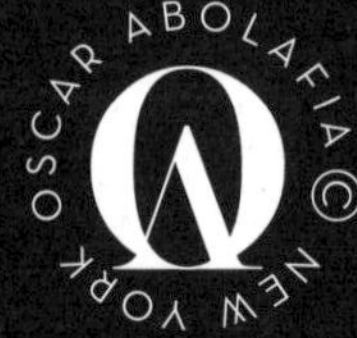

TERRA